THE
TOYOTA
WAY
to CONTINUOUS IMPROVEMENT

THE
TOYOTA
WAY
to CONTINUOUS
IMPROVEMENT

LINKING STRATEGY AND OPERATIONAL EXCELLENCE TO
ACHIEVE SUPERIOR PERFORMANCE

JEFFREY K. LIKER
JAMES K. FRANZ

New York Chicago San Francisco Lisbon
London Madrid Mexico City Milan New Delhi
San Juan Seoul Singapore Sydney Toronto

1 2 3 4 5 6 7 8 9 0   DOC/DOC   1 6 5 4 3 2 1

ISBN: 978-0-07-147746-8 (print book)
MHID: 0-07-147746-2

ISBN: 978-0-07-176215-1 (e-book)
MHID: 0-07-176215-9

This publication is designed to provide accurate and authoritative information in regard to the subject matter covered. It is sold with the understanding that neither the authors nor the publisher is engaged in rendering legal, accounting, securities trading, or other professional service. If legal advice or other expert assistance is required, the services of a competent professional person should be sought.
—From a Declaration of Principles
Jointly Adopted by a Committee of the
American Bar Association and a Committee
of Publishers and Associations

McGraw-Hill books are available at special quantity discounts to use as premiums and sales promotions or for use in corporate training programs. To contact a representative, please e-mail us at bulksales@mcgraw-hill.com.

This book is printed on acid-free paper.

To my father, who taught me the values
of hard work, integrity, and love.
—Jeff Liker

To my father-In-law, a brilliant mind and
a true gentleman whose example continues
to inform and inspire.
—James Franz

Contents

Section Three Making Your Vision a Reality

Chapter 13 One Time around the Plan–Do–Check–Adjust (PDCA) Loop: A Lean Short Story at Alte Schule

Chapter 14 Sustaining, Spreading, Deepening: Continuing Turns of the PDCA Wheel

Chapter 15 Continuous Improvement as a Way of Life

Acknowledgments and Guest Author Biographies

We feel very fortunate that we can make a living studying and doing what we love—applying what we have learned from Toyota to help organizations succeed in their desired goals. Along the way, we continually expand our network of people who are also dedicated to that mission. These include lean advisors, both internal and external to companies, and executives who have learned the power of striving for operational excellence. Some of our valued colleagues were willing to share their passion and experiences by cowriting the case studies in Section Two of this book. We use the term *sensei* (treasured teachers) in this book to refer to these people, as they are all true lean leaders who dedicate every day to learning and teaching others. We believe that the message of this book is much stronger because it comes in different voices from the people leading the transformation. Here are our associate authors (alphabetically).

Charlie Baker was the first American chief engineer (large program leader) and then the first vice president of engineering for Honda. He has been taking what he learned and teaching American companies as vice president of engineering. His depth of knowledge of lean product development is humbling, but what is more impressive is his dedication to continuous learning.

John Drogosz works with us supporting Liker Lean Advisors. He is one of the few individuals who have become great lean advisors without ever working for Toyota or an affiliate, although he has been taught by many Toyota alumni. He is a natural facilitator and instinctively grasps how to approach transformational change wherever he goes.

Steve Hoeft was trained by some tough Japanese *sensei*, learning by working for a supplier to Mazda. He also worked with us for years at Optiprise and now leads a lean health-care consulting practice at Altarum. He electrifies crowds as a classroom teacher and pushes everyone he advises to higher levels of excellence.

Robert Kucner was Jeff Liker's Ph.D. student and thoroughly exploited that opportunity to learn lean by doing at a shipyard that repairs and overhauls submarines. Since then, he has been collaborating with Liker on consulting and brought his natural transformation skills to a rental car company, a maker of construction and mining equipment, a software engineering company, and product development organizations.

Tony McNaughton has direct lineage to Taiichi Ohno as a student of one of Ohno's best students. After doing his time at Toyota in Australia, he has become one of the world's best Toyota Production System (TPS) advisors to companies across the globe. We had the pleasure of working with Tony on an assignment for a global complex company focused on plants in Asia.

Richard Zarbo is a natural learner and a leader who finally got tired of playing at Deming's teachings and decided to do it as the master intended. He dedicated his life to applying Deming's teachings, as best exemplified at Toyota, within his purview of pathology and lab medicine. His self-transformation and that of his group has been inspirational.

We are grateful to all these people for learning with us, teaching us, and participating in the book.

We are also grateful to many people at Toyota. Jim got his start working there in Japan as a production engineer, and Jeff has been learning from them since 1983. Wherever we go and whatever we do, we are always trying to live up to the high standards of excellence that we have learned from our colleagues and friends at Toyota.

An earlier version of this book was started with David Meier. The original concept was to write a book for each of the 4Ps in *The Toyota Way*, with this being the "Process" book. As time went on, David could not participate in the book. Since processes, people, and problem solving are so integrated, we decided to write this one book on continuous improvement. David's deep thinking and expertise was an inspiration and we built off of some of his key ideas. For example, it was David who emphasized that the system surfaces problems that poeple solve, in turn developing themselves. We are very grateful to David for all he taught us and contributed.

A project such as this couldn't be successful without the patience, understanding, and support of our families. Team Liker has been at this for decades, and Jeff's wife, Deb, his son, Jesse, and his daughter, Emma, are veterans. All have been supportive and have helped the project along the way. This is Team Franz's first foray into a project such as this, and Jim's wife, Kate, has been there 24/7 with unwavering support. Jim also got creative inspiration from his daughter, Taylor, whom he claims is the truly gifted writer in the family. To all of our loved ones who had to deal with us during this, our labor of love, we humbly and honestly say thank you.

With more than half a century working in and with industry between us, individually acknowledging all of those great people in countless industries all over the world with whom we've had the pleasure of working would be an impossible task. Our journey thus far has taken us all over the globe; we've worked with countless companies at various stages in their lean journey, and we have grown with them. We continue to develop and expand in our knowledge and skills as *sensei* as a result of our guiding and teaching you in your efforts. Thank you all.

We have added more formal biographies of each of our guest authors in alphabetical order. While we worked with each on the writing and editing, their chapters are their stories. We hope you will share our view that there is remarkable consensus across all of us on the key role of leadership in lean transformation and the centrality of building a culture of continuous improvement especially at the working level of the organization.

Charlie Baker is a leading authority on transforming product development to Lean. Mr. Baker is currently employed as vice president for advanced technology at Harley-Davidson. Previous to this he spent four years as vice president for engineering for NAAS (pseudoname), a leading supplier of complex and highly engineered automotive subsystems. As a direct result of the successful transformation to lean, cost, quality, and speed of development as well as product competitiveness were dramatically improved. Before his responsibility at NAAS, Mr. Baker spent 15 years in executive positions at Honda R&D in both North America and Japan, both as chief engineer of development as well as VP of Honda R&D Americas. He was the first American to lead a major Honda global development in Japan as chief engineer—the 2003 Accord. Previous to this he led the 2001 MDX development in Honda R&D Americas, the first time a major new vehicle was developed in Honda's American R&D. Mr. Baker started his career with General Motors, where he worked in engine design and development at Pontiac Motor Division and Saturn Corp. Mr. Baker holds a BSME from General Motors Institute and is a Registered Professional Engineer.

John Drogosz, Ph.D., is an independent consultant who supports Liker Lean Advisors, LLC. He has 15 years of Lean manufacturing and above-shop floor experience. Dr. Drogosz currently teaches classes in lean manufacturing and lean product and process development for the University of Michigan's Center for Professional Development's Lean Certification course in Ann Arbor. Before joining Optiprise, John worked through John Shook's TWI Network as a Ford production system consultant at the Dearborn engine plant while writing a Ph.D. dissertation developing a mathematical model to optimize capacity utilization. Dr. Drogosz also held a management role at Delphi Automotive in enterprisewide lean implementation, including running numerous value stream mapping workshops in plants, developing corporate training materials, and leading the transformation to lean. Dr. Drogosz holds a bachelor's degree in Business Administration from the University of Western Ontario and a master's and Ph.D. in Industrial and Operations Engineering from the University of Michigan. He is also a Six Sigma black belt.

Steve Hoeft, BS, MBA, PMP, is a practitioner, teacher, and thought leader in applying lean principles to unique processes, including health-care systems. Steve is the developer and key instructor for several modules in the University of Michigan's Lean Healthcare, New Product Development, and Manufacturing certificate programs. Steve wrote *Stories from My Sensei*, published by Productivity Press. From 1995 to 2003 he helped create and lead Optiprise, Dr. Jeffrey Liker's lean consulting firm. His projects have won many awards and recognitions, including Shingo Prizes and a 2002 Most Improved Plant Worldwide award (Tenneco Automotive). Steve was the performance improvement manager for Johnson Controls, Inc., from 1993 to 1995. During this time he received significant coaching and training from Toyota *sensei* and leaders in Kentucky. Steve started his career as a production supervisor and engineer at General Motors, receiving training and Jonah certification from Eli Goldratt (TOC and OPT). Steve holds a dual BS degree in Industrial Engineering and Operations Research from Wayne State University. He also holds an MBA from the University of Toledo. Steve is a Certified Project Manager Professional (PMP) through the Project Management Institute.

Robert Kucner, Ph.D., is an independent consultant who supports Liker Lean Advisors, LLC, with 10 years of experience, specializing in lean product development, lean manufacturing, and Lean Six Sigma deployment. Recent clients have included Caterpillar, Alcatel-Lucent, the U.S. Navy, Hertz Rental Car, and Orgprom. Bob has recently worked with these companies in a wide variety of lean product development applications, including software development, tractor development, automotive development, and ship design. Bob completed his doctoral dissertation, "A Socio-Technical Study of Lean Manufacturing Deployment in the Remanufacturing Context," in Industrial and Operations Engineering at the University of Michigan, Ann Arbor. Previously, Bob was the Naval Sea System (NAVSEA) National Value Stream black belt for naval shipyard transformation. Bob holds a Ph.D. and master of science degree in Industrial and Operations Engineering from the University of Michigan (with Dr. Liker as his advisor), and a bachelor of science degree in Mechanical Engineering from the University of Maryland.

Tony McNaughton worked for Toyota Motor Corporation Australia for more than a decade. This was at a time when Toyota Japan was learning how to manufacture outside of Japan and to deal with non-Japanese suppliers and trade unions. As a member of the Toyota Australia staff engineering group and supplier development group, Tony was instrumental in defining and implementing the Toyota Production System internally within Toyota as well as their Tier 1 suppliers. He was mentored by Toyota Japan's Toyota Production System experts, Operations Management Consulting Division (OMCD). Tony McNaughton is now the managing director of Lean Thinking Pty Ltd. and is a senior advisor to Lean Enterprise Australia.

Richard Zarbo, MD, DMD, is the senior vice president and chairman of pathology and laboratory medicine in the Henry Ford Health System. He received both medical and dental degrees from the University of Connecticut. He is a board certified anatomic and clinical pathologist and an expert in head and neck pathology, laboratory quality, and lean management. Under the leadership of Dr. Zarbo, all laboratories of the Henry Ford Health System have been integrated into one corporate service line that includes five acute-care hospitals and 30 clinic laboratory sites. He has been one of the pathology profession's early pioneers in applying quality techniques and principles of lean manufacturing to laboratory medicine and these integrated laboratories. Dr. Zarbo's curriculum vitae contains over 200 peer-reviewed publications, with over 50 directly related to laboratory quality. Dr. Zarbo is the past president of the United States and Canadian Academy of Pathology and current president of the Michigan Society of Pathologists.

Prologue

Is Toyota Still a Great Company Others Can Learn From?

When Toyota recalled more than 10 million vehicles between late 2009 and early 2010 because of safety issues, accusations about precipitous drops in quality started flying, and critics claimed that Toyota had been intentionally hiding potential safety issues. This naturally led some people to question the Toyota Way. We still believe that the core of Toyota's engineering and manufacturing processes are exceptional, and that the three main recalls (misused all-weather floor mats entrapping accelerators, Prius brake feel, and slow to return "sticky" pedals) were three specific errors—not an indictment of all the company's processes. We have studied the recall saga thoroughly and found no evidence that Toyota was intentionally hiding any safety issues.[1] On the other hand, the Toyota Way says that Toyota should bring all problems to the surface, find the actual root cause, and solve the problems one by one, and it seems that the company was slow to respond. That does not mean that the Toyota Way is invalid; in fact, it reinforces the importance of following the principles in every part of the organization all the time.

The point of *The Toyota Way* was not to chronicle current events at Toyota or suggest that the company is perfect but rather to identify sound management principles from many sources, such as Deming,

Henry Ford, Training within Industry, and organization theory, that any company can learn from, using Toyota as an example since they integrated these principles into a total management philosophy. We suspect that all would agree that Toyota's remarkable success in growing from a small, local Japanese company to the world's largest automaker, based on innovation, quality, and safety, was exceptional. That there have been growing pains along the way is not surprising. Organizations throughout the world have used the principles of the Toyota Way with great results, in health care, industry, mining, banking, government, and countless other fields. As you will see in this book, we always encourage companies to find their own way, using the principles as guidelines. So what was the real story as Toyota seemed to stray so far from excellence?

In the fall of 2009, and leading into 2010, the U.S. government and the media relentlessly attacked Toyota. Toyota was a fraud, they claimed. It lies, cheats, and puts profits before people. It knowingly endangers its customers, putting their lives at risk, and hides the problems. The culprit was sudden unintended acceleration, in which Toyota vehicles, but not those of other car companies, can take off on their own, and no attempt to stop the car works. At least, that was the story relayed breathlessly day and night by an endless stream of "expert commentators." We have to admit, we had an unfair advantage over the 24/7 news crowd. We could be patient enough to find out the truth. We could research and follow up on the stories and read the police reports, claims, and other material without the daily pressures of having to produce over-the-top, scandalous headlines. As the litany of media stories broke, each more fantastic than the last, we were able to look with calm and clear heads at what was really happening and draw conclusions of our own.

We will start by saying—balderdash! As you might imagine, we find these claims to be without merit, or, in less polite terms, utter nonsense. The underlying claim of electronics problems leading to sudden unintended acceleration was little more than a baseless witch hunt, as revealed by a thorough NAAS investigation in a report released on February 8, 2011. Certainly mistakes were made that led to sticky pedals in a small number of cars and Prius brakes that felt funny when the antilock break system (ABS) unexpectedly kicked in under unusual conditions. Even the Lexus vehicles, the hallmark of near perfection, have had a series of nagging errors. As of the time of this writing, the government's safety arm, the National Highway Transportation Safety Administration (NHTSA), has validated two cases of tragic accidents related to unintended acceleration in Toyotas—a Camry accident due to a poorly designed floor mat recalled in 2008 and a San Diego police officer and his family who tragically died in August 2009. In the San Diego case, the police report indicated that the problem was that the wrong all-weather floor mats had been placed in the passenger compartment and not secured, and the mat entrapped the accelerator pedal, causing the car to race at over 100 miles per hour. The real problem turned out to be at the Lexus dealership, where the police officer picked up his loaner passenger car; the dealer had installed an all-weather floor mat that was designed for a much larger sport utility vehicle—it entrapped the pedal because it simply didn't fit right. Without the error by that dealer, we doubt that it would be necessary to write this prologue. Unfortunately, it did happen, and all the hoopla in the press has called into question the integrity of the company and its legitimacy as a model for excellence.

The Truth about the Recalls

Let's put aside what Toyota did wrong or right and whether it deserves disdain for the way it handled the safety concerns. It is absolutely clear that none of the defects had anything at all to do with the company's manufacturing system. The root causes of the technical issues were a small number of engineering design errors made over a 10-year period. Most of what companies have been learning from Toyota comes from the Toyota Production System (TPS) in its factories, which is as intact as ever and continues to build exceptional-quality cars at comparatively low cost. Anyone who has spent time in a Toyota factory recently knows that excellence abounds. Watch the painstaking approach to training a team member to perform a one-minute-cycle-time job. Watch how parts come to the assembly line in sequence in a precise orientation so that there is almost no waste as the team member grasps each part in the course of her routine. Witness the launch of a new vehicle with thousands of new parts and new tools, where every team member, team leader, and group leader has precisely planned every minute detail so that the vehicle launches flawlessly and the line is up to full speed within days. Parallels to a fine symphony orchestra immediately come to mind.

Now let's consider a few facts about the recall crisis to assess the legitimacy of claims that it represents a collapse of quality and integrity:

- *Defective carpets that are not defective.* Let's say you bought a Toyota or Lexus that is on the carpet recall list and drove it home. What would be wrong with it that could cause sudden acceleration? The answer is, nothing at all. There is no defect, unless either you or the dealer added a rubber all-weather floor mat to the passenger compartment and stacked it on top of the existing mat rather than first removing the existing mat and then fastening the rubber mat to the retaining clips on the floor of the car. If that happened, the rubber floor mat could slide forward and entrap the accelerator pedal, causing serious danger. Was that a defect in the car? Your call. You should also know that the same problem can occur in many other companies' cars if you stack mats one on top of another.

- *Sticky pedals that do not get stuck.* In less then 20 confirmed cases out of 2.2 million cars sold, the pedal got sticky and returned to the neutral position more slowly than normal. The car does not suddenly accelerate in this case, of course, but it does not decelerate as quickly as you would expect. The brakes will still stop the car. There have been a couple of cases in which the pedal actually stuck in position, but this was in a fast idle mode, and the brakes were more than enough to stop the car. Fortunately, this has not caused any accidents as far as we know. It did lead to federal investigations of Toyota and the largest fine ever levied against an auto company.

- *Unusual-feeling brake pedals that still stop the Prius.* You are driving your 2009 Prius at slow speed, hit a pothole, and apply the brakes. There is what feels like hesitation for a second before the ABS system kicks in. Actually, what happened was that the

ABS was set more aggressively and kicks in, a condition you do not expect, and the strange sensation is the ABS working to actually stop the car effectively. Again, there were no known accidents. Interestingly, around the same time as the Prius recall, Ford announced a different but similar problem in its Fusion hybrid that actually led to slight hesitation in braking. Ford did not issue a recall and reported that it was not a safety issue. No problem!

- *A Lexus that spins out in unusually tight turns and fails.* Consumer Reports *tests, but passes government tests.* The 2010 Lexus GX 460 sport utility became notable as the first car in more than a decade that was put on the "do not buy" list by *Consumer Reports.* In a test, its drivers drove the vehicle into a sharp turn at 60 miles per hour and at the last second took their foot off the gas and did not apply the brakes to see if the vehicle stability control (VSC) system would kick in and adjust the car. The Lexus rear end spun out to an unacceptable degree before the VSC system kicked in and righted the vehicle. How could Toyota have missed this in its own tests? It turns out that the test is not required by NHTSA and Toyota does not run it in this way. When *Consumer Reports* explained how it was testing, it was easy for Toyota to replicate the results and tune the vehicle stability control system (a change in computer parameters), solving the problem in no time. Toyota actually stopped sales of the car the same day that *Consumer Reports* reported the problem.

United States Disease

Toyota builds and sells cars all over the world using common parts on common platforms; many of them are shipped from Japan. Yet only one country had a rash of sudden unintended acceleration reports. The company has been sued and brought in front of the government in only one country. Massive recalls were initiated primarily in one country. Why did the same cars change when they came across the border to the United States and become Stephen King nightmares? By the way, the United States is the only country that uses all-weather floor mats extensively.

Recalls are a fact of life in the U.S. auto industry—before 2009, Toyota had not stood out over time as being particularly high or low on recalls. Recalls themselves are quite subjective and have a lot to do with judgments by the company and government policy. For example, the decision to issue a recall is made either by the company alone or after a dialog with the NHTSA. The NHTSA and the manufacturer are trying to assess whether other cars may have the problem and the safety risk if the problem were to occur. At times, both parties easily agree that a recall is the right remedy. But given, as the previous examples show, that it is not always clear what is and what is not a safety concern, it's also easy to see why disagreements would occur and manufacturers might resist recall demands from the NHTSA—demands that from a manufacturer's perspective sometimes seem capricious. There also seems to be some political motivations. After the NHTSA was criticized in the fall of 2009 for being too "soft" on Toyota, recalls increased precipitously—for all auto manufacturers.

In 2008, there were 119 separate recalls affecting more than 12 million vehicles in the United States. Toyota was responsible for three of these, affecting about 1 million vehicles total. In 2009, with the carpet recall, Toyota jumped up to nine recalls affecting about 5 million vehicles. After the NHTSA became more aggressive, the top five automakers in U.S. sales (other than Toyota) went from 47 recalls in 2009 to 80 safety recalls in 2010. General Motors Co., Chrysler Group LLC, Honda Motor Co., and Nissan Motor Co. recalled more vehicles in the first half of 2010 than they did in all of 2009. It seems clear from this that recalls have as much to do with government policy as with the underlying risks to the public—the same automobiles did not suddenly become twice as unsafe in a six-month period.

As time has passed, there have been several objective investigations of cases in which Toyota customers claim sudden unintended acceleration. Toyota investigated more than 2,000 cases in the first half of 2010, finding zero instances of sudden acceleration caused by electronics and a lot of cases of driver error or misunderstanding. The U.S. government investigated dozens of cases. The verdict—other than stacked carpets entrapping the accelerator—was that customers mistook the gas pedal for the brake pedal or misinterpreted the normal functioning of the vehicle as sudden acceleration. Toyota has an event data recorder in most of its vehicles. It was not required by law (until after the Toyota crisis in 2010), and different models capture different amounts of data, but in the cases that the government investigated in which customers claimed that their cars took off on their own and that steady, forceful pushing on the brake pedal did nothing, it was clear that the throttle was wide open and that there had been no application of the brakes. In other words, the driver was forcefully applying the gas pedal, not the brakes. It is also interesting that the vast majority of these cases were at speeds under 15 miles per hour, most of them from a static start. This brings to mind the Audi witch hunt of 1986, when the Audi 5000 was linked to six deaths and 700 accidents because of sudden unintended acceleration. The show *60 Minutes* actually faked sudden acceleration to dramatize the Audi 5000 problem, fitting a canister of compressed air on the passenger-side floor, linked via a hose to a hole that had been drilled into the transmission. The only problem detected turned out to be drivers hitting the wrong pedal, but the negative publicity was enough to reduce annual sales from about 74,000 vehicles in 1985 to 12,000 the following year.

Is Toyota Still an Excellent Company?

Does this mean that Toyota did nothing wrong and was simply framed? No, we do not believe that. Any errors are too many for a company that strives for zero defects. And Toyota has concluded that it was slow to respond to customer concerns, leading to major changes throughout the company. On the other hand, 99.9 percent of the engineers and everyone in manufacturing had nothing at all to do with any of the recalls. By every objective statistical measure through the end of 2009, other than recalls, Toyota vehicles were of higher quality and safer than at any other time in the history of the company.

What does all this have to do with continuous improvement and excellence? First, there is no evidence that the decades of excellence through continuous improvement at Toyota were a lie. Certainly manufacturing had nothing to do with any of these problems, so we can comfortably look at TPS as an excellent model and learn from it.

Second, the purpose of looking at Toyota is not to judge whether it is perfect all the time and every Toyota manager is a model citizen. The purpose is to learn so that we can improve our own organizations. Tens of thousands of organizations have applied the basic lean concepts that Toyota pioneered, with stunning results. Unfortunately, most often those results have been localized and poorly sustained, as the companies did not carry them far enough to make the kind of transformation that is possible through true continuous improvement.

Using Toyota's own standards of excellence, we will admit that we were disappointed by a number of Toyota's decisions revealed through the recall crisis. Fundamental concepts in the Toyota Way were violated. Customer first says that you always listen carefully to the customer and translate any concerns into problem solving and then into immediate action. Problems should not accumulate in batches to be solved later. The foundation of the Toyota Production System is bringing problems to the surface, scientifically analyzing the root causes, and putting countermeasures in place.

In February 2010, a lightbulb came on, and Toyota began to act more in line with what the Toyota Way would demand. It started a very aggressive recall program that targeted the smallest customer concerns—even those that were not serious safety issues. It also took an aggressive stance in evaluating virtually every aspect of its engineering and communication process, including reviews by outside panels of distinguished experts; in response, it put significant countermeasures in place.

In engineering, the company concluded that as it was growing and putting out a multitude of new cars, it had relied too heavily on engineering contractors (about 30 percent of the workforce) and young engineers who did not have the rigorous training of earlier generations of Toyota engineers. Toyota has since reduced its reliance on outside contractors and actually added management positions so that there is a smaller span of control and more direct mentoring of young engineers. It reassigned 1,000 engineers to focus on quality and safety. It has also taken organizational steps to strengthen regional autonomy in making recall decisions, such as creating a chief quality officer position for each local region, strengthening field office engineering, and organizing SMART (Swift Market Analysis

Response Team) teams that go to the customer to investigate complaints firsthand.

We believe that the model of continuous improvement that Toyota applied broadly in the company, especially in manufacturing, is the best path toward excellence that we know. We have worked with many companies, and opportunities for improvement using lean methods are everywhere, but there is an important caveat. To truly capitalize on these opportunities, the leaders of the organization have to think differently about improvement. The theoretical foundation for this new way of thinking is an old American idea: plan–do–check–adjust (PDCA). In this book, we argue that the simple idea of PDCA can be applied to make an organization innovative and adaptable to take on major challenges from the environment. It is the path to the ever-elusive learning organization that so many companies have only dreamed of. Toyota remains, in our opinion, the best example of a learning organization. It began learning almost immediately from the recall crisis and will come out stronger. Outlearning the competition is the only sustainable way to win the race . . . in the long term.

Section One

The Journey to Continuous Improvement

We are what we repeatedly do. Excellence then is not an act, but a habit.

—Aristotle

The term *kaizen*, which literally means change (*kai*) for the better (*zen*), has been around for so long that most non-Japanese books do not even italicize it as a foreign word. There is a danger that familiarity breeds complacency. How many companies have, or have had, a continuous improvement office with continuous improvement coordinators? It is old hat, yesterday's news—a fine concept, but nothing earth-shattering. Yet, would it surprise you to hear that in our collective visits to literally hundreds of companies in the last 10 years, we have never seen honest-to-goodness continuous improvement outside of Toyota? We are sure that there are cases, but we have not seen them. And even Toyota struggles to maintain continuous improvement, particularly in its overseas operations. In 2001, then Toyota president Fujio Cho issued a detailed booklet called *The Toyota Way 2001* based on a model with only two pillars reflecting the core practices of the company—continuous improvement and respect for people. He did that because he saw too much inconsistency among Toyota managers in their understanding of what made the company tick. He needed to continually drive home the importance of this seemingly simple concept: continuous improvement.

Now let's consider what continuous improvement means. It does *not* mean that the company values only small, incremental changes and avoids fundamental innovation. It does mean being committed to the ideal of improving continuously in every part of the organization. In reality, we know that doing so is impossible. At some times and in some places, we have to be just doing our jobs the way we did them the day before, and perhaps we even make mistakes that send us backward. In reality, continuous improvement is a vision, a dream, and no company in real life can possibly always get better. Witness the Toyota recall crisis. That hardly represented a leap forward. The leap forward should come as a result of the crisis as Toyota reconnoiters, reflects on what happened, and drives change throughout the enterprise. The key word there is *throughout*. Every part of the organization (sales, engineering, manufacturing, communications, government affairs, quality), down to the level of the working stiff, has to work actively at countermeasures to safety recalls and the resultant damage to the company's image. In our experience, no company does this better than Toyota.

We've been actively part of the "lean" movement that was launched when Womack and associates put out the seminal book *The Machine That Changed the World*,[1] and labeled what they saw at Toyota "lean production." We have led countless *kaizen* events, getting together teams of people for a week to attack a process with a vengeance, dissecting it, picking it apart, finding waste, developing imaginative leaps forward, implementing the best ideas, and then measuring the improvements. These have been some of the most exciting weeks of our careers. We have also led companies toward longer-term, deeper transformations of value streams in manufacturing plants, iron-ore mines, car rental sites, product development offices, software development projects, and more. This is more satisfying in a deeper way than one-week *kaizen* events, but our intent in everything we have done is always the same: to teach, illustrate, and sell the concept of continuous improvement. For us, success is when lightbulbs come on and people say: "Wow! That is what it feels like to open our minds to the possibilities for improvement. That is what I want to dedicate my career to."

The good news is that we get those lightbulbs coming on quite often. The bad news is that rarely do enough lightbulbs come on in enough of the organization's leaders to drive it aggressively toward the vision of continuous improvement. The most obvious problem is made apparent when we realize who is part of the demonstration *kaizen* events and who is not. Most of the key executives are conspicuously absent. They are busy looking at the reports to decide whether there is enough payback from this lean program to keep funding it. They are managing the company as if by remote control, and they are remote. Being analytical is fine, even a virtue, but the only hope of seriously marching toward the ideal of continuous improvement is to have passionate executives leading the charge. They are simply not there in very many organizations.

As we thought about this conundrum, it occurred to us that we might have been framing *Lean* in the wrong way, which could even have contributed to this problem. Lean has become framed as a "war on waste." A war is something that you prepare for, fight, and hopefully win, and then you move on. For far too many organizations, lean is a war that requires some trained troops (i.e., black belts) to go into the organization, win the war, declare victory, and move on to something else. This is not continuous improvement.

Our search for better models led us to some of the great management books on companies that are consistently high performers. Lo and behold, these companies share many of the same characteristics that we have come to admire in Toyota—a passion for excellence, an obsession with satisfying customers, striving for perfection, driven by core values, highly self-critical leaders who are humble and leave their egos at home, a desire to build something that will endure forever, and complete faith that investing in people is the only way to succeed.

What we think is missing from some of the great books about searching for excellence or striving to be great is the playbook. How do you do it? This is where what we learned from Toyota about the journey to continuous improvement comes in, as does what we can learn from other companies on the lean journey. There is some magic in what happens in those *kaizen* events, and it is the delight of freeing our minds to challenge today's way of doing things and moving toward a deliberate, planned better state that meets our objectives.

In this first section, we bring you the background concepts that we will illustrate through detailed case studies in Section Two. We consider the culture needed to embrace continuous improvement to be what we describe as "organic," as distinct from the mechanistic approach to lean that too many companies continue to take. The cases in Section Two are written from a vantage point that is missing from much of the literature—the perspective of the change agent. In Toyota terms, this is the *sensei*—the master teacher. The *sensei* can be a hired consultant or, better yet, a full-time member of the organization. We dug into our network of exceptional *sensei*, both internal executives and external advisors. Together we are bringing you this book to share our understanding of continuous improvement and examples of how we attempt to move organizations along on their journey toward this elusive ideal state. The goal is to help executives, managers, and change agents envision what continuous improvement can look like in any organization, and plot a path toward that vision.

Chapter 1

Continuous Improvement toward Excellence

The reason behind the absence of focus on product and people in so many American companies, it would seem, is . . . overreliance on analysis from corporate ivory towers and overreliance on financial slight of hand, the tools that would appear to eliminate risk, but also, unfortunately, eliminate action.

—Thomas Peters and Robert H. Waterman Jr.,
In Search of Excellence

Continuous Improvement as the Pursuit of Excellence

It is hard to imagine any self-respecting CEO saying, "My vision for my company is mediocrity." Excellence seems to be a universal goal. Yet our experience working with many companies has been that the actions of their chief executives tend to lead to mediocrity, not excellence. Perhaps it is a matter of definition. When the CEO sets business goals, they're typically in terms of profitability and growth. Is being the profit leader in your industry or the growth leader in your industry equivalent to the pursuit of excellence? If a company grows rapidly through mergers and acquisitions and becomes the largest company in its industry with the fastest-rising stock price, has it achieved excellence?

Let's go back to basics. Your child is passionate about golf or music or cooking and thinks that he wants to make a career out of it. You explain if he is really serious about this, he will need to dedicate himself

5

to what he loves, perhaps for the rest of his life. Above all, he will have to obsessively practice, practice, practice. If he would like it to be a hobby, that is also fine, because he can always pick it up and have some fun in his spare time, but treating it as a hobby is different from treating it as a vocation. Let's say your golf-loving son Johnny replies: "I don't really know about dedicating my life or sacrificing, but I really want to win the juniors tournament next summer so that I can impress Judy enough to go to the senior prom with me." As a parent, you might feel deflated and think that Johnny is not really dedicated and this will be a passing phase. The passion for excellence is just not there.

Defining excellence in an absolute sense is challenging. Is the standard for excellence in playing the violin being among the top 10 in the world, being the best in your country, or being the best in your town? Is the town virtuoso not excellent just because the best in the world are so much better? Is excellence an absolute value, as in achieving an A in the course? We believe it is more useful to define excellence as a pursuit rather than as an absolute value. If we improve, we're closer to excellence than we were before. The highest levels of performance give us a vision of excellence that provides a direction for our efforts—a "true north."

Now suppose that Johnny grows up, gets his MBA, and rises quickly to become the CEO of a global food-processing company. He is a brilliant public speaker, and he extols the virtue of making the highest-quality food for a competitive price. It all sounds good, but at the same time, his business decisions are all focused on short-term transactions to increase the company's share price—mergers, acquisitions, selling off businesses, moving production to low-wage countries, and training legions of "black belts" to drive cost-reduction projects. Costs are going down, down, down. Quality is acceptable; there are problems, but none of them are big enough to shut down the company. There is nothing distinctive about the products. The bottom line looks great. Is this true excellence as a producer of high-quality food, or is making food simply a means to quick profits, like a hobby? Johnny may be excellent at making money, but he is not excellent at making food.

There is evidence that over the long term, companies that are striving for true excellence in the products they make and the services they provide outperform companies that are focused only on short-term financial goals. One of the best-selling business books of the 1980s was *In Search of Excellence*.[1] Peters and Waterman identified the most successful American companies based on long-term financial performance and came up with a list of generalizations of what they had in common. Excellent companies "stuck to their knitting"; that is, they focused on what they were good at and worked to be the best at it. At the core of their model were shared values. The managers in excellent companies valued customers and had a passion for innovation within their industry:

> *The rational model causes us to denigrate the importance of values. The top performers create a broad and uplifting, shared culture, a coherent framework within which charged-up people search for appropriate adaptations. Their ability to extract extraordinary contributions from very large numbers of people turns on the ability to create a sense of highly-valued purpose.*[2]

Some people have pointed out that many of Peters and Waterman's "excellent" companies did not perform so well in the 10 years after the book came out. But there is further evidence that pursuing excellence pays over the long term. In *Built to Last* Jim Collins and his associates[3] chronicled 18 "truly exceptional and long-lasting companies" and compared them to less competitive counterparts in terms of growth and financial performance over many years. Almost 20 years after *In Search of Excellence*, Collins and his associates also found that the most successful American companies had vision, were innovative, and had developed a strong set of shared values. The leaders of these companies were uniformly passionate about their customers and their quality and intentionally developed next-generation leaders who shared that passion. Among Collins and his associates' many insights was that the company itself is the ultimate creation. "We had to shift from seeing the company as a vehicle for the products to seeing the products as a vehicle for the company."[4]

In many companies, we hear inspiring speeches by CEOs who are very convincing about their commitment to excellence. Unfortunately, when we have had an opportunity to investigate the actual state of the company, we have seen something entirely different. We have seen disarray everywhere, people coming to work who seem more interested in watching the clock so that they can go home than energetically doing excellent work, department managers who are more interested in growing their budgets than in performing a real service for customers, and poorly organized work processes.

In *The High Velocity Edge*, Steven Spear documents the success of leaders like Boeing, Toyota, and Pratt & Whitney that are out front in business success while their competitors huff and puff and struggle to keep up.[5] He identifies operational excellence as a key differentiator. In a personal interview, he explained that the lack of interest in operational excellence starts with deficiencies in our business education system:

> *Current management training, especially the typical MBA, suffers a fatal flaw. It is largely "transactional" in orientation, with students taught to think in terms of buy/sell, enter/exit, hire/fire decisions. Business strategy courses are mainly about transactional decisions—entering or exiting markets, licensing, outsourcing and so forth to gain a positional edge over competitors, suppliers, and customers. Even many operations management courses have taken on a transactional bent, with focus on facility site location, technology selection, production control tool use, and the like. However, outside of a few courses, missing is the critical idea of actually managing work in a way that uses operational excellence to give the firm competitive advantage, not merely finding a defensible position, but relentlessly outracing the field with ever better products and services, and ever better ways of bringing them to market.[6]*

The Toyota Way as the Path to Excellence

The Toyota Way provides an in-depth case study of one company's pursuit of operational excellence through continuous improvement and how it turned that pursuit into a strategic differentiator. From the senior executives to small groups of team members on the shop floor,

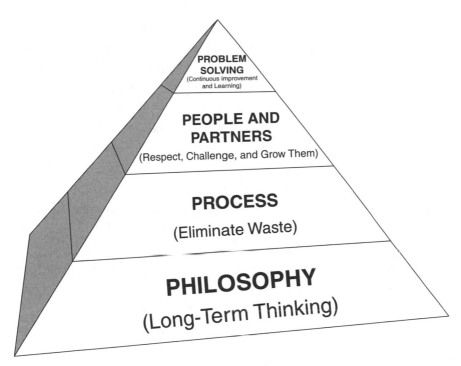

Figure 1.1. The Toyota Way 4P Model

there is a feeling of intense energy focused on getting better. Liker summarized the management principles he derived from intensively studying Toyota as a 4P model: an integrated system of philosophy, processes, people, and problem solving. The 4P model is shown in Figure 1.1. The philosophy is the foundation: "Base your management decisions on a long-term philosophy, even at the expense of short-term financial goals."

The most striking thing about Toyota is the consistency of values and the sense of mission up and down and across the company. The external focus is consistently on adding value to customers and society. The internal focus is on developing exceptional people and continually *challenging* them to push the boundaries of their abilities. "Challenge" is one of the five core values of the company. Toyota's internal document, *The Toyota Way 2001*, summarizes it this way: "We accept challenges with a creative spirit and the courage to realize our own dreams without losing drive or energy." Throughout its history,

Toyota leaders have been expected to distinguish themselves by accepting and delivering on a great challenge. For example, Takeshi Uchiyamada, head of research and development (R&D) at the time of this writing, took on the challenge of leading the development of the car for the twenty-first century, resulting in the creation of the first Prius.

In 2010, I (Jeff Liker) visited Herman Miller, an office furniture company that Toyota adopted as a student of the Toyota Production System (TPS). When the Toyota experts first visited Herman Miller's file cabinet plant, chosen as the pilot for TPS, they issued a challenge. At the time (around the year 1998), the plant was assembling file cabinets on two assembly lines (two different product lines), running three shifts, with 126 assemblers. The challenge was to build the same volume with one assembly line, working two shifts, with 16 people. The Herman Miller managers thought this was crazy, impossible, but with guidance from the Toyota experts, they worked at it, and worked at it, and are still working at it. Ten years later, through thousands of improvements, they had increased file cabinet production from 6,000/week to 7,250/week, on one assembly line, running two shifts, with 30 people. Twenty-minute changeovers were reduced to zero changeover. Lead time to produce a file cabinet dropped from 62 hours to 4 hours. This was the result of years of continuous improvement in practice.

In the fall of 2008, Toyota shocked the world when, like other companies, it faltered in the Great Recession. In fact, for the fiscal year ended in March 2009, it reported a financial loss for the first time in 60 years—$4.4 billion. The *New York Times* wrote: "The Toyota Motor Company booked its first annual net loss in six decades Friday and warned that it would plunge even deeper into the red this year, a stunning reversal for an automaker whose breakneck expansion and record profits seemed unstoppable just 12 months ago."[7]

Is the important news here six decades of profitability year after year, or one year of loss in the worst industry downturn since the Great Depression? In reality, Toyota's system did not fail. It performed exactly as planned, but the plan was not designed to deal with a drop of 35 percent in the market. The plan for operations was designed to give Toyota the flexibility to adapt to a ± 20 percent change in the market, which had worked just fine for decades. When sales declined to 65 percent of planned capacity, Toyota predictably lost money. Granted, Toyota could have softened the financial impact somewhat by acting like its competition: aggressively lay off workers and idle plants. Instead, no regular employees lost their jobs; they came to work and participated in training and improvement activities. The 4P model shows that the philosophy is based on long-term thinking, not knee-jerk reactions to the latest change in the winds of the economy or the speculations of various "pundits" on the financial channels.

To support its long-term philosophy, after decades of consistent profits (for example, $18 billion in fiscal year 2008 alone), Toyota saved plenty of cash reserves to weather the recession without involuntary layoffs or plant closings. Toyota's emergency system did kick in right away to find creative ways to cut costs and restore profitability. In April 2009, Toyota was forecasting a loss of more than $6 billion for the fiscal year. By the fall of 2009, this projected loss had dropped precipitously to an expected loss of $2 billion. At it turns out, this was overstated, as the market picked up, and for the fiscal year ending in March 2010, Toyota posted a net profit of over $2.2 billion. Even the comparatively minor pain that Toyota experienced was unsatisfactory to president Akio Toyoda and the board of directors. They ordered the company to significantly reduce its fixed overhead and operating costs so that in the future, Toyota could break even at 70 percent of planned sales.

This is not to say that Toyota is perfect; far from it. The recall crisis in some ways made the Great Recession appear easy to conquer. But imagine how difficult it would have been to address the recall crisis if the company had laid off tens of thousands of employees and slashed R&D spending during the recession. Instead, its investment in training and developing people at all levels gave it a formidable army to undertake the changes required by the recall crisis.

Toyota will always have ups and downs and some leaders who fail to act according to the Toyota Way. The ideal that the company is striving for is always so far ahead that it seems impossible to achieve, but the leaders do know in what direction they're headed, and it is about far more than being profitable or being the biggest. They're striving for their vision of excellence.

Lean and Why Companies Fail at It

Toyota's success has inspired tens of thousands of organizations to adopt some form of a "Lean" Program. The term was introduced in *The Machine That Changed the World* and later in *Lean Thinking* as a new paradigm that was as monumental as the shift from craft-style to mass production. The focus of lean is always on the customer and the value stream. It is a pursuit of perfection by constantly eliminating waste through problem solving. Certainly an organization that is truly dedicated to becoming lean is on a path toward excellence. Yet, a large survey conducted by *Industry Week* in 2007 found that only 2 percent of companies that have a lean program achieved their anticipated results.[8] More recently, the Shingo Prize committee, which gives awards for excellence in lean manufacturing, went back to past winners and found that many had not sustained their progress after winning the award. Why is the pursuit of excellence through lean not working?

To answer this, we might ask: is lean a hobby, or is it a lifelong commitment to becoming something great? A Lean Program with a short-term focus on cutting inventory or head count is much more like Johnny wanting to win the summer golf tournament to get the girl than like someone who is passionate about becoming the best golfer that he can be. Somewhere along the line, we developed a disconnect between the passion for excellence of highly successful companies like those that Peters and Waterman, and later Collins, were writing about and the implementation of process improvement methodologies. Companies have to do something if they're serious about excellence, and improving processes to better deliver value to customers seems like the obvious thing to focus on. So what is the source of the disconnect?

The Shingo Prize committee compared past award winners that had continued to improve with those that had gone backward and found that those that had gone backward were simply copying the tools, and those that had continued improving had turned the initial improvement efforts into a culture, starting with leaders who were passionate about striving for excellence. The committee revamped the award, calling it the Shingo Prize for Operational Excellence, and changed the criteria to emphasize developing a culture of continuous improvement.

We will talk a great deal in this book about problem solving, which is different from the connotation of firefighting. In firefighting, we are running around putting our finger in the dike and hoping that the dam will not collapse. In true problem solving, we are deeply trying to understand the root cause of a problem so that we can ultimately prevent the problem from occurring again. Toyota uses the "five whys" method: keep drilling down by asking "why" until you find the root cause. We did a five whys analysis to understand why so many companies are failing at lean. This is summarized in Figure 1.2.

What we see when we walk the operation is spotty implementation of lean and the basic discipline degrading over time. When we trace through the causal analysis, we discover that lean, as understood by these companies, is really a staff-driven program that is designed to quickly find and eliminate waste, with little understanding or commitment by the people who manage the process day by day. This is because of the lack of understanding by senior management, who think in simple mechanistic, cause-and-effect terms, believing that they will get results by using rewards and punishments to pressure the

Figure 1.2. Root-Cause Analysis of Why Lean Isn't Sustained at Large, Traditional Companies

system. This lack of serious commitment to understanding how they can develop true operational excellence, in turn, stems from the way senior managers are measured and evaluated—the bottom line. At the root cause are investors who don't understand or care about operational excellence and view the organization as a black box in which decisions lead to results, which either do or do not include large profits. As Steven Spear noted, their own training is transactional, and long-term efforts to make the company competitive based on operational excellence seem too distant and abstract.

By contrast, Toyota's record of continuous and persistent operational improvement (Figure 1.3) is attributable to a very different worldview on the part of those who hold the purse strings. There is no external board of directors representing investors. At the top is an internal board of directors made up of lifetime employees like Fujio Cho, who helped evolve the Toyota Production System, and Takeshi Uchiyamada, the chief engineer of the first Prius hybrid. Early in his career, President Akio Toyoda was sent by his dad to work in the

Figure 1.3. Root-Cause Analysis of Why Lean Processes Are Sustained and Improved at Toyota

Operations Management Consulting Division (OMCD), formed by Taiichi Ohno, to learn the Toyota Production System from the ground up by getting his hands dirty. Managing officers from every region of the world report to board meetings, providing detailed accounts of the current state of operations, and have input into strategic decisions. Informed discussions of philosophy, purpose, and operational capability are standard fare in Toyota board meetings. Executive officers get a salary and bonuses, but a fraction of the compensation of American CEOs. For example, one analysis showed that in 2010, Alan Mulally, CEO of Ford, got more compensation than the entire 20-plus-person board of directors of Toyota. The Toyota directors aren't given incentives to drive up the share price to make themselves rich. Running the company is driven by passion and striving for excellence.

Is Lean More than Mediocrity at a Cheaper Price?

We have been trying to understand Toyota, as well as help other companies that are trying to improve themselves with Toyota as a model, for more than 15 years. I personally have been studying Toyota for almost 30 years. When a new organization seeks us out as advisors, we're always excited by the possibilities. We try to grasp the current situation by going to the *gemba* (where the work is done) and observing. What we see is chaos and disorder in all processes, with little understanding of a method for systematically attacking the problems.

Our beginning point is always to explain our philosophy of lean: it's a long-term commitment, it's a process, we're only guides, and the most important thing is how your own people develop their ability to lead continuous improvement. We then do projects, and each individual project is successful in improving a process and the results from that process (e.g., quality, cost, safety). We work with teams that do wonderful work eliminating waste and feel inspired by their own power to make change for the better. Everything is upbeat and rosy until . . .

In many organizations that we work with, something happens that derails the process. That something always involves lack of commitment by senior management. It could be that sales are down and budgets are cut, including the continuous improvement budget. It could be a reorganization in which the Six Sigma department is now taking over lean, and the direction of lean shifts from continuous improvement to stand-alone projects. In some cases, the senior executives have decided that one or two years have passed and the bottom-line results aren't as impressive as they had hoped, and so they want the whole Lean Program to go in "another direction."

We're talking about large companies, and some of our colleagues have had more success with medium or small companies. In large companies, with dozens of plants, even a breakthrough on one value stream in one manufacturing plant may be insignificant when it is rolled up to the company level. Of course, we can extrapolate what will happen if we keep this going for a few years, but that often seems too abstract for key decision makers.

When it comes right down to it, the success of lean depends on the very top leaders of the company. If they're striving for excellence and are committed to lean as a vehicle for progressing on that journey, lean is bound to be successful. If they have a short-term operational objective (e.g., cut head count by 20 percent) and see lean as a toolkit for achieving it, lean may help them do so, but this alone will not achieve operational excellence.

On the other hand, there are ways to approach lean that will get impressive results in a defined domain while still developing people. A top leader who is willing to be convinced and is at least open to some extrapolation will be able to see the benefits within defined areas of practice, and the lean zealots will buy some time to convince the senior leaders that lean should be a way of life at the company. Focusing lean activities intensively on critical business issues is essential for all but the most patient and committed of senior executives.

The Real Journey to Excellence Follows PDCA

We decided to write this book because of the urgency of helping companies understand why their great individual projects are not adding up to the stunning business results that they expect. What we have observed time and time again is a very large difference between what senior leaders think is happening with their Lean Program and the reality in the trenches where the real work is done: at the *gemba*.

As we work with companies and compare their Lean Six Sigma programs to the philosophy of the Toyota Way, we see a striking gap. One thing we have observed is that Toyota almost always gets the results it sets as targets, and it almost always sustains the new process—not for days or weeks, but for years. How is it that with the same lean toolkit, Toyota achieves so much more than other companies? When we're in the trenches with our clients, it seems quite apparent why they're doing so well on individual projects and so poorly at growing and sustaining the momentum. The simplest summary is that they see lean as a toolkit and don't understand the deeper philosophy.

One warning as you read this book is that we say some pretty critical things about Lean, Six Sigma, and Lean Six Sigma. We try to be equal-opportunity bashers. Heck, we would be happy to throw in some slams on the theory of constraints and agile, for that matter. There is a long-standing debate, and some down and dirty political conflict, between the lean factions and the Six Sigma factions within many companies, and in the software development world a conflict is growing between lean and agile. We're often assumed to be in the lean camp, so the lean zealots are often startled when they hear us criticizing what they are doing.

A Note on Lean Six Sigma

Throughout this book you will hear various references to Lean Six Sigma Programs that may sound negative. The truth is that we have had some pretty negative experiences being brought into organizations to help them on the road to operational excellence only to run into the Lean Six Sigma bureaucrats who blocked our progress. So partly you are hearing frustration.

(Continued)

The basic problem is that Total Quality Management, a beautiful philosophy that puts customers first and strives to perfect processes to deliver what the customers want when they want it morphed into something else as it traveled through Motorola to Allied Signal to General Electric and on to companies all over the world. At its worst it became a fairly mindless application of statistical tools to remove variation from processes with the sole measure of success being dollars saved. Young people good at math were trained in statistics and set loose on operations run by experienced people trying to get through the day. These young black belts who were often inexperienced and lacked leadership or even strong interpersonal skills, collected the data, gave their list of recommendations (which ended in dollars saved), and got paid big bonuses. This is an unimaginable scenario in Toyota. Young, inexperienced people are the apprentices who are there to learn and to be developed by the experienced masters.

Total Quality Management as practiced by the best companies in Japan and some of the best companies outside of Japan was primarily an organic system, while Six Sigma was primarily a mechanistic knock-off that fit the Western mindset. At its worst, the experts come in, do their projects, and leave an unstable process without local ownership. When "lean" was getting attention and acceptance, the Six Sigma black belts picked up some of the key tools and declared that they were now Lean Six Sigma experts. It is interesting that no one in Toyota would ever declare themselves TPS experts. They all sincerely believe they are just learning.

Because of this underlying philosophy and mindset, we have reservations about the Lean Six Sigma movement. On the other hand, the tools are all great if applied in the right way at the right time, and all are used by Toyota and many other excellent companies. And there are certainly many Lean and Six Sigma black belts with excellent change management skills and strong leadership skills who take the kind of teaching and cultural development approach we are advocating here.

Our criticisms have one common root cause. When individuals armed with a new tool or method go into a process on the attack to remove waste (lean), reduce variation (Six Sigma), or eliminate the constraints (theory of constraints), we have some serious concerns. They're seeing the system as a mechanistic set of processes that they need to fix. Unless the people in the process learn a new way of thinking, and some real skills to enable them to improve the process themselves, it will be a one-off change in their process, and over time you will see it degrade. Continuous improvement is more than a buzzword. It is a necessity if you truly want sustainable improvement.

Throughout the book we will be repeating one mantra above all: PDCA. Plan–do–check–adjust was taught to Toyota by Dr. W. Edwards Deming, who learned it from his mentor, Dr. Walter A. Shewhart. Deming originally came to Japan as a statistician to improve the census, but he got caught up in a national transformation that he could not possibly have imagined—the transformation of Japanese industry from rank amateurs in manufacturing to the best quality in the world. We believe the philosophy underlying PDCA is the reason for that stunning turnaround. The best Japanese companies resonated with PDCA as a way of thinking:

- Deeply question every process; bring problems to the surface and carefully define them.
- Understand the root cause.
- Develop countermeasures that are viewed as provisional until proven.
- Plan implementation in great detail (all *plan* to this point).
- Run the experiment (*do*).
- Closely monitor and analyze what is going on in the experiment (*check*).
- Learn from what happens and turn that into further action (*adjust*).

Run the loop over and over and see individuals learn, the organization learn, and operational excellence grow, and then connect that capability to a well-planned and well-executed business strategy.

The concept of PDCA was introduced by Walter Shewhart in a book about quality control in 1939.[9] Some trace it back to Bacon's work defining the scientific method in the thirteenth century. We still believe that there is something fundamentally different about what Toyota did with PDCA compared with what Shewhart wrote about, or even what Deming was teaching in Japan. The difference is between certain individuals using tools to control quality and the way Toyota's approach made PDCA an organizationwide philosophy. It is also a difference between individuals using PDCA to learn about a specific problem domain and a company embracing PDCA for organizational learning. *Individual learning often doesn't equate to organizational learning.* Robert Cole, one of the early Western experts on Japanese management systems, argues that organizational learning is essential for long-term success:

> *The interest in organizational learning stems from the premise that flexibility and speedy response are characteristics of learning organizations, and these are seen as critical to organizational survival and success in the new world of global competition. Learning organizations are adaptive organizations, and under the best circumstances they develop organizational practices that help them learn how to learn.*[10]

When an organization embraces PDCA, it starts to grow to become a learning organization. Projects go beyond one-offs and become a continuous stream of learning opportunities on the road to excellence. Excellence is an attitude as much as anything. Companies that think that tough, single-minded executives can, through brute force using shotgun-blast lean, drive the organization to achieve the metrics will not learn and will never understand real excellence. There is evidence that they also will not enjoy long-term success.

Learning Organizations Need Managers Who Are Teachers

The damage was done when Frederick Taylor defined "scientific management" as a body of knowledge owned by expert industrial engineers who are the thinkers, while the people who do the work *and* their managers/supervisors are the doers. While few managers today would agree with this philosophy overtly, it penetrated much of the global culture to a far greater degree than we realize. It put middle management in the role of the mindless pawns of the "experts" who were doing the thinking.

At various points Toyota executives have tried to redefine TPS as the "Thinking Production System." The idea was never to improve lifeless processes and make them "lean." It was not to develop lean material handling or lean cells or lean IT or lean engineering or any lifeless lean things. It was to develop thinking people who learn how to learn and grow and continually challenge the current work methods. Toyota wanted an army of process improvers spread across every value-added job thinking, planning, and doing, not a small number of staff experts and clever CEOs for hire to turn around the business. Improvement requires innovators and continuous improvement requires continuous innovators everywhere all the time. This was the paradigm shift, not the movement from mass production processes to lean processes.

It is interesting that the earlier tectonic shift was from craft production to mass production. Craft production was inefficient with the lone craftsperson doing every task, moving about the shop wasting motion and working on lowly and challenging tasks. In mass production the work was dissected into tiny pieces, each scientifically optimized and taught to an unskilled worker to perform repetitively throughout the day with the work defined in detail by an efficiency expert. Higher-level thinking tasks were assigned to managers and professionals who could be freed of the drudgery of mindless repetitive work. Craft production is inefficient and outdated, whereas mass production is efficient and provides lower-cost products in mass quantities to customers. But we lost something in this transition.

The excellent craftsperson was also thinking about how he or she could better do the work, save materials, improve the quality of the product for the customer—in short, innovate in the product and the process. The craftsperson usually did have someone to delegate the lowliest tasks to—an apprentice. The apprentice did the dirty work in exchange for an education—for learning at the feet of the master whose job was to teach. The harmony of planning, doing, teaching, and improving in this relationship was magical and somehow got lost as we rushed to get lower and lower piece prices through economies of scale and ever more elaborate bureaucracy.

There have been many experiments in "enriching work" by putting the pieces back together into whole jobs done by individuals or self-directed teams, but Toyota found a unique way of balancing the efficiency of the division of labor with the magic of the craft system. Work groups at the *gemba* (where the work is done) took responsibility for doing the work and studying how to better do the work with a teacher—the group leader—who was herself a student of PDCA. The group leader's job was to learn and teach, learn and teach, continuously. Teaching for the group leader meant learning PDCA by doing, starting with deeply understanding the work. Of course, learners are open to all input, including from staff experts, but the integration of that knowledge happens at the work site and is carried on across generations as masters teach apprentices who become masters to teach apprentices.

When Toyota says, "We build people before automobiles," it recognizes that it is people who improve processes and build products, and the capabilities of those people matter. The capabilities include continually upgrading their skills in performing the work, just like any artisan striving to master his art, and at the same time upgrading their skills in improving the processes by which they do the work. The duality between process improvement and skill development is inseparable, and if split between the staff thinkers and line doers, destroys any hope of continuous improvement.

In *Toyota Culture* we introduced Toyota's concept of "servant leadership."[11] Unfortunately, at times that concept was misunderstood. It does not mean that management becomes servants of the workers and does their bidding. It in no way weakens the role of management, but in fact strengthens it. Managers become responsible for how the value-added work gets done and for the development of the people doing the work. Managers are the master craftspeople who are teaching and developing the apprentices and in this way supporting the value-added workers. If managers do not themselves understand the work, or the process of continuously improving the work, they cannot add value, but are left to mindlessly monitor and control the workers to get out "pieces." The servant leader must earn deep respect. The teaching method can at times be harsh and challenging to the student. The goal is excellence in methods and results and continuously upgrading skills levels to achieve excellence.

The *Sensei* Perspective of This Book

You may sense some underlying frustration. We're often disappointed at the gap between what we see is possible in organizations and what actually happens in their lean transformation efforts. Those of us who share a more or less common perspective on what we're trying to accomplish with lean get together and complain about the concrete-headed executives we work with and what we would do if we were in charge. We're not in charge, but we thought it might be useful to share how we see things when we enter a company, help people see better ways to work, and try to teach what we have learned. We would like to convey through our eyes why lean so often fails and the path forward to a true journey toward excellence.

The perspective we will take in this book is that of a *sensei*, and we would like to take you on a learning journey. In Japanese, *sensei* literally means "teacher," but it implies much more. It implies the respect granted to a master at his craft by the apprentice who is struggling to learn that craft. We believe that the relationship between the *sensei* and the student (*deshi*) in Toyota is a key success factor, and one that is very much underappreciated in the lean movement. We have invited a number of *sensei* to help us with individual chapters. Through actual companies that they helped coach, we will see the situation they faced through *sensei* eyes: what happened, what worked, and what didn't work. All of our *sensei* are passionate about excellence and about helping others who want to be excellent. We all see process improvement and people development as two sides of the same coin in organizations. We aren't "leaning out processes" or "implementing lean solutions" but rather developing people to achieve challenging goals through a clearly defined improvement process and, in so doing, stretching themselves to become better people.

Most of us have learned from Toyota or Toyota suppliers. Our guest coauthor of Chapter 11 learned about lean product development mainly by working inside Honda as a chief engineer and engineering executive and then taking that to an American company as the vice president of engineering. When we compare notes among ourselves, we debate specific terminology or techniques, but we all share a common philosophy of solving problems through PDCA. This is a systematic way of solving problems as a step-by-step journey toward excellence that has made companies like Toyota and Honda so consistently successful over decades. That is what we wish to share.

Chapter 2

PDCA and Striving
for Excellence

*Long-term commitment to new learning and new philosophy is
required of any management that seeks transformation. The timid
and the fainthearted, and the people that expect quick results, are
doomed to disappointment.*

—W. Edwards Deming, American consultant,
statistician, and educator

PDCA as a Way of Thinking
and Learning

The concept of plan–do–check–adjust (PDCA) was taught to
Toyota by Dr. W. Edwards Deming, who was teaching what
he had learned from Dr. Walter Shewhart, the statistical
process control pioneer at Bell Laboratories. The focus was on preventive problem solving to reduce variation in all parts and to build each
component, subsystem, and complete product right the first time,
without a need for wasteful corrective action. A key message was that
good problem solving starts with good planning. Good planning is
fact-based. Since any real-life phenomenon is dynamic, not static,
Shewhart and Deming represented the dynamic nature of problems
with statistics.

Consider the example of statistical process control (SPC) charts
from the viewpoint of PDCA. The purpose is to reduce defects sent to
the customer by identifying processes that are moving out of control

before they produce defects. The "plan" includes the design of control charts: identifying the key variables to be charted, the expected average, and the acceptable range of results that are "in control," and then developing an action plan for how to respond when results are getting out of control. The "do" is to implement SPC through introducing the tools on the shop floor and training the workers. The SPC charts themselves are the "check" on the product, and the "adjustments" should be made dynamically when quality measures show that a process is drifting out of control—before defective product is actually made. Note that another PDCA loop can be the implementation of SPC itself, in which the problem may be that there is a gap between how the tools are intended to be used and how they actually are used, and we come up with a countermeasure for improvement. We then check to see if that countermeasure is working and make adjustments based on what we learn.

The key concept here is learning in a deliberate way. The plan leads to identification of a problem—a gap. Then we try countermeasures under the assumption that they may or may not work as expected. The check is so we can learn what actually happened and then make appropriate adjustments based on what we learn.

There are a variety of statistical tools for PDCA, ranging from mundane trend charts and bar charts to more elaborate statistical methods like experimental design and regression analysis. The general formulation is that there is some objective function (y), and we need to identify the right variables (x) and the statistical distribution (e.g., bell-shaped curve) that best fits the data. Then we are in a position to make predictions, implement, and check whether our predictions were correct. If we were correct in our predictions, we can then standardize the practices through various control systems and spread them to other places where the solution might fit. When you finish solving one problem, then you start planning for the next problem to solve so that it becomes a cycle, as shown in Figure 2.1.

Most organizations today have adopted some type of formal problem-solving process. It is a relatively structured approach, and so the full, detailed version should be used mostly on problems that

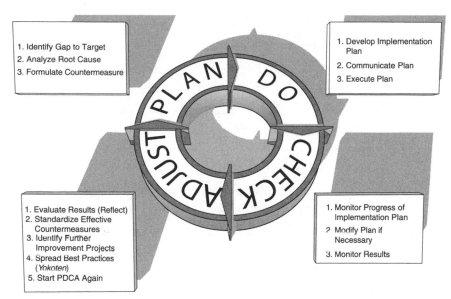

1. Identify Gap to Target
2. Analyze Root Cause
3. Formulate Countermeasure

1. Develop Implementation Plan
2. Communicate Plan
3. Execute Plan

1. Evaluate Results (Reflect)
2. Standardize Effective Countermeasures
3. Identify Further Improvement Projects
4. Spread Best Practices (Yokoten)
5. Start PDCA Again

1. Monitor Progress of Implementation Plan
2. Modify Plan if Necessary
3. Monitor Results

Figure 2.1. PDCA Problem Solving Is the Core of Lean Thinking

justify the investment in time and effort. In one structured form, it is part of the Six Sigma Program led by black belts. The job of the black belts is to identify problems that are worthy of their time and effort, which mainly means justifying them in terms of dollars saved. The core methodology that evolved in the Six Sigma movement is DMAIC: design, measure, analyze, implement, and control. Notice that the final step is "control": this assumes that if it all works out, you can tie a ribbon around the problem, and it is solved.

Toyota grabbed PDCA, applied it, and ultimately absorbed it as a core part of the Toyota Way. You can see PDCA loops in many figures and models throughout Toyota, and it is talked about constantly. It clearly made sense within the context of Toyota's culture, but is it the same thing that we now learn in Six Sigma training? We think that there are subtle, but important, differences. For Toyota, PDCA has become more than a set of methods for solving and closing out problems and far more than statistical analysis. It has become a way of thinking and the core of Toyota's learning philosophy.

What Is PDCA?

PDCA is short for plan–do–check–adjust and is the basis of problem solving as taught by Walter Shewhart at Bell Laboratories beginning in 1925. Shewhart's disciple, W. Edwards Deming, taught the PDCA method of problem solving in Japan in the 1950s and found an eager audience at Toyota. The PDCA way of thinking recognizes that life and business are dynamic and drives people to develop a disciplined method of identifying, defining, and solving problems as they occur, ideally one by one. Planning is critical and essential in that you need to first identify a gap between the actual situation and a target and identify the root cause of the problem. Once the root cause has been identified, countermeasures can be developed and tried by doing. The act of checking and adjusting means that you're comparing the expected outcome with the actual outcome and modifying your planning for the next cycle. New, standardized best practices are shared, and the process starts anew. Often the term *act* is used for the A, but we prefer the term *adjust* because it reflects the dynamic of learning. As you continue to run through numerous PDCA "loops," your understanding and expertise grow and deepen.

Toyota would like to spread this way of thinking to all people at all levels, not just among black belts. The focus is on thinking deeply and rigorously, based on the facts. This starts with *planning* and asking what the real problem is that you should be working on. Then you set a vision for the future and define specific measurable targets. Planning continues by asking where the real problem originated (point of cause) and then what is the root cause of the gap between the current situation and the targeted level. Then many ideas are generated that may solve the problem, and through some defined criteria, the most likely one is selected.

Now here is one of the key points for real learning. At this point, the proposed solution is still provisional. Toyota calls it a countermeasure.

We do not really know what will happen until we try it. The *doing* is to try it. Steven Spear calls this "running an experiment."[1] It is not really a controlled experiment with an experimental group and a matched control group, but it is a test of the hypothesis that we formulated in the *plan* stage. The *checking* is to see what actually happened in the experiment. What worked? What didn't work? What can we learn from this? In the *adjust* stage, we standardize what is working for that process, we come up with additional countermeasures for what did not work, and we share what we learned with others. The process of sharing with others is called *yokoten* (see the sidebar later in the chapter). It is more appropriate to say that others will choose to learn what they can from us in order to solve their own problems. There are always unresolved issues and things we can do better that flow right into the next PDCA loop. Thus, PDCA is a way of thinking and how the organization learns.

The difference between PDCA as a method of control seen in many companies with Six Sigma programs and Toyota's view of PDCA as a way of thinking and learning is summarized in Table 2.1. The starting point is the purpose of PDCA. In the DMAIC formulation, the purpose often seems to be control. In Toyota, the purpose is to

Table 2.1. Western View of PDCA as Control versus Toyota's Learning Perspective

	Western PDCA	**Toyota's PDCA**
Purpose	Predict and control process	Learn by trying
Goal	Solve problem	Improve process and develop people
Assumption	World is predictable, like a machine	World is dynamic and uncertain, like a living organism
Planning process	Statistical tools	Deep understanding and build consensus
Analyst	Expert with group input	Work group with expert support
Do	Implement solutions	Try countermeasures
Check process	Confirm hypothesis	Find further opportunities for improvement
Adjust process	Standardize proven process and replicate best practices	Standardize what works, share learning, ID further problems for PDCA

achieve breakthrough levels of performance and in the process learn by trying, but since Toyota sees the organization as a complex system of people, processes, and equipment, it sees a great deal of variability and uncertainty. Each PDCA project does in fact control some aspect of that variability for a time, but then as conditions change, new countermeasures must be put in place. This is why it is critical that the group responsible for the daily work is trained in PDCA so that its members can immediately notice new problems that arise from changing conditions and develop new countermeasures.

The term *countermeasure* is important because it suggests the provisional nature of any action to counter the unwanted variability. Toyota does not believe that a countermeasure is *the* solution; rather, it is the measure that is currently being tested. If the check shows that it has worked to move toward the target, then it is kept in place until a better countermeasure is developed. PDCA at Toyota never ends, not on any process. You do not close out the project and then control it and walk away. PDCA truly is a process of continuous improvement and thus continuous learning.

The Folly of "Lean Solutions"

The Western "control" orientation toward PDCA implicitly assumes that solutions to problems can be context-free. By this we mean that what works in one context should work the same way in another similar context. If we come up with a solution that is proven to work in the check stage, then in the adjust stage, we are told to spread the "best practice." This suggests that what worked in this particular case can work in other cases in the same way, so we merely have to replicate it. It is like any other fixed object, say, a gear: we can copy one gear design that works and insert it into another engine of the same design, and it will work—interchangeable parts, interchangeable best practices. Toyota uses the Japanese term *yokoten*, instead of spreading best practices. *Yokoten* is an organic concept rather than a mechanistic one. Technically it means "across everywhere," but you must understand what you're transplanting and the conditions where you are transplanting it and adjust appropriately, or it will fail.

What Is *Yokoten*?

Yokoten is a term in Japanese that describes the process of sharing practices horizontally in the organization. It means that during the sharing of a "better" practice, the environment into which the new idea is to be adopted must be understood, or the idea is not likely to succeed. It is in contrast to the forced, context-free replication of ideas without modification that is commonly known as "sharing best practices." *Yokoten* recognizes that ideas cannot always be copied without modifications to adapt them to the new environment.

Seeking prediction and control through immutable laws of lean that can be applied in any context leads to questions like

- What is the optimum mix between pull and push?
- When is electronic *kanban* better than a physical card system?
- What is the best practice in organizational design for structuring work groups?

Someone from Toyota would immediately recognize that these questions simply cannot be answered, or rather that the answer to each is: it depends, it depends, it depends. PDCA thinking leads you to recognize the complex interdependencies of systems. Every system is different from others. Moreover, something that is a best practice at one point in time might not be a best practice in the same setting a few months later, when conditions have changed and we have learned more. Remember that solutions are provisional.

As an example, our clients often ask us about a specific piece of "lean software"; they want to know if we recommend it. "There is no such thing as 'lean software,'" we answer. "There are lean systems, and you can find ways to use software as countermeasures to problems in lean systems, but there is nothing inherent in a piece of software that makes it lean or not lean." They find that confusing and persist. "But this is an enterprise resource planning system, and it has a *kanban* module." (*Kanban* is the signal to replenish inventory in a pull system. For example, as the assembly line uses parts, it might send back *kanban* cards signaling that it needs new parts to replenish what it has used.[2]) "Isn't *kanban* part of lean?"

We patiently answer, "Yes, it is true that under certain conditions, *kanban* can be used as part of a pull system, and this can be an important part of a lean system, but *kanban* can also be misused to create a non-lean system, and both electronic and manual versions can be used effectively under the right conditions." You can get the point of this endless dialogue, which leads to questions of what the right conditions are and how they can be specified so that the decision can be optimized, and on and on. The truth is that *kanban* represents today's countermeasure. We cannot produce exactly what we need when we need it in one-piece flow, so as a countermeasure we hold a small amount of defined inventory in a "marketplace" and replenish it as it is used. Over time, as we improve, we may get to the point where we can eliminate the inventory, and thus the *kanban* system, completely.

The mechanistic way of thinking about cause and effect was epitomized by Frederick Taylor's quest for "the one best way." Using his brand of "scientific management," he would time workers with a stopwatch and observe what the fastest worker did so that he could define the "one best way" of doing the job.[3] That "best way" would become the standard, and the foreman's job was to enforce this way of working. Taylor separated planning from doing. The doers, the workers, could not be trusted to contribute to the one best way. In fact, according to Taylor, they could be trusted only to be creative about ways of getting out of work:

> *Hardly a competent workman can be found who does not devote a considerable amount of time to studying just how slowly he can work and still convince his employer that he is going at a good pace.*[4]

Since Taylor, industrial engineering has morphed mostly into a discipline of mathematical modeling to find the "optimum" using operations research methods. The lean movement came about in a different way. It was case-driven, rather than mathematical-model-driven. *The Machine That Changed the World* documented the relative success of Japanese practices, and then later, in *Lean Thinking*, we learned that Toyota was the best of the best.[5] So a best practice in lean became whatever Toyota does. There are very few mathematical formulations that tell us the "lean best practice" for a given situation. Since Toyota is the best model for lean and we are trying to imitate best practices, the questions are then of the form, "What does Toyota do in this circumstance?" Presumably whatever Toyota does is lean, and if we copy it, we will get the best results. This also leads us down the wrong path. The idea of copying "lean solutions," even from Toyota, is completely alien to the Toyota way of thinking. Toyota does not even want one of its own plants to simply copy what another Toyota plant is doing. They want each plant to be aware of successful practices in other plants, deeply understand their own problems and circumstances, and consider how these ideas might be useful. But simply copying would be inappropriate and would kill *kaizen*.

If we go back to the case of Taylor's time studies and search for the one best way, you might notice that Toyota also has standardized work and uses stopwatches quite a bit. Isn't it following Taylor's methods? In a sense it is, but its philosophy is 180 degrees different. Toyota wants the work group to follow PDCA religiously. If someone in the work group says that we need to time our jobs and rebalance the work, the first question a good *sensei* will ask is, "What is the purpose of this exercise?" This leads not to lean solutions but rather to questions like

- What is the rate of customer demand (called the *takt*)?
- Is the current system meeting the *takt* consistently?
- If not, what are the causes of variability in production that prevent meeting the *takt*?

Based on the answers to these questions, we may, or may not, decide that the focus of problem solving should be on productivity using time and motion studies. If the analysis does reveal that we are not consistently meeting *takt* (see sidebar) or that we are not meeting our targets for cost, the analysis might lead us to want to improve the productivity of individual work processes. The question then becomes, "Where is there waste that is contributing to the gap between the target and the current condition?" In this case, we would want the work group to use a stopwatch to understand the current situation and identify waste. It would then seek to understand the root cause of that waste. This would lead to countermeasures to eliminate that waste, which the group will test, and based on the results of these tests, it will develop new standardized work for the improved jobs. These standards are not necessarily the best for everyone who is doing that job anyplace in the world, but the work group has demonstrated that the new approach will more consistently help it achieve its targets in this process right now, until it comes up with something better.

What Is *Takt*?

Takt is a German word for meter or rhythm. In music, a metronome sets the *takt* for the rhythm. In lean, it is a measure of the average rate of customer demand, expressed as time per unit. A 60-second *takt* on an automobile assembly line means that a car should come off the end of the line every 60 seconds. If we have perfect one-piece flow, this also means a car body should be produced in the welding shop every 60 seconds to match production to demand. When we balance the work, we are trying to load each worker on the assembly line so that the amount of value-added work that he does is as close as possible to the *takt* (e.g., 60 seconds of work per cycle). Of course, this is impossible, as there is always waste, and also it would be extremely stressful to the worker to be fully loaded, with no opportunity to compensate for any variation. So we assign each job a little less than 60 seconds of work.

Having done this productivity improvement project, the work team is now more capable of understanding waste and the PDCA process so that it will be more adaptable as conditions change. For example, when market conditions change and the *takt* changes, the work team will have to rebalance the workload for all of the jobs and develop new standardized work. Adaptability through PDCA thinking is what Toyota strives for, not mindless copying of "lean solutions." Adaptability comes from highly developed people who are continuously improving processes. That will not happen if the people in the work group wait for engineers or black belts to do the thinking for them.

Toyota Business Practices to Grow People and Processes through PDCA

For Toyota, PDCA is more than a way to get results from process improvement. It is a way of developing people. This was formalized in 2002, when Toyota Business Practices (TBP) was introduced. Fujio Cho, as president, introduced *The Toyota Way 2001*, an internal document that first formalized Toyota's culture. It was laid out as a set of principles with historical quotes. However, Cho realized that something more was needed to translate the principles into action. Toyota Business Practices is the concrete methodology that does this. At first glance, it is not all that different from other eight-step problem-solving methods (often called 8D methods, for eight disciplines).

There are eight steps to TBP, as shown in Figure 2.2, that collectively follow the PDCA cycle. (Actually there are nine steps if we include "grasp the situation," a prerequisite to beginning to define the problem.) As usual, Toyota was deliberately improving on its past method, called *practical problem solving*. The starting point is to clarify the problem versus the ideal state. Defining the ideal state is a critical step. This is to avoid settling for incremental fixes to the current state. It is usual to think of 10 or 20 percent improvement as a big change, but in some cases doubling performance is feasible. To think big, we must have a vision that pulls us, rather than tinker with the system as it is. What would be the realistic ideal state of the system? It may be defined by benchmarking the best process like this in the

	Process Improvement	People Development
P	Grasp the situation	Understand people development needs (Who? What? Why?)
	Clarify the problem vs. the ideal state Break down the problem Set the target Root-cause analysis Develop countermeasures	Vision of ideal team member Targeted areas to develop Skills matrix Strengths and weaknesses Personal development plan
D	See countermeasures through	Coach through the process
C	Monitor both results and processes	Reflection (*hansei*)
A	Standardize successful processes and identify gaps for next steps	Reinforce positive behaviors and identify next learning needs

Figure 2.2. PDCA of Processes and People through Toyota Business Practices

world. Having agreed on this vision, we will not be motivated by the ideal state if it seems impossible to achieve. To get to a challenging but achievable goal we must "break down the problem" into smaller, more tractable pieces and set priorities. For the pieces we choose to work on, we should go even one step further and set concrete, measureable targets. How will we know if we have succeeded? The targets are short-cycle, measurable guideposts along the journey.

The gap between the actual and the target becomes our definition of the problem. A common saying at Toyota is that without a standard, there is no problem. A problem is always stated as a gap between the target (standard) and the actual condition. Now that we know what specific problems, or gaps, we will work on, we can search for the root cause of these gaps, develop countermeasures, try the countermeasures, monitor how we did, take follow-up actions to standardize, and identify further actions to improve.

Compare this problem-solving process to that of other organizations, and you might see some important differences. Very few problem-solving processes explicitly call for identifying the ideal state as a point of comparison. Most 8D processes miss this critical step, and it was not even explicitly called for in Toyota's previous method of practical problem solving. The next critical concept is breaking down the problem and developing a plan for each piece. Most other approaches would start after the problem has been broken down, that is, with a more specific problem to solve, which very much limits the scope and effectiveness of problem solving. Beyond that, the differences are mainly in the philosophy of control versus learning, discussed earlier.

In many companies that we have worked with, we have encountered a "just get it done" mentality that was pervasive throughout the operations and the organization structure. When organizations lack a coherent vision and instead focus on the short term, they tend to gravitate to an "action" bias, where it doesn't really matter if what you're doing is going to benefit the organization in the long term; rather, it matters that people are "getting things done." In this type of organization, we find that the PDCA cycle gets abbreviated to simply a strange, short-circuited *do* mentality. Heroes replace process adherents. Planning for an experiment, checking, and adjusting based on the outcomes of a particular action are nonexistent. This type of organization breeds a "firefighter" mentality, in which swift, bold action is rewarded, regardless of outcomes or causes. Indeed, we find that many of the "fires" that are being put out are directly related to prior blazes. This type of action bias is shown in Figure 2.3. It should be obvious from our discussions this far that a company that embraces, supports, and promotes this type of behavior will find sustaining any lean transformation efforts to be a difficult, if not impossible, task.

A key part of the learning philosophy is to ask how people develop when they go through the process. We have added a column in Figure 2.2 on people development (our words, not Toyota's). At each step in TBP, there is an opportunity to develop people. It starts by having a vision of what the ideal team member would be so that we can see the gaps. It's also important to point out that the gaps that exist are not the "fault" of the team member but rather the responsibility of the leadership to address. Then we would ask whom we want to develop, what we want them to learn as a result of working on solving this problem, and why. The skills matrix is a simple way of keeping track of learning targets versus actual achievement.[6] For each person, we list the

Figure 2.3. A "Get It Done" Mentality Destroys the PDCA Cycle

skills we desire and fill in circles in quartiles for percentage of skill development. The team members will not learn unless they get feedback, so a coach is needed. When we do the check, we can check not only the results but also the process of achieving the results. Individual team members can reflect on their contributions. What did they do well? What were areas of weakness that should be worked on to improve further? This leads to further action on people development to bring them to the next level.

Toyota does not specifically come up with a formal people development plan every time it solves a problem, but this is always in its awareness. Every problem-solving project is an opportunity to develop people. To consciously develop people, we must have a plan, and we must do, check, and take further action based on what we learn.

Mike Rother uses the term *kata* to refer to the routine behavior patterns that we wish to teach and reinforce.[7] The Japanese term *kata* is often used for the routines we must use to be successful in the martial arts. If we think about a karate master black belt training a novice, the master must first break down complex routines into teachable pieces. These pieces are practiced over and over by the novice with critical feedback from the master. At first they must be copied exactly as the master demonstrates—no innovation is expected or permitted. At some point, the student passes on to the next stage when she has achieved a degree of mastery of each earlier piece. Only the master can judge when the student is ready for the next stage. Then she will be able to perform each step without thinking—it just comes naturally and does not need to be closely monitored by the master. Eventually the student learns entire systems of routines, which must be practiced over and over with critical feedback. When the routine becomes natural, the student might innovate in small, but deliberate ways. She has the freedom to start to think for herself. Only through this intensive and lengthy process can the student, over some years, eventually earn a black belt and from there a master black belt to teach others.[8]

Rother describes in detail an improvement *kata* for achieving challenging objectives and a coaching *kata* for teaching the improvement *kata* to others.[9] We can think of Toyota Business Practices as Toyota's improvement *kata*. It applies equally to focused process improvements in a plant, e.g., increasing productivity in the tire installation operation, and large innovations, e.g., developing a car for the twenty-first century, which turned out to be the first Prius.

Is this how we train black belts in Six Sigma? Occasionally, perhaps, but in our experience, rarely. More typically, there is classroom training on the entire process, focusing mainly on the statistical tools, then the student does a project with occasional interaction with the black-belt teacher, then he presents the one project listing the purported savings, and then he probably gets the black belt. In some cases, the entire black-belt certification process is done online, with the project being reviewed by someone who has never even met the student or seen the actual situation. Try to get a black belt in karate online. It is comical to even consider it.

To get the daily coaching needed, Toyota relies on the direct manager to act as the coach. He must first develop a level of mastery of Toyota Business Practices, and then he can teach, coach, and judge his subordinates. Toyota developed a method to teach and cascade down

TBP that follows a learning model much like that used in karate. Toyota started teaching TBP at the very top of the organization—president, executive vice presidents, and so on. The original master trainers were in a special Toyota Institute, but eventually the executives could teach and become the board that judged projects, and this continued to be passed down through the management ranks until group leaders on the shop floor could teach and coach the hourly production workers. Going through a TBP process once does not lead to "certification." It is expected that you will continue to practice TBP over and over, learning more each time.

Six years after the launch of TBP, it was still being cascaded down to lower levels. The Great Recession of 2008 turned into the ideal opportunity to develop the group leader, team leader, and team member levels in TBP. By contrast, most problem-solving programs in other companies would not even *last* for six years, let alone be accelerated during difficult times. In fact, it is more likely that people will be laid off and the training programs cut in difficult times.

For Toyota employees in Japan there are periodic updates of TBP training. Each time a manager is nearing a point of getting promoted, he or she must do a serious TBP project that is judged by a panel. The projects evolve in complexity as the employee matures, both in the scope of the project and in the number and level of people who must be influenced to get the solution implemented.

If we think about TBP as the concrete actions that put the Toyota Way into practice, we can see it as being far more than a problem-solving method. The Toyota Way is based on twin pillars: continuous improvement and respect for people. Continuous improvement is practiced through TBP, and it is practiced in a respectful manner. Each step should reflect the core values of the company that focus on respect for people. For example, the ideal state for the process should always be ideal from the point of view of the customer. So to define the ideal state, the problem solver is thinking carefully about what "customer first" really means.[10] And it continues through the process. Values get put into action, and the actions reinforce the values. Through repeated cycles of learning, we eventually build a culture of continuous improvement and respect for people.

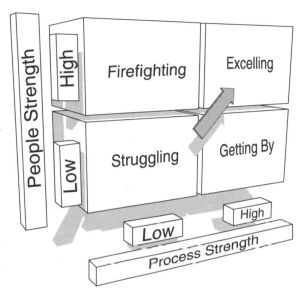

Figure 2.4. Exceptional People and Exceptional Processes Must Go Hand in Hand

The search for excellence requires both exceptional people and great processes (see Figure 2.4). Some companies have neither and are simply struggling to get by. More typically, a company that has been around for a while has succeeded on the backs of some exceptional people who have prevailed in spite of poorly organized processes. Every day is a fire waiting to be fought, and these people are good enough to manage their way through the day. We also know of companies with very strong engineering departments that have developed well-designed processes but see the people who operate them as a necessary evil. People are interchangeable parts, and there is relatively little investment in developing them. Our experience is that those firms are getting by but will never be excellent. Only companies with excellent processes *and* excellent people will truly excel.

PDCA Is a Way of Life; Copying Shouldn't Be

We are often challenged by the audience on a number of issues when we make presentations about Toyota. Can we really use Toyota as a model, since it is a Japanese company, and our culture is so different?

What is this lean management process really, and is it better than our Six Sigma/theory of constraints/agile program? Isn't Toyota showing signs of weakness in quality and profitability, and if so, why should we follow it?

The answer is that no organization should try to copy another. Trying to imitate a successful company like Toyota, and we do think that 60 years of consistent growth and profits is remarkable, is as big a folly as trying to implement lean solutions.

What we really advocate is copying the PDCA way. It is actually not something to copy but rather to live. It was invented not in an exotic Asian culture, but in America. It just happens to have been practiced and refined to a level of mastery by a Japanese company. Toyota gives us a model of the value of using the philosophy of PDCA to become a learning organization. Its key to success is to adapt at all levels of the organization all the time through continuous improvement.

When we speak of lean processes in this book, we will always be referring to PDCA. There is no lean process per se, but by following PDCA, we can make processes leaner and leaner through the constant pursuit of eliminating waste. If someone shows us a process and asks if it is lean, we will always ask one question: what is the problem that you are trying to solve? If the person cannot answer that question, we will go back to the first principles of PDCA. As we continue through the book, we will repeatedly return to the fundamental concept of PDCA, but first we must clarify some critical concepts in the next three chapters. Why is it essential to use process improvement as a training ground for developing excellent people? How can we connect each of our *kaizen* activities to a more basic business purpose? What is the difference between "leaning out a process" and building a lean system?

Chapter 3

How Process Improvement Can Develop Exceptional People

While at work I was thinking about the lack of care in the digital computer manuals I was editing. . . . It then occurred to me, there is no manual that deals with the real business of motorcycle maintenance, the most important aspect of all. Caring about what you're doing is considered either unimportant or taken for granted.

—Robert Pirsig, *Zen and the Art of Motorcycle Maintenance*

Not Excellent: A Tale of Refrigerator Baskets

One day Jeff Liker received a call from a prospective client. In a gruff and impatient voice, the caller explained that he was the vice president and chief operating officer of a company that supplies wire baskets to refrigerator manufacturers. These are baskets that slide in and out. The company had been doing lean for a while, he explained, and he was a believer, but it was moving too slowly. Recently he had visited the company's Mexican plant, and it had showed him the results of *kaizen* workshops. The plant had got a team together to focus intensively on improving a process, and in just five days it had done more than his other plants had done in months of lean activity. The cost savings were phenomenal, and this was a very low margin business. "Do you have a course up at the University of Michigan on *kaizen* events?" he asked. "That is what we need."

Liker explained that a conventional course would not teach his employees real skills. "You can learn *kaizen* only by doing." He offered to send down one of his consultants to lead a one-week *kaizen* workshop at a plant and teach people how to do *kaizen* at the same time—teaching and doing. The COO agreed with that plan and said that he would get all of his plant managers together at one site—the plant that needed the most work.

Our *sensei*, Keith Leitner, went out to the plant and walked the floor, and the low-hanging fruit was obvious. There were mountains of inventory everywhere. The reason was clear to Keith. Different steps of the process were spread to and fro throughout the plant, and each process was scheduled as an island, spitting out large amounts of product, which was stored in inventory and then pulled out of inventory for the next process. The current situation was

- Wire straightening and cutting in batches in the Fabrication A area of the facility
- Frame manufacturing in the Fabrication B area of the facility
- Final assembly (prior to paint) in the Fabrication C area of the plant
- Work-in-process (WIP) inventory storage in large batches between processes
- Three-shift operation most of the time (not always needed)

In the actual *kaizen* event, the team of plant managers, along with local production managers of each area, gathered data on the current situation. They developed a spaghetti diagram showing the path of the material, which traveled 2,500 feet. A total of 1,900 square feet of floor space was taken up by inventory—33 days of work-in-process inventory, cut parts, for the large and small baskets. The lead time from when they first cut the wire for the baskets to when the baskets were assembled took eight working days (mostly time parts were sitting in inventory).

The teams sketched out various alternative designs for cells and settled on a final design. They moved equipment and set up a single cell to make the small and large baskets. By the end of the week, the cell was functioning. The before and after statistics were stunning:

- There was 54 percent less inventory between processes.
- There was 97 percent less inventory in the cell.
- The cell occupied 56 percent less floor space.
- There was 98 percent less lead time from cut wire to assembled baskets (8 days down to 0.2 day).
- Labor productivity was 61 percent greater.
- The third shift was eliminated.
- Capital equipment valued at $70,000 was released.

A telephone report out was given to the COO, who was delighted with the results and wanted more. A second workshop was scheduled for the plant two months later to create a cell for the other major product family in the plant, with similar results. While this was going on, Keith and the plant manager developed a six-month plan based on value stream mapping of the model product line that included pull systems between all processes, establishing work teams, setting up standardized work, establishing pull to suppliers, and a program of Total Productive Maintenance. After the second workshop, which was equally pleasing to him, the COO announced that he had spent enough money on consulting (a tiny fraction of the savings), and that he now expected the other plant managers to apply what they had learned in their plants and get similar results. The education was over, and it was time to show the money. In our informal follow-up, we learned that little in the six-month plan ever got done and that the other plant managers had done relatively sloppy workshops to set up cells and produce the requested cost savings. Many hourly workers had lost their jobs as a result of the *kaizen* workshops.

What was the purpose of this so-called lean activity? From the point of view of the COO, it was clear: shake up the plant managers and give them some training, and then get the fast dollars. The one-time cost reduction was the goal, and the COO seemed happy with the results.

Obviously, that is not what we were trying to accomplish. We saw a company that was in a sad state, without vision, with no real system of production, with poorly trained people, and with no understanding of the tools that could help it improve. We saw huge opportunities for improvement to attain operational excellence. The few workshops and creation of crude cells had barely scratched the surface. We admit that we should have questioned the purpose more vigorously and probably not taken the job to begin with, but we had hoped that the initial results would convince the COO that there was a great deal to be gained through lean done right. We were wrong. The problem was that the COO lacked any vision for his company beyond meeting the budget. He certainly saw limited value in investments to develop people. We have learned from a number of similarly bad experiences that isolated process improvement projects have very limited benefit if they are not tied to a broader purpose.

The Torque Wrench Problem: Developing a Manager to Find the Real Root Cause

The wire basket case is in stark contrast to what we have seen repeatedly in every part of Toyota. Process improvement at Toyota always has the dual objectives of getting business results and developing people. Let's consider an example of how Toyota used process improvement to develop a young up-and-coming engineer.

Yuri Rodrigues had been on a fast-track career path in an innovative model lean engine plant in Brazil that was part of a joint venture between BMW and Chrysler. In 2003, he crossed paths with Gary Convis, then president of Toyota's plant in Kentucky, who offered him a job with Toyota. The Kentucky plant had lost a number of excellent managers, and Gary saw the need to bring in some fresh blood from outside. Yuri could not get a work visa right away, so Gary arranged for him to spend his first year in Toyota's assembly plant in Brazil. Gary would pay his salary out of the Kentucky budget and viewed this as a developmental opportunity for Yuri. Yuri would start in Brazil as an assistant manager in the assembly plant over trim, chassis, and final assembly, at least a grade level below where he was in the joint venture, but he would have an opportunity to learn the real Toyota way and work his way back up.

Yuri's *sensei* was a Japanese coordinator, a 35-year Toyota veteran who was one of the leading Toyota Production System (TPS) experts in the world. One of his first major *kaizen* opportunities was to solve a debilitating quality problem in which 55 defective cars were sitting outside in the yard waiting for repair because of low torque on accelerator bolts—completely unacceptable by Toyota standards. Trim assembly was the department that put most of the cars there. The goal was to get the trim department capable of building to *takt* (customer demand rate) without producing defective cars that had to be set aside for repair.

Toyota plants set a standard for the maximum number of cars waiting to be repaired and usually make it visible. If a plant exceeds the maximum, it shuts down production until the problem is solved. It was clear to Yuri that 55 was too many, and that started the problem-solving process.

Using his engineering expertise, Yuri figured out that the defects were the result of inconsistent torque in attaching bolts on the trim line, particularly at a few workstations. This provided a more specific target condition—a process in which all of the bolts are attached to the proper torque (tightness) in the allotted standard time.

To diagnose the cause, Yuri noted that the team members were using relatively primitive impact wrenches that required judgment in tightening the bolts, something that he had not experienced in his last job, where team members always used more sophisticated wrenches that would automatically measure the torque and shut off when the precise level was achieved. Yuri's idea for a countermeasure was to purchase a sophisticated automatic torque wrench so one team member could tighten all the bolts.

When Yuri presented his countermeasure to upper management, he thought his coordinator would be proud. Instead, the coordinator interrupted Yuri's presentation to say, "Okay, so I see you contained the problem. But do you want me to buy new $400 wrenches for everyone in the whole plant? Because if you are telling me that's your solution for that problem, that's what we are going to have to do."

Yuri got defensive and said, "I'm not saying that." His coordinator calmly said, "So go back and think some more. That's no good."

A week later, Yuri went back to his coordinator and gave another solution. He had figured out that some of the older wrenches were too weak to achieve the desired torque. So Yuri wanted to purchase more of the inexpensive impact wrenches to use as backups. He presented this solution to his coordinator and received an abrupt response—"No good"—then his coordinator walked away.

So Yuri thought about it and realized that if his solution was to buy new guns, he was going to have to keep buying them, so he still hadn't gotten to the root cause of the problem. In the end, it took him about a month, but eventually he realized that he had been going in the wrong direction for a solution, and his coordinator had never told him! The coordinator just said, "No good."

When Yuri was at his wit's end and wondering when he was going to be fired, he remembered what he had learned in TPS training about the "five whys"—when solving a problem, a Toyota leader needs to keep asking why until she gets to the root cause. Yuri had not asked why enough times.

When he asked enough whys, Yuri uncovered three important root causes of the trim assembly problems. First, the team members were not well trained. When a team member shoots the bolts using the more primitive impact wrenches, he should be able to hear a different sound and get a certain feel when he reached the right level of torque. The team members did not know that. Yuri spot-checked team members throughout the line, and about 40 percent did not know how to feel and hear when the proper torque was achieved. The second cause was that the maintenance system for the impact wrenches was deficient. The wrenches were getting weak, but no one was maintaining them or changing them out before they got to that stage—there was poor preventive maintenance. Yuri also checked the maintenance of other tools, and saw that preventive maintenance was poor throughout assembly. The third cause was a product design issue that he knew would take a long time to get through the engineering organization, so he decided to focus on what he could control—team members' knowledge and tool maintenance.

To deal with the team members' knowledge issue, Yuri decided that he needed to personally train each team member who used a torque wrench. He had to go beyond the one-off short training that he had experienced at the joint venture. To ensure that each team member had the actual skills needed, Yuri had to teach those skills on the job, let the team members practice, and continue checking until he was confident that each of them had learned the correct way to use the gun. He was interested in changing behavior patterns, which was much harder than getting team members to nod their heads in agreement that they understand the correct method.[1]

To address the maintenance problem, he set up a visual management system called a *kamishibai* board. *Kamishibai* means a storyboard. In Japan, parents will take children's books and rewrite them on a series of cards. Using these cards, when parents read at night to their sleepy children, they can easily keep track of where they are in the story when the children fall asleep. The parent reads a card, and if the kids are still awake and want to listen, the parent puts that card at the back of the pile and goes on to the next one until the children doze off. The next night, they start where they left off.

Kamishibai for preventive maintenance functions in much the same way: there is a card for each item that needs to be checked at each hour and on each day. Not everything needs to be checked every day, and new tools do not need to be checked as often as old tools. On the *kamishibai* board, the cards are arranged hour by hour. The maintenance person pulls the first card, does an hour's worth of work, signs off on the card that it was done, and goes on to the next one. This focuses attention on what needs to be done hour by hour for that day and gives direct and immediate feedback if maintenance gets behind. Before Yuri implemented the *kamishibai* board, it took three people to check all the tools in assembly. Yuri was able to get that down to one person doing only the checks that were necessary that day.

Yuri worked at implementing these ideas, and when his *sensei* came to him now, instead of saying, "No good," he would look at Yuri, give a small smile, and say, "Continue." During the following months, Yuri continued to develop. Sometimes he made mistakes and sometimes he was on the right track, but he would always know which depending on whether his *sensei* gave him a smile and told him to continue, or whether he said, "No good." After five months, the faulty cars had disappeared from the yard, and the loose bolt problems were reduced to almost zero. Quality defects were reduced from 0.3 defects per car to 0.1, and the cost of maintenance of the tools was reduced from $9 per unit to $1.50 per unit. Yuri didn't have to buy those expensive torque wrenches after all.

The Business Purpose and the People Purpose

What is different about the refrigerator basket case at the beginning of this chapter and the Toyota torque wrench example? It starts with the purpose. The purpose in the refrigerator basket case was to get the cost savings that the COO desired—end of story! How that was done was of no particular importance as long as the results were achieved. As it turned out, it was achieved by an external expert coming in and guiding a team through a couple of *kaizen* events in a way that left the team members with a very limited set of skills for approaching further process improvements that would get the additional cost savings that the COO wanted. They were now between a rock and a hard place.

In the Toyota case, there was both a business purpose and a people purpose. The middle manager responsible for production, Yuri, had identified the business purpose, which was to fix the bottleneck that was impeding production of cars. His *sensei* identified the people purpose, which was to develop in Yuri the right way of thinking about and solving problems. From the point of view of his *sensei*, who was also a high-level and powerful Toyota executive, developing Yuri was a far higher priority than solving that particular problem. He knew that there would always be problems, and that if Yuri solved this one superficially, he would solve all of them superficially, and the errors would keep compounding. On the other hand, getting Yuri to be a well-trained Toyota leader would benefit the company a thousandfold more than solving this one problem. The return on investment (ROI) for this investment in training was obvious.

Notice that the *sensei* never lectured Yuri on TPS or told Yuri exactly what to do. At Yuri's former company, he was already viewed as a lean expert. His reaction to lectures on basic principles by his *sensei* would have been: "I already know this, so why is he wasting my time?" Instead, the *sensei* wanted Yuri to struggle through the problem-solving process and discover for himself what he did and did not know. Yuri's actual reaction was: "I came to Toyota thinking that I knew everything, and I quickly discovered that I knew nothing."

The *sensei* could have led a *kaizen* event, solved the torque problem easily, and implemented the solution within a few days. Instead, the problem dragged on for weeks as Yuri suggested things and tried things, and the main coaching response was, "No good." Each idea Yuri had that was "no good" led to learning, maybe more important learning than when he finally got things right. Curiously, the *sensei's* negative responses did not cause Yuri to get frustrated and give up. Instead, they challenged Yuri to think more deeply and use his creativity instead of resorting to the easy way out, like buying new wrenches. The combination of respect for the *sensei*, a desire to learn the Toyota Way that the *sensei* represented, and the fact that Yuri was working on a concrete project where it was clear what he was trying to achieve kept driving him forward. At the end, he had a rush of deep satisfaction that he could not have achieved if he had been told what to do.

It is also interesting to note that Yuri was in this particular plant in Brazil only on a short-term assignment until he could get a visa to move to the Kentucky plant. That means that his *sensei* had to have a big-picture view and long-term concern for the future of Toyota as a company, not only a local concern for what was happening here and now in the Brazilian plant.

Innovation Comes from Working toward the Targets and Purpose

Thomas Edison invented the lightbulb, Alexander Graham Bell invented the telephone, and Steve Jobs single-handedly led Apple to invent the iPhone. After the fact, we see breakthrough technologies and try to trace them back to some individual hero who had a big idea. A team went to work, and history was made. Get the right genius with the right big idea, and she should become rich and famous and change the world. There is a romantic appeal to that notion, but when you strip it away and see what actually happened, there was seldom a linear relationship between some individual's big idea and a breakthrough innovation. In fact often the fundamental ideas came from people other than the individual who was given the credit.

When we think about Toyota and lean, a common assumption is that continuous improvement is synonymous with incremental innovation in small steps. We say that Toyota is like the tortoise, slow and steady.[2] The assumption is that the company does not want to rush along and does not value big ideas. Base hits and sacrifice outs are just fine. Let our competitors hit the home runs. There is some truth to this view, but not in the way we think.

The real problem with depending on home runs is that they are unpredictable. When everything lines up right—the pitch, the skill level of the batter, the swing—they are a thing of beauty. Toyota is happy to take all the home runs it can get, but it wants more predictability so that it can adapt appropriately to the environment and consistently deliver customer value. To survive long term, you absolutely must have innovation. Toyota believes that it is possible to have planned innovation with a clear purpose.

This may sound like a contradiction in terms, but Toyota has done it over and over. We see the Prius hybrid and some Lexus models as breakthroughs,[3] but new technology like this is only the tip of the iceberg of innovation. When we look at a process and define the future state as half the space and half the people, we are preparing for innovation, just as when we define the goal for a new automobile as the same size, twice the fuel economy, and more spacious inside, we are defining the requirements for innovation. We start with the future state vision and targets, and then innovation is deliberately focused on achieving the targets on a predefined timeline. In Chapter 11, Charlie Baker explains how this process works in the case of new product development.

People are responsible for innovation—it does not come from computers or from lean. It comes from individual imagination and persistence. Every small *kaizen* leaves people stronger in terms of their confidence and innovative capability. Obviously, big *kaizen* do this as well. Some people within Toyota have speculated that one of the reasons for the original Prius was to shake up the R&D organization to think about more fundamental innovation. It was as much a people development project as a breakthrough product for Toyota. In fact, Charlie Baker's first project as chief engineer at Honda in 1993, and the first time an American team led a program, was to develop the Acura CL sports coupe. He later discovered that Honda had not had a two-door sports coupe in its product plans, but had added it as a relatively low-risk way to develop the ability of the Americans to lead a complete product development program. The Acura CL was a Honda Accord with a new body, a V6 engine, and additional features—essentially a $100 million training program for Charlie and his team.

Innovation can be big or small in scope. Starting with a challenging target of eliminating quality defects that result from torque problems will drive a certain type and level of innovation. Starting with a target of a new vehicle with twice the fuel economy and zero emissions is obviously a different level of innovation, but the innovative process is the same. To achieve innovation in a planned and deliberate way, we need to break the big problem into many little problems. Thus, we talk about nested plan–do–check–adjust (PDCA) loops. Many small steps will eventually lead you to the big innovation if you are persistent.[4] This has been proven time and time again in the innovations of great inventors like Edison, and also throughout Toyota. In the next chapter, we will consider more broadly how *kaizen* is driven by a clear business purpose and defined targets.

Chapter 4

Lean Processes Start
with a Purpose

*A vision is not just a picture of what could be; it is an appeal to our
better selves, a call to become something more.*

—Rosabeth Moss Kanter,
Harvard professor and business author

A Tale of Two Lean Transformations
(Composite Cases)[1]

Mecheng makes engineered-to-order control panels that are
used in power plants, oil rigs, manufacturing plants, and
other complex applications. It has tens of thousands of versions customized for each application. The company could not imagine
how it could possibly use lean concepts with such a diverse product
mix, where cycle times for individual processes can vary by a factor of
10 and demand can double from one week to the next. There were
frequent complaints from customers, who waited months for their
product and were particularly unhappy to find quality defects. A competitor in the marketplace was undercutting the company on price,
and to compete, it had to lower its prices, so profit margins were razor
thin. Mecheng hired BigLean, a consulting group, to help turn things
around.

BigLean sent in a team of consultants with years of lean manufacturing experience. The consultants asked Mecheng to establish a lean
department at the corporate level that could lead the charge. Mecheng

assigned its best Six Sigma black belts to the new Lean Six Sigma department. The consultants and the members of the internal group were all over the plants with frenetic energy. They mapped processes, timed processes with stopwatches, pored over data, and developed a set of recommended changes. The recommendations included reorganizing around product families, like a focused factory, and creating flow lines based on a new layout of the plant. Within each product family, the workers would build to a *takt* time (which was actually a range because of different products in the mix). Standardized work was developed for the most profitable and largest-volume products. An analysis of the current staffing levels versus what they could be with lean showed that a 50 percent productivity gain was possible, so the company set a more achievable target of 30 percent. Management agreed to all the changes and assured the consultants that it would fully support everything.

Within nine months, the changes had been made, and the 30 percent productivity improvements were booked—many people had lost their jobs. Throughput was improved, so more products reached the customers on time, although quality problems continued. The internal lean team developed auditing methods to audit the managers in each plant: follow the new standard procedures or else. The environment became regimented, almost like a police state, but there were improvements on all key metrics. Management was won over by the power of the lean methodology.

FriendlyHealth is the largest urban hospital in a midsized city and has branch offices in the suburbs. It is a public hospital and has a reputation for friendly, responsive staff members who always put the patient first. It boasts some of the best cardiology specialists in the world and the latest technology. It had gone through many programs in the past for quality, teamwork, and leadership training. Each program had been positively received, but none had lasted. Now the hospital was facing its third year of losses, and the board of directors was asking for real change. "Lean health care" was sweeping the country, and FriendlyHealth's CEO decided to jump on board. The promises of reduced patient waiting time, streamlined processes, large decreases in operating costs, and greater patient safety were too good to pass up. The CEO assigned the director of quality to lead the lean effort.

The director of quality went in search of consultants. She found a small group of former Toyota employees who took a learning-by-doing approach to lean. She emphasized that customer quality and safety were the highest priority and employee morale was a close second, but the hospital also needed to become more efficient. The consultants suggested a few projects in model areas to demonstrate that lean is not mean and can help employees do their jobs better and more easily. By the end of the first year, each project was successful, and all the people involved were turned on by lean. T-shirts were made up extolling the virtues of being on the lean team. Everyone was happy except the CEO and the COO, who were looking at a fourth year of financial losses.

Mecheng had a clear set of objectives for its lean transformation and achieved those objectives. It wanted quick cost reduction with more throughput, and it got it, but at what cost? Along with low employee morale, customers remained unhappy with the quality of the panels. In an environment in which the people who are doing the work are not respected or empowered, is it likely that they will take the care to improve the quality of the panels? Will this highly mechanistic organization be able to adapt to change to stay ahead of its competitors?

In many ways, FriendlyHealth did lean the right way. It was beginning to develop capability in those of its people who were engaged in the process of change, but somehow it lost sight of any larger business purpose to the lean transformation. Was FriendlyHealth more or less successful than Mecheng?

Inspiring People through a Sense of Purpose

Companies might ask, "In our company everyone has his or her objectives for the year and is judged based on those objectives in the annual performance review. So what is different about Toyota's system?" There is an important difference between measurable objectives and purpose. Toyota has both, but we find that most companies have only measurable objectives. If we ask what the purpose of the company is, we get an incredulous: "We are in business to make money!" Perhaps that is the only purpose of that company. When we invest in a mutual fund, our reason for investing in it is straightforward: we want to make money. So if a company is like a mutual fund, it is just another invest-ment to be judged by how much income it produces. Of course, we should put our money where the best return is, so if our company is not doing well, we should shut it down or sell it and find someplace else to put our money. It seems that private equity firms often operate that way when they take over a company: invest only when it is the best place to put the money *today*, and if the market is down, sell off assets (especially employees) and find a different investment.

In the book *Built to Last*, Collins and Porras find that leaders of the most consistently financially successful companies in fact think about the business as more than a short-term investment. They strive to create an institution that will serve a greater purpose:

> *People feel inspired by the very notion of building an enduring, great company. We've met executives from all over the world who aspire to create something bigger and more lasting than themselves—an ongoing institution rooted in a set of timeless core values, that exists for a purpose beyond just making money, and that stands the test of time by virtue of the ability to continually renew itself from within.*[2]

Collins and Porras[3] cite the vision of Walt Disney to "bring happi-ness to millions," the vision of Merck to always remember that "med-icine is for the patient and profits will follow," the Sony Way to "serve the whole world" by being a pioneer in technology that always "brings out the best in a person," and Ford's former CEO Don Petersen pronouncing that the company existed for the three Ps—people, prod-ucts, and profits—but "people should absolutely come first," followed by products and finally by profits.

Let's go back to the Mecheng case and consider the implied pur-pose. The purpose is to make profits, which equal revenue minus costs. So reducing costs increases profits, and since people are one of the easiest costs to control, the company focused on reducing head count. End of story. Who was motivated by this vision? Surely the people who lost their jobs were not. Those who were left behind were motivated in a negative way—that is, by the fear that they might be next.

There is a good deal of research evidence to suggest that people are motivated by a positive vision to a much greater degree than by a localized objective with no apparent purpose, or by general fear. Let's consider one example from the field of organizational development.[4] Ron Lippitt is one of the pioneers of a method called preferred futuring.[5] Groups of people are carefully selected to represent a critical mass across functions in the organization, and they move through a series of exercises that culminates in building a vision of their preferred future. The method evolved from some work that Ron Lippitt and a group did in the 1960s to try to improve openness to racial diversity. They used racially diverse groups of people as focus groups, and at first they asked the members of those groups to identify barriers to racial harmony so that they could work on breaking down those barriers. As this was a research project, they were tape-recording the responses. When they played back the tapes, they noticed a trend, so they coded the responses based on the level of energy in the voices of the participants. They found that as people came up with barriers to change, their energy levels were going down and down to the pits. So they tried something different. They asked those same groups to envision a future of racial harmony and describe it in great detail, as if they were actually there observing it up close. In this discussion, energy levels went up and up, and the groups were on fire, ready to change the world.

Rallying the troops by saying that our owners are our key stakeholders and that we must eliminate jobs to help them get richer is likely to fizzle. Is that a good reason to sacrifice? What about the following?

- We will give customers a better product to enrich their lives and strengthen local communities by providing jobs.
- We will save lives through our health-care efforts while providing a secure and fulfilling work environment for our team members.
- We will provide the best shopping experience in the business, giving customers high value for every dollar spent, served by highly motivated associates.

The way to inspire people is to sell them on a positive vision that is more than money, like the great companies in the work of Collins and his associates. The vision should include ways in which customers will benefit, society will benefit, and the company will provide for the well-being of its employees. That makes it worth getting out of bed in the morning and even working long hours.

Is a broad and grandiose vision enough? Lippitt and his associates found that the vision is a critical step, but that without a realistic plan for achieving the vision, at least a first step, the vision quickly loses its motivating power. So how do we turn the vision into action?

From Vision to Plans

Over the years, Toyota has evolved an elegant, but simple system of tying a broad vision for the company to concrete plans and actions. It is based on a well-known method in Total Quality Management called *hoshin kanri* (management and control of the company's direction),[6] and it can be thought of as a hierarchy of purpose, from broad, timeless values to increasingly specific visions, goals, and plans. It touches every part of the organization from top to bottom and sideways. Let's consider each step in the process.

The Organization's Mission

Toyota's mission can and does change over time, but it always includes at least three elements, in this order:

1. Contributing to customers, society, and local communities
2. Contributing to team members and partners
3. Contributing to the growth and health of Toyota

Profits are never explicitly mentioned as part of the mission, but it is well understood that Toyota cannot do any of the three things without profits. From a Toyota perspective, profits are an indication that what Toyota does is valued by society, and they provide the input necessary to renew the system and continue to evolve.

True North

At Toyota, there is a right and a wrong way to achieve the mission. Some companies call this the North Star, and the concept is the same.

Wherever we are in the world, and even as time passes, the North Star is a constant guiding light. It is used by sailors and travelers as a reference point, even though their destination is not the North Star. In the case of True North, which represents perfection, we are striving to move toward it, but the path is never clear at the outset, and we know that we will never completely achieve it.

The concept of True North is often referred to within Toyota, but in the past, if you had asked different people what it meant, you would have gotten somewhat different opinions. *The Toyota Way 2001*, an internal company document (see Liker, 2004[7]), helped a good deal to clarify True North. It represents the company as a house with two pillars: respect for people and continuous improvement. That is what the company is about—striving to act with perfect respect for its customers, society, partners, and team members and continuously improving toward perfection in every part of the company. The house of the Toyota Way also provides a foundation of five core values for the two pillars:

1. *Challenge.* This is a spirit and a confidence that the company can succeed at achieving its goals regardless of the vagaries of the environment. In fact, without challenge, in calm waters, the company would drift aimlessly and become complacent. It also applies at the individual and group levels. Challenging targets spur people to stretch themselves and innovate to levels that often seem impossible at the outset. Challenge is not a single race where you reach the finish line and you are done, but is more like an endless obstacle course where you are constantly working to get better, and quitting at any point means that you lose the race.

2. *Kaizen.* This is a passion for constantly finding ways to improve every square inch of the company toward perfection. Good enough is never good enough. It can always be better. Interestingly, one component of what Toyota calls *kaizen* is lean processes, so it is just a small part of the overall Toyota Way. The True North definition of a lean process is one in which all the waste has been stripped away and what is left is pure value-added for the customer—also called one-piece flow.

3. Genchi genbutsu, *or go and see to deeply understand.* From the founding of the company, Toyota has been successful because of a deep appreciation for the value of deep knowledge of the actual situation—the customer, the manufacturing process, the parts being designed, the supplier's shop, and on and on. Databases of statistics will never tell the whole story from the Toyota perspective. Toyota leaders and team members must have a gut feel for whatever they are doing that comes from directly observing and being immersed in the actual situation. The Toyota leader must be a part of the team, working in the process and getting his hands dirty improving the process directly. Kiichiro Toyoda was famous for saying after the decimation of Japan in World War II,

> *I would have grave reservations about our ability to rebuild Japan's industry if our engineers were the type who could sit down to take their meals without ever having to wash their hands.*[8]

4. *Teamwork.* It seems to be a truism in today's world that the team is more powerful than any individual, and that is certainly part of the True North vision of Toyota, but many companies stop at teaching people to have effective meetings and rewarding the team for accomplishments. Toyota wants its members to feel that they are part of Toyota as a team and to identify with the values and goals of the company so strongly that they will always want to help other Toyota members to achieve important company goals. This means taking all individual responsibilities seriously and being accountable for contributions to the team. Being a good team member starts with being a good person—honest, reliable, and capable—so as individuals grow, the team becomes stronger.

5. *Respect for humanity.* Ultimately, Toyota believes that the company exists to serve humanity. Building cars is of no value unless Toyota is in some way advancing society in the process. Respecting local customs throughout the world is a necessary condition for respecting humanity and contributing to society.

This is why the recall crisis in America, in which Toyota was accused of horrific crimes against humanity, sent a shock wave throughout the company. Hiding potential safety defects is an unimaginable violation of Toyota's core principles. An intensive root-cause investigation of the system that allowed whatever problems there were to fester was an absolute necessity.

The "True North Vision" Gives Us a General Sense of Right and Wrong Direction

First principles are useful. We have some sense of when we are on course and when we are off course. One-piece flow is a first principle. It means having the right parts at the right place at the right time at every step in the process. We all want it our way and we want it now, and that is the ideal of one-piece flow. If we are adding extra steps in a process, information or materials are being batched, or there is a time gap between when one step is finished and another begins, we know that we are adding waste and we are on the wrong path.

Another first principle is respect for people. In Toyota's definition, if a person is not being challenged and learning, she is not being respected. Simply being polite to people is not enough. When the leader is doing the thinking for everyone, that is disrespectful. When people are expected to carry out tasks in a prescribed mindless way and are not asked for ideas for improvement, that is a violation of the human right to grow and develop.

A colleague visited a Toyota plant in Japan and saw people doing one-minute tasks like putting wheels on the vehicle with four bolts over and over all day long. He asked his host how a person doing that mindlessly and repetitively was being respected. His Toyota host agreed that this was far from ideal and that the company needed to continue to work on developing a better way.

The point is that anyone who walks around Toyota factories and offices can find endless examples of Toyota violating its own principles. Why is there any inventory anyplace? Why is any person doing a repetitive job without thinking? Why is there so much inspection when inspection is waste? If Toyota is serious that it believes in these things, why does it allow any deviations?

The answer is that Toyota uses these principles as a North Star: "This is the ideal and the direction in which we try to head." You cannot "implement" respect for people. You cannot mandate zero inventory. These are ideals. You have to spend your life working toward them step by step. At Toyota, people are painfully aware that the company is far from perfect and will never achieve perfection, but that does not stop them from trying. In fact, the gap between the actual and the ideal is what motivates continuous improvement. On the other hand, having that general direction by itself does not tell people what problems to work on. Should the company immediately redesign all its factories so that no person does a repetitive, short-cycle job? Should it mandate zero inventory? Both of these decisions would shut down the company, and it would go bankrupt. How do people know what to work on? The answer is that they need more specific and shorter-term targets to make progress toward True North.

Ten-Year Vision

Toyota develops a new vision every decade. The Global Vision 2020 is represented by two interlocking rings representing cycles of nature and cycles of industry. In the past, industry often advanced at the expense of the natural environment, wasting natural resources and even physically damaging the environment. It is never acceptable at Toyota to think in this *or* that terms. Growing industry *or* a healthy environment is not an acceptable compromise. Only growing industry *and* a healthy environment is acceptable.

That is fine. But how do we break the negative cycle that harms the environment? The only answer that Toyota has ever known and will ever know is innovation. Toyota includes in Vision 2020 the concept of *monozukuri*, which means the art of making things. Toyota is constantly innovating new and better ways to make things, and for this decade it will focus on how to make things in a way that is in harmony with the environment, both environmentally friendly products *and* environmentally friendly processes.

Five-Year Intermediate Plans

This is what many companies call their business plan. Sophisticated companies have such a plan. At a company level, Toyota knows what new vehicles it will launch and when, what vehicles will be refreshed, what volumes it expects, and so on. Every unit in Toyota has a five-year plan at the plant or organization level. There are plans for new car models, financial plans, quality improvement plans, and people development plans. These are rotating plans, following the PDCA cycle, that keep getting updated to reflect changes in the environment and what is actually accomplished.

Annual *Hoshin Kanri*

Probably the biggest difference between Toyota and most other companies is the level of detail in the annual plan. It connects more general goals to very concrete activity in each part of the company. This is also the way in which Toyota coordinates horizontally so that different parts of the company are aligned toward common goals. Moreover, progress is checked day by day throughout the company to determine how groups and individuals are performing relative to the annual objectives they have set. Constant reflection relative to clear and measurable objectives is the engine that drives continuous improvement.

Hoshin kanri means both direction and management control to achieve this direction. Toyota did not make this up, and it is not unique to the company. It became a centerpiece of Total Quality Management in the 1960s, and Toyota picked it up to greatly improve quality in order to compete in the global market. Like all things, it has been refined and refined through *kaizen* in Toyota.[9] Now it is part of the annual routine throughout the company. As the year progresses, there is a great deal of reflection and some initial planning for the next year. Each January, the president of Toyota Motor Company makes a speech reflecting on the past year, discussing market conditions, and laying out his vision for the year. January through the end of March (when the fiscal year ends) is the window for each region, function, business unit, and individual to work on its *hoshin kanri* plans for the next fiscal year and get them approved. By the middle of the year, all parts of Toyota conduct a major reflection on what has actually happened compared to the plan and have an opportunity to modify the *hoshin kanri*, and then the rest of the year's reflection will influence the plan for the next year.

So what is different compared to traditional management by objectives? The simplest way to describe the difference is that *hoshin kanri* follows True North processes.

Traditional management by objectives (MBO) is typically part of the command-and-control system. Senior management gets together, decides what the business needs, and orders the middle to deliver . . . or else. This is not to say that all companies have a hostile employee relations environment. Middle managers will often buy into the business needs and sincerely want to help the company be successful, so they take their marching orders and do their best to deliver the desired results. What happens next is the tragedy. They actually have few tools in their toolkit for delivering the results. If it is a short-term cost issue, they can only look at their portfolio of costs and start cutting things— labor is usually the most obvious culprit. If it is a quality issue, they can pressure people to be more careful and develop more quality standards. Whatever it is, they start paying attention to it, and that means paying attention to the people responsible for it. The typical middle manager does not have any direct means of improving the situation other than to put pressure on the right people who can work harder or more carefully or can follow the process provided by a staff group like quality or engineering more strictly. This is a very pressure-packed situation for both the middle manager and the people doing the work, even in an otherwise benevolent environment. And pressuring people to get better results out of a process that is not well designed does not work very well!

By contrast, *hoshin kanri* is a participative goal-setting process that is more consistent with respect for people. "Catch ball" is the term used for the give and take that ultimately leads to targets that all agree on. This sounds really good, but in the traditional situation we just described, would catch ball help the middle manager who does not have the tools to achieve the objectives that he helped to set? The truth is that when Toyota decides that the business needs something, whether it is cost reduction to deal with the recession or improvements in quality to deal with slippage in quality rankings, senior executives do not leave it to democracy to decide if they will pursue that objective. The only real wiggle room in catch ball is how much a particular unit will take on. Plant A is going through a major model change that is bigger than it has ever experienced before, and will have difficulty dealing with the cost reduction and quality improvement targets needed next year. Through discussion, Plant B, which is in a more stable situation, agrees to take on a little extra burden.

If the business objectives at Toyota are not subject to a great deal of negotiation, then how is this different from management by objectives? It is what happens next that makes all the difference in the world. What happens next is plan–do–check–adjust (PDCA) as it was meant to be done. This starts with a big-picture plan for the year that is broken down level by level until it is clear to every team member in the company. The form, meaning, and level of detail of the plan are as different from MBO as night and day.

Toyota Business Practices as the Improvement *Kata* That Turns Abstract Visions into Practice

When we look at a Toyota plant, we see many good ideas, and it appears that the company has a department of Toyota Production System (TPS) geniuses who design and implement all these "lean innovations." We might ask whether these ideas are standardized and implemented in all Toyota plants in the exact same way. Are the TPS experts telling the plants what to do and auditing them to see if they are following the best practices? The reality is that very little that you see at a Toyota site is the result of one person with a big idea that got standardized across plants. More often, what you see is today's condition, which is the result of many small steps, some of which were discarded and others embraced. It was the result of many cycles of PDCA, and it is different throughout Toyota because different organizations are on different learning cycles.

Mike Rother, who spent years researching how Toyota does what it does and how he could better teach companies that were on a quest for excellence, distilled what he learned into the concept of the improvement *kata*, which he suggests underlies human striving to meet challenges. A *kata* is a well-rehearsed routine that eventually becomes second nature. In this case, the routine is the process by which we make improvements. We discussed it briefly in Chapter 2.[10]

Rother concluded, as we have, that people have a fundamental misunderstanding of what the Toyota Production System is in practice. They have mistaken lean solutions for the process that leads to what we see in a Toyota plant. We need to look more deeply at the human thinking and processes that underlie specific practices that we observe. Rother notes recent findings in neuropsychology that people develop well-worn neural pathways that make it comfortable to do things the same way again and again. He points out that while humans derive a lot of their sense of security and confidence from this, the *content* of what we do will change, whether intentionally or not, because conditions always change.

The trick, according to Rother, is to develop well-worn mental circuits not for solutions, but for how to *develop* solutions. The management task, then, is to have the organization's members practice a behavior pattern, like the improvement *kata*, that achieves this. We need a routine not just for doing the work, but for continually improving the work. That routine is missing in organizations that use top-down management objectives, so managers have no choice but to blindly start cutting things. He introduces the improvement *kata* as the way we can break down an abstract vision into a concrete objective and through striving to achieve it develop and utilize the creative powers of people. It involves teaching people a standardized, conscious means of grasping the essence of situations and responding scientifically. The improvement *kata* is a routine for teaching and learning that mobilizes people's capability to achieve desired conditions.

Toyota's improvement *kata* has been taught implicitly in some parts of Toyota for decades. We saw Yuri Rodrigues learning it in the traditional way in Chapter 3. The wisdom of his TPS master was evident, but it was not explicitly documented and taught until 2002, when Toyota Business Practices (TBP) was introduced. We introduced Toyota Business Practices, which is Toyota's improvement *kata*, in

Chapter 2. The improvement process must start with the direction. True North helps, but it provides only a very general sense of direction. A more near-term and specific objective is needed. The *hoshin kanri* process breaks down True North into an annual plan in layers and layers of detail so that there are clear targets for all. The targets may be different for each person, but they have been defined in a way that adds up to what the overall business needs.

When you walk around Toyota these days, you will see TBP in action everywhere. Any Toyota employee should easily be able to answer these three questions: (1) What are your biggest problems? (2) What specifically are you trying to achieve in solving those problems, and by when? (3) How are you doing it? The biggest problems should be linked to the employee's *hoshin kanri* objectives. What people are working on and when should be clear, simple, and visual. They should be able to walk you to the actual workplace, perhaps refer to documentation on the wall, and easily explain what they are working on. The question of how should be through TBP. You should see a well-defined statement of the problem, a clear vision for the process, the problem broken down into manageable steps, and the progress they are making on the current step. And the employees should know up to the day (or at least the week) how they are doing relative to their target.

A Target Is a Concrete Guidepost to Compare Against

One important distinction that Rother makes is between a target as an outcome and a "target condition." An outcome that provides specific business results might be a certain percent cost-reduction target, but that in itself is not actionable other than by looking at a spreadsheet and cutting existing cost items. What Toyota seeks is creativity—coming up with new ways of working that will help us achieve the results. For that we need a clear picture of what we desire in the future, a target condition that is challenging yet achievable.

Few companies other than Toyota get to the point of having clear target conditions. There are many things that are measured and many quantitative objectives, but not a clear, actionable condition. The actionable condition can be visible, such as no more than four cars in each repair lane, or it can be a quantitative target, such as half the defects without adding any quality inspectors. When a clear condition that is visible and measurable has been set, then the people who are responsible for the work must be taught a clear method to work on solving the problem that conforms to the PDCA process.

Problem solving starts with "grasping the situation" to understand the business needs and, roughly, the current state of the processes. Based on this, an area that needs work is picked, and an ideal state is defined. For example, in the paint shop in an assembly plant, we may want to increase our flexibility to respond to customer demand. One obstacle to this is the large number of cars that we paint ahead and keep in a buffer of painted car bodies. Why do we have the buffer? It is because we have to repair paint defects in most car bodies. We might observe that the best Toyota paint shop in Japan has a buffer of only 10 cars that need any repair of the painted body compared to our current condition of 40 car bodies on a paint repair line. We might say that 10 cars is the ideal state, but we realize that this is too challenging a goal in our current condition. So we choose a target condition of keeping a maximum buffer size of 15 cars in need of repair. The business benefits will be less space needed for painted car bodies, fewer team members needed to do the repair, and a process that is more responsive to customer demand.

The targets should be broken into small steps so that the time between trying something and seeing the results is short. When one target condition is achieved, the next can be set. We are planning to go from 40 cars to 15 (a 25-car reduction), so we might break that into steps of 5 at a time—every two weeks over a 10-week period, our target will be to reduce the number of cars in repair lanes by 5. At this point, we still do not know how we will achieve the target condition, but we have a clear idea of the direction for short bursts of creative activity. We then need to analyze the causes of cars in repair, which would lead to an even more specific target condition that might be worked on today.

The role of managers is to coach the process, so they must themselves be experts on improvement and therefore coached. When there is a clear and visible target condition and people have been trained in the improvement process, Rother suggests five questions that a manager should ask whenever she is visiting the work area:

1. What is the target condition at this process?
2. What is the actual condition now?
3. What obstacles are now preventing you from reaching the target condition? Which one are you addressing now?
4. What is your next step (start of the next PDCA cycle)?
5. When can we go and see what we have learned from taking that step?

The result of this thinking process is one-by-one problem solving. At the beginning of each PDCA cycle, it is not clear how the target condition will be achieved. As we try ideas, some will fail, but we still learn something important from each thing we try. When the target condition is clear and a team of people follows the problem-solving process, and management pays attention, it is amazing how often those people achieve or exceed the target.

Figure 4.1 shows how this overall process fits together. Grasping the situation leads to an overall purpose for the business and for developing people. Further investigation at the *gemba* will help us define a realistic ideal state to move toward. However, while it is realistic in theory, the ideal state may be too big a stretch under present conditions, so we need to establish an achievable target, output, or condition. This, itself, needs to be broken down into smaller actionable steps. As we take each step toward short-term targets, we are following the PDCA process and learning so that we can better plan the next step toward the target. It may be a small loop that takes minutes or a larger one that takes days, but a PDCA loop that takes months is too big to grasp, and feedback is too slow. Continuous improvement does not mean that Toyota prefers small, incremental changes, but that breakthrough goals are broken into small steps so that exploration and learning will move us toward the breakthrough. Assuming that we will achieve a breakthrough in one fell swoop requires a good deal of luck. Toyota does not want to leave its most important business objectives

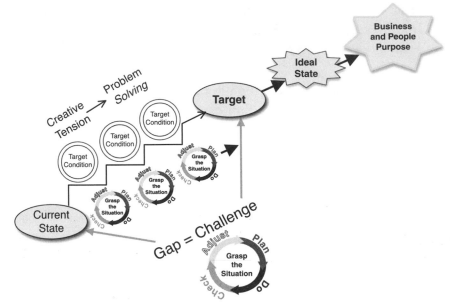

Figure 4.1. Work toward the Purpose and Clear Targets through Creative Problem Solving

to chance. The improvement *kata* provides a systematic way to achieve the target with high reliability, and along the way develops some new neural pathways so that people will think and behave differently—simultaneously developing people and processes.

As *hoshin kanri* moves down through the organization, it becomes increasingly specific and focuses more on *how* we will achieve the outcomes than on the outcomes themselves. At the work group level, a visual board is constructed, called the Floor Management Development System (FMDS), and the top line displays graphs with outcome metrics and targets. As we look down the board, we see how this is translated into process metrics and activities.

For example, the most common quality metric used in Toyota assembly plants is defects per vehicle (DPV). These are measured in a final inspection process inside the plant, and whatever is caught there is fixed before the vehicle leaves the plant. Not only does final inspection, a non-value-added activity, prevent defects from escaping to the customer, but it is also used to drive improvement back to the individual processes where quality is built in instead of inspected in.

Consider the production line that assembles the door. Let's say it is creating 8 DPV, and the target is set to get to 5 DPV. This would be the main key performance indicator (KPI) on the top line of the FMDS board. In the next row down, for a specific process (e.g., attach window regulator and window) that is found to be the cause of an unusual number of defects, there would be a sub-KPI—for example, actual = 3, target = 1. One level down would be a process KPI that breaks down that specific process into work elements, and for a particular work element (e.g., attach window regulator in place) that is causing problems, we might have actual = 1, target = 0. Then at the bottom of the board we would have activities that we are doing to go from 1 to 0 on that work element. This might include improving a tool like an air gun or training the operators who do that job (as we saw Yuri work on in Chapter 3). When a particular work element is improved, we might then shift our focus to the next most critical process, breaking that down to the work element that is causing the problems. Getting to the overall target DPV for doors may take one month, and then we would shift to another quality problem and set of targets.

Combining Short-Term and Long-Term Thinking in a Crisis

The concept of developing a perfectly aligned set of visions and goals and targets guided by a 10-year vision is seductive. Who would not want that? The reality of doing it is very difficult. The gap between what Toyota has accomplished to date and the current situation for most companies is the decades of accumulated experience and commitment at Toyota. You cannot get from here to there in one step. For a variety of reasons, including years of neglect, many companies today find themselves in a struggle for their very survival. Sometimes we are asked: "Before we even start on any lean activity, should we spend the next six months getting all of our goals and targets aligned?" Is that a prerequisite for starting a lean process for those in the early stages of adoption? Obviously the answer is no.

Dana Corporation, a global supplier of truck chassis components, was one company that decided to turn the corner on a commitment to lean while trying to get off of its deathbed. In March 2006, Dana filed for Chapter 11 bankruptcy protection, emerging from Chapter 11 in February 2008. Within six months, Dana was right in the middle of a major downturn in sales when gas prices spiked and soon after the Great Recession hit. Sales were down by 40 percent or more, and the company was threatened with permanent dissolution. At the time it emerged from bankruptcy, Dana was led by the chairman of the board, a former chief financial officer from General Motors, who then hired a former American Toyota executive, Gary Convis, as temporary CEO. The former GM CFO took the main responsibility for driving the financial improvements in a traditional top-down manner, while Gary worked to lay the foundation for future operational excellence.

Gary did not spend the first six months cascading *hoshin* down the ranks. There were small pilot projects and across all plants a basic cleaning up and organizing of the workplace (called 5S in lean) to engage the workforce throughout the company, but the main driver for survival was senior management-led *kaikaku* (radical process improvements), in this case focused on cost reduction. There were massive layoffs and plant closings driven by the need to downsize capacity. While this was a tragedy, it did provide an opportunity for the former Toyota executive to identify the leaders of the future based on how people responded to the crisis. The few who were capable of leading the radical improvement efforts were selected as future company leaders. In addition, Gary tapped his deep network to hire in seasoned TPS veterans, including former Toyota employees, as coaches to drive major improvements while teaching and developing others along the way. His goal was not only to get through the crisis but also to build the foundation for long-term operational excellence.

For example, Marty Bryant, a former Toyota employee, was put in charge of global operational excellence. He decided to put TPS into practice just as it had been taught to him—"no watered-down version." Marty led aggressive *kaikaku* activities (breakthrough changes), all focused on major cost reduction, but he refused to focus only on achieving target costs:

The results take care of themselves, but I was trying to teach people a good way of thinking about problems. The method was not to try to teach people how to go out and look for job reductions, because then you usually get short-term results. The method was go out and design the most efficient process and then we will clearly see the gap between what should be happening and what's actually happening.[11]

Marty also wanted to do this by engaging the hourly workforce and the union. In fact, the union had to be there with the manager making the presentation. Nobody lost his job as a direct result of these workshops—extra people would be moved to a different job or to a *kaizen* team. On the other hand, when a head-count-reduction order came from corporate to downsize, at that point they would downsize. The union and the workforce understood the economic crisis and generally seemed able to separate what was happening through the *kaizen* workshops from these downsizing decisions. When the company did downsize, the remaining workforce was able to produce the quantity and quality of parts needed—it was not a mad scramble. As Marty explained:

The hourly workers and union representatives had to be on the teams that were doing it. Before management was allowed to present the ideas to me, they had to bring the workers of that process into the boardroom or the meeting room, present to them, and truly get their approval. And the learning of the managers was twofold. One is teaching them that you really do respect everybody, and the second is they learned how to sell a difficult idea to an audience that wasn't necessarily complimentary. The end result was very good engagement. It really started to change the culture of the plant.[12]

What You Work on Now Depends on Your Situation

We are often asked for the best way to approach lean transformation in a company, and we fire back the ubiquitous answer: it depends! It depends on the business needs, the past history of process improvement in the company, the maturity of the people and the culture, whether people are enthusiastic about learning or jaded by many programs of the month, and more. The only way we can assess this is to go and see and observe firsthand. Toyota uses the phrase "grasp the situation," which happens before a particular PDCA cycle. We must get a picture of the whole situation before diving into specific targets and improvement projects.

While we cannot give a prescription for the best way to approach lean, we can say that the company needs to define a clear purpose for any activities. The purpose should include two elements: business purpose and people development purpose. Table 4.1 gives a high-level view of a variety of situations and a general picture of the business purpose and people development purpose.

In general, organizations that are in a crisis will need to focus on the crisis and use that opportunity to train and develop leaders, as Dana did. The crisis might be financial, with the threat of bankruptcy,

Table 4.1. Examples of Focus for Lean Improvement under Different Conditions

Business Purpose	People Development Purpose	Approach to Change
Company survival	Identify and develop leaders/lean coaches for future of company by observing who can lead *kaikaku*	Identify business needs to survive with key performance indicators and use radical *kaikaku* of processes to achieve them
Critical customer issue (quality, cost, delivery)	Targeted leadership development/lean coaches on how to achieve target condition through PDCA	Targeted *kaizen* of processes critical to customer-facing issue based on target conditions
Business need for specific results (e.g., productivity improvement)	Coach leaders on how to achieve target condition through PDCA	Set appropriate target condition and work to achieve in manageable steps with feedback
Begin journey to operational excellence in stable/growth environment	Convince leaders of value of improvement and develop lean coaches	Build "showcase" process or demonstration projects by driving toward target conditions and target outcomes

and then finances will be the focal point. The crisis might be a major customer satisfaction issue, such as quality or on-time delivery, and the risk may be losing a major customer and going out of business. In following Toyota Business Practices, the response to the crisis needs to be broken down into manageable elements. It is still possible to develop target conditions for different parts of the organization. Those target conditions should be measurable and visible, and people need to be held accountable for achieving them in the right way. It should be clear who will be learning from this project, what they will learn, and how they will be taught. This is an opportunity to teach the improvement process, but the "teachers" also need to be aggressively driving the changes. In calmer waters, when the company is stable or growing, it can afford a calmer, more patient approach to winning over doubters and developing people.

The "lean program" will look different in different business circumstances, but not completely different. We provide a picture of the extremes in Table 4.2. In an extreme crisis, the challenge is to get through the crisis but at the same time use it to set the stage for prospering coming out of the crisis. Leading the way will be leaders. The crisis is an opportunity to identify and promote the right leaders, as we saw in the Dana case. These are people who are open to learning the right way to solve problems and coach people, in addition to getting results.

When times are good, the challenge is that there is no crisis to motivate change. Many leaders have found this to be even more challenging. At least in a crisis, it will become clear what has to change

Table 4.2. Different Approaches in the Extremes of Business Conditions

	Range of Business Conditions	
	Crisis	**Healthy**
Primary purpose	Drive rapid results	Build foundation for lean enterprise
Secondary purpose	Develop future leaders	Develop people and culture
Leadership	Top-down turnaround	Top-down coaching
Focus	Results through process improvement	Process to drive results and learning
Time frame	Short-term to get to stability	Long-term

and why. Toyota has found that good times are some of the most dangerous because people tend to become complacent. In fact, Akio Toyoda identified complacency as one of the root causes of the recall crisis. So a crisis actually helps the company move forward. By setting challenging targets and holding people accountable, the people involved will feel the crisis, whether it is externally imposed or internally created.

Notice that top-down leadership is essential regardless of the business condition. We might think that in a crisis, we need hard-driving command and control, and when the organization is financially healthy, we can allow improvement to surface from the bottom up. In reality, a good process for problem solving will not naturally occur in either situation. The natural inclination is to attack urgent problems as they become fires to fight; to combat that tendency, people need leadership. That leadership starts from the top. In a crisis, the role of top leadership is to teach a good process for solving problems, as Marty was doing at Dana. In calm waters, it is even more critical for top leaders to actively teach and coach improvement because there is no burning platform.

Lean as a Culture of Continuous Improvement

The book by Womack and Jones was titled *Lean Thinking* for a reason.[11] It is clearly more than a toolkit to be mindlessly applied. We must change the way people think. When we change thinking, we will change behavior.

How do we approach a mammoth cultural change like this? In the next chapter, we suggest that there is a mechanistic approach that specifies what to do in great detail and an organic approach that grows capability gradually through deep experience. It would seem obvious that organic development is better and more compatible with lean thinking, but what is obvious is not always correct. We will argue that a balanced approach is needed, and that in fact, in the early stages of lean deployment, there is often a need for a greater degree of structure through a more heavily mechanistic approach.

Chapter 5

Lean Out Processes
or Build Lean Systems?

A system is a network of interdependent components that work together to try to accomplish the aim. A system must have an aim. Without the aim, there is no system. . . . What we need to do is learn to work in the system, by which I mean that everybody, every team, every platform, every division, every component is there not for individual competitive profit or recognition, but for contribution to the system as a whole on a win-win basis.

—W. Edwards Deming, American consultant, statistician, and educator

"Leaning Out" Processes

A *process* is a series of actions, changes in state, or functions that brings about a result. We can look at a process as one transformation step, e.g., drill a hole, or as a value stream, which is all the steps from start to finish to produce the desired output. For our purposes, both would be considered processes. You can "lean out" one step or the entire value stream. Generally, process improvement refers to the technical transformation itself, without regard to the people or the broader context. As we will see, focusing on the process without the people is often misleading and even destructive.

When we teach the basic concepts of lean in public courses we ask participants what they expect to get from the course. We hear things like

- "I'm a manufacturing engineer, and my manager asked me to get trained up because we need some major cost reductions at our facility."
- "There are four of us here in the course, and for us lean is a necessity because we have to either cut costs or go out of business."
- "I'm the head of continuous improvement, and we have inventory everywhere. We are growing and we need the space, so I'm leading an effort to lean out the facility."

At the risk of sounding disrespectful, what do all these people think they are doing by leaning out this or that? Obviously they think that there is some physical thing that has waste in it, and the objective is to remove that waste. It is sort of like cleaning your pool. Remove the dirt and debris and your pool is clean, but even your pool will not stay clean for very long. Removing waste as a technical process can work, at least in the short term. In fact, many traditional industrial engineering methods do this quite well. Frederick Taylor routinely increased productivity by 20 to 50 percent through time and motion studies. Henry Ford increased productivity by 5 to 10 times by shifting from building cars in place to using a moving assembly line. In each case, it was a change in the technical process that drove the improvements. Another way to think about the "lean-it-out" mentality is to picture a brick wall like the one shown in Figure 5.1. If we put on our "eliminate waste" blinders, we begin chipping away at the wall, hoping that taking out the next "brick" doesn't cause the entire structure to come tumbling down around our ears.

Companies continue to focus their lean efforts on *kaizen* "blitzes" to identify wastes such as excessive inventory, downtime, operator walking, imbalance in workload, movement of material, and so on, while not understanding that they aren't actually building anything long-lasting. After all of the effort, they are left with a hollowed-out structure that can topple at the slightest introduction of variation. In effect, what they leave in their wake after a series of blitzes tends to look like the wall in Figure 5.2, a structure whose stability or value is questionable. While it certainly takes fewer bricks to maintain the

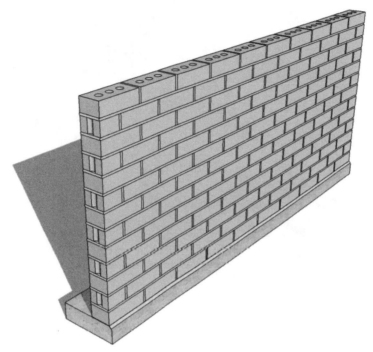

Figure 5.1. A Typical Process or System as a Brick Wall

basic structure, what do you think will happen when a load is applied from any direction?

The common lean method for a repetitive manual process is to calculate the rate of customer demand, the *takt*, and then balance the jobs on that line so that each operator has a cycle of work equal to the *takt*. For example, if average customer demand is for a car every minute, then ideally every job should have one minute's worth of work. There is some natural variation, so you need a little bit of slack, but it is not uncommon to find workers in many companies spending 40 or 50 percent of their time doing value-added work, with the rest being waste. If the operation has not been well balanced in the past, this simple exercise can easily free up one-third or more of the people. In repetitive service processes, such as those in banking, that were rarely studied by industrial engineers, it is easy to get these kinds of gains. We can also calculate the inventory levels needed to support the

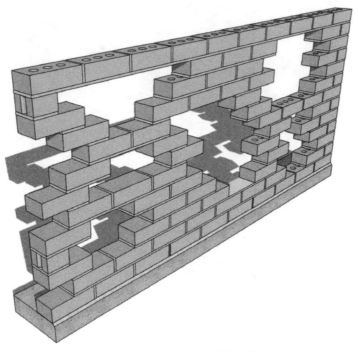

Figure 5.2. The Brick Wall Has Been "Leaned Out"

takt, and we typically find that lopping out half the inventory will have no adverse effects on production because there is so much excess inventory. It is low-hanging fruit.

The next question we get is how to sustain the process in the leaner state. In Taylor's day, the job of the supervisor was to use a tasty carrot and a big stick to maintain the new work methods, generally paying the worker for each piece produced. The carrot and stick works, but you get what you reward, and not much else. If you reward productivity, do not expect top quality or safety. This was the problem with the piece-rate system. If you pay by the piece, people will produce a lot of pieces, but whether they are the right pieces or the best-quality pieces is another matter. Try to change their work methods and you get resistance because the workers will accept nothing that will even temporarily slow them down and lower their pay. Forget about standardized work. Each person wants to do the job the way he personally believes is fastest.

Those of us in the lean community may have created our own problem by defining *lean* simply as waste reduction. Get out your hammer, chip away at some waste, and you are doing lean. We will learn in this chapter that lean is far more than a waste-reduction methodology. When people say that they use the tools of lean or Six Sigma or theory of constraints to lean out the process, reduce variation, or increase throughput, they are completely missing the point, at least from the Toyota perspective. Lean is a system of philosophy, processes, people, and problem solving that is striving for excellence. Strangely, a lean system is *not* one in which all the waste has been eliminated, since all real organizations always have waste. A lean system is one in which waste is made visible every day, and there is pressure from the process for people to fix the problems. When we look at an operation that someone proudly displays as a lean model, we are not looking to see if the *kanban* is well designed or the standardized work is neatly displayed. We are looking to see whether the team member doing the work knows, without a lot of effort, what she should be working on right now, what her biggest problems are, how she will address the problems, and when. Does the system reveal the next set of problems to be solved? People and processes are inextricably intertwined in real lean.

Are Organizations Like Machines or Organic Systems?

Recently we received an invitation to a conference called "Transforming Business Results through Process Optimization." Wow! We need to go to that. We all want results, and who wants suboptimal processes, but what does it mean to "optimize" a process? This brings to mind that old algebra course that many people would like to forget, in which we had a set of equations and we tried to solve them as a system, but we always had one more variable than we had equations. In operations research, we can in some cases optimize a set of equations even when we have too many variables. Can we actually optimize a value stream and figure out the best parameter for this and the best parameter for that? When people are involved, is there an optimal mix of rewards that we can tweak and adjust to get precisely the behavior we desire? Yes, if the organization behaves like a machine, but not if it behaves like a complex system of people and machines. Unfortunately, people do not follow the rules precisely, and because of changes in the environment, even the technical system has way too many variables to "optimize." It can certainly be improved, but optimized?

Machine thinking is not a new idea; it can be traced back at least as far as the Industrial Revolution. Once people and machines were centralized in a factory, it seems that the people faded into the background and the machines became the prominent feature that managers sought to optimize. This led to keeping machines running at all costs to maximize economies of scale and created all the problems that lean production is supposed to solve.

Thinking of organizations as machines is convenient. We can ignore all those messy interactions between the parts. When there is a problem, it can be traced to a specific person or machine. When we fix something, we assume that it stays fixed. Simple linear cause and effect is easy to understand. Unfortunately, there are severe limitations to lean if we continue to view organizations as machines.

Lean production is not the first new idea that has come along as a counterperspective to machine thinking. Systems thinking has been studied and advocated for well over a century. One of the most cited scholars in this area is Karl Ludwig von Bertalanffy, a founder of general systems theory, who started his writings in the 1920s. A biologist, he argued that the then-widespread physical science view of closed systems led to gross misunderstandings of biological systems, which interact in complex ways within the ecosystem and with the broader environment. Even components of the body, like organs, interact in ways that go far beyond simple linear processes. He then extended this theory to the operation of social and economic systems.

This evolved into open-systems theory.[1] If the outside environment did not exist, or did not change, organizations could act like closed systems, and we could develop ever more elaborate internal control mechanisms to achieve efficiency. Since organizations are open systems that are in constant interaction with a changing environment, they need to be adaptable, with more flexible policies and procedures, and people are the source of adaptation. This led to a rich vein of applied research in the area of "socio-technical systems" (STS) theory. It was applied in many settings to make organizations more successful by jointly "optimizing" the technical and social systems. The term *optimizing* in STS sounds very technical and scientific, but actually the goal is to set up the technology so that it can run and so that it facilitates teams of people to innovate and solve problems. When we compare machine thinking (mechanistic) to the view of organizations as socio-technical systems (organic), there are striking contrasts, as summarized in Table 5.1.

In machine thinking, the goal is to create a tidy environment for our core production processes by buffering them from the vagaries of the environment. One way to do that is to build lots of inventory, so that when demand changes, you can ship from inventory. People are another source of messiness, so they are also controlled by close supervision, technical specialists, and extensive rules. Managers give orders, and working people obey. People are assumed to work only for money, and management, through employment contracts, purchases the right

Table 5.1. Comparison of Machine Thinking and Systems Thinking

	Mechanistic (Machine) Thinking	Organic (Systems) Thinking
Worldview	Simple linear chain of cause and effect	Interdependent, interacting systems
View of environment	Control it; buffer organization from change	Embrace it; respond flexibly to environmental change
Role of people	Extensions of machines	Thinking and improving
View of people	Interchangeable parts	Appreciating assets
Controls	External supervisors, specialists, standard operating procedures	Internal self-regulating subsystems
Management style	Autocratic, command and control	Participative, collaborative
Purpose	Organization's goals only	Members' and society's goals
Risk taking	Discouraged; "If it ain't broke, don't fix it."	Encouraged; "Experimentation is the best teacher."
Change management	Primary responsibility of management and staff specialists	Primary responsibility of work groups

to have people do whatever is needed to pursue the organization's goals. People follow the "one best way" of working as specified by managers and engineers, and are discouraged from experimenting with their own methods—they stop thinking.

The socio-technical systems perspective sees the world as a set of interdependent, interacting systems of people and technology that have a defined purpose and must respond flexibly to changes in the environment. Adaptation is best done by people working in the process, who are empowered to think, experiment, and learn new methods. People will participate in the running of the business only if they feel like a part of the business, so new reward systems that paid people for knowledge and even shared profits with the workers were often developed. The participative, collaborative work systems were a stark contrast to the traditional command-and-control environment. Many studies found higher productivity and quality in companies run using socio-technical systems principles.[2]

Entropy: The Antagonist to Mechanistic Lean Deployment

One of our clients was a global auto parts supplier with operations in the United States. One of its plants in Michigan had been a leader in lean, winning a Shingo prize as a best practice model. We were asked to advise the corporation because "lean had gone backward." As part of our initial investigation, we visited the award-winning plant. The trophy was proudly displayed in the lobby. The plant looked anything but lean—boxes of parts everywhere; machined parts being built up in large batches; evidence of overproduction and poor 5S. There were some whiteboards with metrics, but the last entries were more than a year old. People explained that those boards had been used when the company had a big lean program, but the plant manager who had been its champion had left the company, and things had not been the same since. The former internal lean coach was now managing a production department. He recalled the good old days when they could change over machines in 15 minutes and built only what was needed by the next process, but now changeovers took hours, so they built big batches and held extra inventory. We started to feel more like archeologists then lean advisors—trying to infer from decaying artifacts what the plant had been like in its pre-apocalypse state of lean.

What was the problem here? Obviously the great Lean Program that the company had had in place when it won the award was not being sustained. In fact, one of the most frequent questions we are asked is whether Toyota has any special methods for sustaining the improvements.

The underlying thought process behind this question is pure machine thinking. If lean is like tools that we pull out of the toolbox to do work on the operation, then we should see a clear improvement from before to after we "lean out the process" (see Figure 5.3). Now that we have a lean process, we should have another set of tools to "sustain the gains." Once we shore up that process, it is leaned out, and we can move on to lean out the next process.

Unfortunately, there is no magic sustenance pill to take. The real problem is that organizations are systems, not machines. A useful concept from systems theory is *entropy*. Entropy can be viewed as the

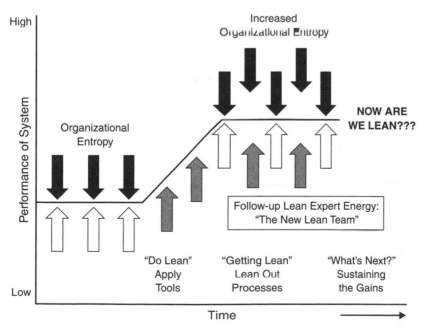

Figure 5.3. Can We "Sustain the Gains" of Lean like Maintaining a Machine?

amount of energy in a physical system that is not available to do work. Anyone who took a thermodynamics course learned the second law of thermodynamics, which states that entropy, or disorder, will naturally increase over time. The universe seems to be lazy. It does not like having concentrated amounts of energy actively doing work and tries to take some of that energy and redistribute it to a more passive state of lower energy. Take the example of boiling water. It boils only when we apply energy, and when we stop applying energy, the heat dissipates into the surrounding environment, and the water cools down. In other words, the energy level of the water decreases naturally if we do nothing and increases only when we add energy to the water by lighting a fire under it.

If we consider the law of entropy applied to lean, it looks like Figure 5.4. We do lean by applying the tools, and we see an improved state, but if we do nothing more, the improvements will decay, and the process will tend to go back to its pre-lean state. Think of mass production as a state of high entropy, with disorder everywhere. There is

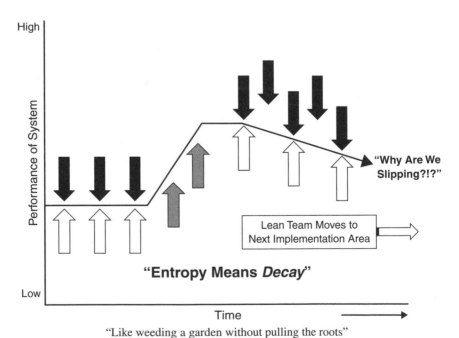

Figure 5.4. The Reality Is That Entropy Will Always Set In, Degrading the Perfect Lean Solution

a lot of potential energy in the form of piles of inventory. They are comfortably sitting around not doing work, and they allow the manufacturing processes to operate at a low level of energy—quality defects, machine breakdowns, low productivity—without disrupting customer shipments. In fact, we might say the second law of manufacturing systems is that mass production is a natural state, and to force the unnatural state of lean requires constant energy. Toyota *sensei* often use metaphors from nature. One Toyota Production System (TPS) master exclaimed that a superficial tools approach to waste elimination "is like weeding a garden without pulling the roots." The weeds will simply grow back, and then you have to start pulling them all over again. Now we have some new technology that we put on the ground that can actually prevent weeds from growing, but even it needs to be renewed every year.

An Effective Work Group Can Overcome Entropy

So how does Toyota sustain the gains? The answer is that Toyota does not see the Toyota Production System as a mechanistic process of implementing an improvement. It sees TPS as an organic process of continuous improvement. Any improvement is simply one more countermeasure to learn from. If we focused on sustaining the gains, we would stop improving. Toyota understands that as the system becomes leaner, with less waste, more energy is needed to operate it. It is harder to run a system with two hours of inventory than to run that same system with two days of inventory. It requires more precision, discipline, and attentiveness (see Figure 5.5). The positive energy comes from people improving the process every day, every hour, every minute. The only people who are continually at the work site are the people who operate the process—the work group. To keep the positive energy of improvement alive and growing within the work group takes leadership. So Toyota works very hard to continually develop leaders who are capable of leading continuous improvement.

   We have given a detailed description of the work group structure in other books.[3] There is ideally a 5:1 ratio between the working team

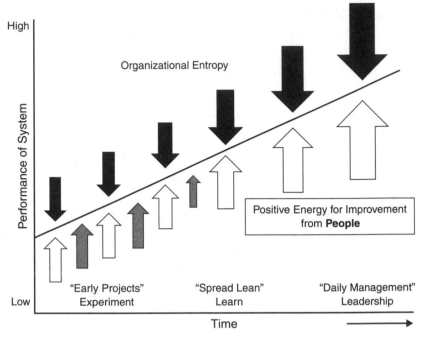

Figure 5.5. Counter Entropy with Positive Energy

leader and the team members. There are 4 or 5 team leaders for every group leader, so each group leader has 20 to 25 people. In a production group, the team leader is generally the most skilled worker who also has leadership abilities, and in engineering, it is the lead engineer for developing a portion of the car. The group leader is the first-line supervisor, the first formal management level. This person leads the daily work that brings the tools and methods of lean to life. Without his or her leadership, checking, cajoling, and coaching, you will see evidence of entropy: metrics will not be up to date, problems will be contained but not really solved, *kanban* will get lost, standardized work will not be followed, and evidence of decay in 5S will be everywhere. You can judge the effectiveness of the leader by the overall condition of the work area and whether there is active problem solving leading to personal growth of team members.

In the heyday of the socio-technical systems movement, the centerpiece of most interventions was "semiautonomous work groups."

This reached a peak in Volvo's plant in Uddevalla, Sweden, in which the entire technical system—the module design of the car and the physical layout of the plant—was designed to support the autonomous work group. The ideal was to give each independent work group a quota for the day—build this number of modules or cars—and let the group have at it. The resulting struggles would lead to innovation and learning. There has been some lively debate about whether this method of empowerment led to less or more operational efficiency than Toyota's more structured approach.[4]

Another Swedish company with considerable success is Scania, a truck company that has had a remarkable run of decades of organic growth and profitability. In the 1980s, Scania was following the lead of other European companies in moving toward autonomous work groups. One radical step was to eliminate all of the first-line supervisors. One manufacturing manager could have 40 or more people reporting to him. The people were organized into large groups of 15 to 20 with a team leader. The system seemed to be working okay, but eventually the company hit a wall and found that its efficiency was behind that of its competitors. The CEO personally sought help from Toyota, and several American Toyota managers came to Sweden once per year as coaches. Scania was a marvelous student and tried everything it was taught. On one of the annual visits, the Toyota *sensei* explained that in the organization structure at the time, group leaders had too big a span of control; they needed a structure more like Toyota's, with functioning group leaders and team leaders. Scania reorganized in this way and has not looked back since.

The fundamental insight for Scania was that its original problem was not too many managers but not enough leaders. The autonomous work group solution was to eliminate a lot of managers, but it still lacked the leadership. What the company learned from Toyota was the role of a leader in a lean system. The problem in a traditional organization is that there are few systems to support the leaders. They are constantly in a firefighting mode. Lean systems provide visibility for problems and the tools necessary for leaders to truly add value.

The Real Purpose of Lean Systems Is to Bring Problems to the Surface

People often have a hard time understanding the real purpose of what they see at Toyota. For example, Toyota has measurements everywhere. It seems to track everything under the sun. So if we have measurements and visually display the data, we are acting like Toyota. If we look more closely, Toyota is not really measuring everything, only very carefully selected items that will be the focus of improvement. Moreover, Toyota is not simply displaying data but using information to show whether or not the actual performance is meeting the target. The time frame of measurement is usually very short; for example, we might measure the process every hour, or in some cases every cycle. The purpose is to have a short time frame for comparing what actually happens with what we had planned (the standard), so that people can tell how they are doing in real time. Since we cannot "optimize processes globally," people monitor processes locally and make adjustments as they work. The greater the time between the action and the result, the more difficult it will be to understand the cause of a breakdown in the plan. As a detective would say, when we get to the scene of the crime too late, the trail is cold, and so many things have changed that it is difficult to reconstruct the crime.

When there is a clear connection between expectations, actions, and results in the short term, we find that people will usually do their best to contribute to the business. People generally want to do a good job. They want to succeed and "win," but if the game is vague and it is not clear what they should be doing to win, they will fail. If our guide to winning simply says be careful about everything you do, follow the plan exactly all the time, and always anticipate all the problems that might occur, people must be either prescient or they're toast. On the other hand, if the vision is clear, they understand the methods to use, and they are well trained in those methods, they will solve the problems that do arise as they go. Moreover, as they do this, they will be learning. They will learn what obstacles to expect and how to respond to them. People will grow in value to the organization.

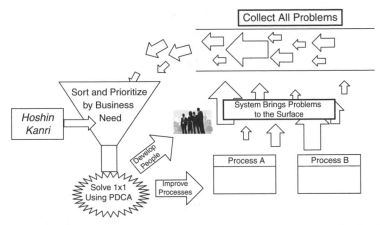

Figure 5.6. Lean Systems Are Processes That Bring Problems to the Surface so that People Can Continually Improve and Learn through PDCA

This dynamic process of bringing problems to the surface and then learning by addressing them one by one is illustrated in Figure 5.6. Our definition of a lean process is one that brings problems to the surface as they occur, making them visible for team members to solve one by one.

Of course, simply bringing problems to the surface does not solve them. Work groups need to be well trained in problem solving using a true plan–do–check–adjust (PDCA) process. The best way of learning is by doing, so the best situation is repeatedly solving problems to improve processes so that people are being developed in real time. As with anything else, we learn a skill by repeatedly practicing that skill. A training class here and there does not help if the skill is not practiced regularly. Without continual practice, the skill atrophies.[5]

We also need a way of sorting all the problems that become visible, or we will be overwhelmed. The method is the *hoshin kanri* system, discussed in Chapter 4, which links the business plan to group and individual plans. Through the *hoshin kanri* process, we can sort out the business priorities from problems that would be nice to solve.

The Toyota Way included seven process principles that can be viewed through the lenses of machine thinking or systems thinking (see Table 5.2). The machine thinker views the process as an isolated technical stream of work and views each principle as a guideline for

Table 5.2. The Real Purpose Behind Toyota Process Principles

Toyota Process Principle	Apparent Purpose: Machine Thinking	Actual Purpose: Systems Thinking
Create process "flow" to bring problems to the surface	One-piece flow is the ultimate in waste elimination	Process flow brings problems to the surface
Use pull systems to avoid overproduction	Reduce inventory, which is the main purpose of lean	Pull systems bring problems to the surface
Level out the workload (heijunka)	Unevenness prevents smooth flow and increases inventory	Leveled flow brings problems to the surface
Stop when there is a quality problem (jidoka)	Do not let defective products leak out	Stop to bring problems to the surface
Standardize tasks for continuous improvement	Standardization is the best-known way and most efficient	Standards compared to actual define problems
Use visual control so that no problems are hidden	Visual control allows everyone to understand the state of the operation by simply looking	Visual controls make the standards clear to identify problems
Use only reliable, thoroughly tested technology	Toyota is conservative about using risky new technology	Using technology as a fix is avoiding the problems and can create new ones

leaning out the process. For example, we implement a cell to create one-piece flow. We minimize the inventory with a pull system. We control the evenness of the work schedule with *heijunka* (leveling) tools. We write up and post standardized worksheets to control how an individual worker performs her job. Visual factory allows us to know where the problems are so that we can jump in and control deviations immediately. We avoid complex new technologies because they add variation to the process. In machine thinking, we see a direct cause-and-effect relationship between the implementation of a tool and the specific result we get by *controlling* the process.

From the time of Taiichi Ohno's early experience with one-piece flow cells, the Toyota leaders concluded that inventory hides problems and that they could cope with variation only by reducing inventory to expose problems and solve them one by one. Like one-piece flow production, this is one-piece flow problem solving. If one person slowed down or one machine stopped, the entire cell stopped, making the problems visible. When we think in systems terms, we realize all of the Toyota process principles focus on making problems visible so that people can solve them and grow as people in the process (see Table 5.2).

Mechanistic versus Organic? Not So Fast

So machine thinking is out and open-systems thinking is in. Let's throw out the rule books and empower people to design their own work, and life will be good. It is not quite so simple. When Paul Adler looked carefully at the Toyota Production System he studied in Toyota's joint venture with General Motors, NUMMI, he noticed a confusing pattern.[6] It was mechanistic like a bureaucracy because of the extensive rules and procedures, down to every scripted movement of every production worker. It was organic because of the extensive engagement of employees, down to the involvement of every production worker in *kaizen*. Within clearly defined boundaries, employees were developing suggestions, using whiteboards to sketch out new ways of working, quickly making changes to the workplace, and were visibly passionate about quality and the customer. How could this contradiction occur in a real organization? Were they really mechanistic or organic?

Adler introduced a new term, *enabling bureaucracy*, to describe this situation. He noted that the traditional view of mechanistic organizations is that they suffer from "coercive bureaucracy." Rules exist to coerce, and deviation from the rules is a punishable offense. Bureaucrats sit in their offices and busily dream up rules and operating procedures for people to follow, with appropriate rewards and punishments. Usually the rules and procedures have nothing to do with what is really needed and simply add layers of inefficiency. On the other hand, in an enabling bureaucracy, people actually are encouraged to break the rules, as long as they know why they are doing so and they document the results. If the new method is not a clear improvement, they follow the existing standard.

Is it possible to use enabling bureaucracy in a top-down manner to change an organization to one that learns and achieves its goals? We suspect that this is the only effective way. Before delving into the complexity of managing change in large, complex organizations, which we will take up in Section Three of the book, we will take a deep dive into case studies in Section Two. In all cases, a relatively organic approach involving a PDCA learning approach was used, but the transformations were top-down, and some level of enabling bureaucracy was created. There was a range of success across the cases, though in all cases the focus area of the transformation improved in dramatic ways. After going through these cases in detail, we will return to some of the general issues of deploying lean in a way that leads to a journey of excellence.

Section Two

Case Studies of Lean Transformation through PDCA

Learning is not compulsory ... neither is survival.

—W. Edwards Deming, American consultant,
statistician, and educator

Most people learn better by example than by abstract discussion. We have given you a heavy dose of abstract discussion in Section One, and now here is the reward—a series of in-depth case studies from the perspectives of different people who acted as *sensei* in lean transformations. Each chapter was written with contributions from either the outside consultant who acted as the *sensei* or the key executive who was leading the transformation, each of whom tells the story from his perspective. We selected these cases carefully to reflect a diversity of industries, technical processes, maturity in lean transformation, and even success with the transformation. We are not arguing that these are the most successful lean transformations on the planet. What they all have in common is that the *sensei* was striving to teach and drive a culture based on plan–do–check–adjust (PDCA). None of these were attempts to "deploy tools to lean out processes," although that may have been what senior executives expected and even wanted. We pause at various points in the cases for a "*sensei* reflection" to get insight into what lessons we have learned up to that point.

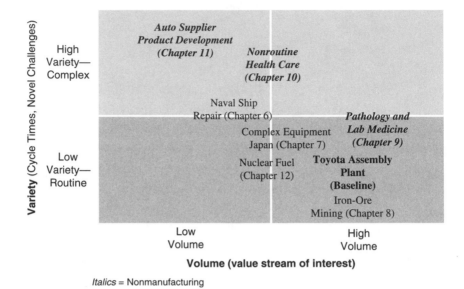

Italics = Nonmanufacturing

Figure P2.1. Categorization of Case Study Value Streams

The seven cases are roughly classified in Figure P2.1 into a framework, with the variety or complexity of the core processes in the organization on the y axis and volume on the x axis. Low variety and high volume is what we normally think of as mass production, and Toyota assembly plants would generally be put into this category. In reality, if you walk through a Toyota plant, you will see batch stamping processes, highly automated body welding and painting, very finicky processes in plastic molding, and a variety of different types of assembly jobs with an enormous variety of different car models and options. Reality is always much more complex than broad generalizations.

Generally speaking, when we have high-volume processes that are relatively simple and repetitive, it is easiest to envision the lean tools in practice. We can physically see the waste. We can calculate the *takt* (rate of customer demand) for a process and measure whether the repetitive process is consistently near the *takt* in its cycle time. When we set up a standard process, the standard applies to a large volume, and each repetition of the process can follow the standard closely. The more complex and variable the process, the more difficult it is to understand how to begin to come to grips with it and identify improvements. What we really are trying to do is move the process toward a future state image of an ideal process. If the process keeps changing from moment to moment, any improvement will apply to one instance of the process but not to the next.

To address low-volume, variable processes, we have to move to a higher level of abstraction in determining what the process is. What are the repeating elements? What are general phases in the process? What are key milestones to judge progress?

Chapter 6 is about lean deployment in repair yards for Navy ships—very low volume and high variety. Two shipyards in the same division of a large organization that repaired and overhauled naval ships took very different approaches to a lean mandate from corporate. The larger shipyard, "Big Ship," took a mechanistic approach, creating a Lean Six Sigma academy. Eventually Big Ship evolved toward a more organic approach. "Small Ship," with a fraction of the resources, took an organic approach, starting with a pilot and building toward a real culture change. Both shipyards had serious ups and downs over a six-year period, and neither was the clear victor as the best example of lean transformation. Bob Kucner, the *sensei* for Small Ship and later the corporate *sensei*, guides us through a number of different phases in their journeys.

Chapter 7 brings us to Japan and a more traditional manufacturing process in a company that makes complex equipment—a bit higher volume, but still with plenty of product variety. It was a subsidiary of a Western global company with elements of both cultures intermingled. Tony McNaughton was trained in the Toyota Production System (TPS) in the traditional way, learning by doing on the shop floor, at Toyota of Australia by a student of Ohno. As the *sensei* for the plant, he demonstrates the traditional way in which a TPS master approaches teaching in a factory.

Speaking of Down Under, we now traverse the ocean to Australia, in Chapter 8, where James Franz takes us onsite to an iron-ore mine. He had the unenviable task of braving an Aussie summer in dry, hot mines and trying to figure out how to apply lean concepts in a very unusual environment. In some ways, the process is very routine, always going from blasting and gathering to a crusher, then a sorter, and then the building of a big stockpile of iron ore. But the ground is highly variable, and no one knows what will be found until the blast. The real key in this case was not physically manipulating the process but changing the way in which the people plan, communicate, and, most important, identify and solve problems.

We repeatedly hear, "We are different," and we hear this loud and clear in health care. "Every patient is different." "We do not know what we will find until we cut the patient open." "We have to be prepared to react creatively to circumstances we could never imagine in advance." One of the most repetitive and high-volume processes in a health-care system is in the labs, where blood and tissue samples are analyzed. In Chapter 9, Dr. Richard Zarbo takes us inside the transformation of the labs he runs at Henry Ford Health System in Detroit, Michigan. The concept of lean was not new to the health-care system, as Henry Ford was its founder and Deming came to the hospital to teach PDCA. Despite this legacy, Dr. Zarbo had a revelation that the labs "did not have a clue what they were doing" with PDCA. So he set out to educate himself and learn by doing, using the laboratory as a, well, laboratory for lean learning. This chapter is more than anything about leadership: how Dr. Zarbo transformed his own leadership in the process of developing leaders down to the work-cell level. The transformation of the culture over a five-year period was stunning.

In Chapter 10, we switch to the less routine worlds of a medical insurance company and a long-term health facility. Steve Hoeft had years of experience with TPS, mostly in manufacturing, so there was an adjustment period as he entered the health-care world. He was not particularly nervous because a process was a process. He led his usual value stream mapping workshops with great "success," only to find that nothing in the great future state vision translated into real action. Dipping back into his past training, he realized that the teams were not getting good feedback, and that no one was accountable. Through simple visual tracking boards and a lot of tough-love coaching, he lit a fire in both cases, with impressive results.

Chapter 11 takes us to an even more complex and difficult-to-measure process—developing a new product, in this case an automotive supplier developing a major subsystem of an automobile (subsystem examples include, braking, exhaust, seating, instrument panel, chassis). Engineers in global companies are geographically dispersed, have different specialties, and do a lot of individual work that needs to come together in the design, testing, and building of a complex product. Charlie Baker got training from some of the best in the world at Honda and was brought into North American Auto Supplier (NAAS) as the vice president of engineering. He had deep knowledge and experience and the clout of being the top engineering executive in charge, so what could be easier? The answer is, almost anything is easier than whipping highly educated and proud engineers into shape, overcoming decades of poor communication, poor coordination, and low expectations. It requires change management at its finest. Charlie probably learned as much as anyone from the experience of leading this challenging transformation. In this chapter, we learn how to transform a complex knowledge-work process and the power of lean even in this unique environment.

Last but not least, we move in Chapter 12 to the highly regulated world of creating nuclear fuel bundles for power plants, where John Drogosz was the advisor for more than 10 years. Once again, we get a sense of how long and arduous the journey is, going through many ups, downs, and periods of stagnation through six distinct phases of development. Murphy's Law is alive and well in real organizations, and everything that can go wrong eventually does go wrong. This case brings to life one of Confucius's wise sayings: "It does not matter how slowly you go so long as you do not stop." They struggled, but they kept going and reaped the rewards.

As we look across these cases, we see differences in the approach of the *sensei*, the cultures of the companies, and the processes that were being transformed. We also see common threads in the problems that these companies faced and the PDCA approach, as we will discuss in Section Three of this book. The actual cases defy simplistic generalizations about issues like going top-down versus bottom-up, deep versus broad, and the best change management strategies. They all illustrate the importance of having a guide, driving lean with clear business objectives, viewing lean transformation as a journey of learning, and the power of learning by doing.

As you read these cases, you will notice they are written in the first person. We wrote the cases with the *sensei* or executive in charge, but in all cases the use of "I" will refer to the *sensei* or executive who was leading and living the transformation.

Chapter 6

When Organic Meets Mechanistic: Lean Overhaul and Repair of Ships

(With Robert Kucner)

You can't move so fast that you try to change the [norms] faster than people can accept it. That doesn't mean you do nothing, but it means that you do the things that need to be done according to priority.

—Eleanor Roosevelt (1884–1962),
U.S. First Lady, lecturer, and author

I t is tempting to include only unequivocal success stories in a book on excellence, especially when the authors were personally involved as *sensei*. Unfortunately, as we pointed out in Chapter 1, the unequivocal successes in lean are few and far between. So we would be propagating a myth if we suggested that every company we touch becomes a lean exemplar.

One of our clients over the years (we will refer to it here as Reman) repairs and overhauls large submarines and aircraft carriers for the U.S. Navy at four shipyards around the country. Bob Kucner, who tells the story in this case, was the consultant, and he can proudly say that he helped make a positive difference in the lives of many working people. This case was written from Bob's point of view and in his own words.

As a whole, Reman exhibited many mechanistic tendencies, but within it existed pockets of organic potential. In this chapter, we compare and contrast how lean manufacturing was deployed at two shipyards within Reman, one relatively organic and the other extremely mechanistic. While our inclination at the time was to applaud the organic pieces and rant over the evils of the mechanistic bureaucracy, looking back over eight years of lean deployment, it is not clear which was more effective in the long run. In fact, it is not even clear whether the overall effort was an unequivocal success or a failure.

How We Got Started on Lean at Reman

In 1998, Jeff Liker became involved in a national program to improve the efficiency and effectiveness of ship production in the United States (called the Advanced Shipbuilding Enterprise Program). Liker, with Thomas Lamb, who had decades of ship design and construction experience, made benchmarking trips to shipyards in Japan and the United States and interpreted what he saw in light of the Toyota Production System (TPS). The fit was actually quite good for the Japanese shipyards, especially one that was modeling its parent company's version of TPS. Ultimately this led to a document called "A Guide to Lean Ship Building."[1] As part of that effort, Liker was a principal in a U.S. government contract to pilot lean production in U.S. ship overhaul and repair yards, sometimes called "remanufacturing."

Reman was part of the nationally funded project, but not directly funded by the grant. Reman's COO explained to Liker that he had recently been put in charge of operations and was interested in lean manufacturing. It was new to his industry, but he saw a great deal of waste, and companies were under increasing pressure to reduce the repair lead time to get naval ships back out on the water for military use; there was also intensified pressure for cost reduction. The COO wanted to take senior leaders from each of Reman's four shipyards offsite to a place where they could visit a lean exemplar plant and develop plans for deploying the techniques in their shipyards.

In the summer of 2001, Liker organized a two-day retreat at an automotive supplier of side-view mirrors in Michigan whose vice president of operations was a former Toyota vice president. The supplier was progressing well on an organic path to lean as a system. Small work groups operated well-designed cells to assemble the mirrors and used *kanban* to pull housings from plastic injection-molding machines.[2] The two days included training on basic TPS concepts, a tour of the plant, and some soul-searching about where Reman as a whole wanted to go with lean.

It was clear from the start that the senior leaders from each of the shipyards had different motivations for coming to the offsite retreat and different visions for their shipyards. The leader of the smallest and most specialized yard, which we will call Small Ship, had taken the time to read some of Womack's *Lean Thinking* and intended to learn and apply what he learned.[3] The leader of Small Ship was relatively new in his position; he saw lean manufacturing as an opportunity both for Small Ship to make a statement within the company and for him to further his reputation and career advancement within the organization.

The leader of the largest shipyard, which we will call Big Ship, was conspicuously absent from the retreat. The shipyard had invested heavily in a set of internal quality and leadership programs centered on the Malcolm Baldrige award criteria and Steven Covey leadership methods. It seemed that Big Ship did not have any particular interest in changing directions to incorporate lean manufacturing.

Reman's COO was respected by the leaders at all four shipyards, yet he was going to be retiring in two years. COOs tend to come and go frequently at Reman, so it was easy for the shipyard leaders to outlast any one of them and even resist their pet initiatives. Reman was highly bureaucratic, yet decentralized, and the individual shipyards were cost centers, not profit centers. If the head of a shipyard delivered reasonable quality without slipping too badly on the schedule and stayed close to budget, he could count on at least a secure if not a distinguished career.

At the conclusion of the offsite retreat, the COO was quite passionate about doing something, but he wanted buy-in from the leadership at each shipyard. He listened intently to their issues and concerns and refused to dictate a direction. Liker laid out options, but also did not dictate a specific path. At the end of the second day, the COO could not get consensus on a way forward, so he finally issued his orders:

> *At this point I will invite Dr. Liker and his consultants to come into each of the four shipyards (including Big Ship) and lead a single one-week* kaizen *event. I will pay for it out of the corporate budget. I want you all to seriously participate and give Dr. Liker your best effort. After that, each yard can decide how to proceed and what they want to self-fund, but I will not force lean on anyone.*[4]

Liker visited all four shipyards to understand their current condition and work with them to identify a focus for the *kaizen* event. In this chapter, we will compare and contrast the experiences of Small Ship and Big Ship, as each in its own way became a leader in the overall initiative, and they provide a vivid contrast in approaches.

Both shipyards had a long and proud history, experienced and unionized workforces, technically competent engineering groups, and risk-averse cultures. These two organizations are loosely aligned as both partners and competitors within the operational arm of Reman. They are partners in that they report to the same COO, serve the Reman mission, and share resources and lessons learned. They are competitors in that they are judged as individual entities, and each desires to be regarded as the leading shipyard.

Each organization was supposedly part of the same lean initiative, but in the early years, they did not have a cooperative relationship as partners in learning. Each organization evolved a different strategy and ideology with regard to lean and struggled to "win out" in pushing its approach to become the standard for Reman. At least early in the deployment, each viewed the other as more of a nemesis than a partner. They frequently checked out the "competition" and plotted ways to get the advantage.

Small Ship was an organization of roughly 4,500 employees that was dedicated to industrial work on submarines. This shipyard was known for its independent thinking and had established itself as the benchmark for submarine repair. As a relatively small shipyard, its culture had been shaped and hardened by multiple threats of closure because of perceived excess capacity within Reman. The shipyard had survived multiple closure threats largely because of its relatively high performance level, but as we started the lean project, powerful political forces were lining up on the side of either sustaining the shipyard or closing it. Lean manufacturing was viewed by Small Ship as one strategy to better ensure its longevity. Small Ship had a close-knit culture that drew people together because of the feeling that it was the underdog compared to Big Ship. The workers there were distrustful of outsiders and of external initiatives led by corporate. Ultimately, the efforts at lean manufacturing within Small Ship were successful in contributing to its ability to avoid closure.

Big Ship was an organization of approximately 7,500 employees and was dedicated to two major product lines—submarines and aircraft carriers. Big Ship was known for its progressive management strategies and was often viewed by corporate management as a model organization within Reman. Prior to lean, it had invested significantly in the training of its managers, drawing on prominent American models such as Stephen Covey (leadership), Mark Graham Brown (metrics), and Malcolm Baldrige (quality).[5] The organization was large and influential, was geographically close to headquarters, and had never experienced threats of downsizing or closure such as those faced by Small Ship on numerous occasions. Big Ship was closely aligned with Reman's corporate initiatives and usually led cross-shipyard directives and guidance. At the time of the kickoff of lean deployment, the most significant management influence at Big Ship was that of the Baldrige Criteria and their use in its "organizational effectiveness cycle." It viewed its approach as a total systems approach that was driven rigorously by metrics and led by experts in the quality department. From our point of view, it was a highly mechanistic approach to organizational effectiveness that used metrics in a carrot-and-stick manner.

Looking back from nine years later, it was a rocky road for lean in this organization, with fits and starts, but many isolated successes as well. We will focus on Small Ship compared to Big Ship and the different paths they took, but first it is important to have a little grounding in ship repair and overhaul.

Overhaul and Repair Compared to Volume Manufacturing

We were incessantly reminded by our clients that ship overhaul and repair is "different." As we have mentioned earlier in the book, the refrain "We are different" is quite usual and even understandable. The natural way that humans learn is by copying from a template, and at the time there was no template for lean remanufacturing. Liker had documented successful lean practices in new ship construction in Japan, but ship construction started with raw materials, fabricated them into components, assembled the components as subsystems, and then finally assembled the subsystems in dry dock to become a new ship. On the other hand, overhaul and repair meant tearing down ships that had been constructed in the past, testing individual components, diagnosing problems, performing repairs or in some cases fabricating replacement parts, then putting the ship back together. There was incredible variety inherent in the different ships that pulled into port and the individual tasks involved from ship to ship.

Nuclear submarines are very large, and aircraft carriers are even larger. Inside, an aircraft carrier looks more like a huge building complex than a ship, with hospitals, cafeterias, living quarters, conference rooms, large engine rooms, firehouses, and more. Both types of ships are scheduled for overhaul and repair far in advance, and it takes two to four years to complete the process. They come into a dry dock, where they sit while being repaired and are out of service during this entire process, unavailable for defense.

There is a great deal of "scheduled maintenance" that is predictable, and some parts are automatically replaced, but in other cases it is not clear what work will need to be done until systems, subsystems, and components are tested one by one. When a part fails, it may be decades old, and a new one might have to be fabricated from scratch.

Basic concepts of lean production take on a different meaning in this environment. Often in pull systems, we build supermarkets that hold duplicated parts and replenish whatever has been used with the same types of parts. This makes sense for standard items like cleaners and oils, but in the case of ship repair, we are often repairing parts for reuse or building unique parts that are not used on other ships.

This was not a problem from our point of view because we understood that the tools were generic and needed to be customized to each situation. We were more interested in the principles of lean than any specific lean solutions. On the other hand, our clients were confused and suspicious, and they wanted a perfectly clear picture in high resolution of what lean would look like in their environment. Often companies ask for a benchmarking trip to a lean company "like us" for just that reason.

It is easiest to test and repair parts of the ship that can be taken off and brought into a shop. For example, many of the ball valves on a submarine go to a repair area that is part of the machine shop. (The ball valves control the flow of water.) Parts that are too large or too integrated into the ship and need to be repaired on board pose special challenges. Eventually, the ship needs to be reassembled, and this is like the construction of a large building—mechanical systems, electrical systems, heating and air conditioning, plumbing, engines, and more. Many surprises arise, and it is difficult to plan precisely.

The greatest portion of total lead time and the largest amount of labor is working on the ship itself in dry dock. That is where the money is primarily expended, so logically that is where a lean transformation should begin. That makes sense from a purely business point of view, but we were interested in both a business purpose *and* a people purpose. The people purpose at first was education and engagement. We wanted to win over key leaders as advocates for lean transformation who would understand lean in remanufacturing, embrace it, and develop internal lean coaches to facilitate the transformation. Thus, we recommended starting lean in the back shops, where it was less challenging to get some small wins and learn the basic concepts.

Phases of Deployment

In writing this comparative case study, six distinct phases of lean manufacturing deployment were identified:

Phase 1: Early awareness. The shipyards were first introduced to the concepts of lean manufacturing through training and the *kaizen* event led by Liker and his team.

Phase 2: Grassroots deployment. The first major steps toward implementation of lean manufacturing were undertaken at both Small Ship and Big Ship with their own funding, independent of any corporate effort at Reman.

Phase 3: Spreading lean broadly. The shipyards moved beyond initial deployment and sought to spread lean manufacturing more broadly in the organization.

Phase 4: Corporate engagement and the next level of deployment. As Small Ship and Big Ship had some success, the head of the corporation funded a corporate office to establish a common approach to lean. The corporate approach was modeled after the mechanistic model of Big Ship, so this shipyard naturally harmonized with the new standards, while Small Ship tried to resist but did minimally comply with the reporting requirements.

Phase 5: Crisis in lean manufacturing deployment. Both Small Ship and Big Ship faced crises in deployment as leaders moved on, energy for lean waned, and natural entropy set in. The result was degradation of the efforts in both yards.

Phase 6: Regrouping and redefinition. In the final phase before I left the company, both organizations found ways to regroup from the crisis and successfully move forward in deployment. Interestingly, the new approach was a blend of the mechanistic and organic approaches and seemed more sustainable than the early, less balanced approaches.

In this chapter, I will analyze both Small Ship and Big Ship as they evolve through these six phases of implementation.

Phase 1: Early Awareness

As we suspected from the offsite retreat, Small Ship was delighted by Liker's initial visit, and Big Ship was polite but disinterested. Small Ship had a prepared tour and selected several potential areas as candidates for *kaizen*, and the head of the shipyard personally escorted Liker while chatting excitedly about lean. Together, they agreed that the area that repaired and replaced ball valves provided the best opportunity, as it was relatively high volume and in the back shop, so it would be easy to get some early wins. There are ball valves all over the submarine to control the flow of water. If they get damaged or wear out they can leak or get stuck in an open or closed position. Small Ship was excited and wanted to start as soon as possible, and within three months of the offsite retreat the one-week event was conducted with high energy and enthusiasm by the participants.

In one week, the Small Ship ball-valve team of approximately 10 workers was able to clean up the workspace, organize tools, and establish basic visual management in the workplace. Equipment was moved to improve work flow. Despite initial skepticism, the improvement effort was well received within the work area, and the positive energy was apparent to the head of the shipyard, who was thrilled by the event. However, Small Ship did not maintain this energy for more than a few weeks after the *kaizen* event. Within months, the work area had regressed to its previous process and performance levels, and there was a growing skepticism among employees in the area, who felt that this was another example of "flavor of the month." There was no deployment in other areas outside ball valve. With budgets tight, even the enthusiastic shipyard head did not want to spend money on further consulting support.

In contrast to the hunger for learning at Small Ship, Big Ship spent most of the time presenting to Liker the various initiatives that were already in process. It had not actually applied for the Malcolm Baldrige award, but it had used the award's criteria internally to assess Big Ship and organized programs around the criteria. It also unveiled a detailed six-week Lean Six Sigma certification course that it was putting together. Liker thought to himself: "This course covers every performance improvement tool and buzzword I have ever heard of and more, with almost no real doing. The students' heads must be spinning just remembering terminology, and they will come out qualified to do absolutely nothing."

The people at Big Ship gave Liker a tour through the shipyard, and there was no visible evidence anyplace of process improvement, but there were signs of disarray, poor flow, and disconnected processes. Toward the end of the visit, they admitted that they were not enthusiastic about doing a *kaizen* event on a shipyard process, but rather wanted to tackle a difficult project management issue, which was the process of repairing large ball valves on a submarine. They delayed the start of the event until six months after the original offsite retreat.

At Big Ship, the *kaizen* event focused on the project management processes associated with onboard valve replacement, specifically work sequencing, readiness of support services, and overall resource allocation. This was a particularly challenging project to undertake, as the work is done in a crowded, nondedicated area aboard the ship. To complete the process, specialized mechanics bring their materials, tools, and instructions to the work site. An additional challenge to this effort was that the consultant did not have the security clearance needed to visit the actual work site, so throw out "go and see." In the five-day *kaizen* event, the team developed a process on paper to change the methodology for repairing the component. Ultimately, only pieces of the new process were implemented, elements that had been identified prior to the *kaizen* event. A full year later, we learned in an after-hours discussion that this difficult process had been selected intentionally to repress the deployment of lean manufacturing, since it did not fully align with the shipyard's existing paradigm for improvement based on the Baldrige approach.

Phase 2: Grassroots Deployment

The *early awareness phase* of lean deployment at both Small Ship and Big Ship did raise some awareness, but it was largely a failure because of a lack of follow-up and organizational commitment. Even at Small Ship, where the head of the shipyard seemed to want lean, he did not know how to lead it. He had assigned lean to a middle manager who was very near retirement. The leadership vacuum allowed lean deployment to languish. Deployment could have ended at this initial stage, had it not been for the high interest of the COO of Reman and a general belief that lean could be a tool to alleviate growing budget pressures.

After about five months of inactivity, Small Ship committed a small but respected internal staff to lean, while Big Ship folded lean into the continuous improvement strategy along with the Baldrige approach of measurement and control.

Grassroots Deployment at Small Ship

Nearly five months after the *kaizen* event at Small Ship, the shipyard took its first major step toward sustained lean deployment by appointing a highly respected senior leader, a production-oriented ex-project manager, as the local director of lean manufacturing implementation. The head of Small Ship had requested a visit to Toyota, and around that time Liker led executives of several shipyards on a trip to Kentucky to visit Toyota's Georgetown plant and a seat supplier plant. The head of Small Ship was "blown away" by the tour, particularly that of the smaller supplier plant, where he could see lean up close and personal. The director of lean deployment concluded that Small Ship desperately needed to develop an internal model area of lean remanufacturing, so that shipyard employees could observe real lean remanufacturing, better understand how to develop a model area, and ultimately get the same feeling of excitement as they got on the Toyota tour. Liker was advising me as I pursued my Ph.D. at the University of Michigan and suggested that I spend the summer at the shipyard to help create the internal lean model in ball-valve repair. The head of Small Ship approved the idea immediately. The local lean director and I became the de facto lean department at Small Ship (since it had not allocated funds for any other positions) and began its efforts at lean deployment.

Small Ship agreed to start in the summer of 2002 with a single-minded focus on developing a model area in ball-valve repair. As it turned out, earlier in his career, the new lean director had been the supervisor for ball-valve repair and remarked: "Even after the original *kaizen* event, it looks about the same as when I ran it. We need to make it a model like we saw in Kentucky, with all the visuals and bells and whistles of lean." A follow-on *kaizen* event was held to rejuvenate ideas and initiatives from the early awareness phase that had not been implemented. Unlike the first event, this second *kaizen* event was followed immediately by daily support. I practically lived in the area all summer. After some initial suspicion, I won over the small team there (12 people) and became close friends with the supervisor and several members of the team, even going to their houses for dinner and getting to know their families.

The ball-valve team repaired a relatively high volume of components, more than 150 per year, but there was still a great deal of variation. There were 10 families of valves, with 5 to 10 sizes in each family, and the valves ranged from 50 to 1,800 pounds and were in a wide variety of conditions of disrepair.

When I first got to the shipyard in the summer, the current condition was typical of mass-production environments that had been neglected for many years. The area was repairing ball valves, but all were late, the cost was prohibitive, and there were frequent quality problems. Here is a summary of the key initial metrics:

- Average lead time of about 175 days for repair of a valve
- No lead-time reductions in the previous six months
- About 70 pieces of work-in-process (large ball valves on pallets)
- Workweeks of ~60 hours
- On-time delivery problems
- Cost overruns

The lean transformation of the ball-valve area was slow, extending beyond the summer and ultimately into the next year as I traveled back and forth from Michigan, but the supervisor and the workers took ownership of the improvements. These were the main changes made:

- A clear, simple process flow was developed. The steps in the process were organized into a clean flow: initial assessment of the ball valves, disassembly and detailed evaluation, repair and fabrication or ordering of replacement parts, reassembly, and test.

- There was a gradual reduction in and then elimination of the pallet racks that were used to store ball valves waiting for work.
- Every valve had to be cleaned, and the blast-cleaning equipment that was used was located about ½ mile from the ball-valve area, with long travel and wait times, thus creating a bottleneck. More than a year after the initial awareness *kaizen* event had called out the need, a new aqua blast-cleaning machine was finally purchased and set up in the ball-valve area, greatly facilitating the flow.
- A work-in-progress cap was applied to control the number of valves being worked on at any point in time. When the limit was reached, additional valves were stored in a holding area and one at a time could enter the process when one valve was completed.
- Usable visual controls were developed, including a board that mirrored the physical process with magnets that could be moved around to show the status of different ball valves in the process and identify with red magnets those that were delayed for some reason.
- Fixtures were built to hold the parts in place while they were being worked on.
- Standard work instructions were written for common repairs that could be completed without engineering approval ("engineering recipes").
- A rapid engineering approval process was developed, with engineers coming to the shop to directly inspect the parts that were visually laid out.

I must admit that compared to other companies we have worked with, including the other cases in this book, developing the model line was a slow process. It was a highly bureaucratic organization, and it had gone years without making any serious process improvements. So it had to get the rust off. On the other hand, as emphasized early in the book, people development is a much slower process than technical improvements, and this company needed a great deal of people development.

Let's consider two examples. I led a value stream mapping session, and in the future state map, I pushed the group to eliminate the pallet storage racks. The group members thought I was nuts. At the time there were 70 pallets of in-process ball valves, mostly on the storage racks. They were in various states of disassembly, often waiting for parts or cleaning. There had even been a study to consider installing a large automated storage and retrieval system—out of sight, out of mind. How could they possibly get by without the storage racks? About six months into implementation, they eliminated the pallet racks. It was so emotional and momentous you would think that the Berlin Wall had just come down. This major cultural event could not have been planned in advance. The team members needed to be ready, and it was a big day when they came nervously to me saying: "It is time to take down the racks."

A second example is the interface with engineering. As in many organizations, engineering was very powerful compared to production. Engineers determined what repairs were needed and signed off on all requests for any deviation from the plans. They sat in temperature-controlled offices and rarely came out to the shop. Yet they were the kings of the hill, making all the decisions about what repairs should be done and how. Having the engineers give up some control and agree to preapproved repairs without engineering intervention was a major cultural change. Getting the engineers to come out to the shop regularly to approve deviations quickly was a genuine cultural shock. This did not happen with one written decree by the head of the shipyard. It was a gradual process of coaching, identifying problems, and discussions with the leadership. I became friends with a number of the engineers and frequented their offices, inviting them to come to the ball-valve shop.

The results were slow to develop, but ultimately impressive:

- Decrease in overtime hours of 95 percent
- Increase in throughput of 28 percent with no added head count
- Increase in productivity per labor hour of 92 percent
- Reduction in lead time of 60 percent

One of the highlights was a high-level visit by the COO of Reman, a three-star Navy admiral, the state's governor, and several U.S. senators. With a large entourage, they came to see the lean model ball-valve area. All the presentations and answers to questions were handled by the supervisor and workers in the area. They were beaming. The visitors were in awe, not of the technical changes, but of the pride and passion of the workers in the area. The COO of Reman declared that it was the best example of lean in the company, and that other shipyards needed to learn from it. Small Ship got a formal citation nationally as a model of lean practice.

The first 18 months of lean at Small Ship focused mostly on the ball-valve area, but not exclusively. While this was going on, there was other important work to spread the deployment of lean. A young engineer had been hired into the lean office, and I was assigned to be his teacher, which was ironic, since I was just learning as I went. A number of other shops had started model lines on their own initiative and were getting some assistance from the lean office. A one-day overview of lean was created and taught by outside lean consultants throughout the shipyard.

Grassroots Deployment at Big Ship

At the same time as the ball-valve model line implementation at Small Ship, Big Ship was aggressively training black-belt experts and senior managers through the newly established Lean Six Sigma Academy. The strategy for deployment at Big Ship was to implement lean manufacturing and Six Sigma jointly via four- to six-month projects, led by the certified experts. Big Ship hired a Six Sigma black belt from an automotive OEM as its lead expert. This individual played a vital role in developing the curriculum for the academy and establishing training programs for green-belt and black-belt change agents and facilitators. Big Ship hired many talented industrial engineers fresh from large universities to serve as these internal experts, and supplemented them with retirees. These facilitators were trained to follow a highly regimented five-step process and were assessed by supervisors based on their adherence to the process and the overall cost reductions from their projects. Big Ship successfully built a large infrastructure to support lean manufacturing and Six Sigma deployment, which was held up by Reman as a best-practice model. If Small Ship's lean office of two full-time people plus me was David, Big Ship certainly had developed a Goliath lean office.

Big Ship also made the decision to work on its ball-valve repair area, but in its case this was one of a number of projects. In fact, it was viewed as the accreditation project for one graduate of the Lean Six Sigma Academy. For six months, the individual worked in the ball-valve area, applying what he had learned in the training. The initial task was to benchmark processes at Small Ship. There was much resentment at Big Ship over the notoriety that Small Ship was receiving from its efforts in ball-valve repair. Big Ship had never had performance problems in that specific work area, and therefore assumed that it was as efficient as Small Ship. (Ultimately, this was proven incorrect when corrections were made for type of work, volume of work, and employee productivity.)

The individual leading the project had no prior performance improvement background. He had been exposed to the many topics in the academy without hands-on experience. He had learned a rigorous method of analysis and spent a great deal of time analyzing the data from the ball-valve area. What he implemented at Big Ship was generally viewed as very shallow compared to what Small Ship had implemented. Mostly he had done 5S to clean up the area and created some boards for visual management. The work area was cleaned, color-coding systems were established, and the overall organization and appearances were improved significantly. No changes were made to the process flow, but paperwork improvements were attempted (but ultimately were not supported by the engineering team). Only minor equipment expenditures were allowed.

At the conclusion of six months, the change agent presented the results of the initiative and the planned follow-up tasks, the project was declared a success, and he received his black belt. Privately, the black belt expressed frustration with the lack of overall management engagement, particularly from groups outside of the production area. After a few months of inattention, the ball-valve area regressed to its previous conditions. Managers in ball valve did not understand the significance of what the change agent was trying to achieve, and several viewed the individual as an annoyance who would go away; he of course did.

 ## *Sensei* Reflection on Phases 1 and 2

I met regularly with Liker at his University of Michigan office, venting about the evils of Big Ship and beaming with pride over the cultural changes taking place at Small Ship. There was no question in our minds that organic was better than mechanistic and that the Lean Six Sigma certification was an abomination. Of course, Small Ship was also the underdog, with paltry lean resources compared to the veritable army of certified black belts at Big Ship. Yet Small Ship was getting deeper and more sustainable results, although in limited areas. I must admit looking back that we had great pride in Small Ship, with a hint of arrogance. Little did we know that Big Ship's investments in lean infrastructure would one day be a source of strength and sustenance, and the lack of formalization at Small Ship would lead to the decline of lean.

A summary of the two shipyards in these two initial stages of deployment is provided in Table 6.1. Big Ship placed tremendous emphasis on widespread deployment (although it was shallow in nature), training, and emphasis on short-term cost reduction. It placed all expertise in the central office, with little opportunity for those outside of the "lean team" to shape the lean deployment process. The lean team was getting a lot of classroom training with some experience, but its members did not have any real *sensei* to coach them on a daily basis. The result was a strong technical emphasis on analyzing data and making recommendations, with little commitment and engagement from the actual operations. There were even more serious implementation problems when the solutions cut across different major departments in Big Ship.

The relatively organic Small Ship focused on only one area for the purpose of organizational learning and showed patience in

(*Continued*)

Table 6.1. Analysis of Big Ship and Small Ship in Phases 1 and 2

	Phase 1: "Early Awareness"	Phase 2: "Grassroots Deployment"
	Illustrations of Mechanistic and Organic Deployment	
Big Ship	Big Ship rejected lean manufacturing because of failure of initial *kaizen* to deliver significant ROI	Big Ship began investment in infrastructure and training; tool deployment of 5S implemented at multiple sites
Small Ship	Small Ship failed to benefit from its *kaizen* because of failure to sustain, but seeds of organizational learning were planted	Small Ship attempted to "just do something and learn," establishing an implementation pilot; organization was very informal
	Indications of Success or Failure of Lean Deployment	
Big Ship	Outcomes of initial *kaizen* had already been planned; little credibility given to this effort	Big Ship was building an effective change management team and training capability
Small Ship	*Kaizen* was well received and produced immediate impact, although the organization failed to sustain the changes	Small Ship developed a very successful pilot and worked to "show lean" to the entire organization

expanding the program. Lean was led by a hands-on doer who had a great deal of respect within all of the operations. I was not experienced enough to be a true *sensei*, so I put a great deal of effort into developing relationships and teaching and coaching the actual work group responsible for the ball-valve repair. Management attention was concentrated on the one model-line area. It emphasized the organic evolution of learning among the employees as it sought to understand how classic lean tools and concepts applied in this environment. At Small Ship, little infrastructure was developed in the lean deployment team—as it turned out, too little. Perhaps this reflected the fact that management espoused support but was really not committed.

Phase 3: Spreading Lean Broadly

At this point, over one year from the original offsite, we can hardly say that either shipyard had built a rock-solid foundation for broader lean deployment. Small Ship had one director, one young engineer, and me part-time to support a shipyard of 4,500 people. By comparison, Big Ship had an army of trained people, led by black belts, but still had no clear successes; you could not go anyplace to see any semblance of a system in action.

At Small Ship, the small lean team chose to focus on multiple model lines and support other initiatives as best it could. The model lines selected each had somewhat different characteristics in terms of the volume and variability of the product: transponder repair, motor generator repair, ball honing, and hatch repair. Each of these lines had a level of success similar to that of the ball-valve model line; however, they were able to move much faster, as senior leadership began to develop a deeper understanding of the implementation process and the overall vision for lean manufacturing. Additionally, the application of tools such as value stream mapping, workplace organization, standard work instructions, *andon* (at Toyota it stops the line; in their case it is used for notifying managers and other workers of problems), and setup reduction began to pop up spontaneously throughout the organization, as middle managers wanted to get on board. These spontaneous attempts at deployment were now considered in the screening process to select future areas on which to focus lean deployment resources. That is, focus areas for deployment models were being developed in areas that had shown significant commitment and personal investment in the lean manufacturing deployment. There was a growing pull on lean resources, replacing the earlier push by the shipyard head.

At Big Ship, black-belt and green-belt experts were deployed to each major department of the organization. A growing number of black-belt change agents were trained, all senior managers were trained on Lean Six-Sigma principles, and Lean Six Sigma objectives were placed in managerial performance appraisals. As additional employees were selected for the lean program, they were trained as black-belt and green-belt facilitators and were embedded in the line organization.

Green belts reported directly to the line organization; some black belts reported to the line organization and others to the director of the Lean Program.

It is important to note that at Big Ship's machine shop, deep-rooted experience and understanding of lean manufacturing began to take hold. This area was the home of valve repair and several other projects that had been in the first round of black-belt accreditation projects. The managers and supervisors in the area were visiting other organizations to see examples of lean manufacturing deployment, including the one at Small Ship. Several of the most experienced black belts were working in the machine shop and were learning from their prior experiences at deployment. An external consultant was hired and facilitated value stream mapping of key processes in the machine shop, which highlighted 12 areas for focus. A buildingwide 5S was conducted (one that reportedly removed more than 35 tons of waste and excess material), and the organization proceeded to conduct *kaizen* events in each of the 12 work areas identified in the value stream map.

Perhaps more important, culturally at Big Ship a rift was developing between the relatively experienced change agents in the machine shop and the classroom training process in the Lean Six Sigma Academy. A very damning observation was made by the most senior black-belt change agent: "Employees go to the six-week training program, and when they get back, the first thing I have to do is retrain them." This rift began to exist as a divergence between the textbook knowledge of the instructors and the "deck plate" experience of seasoned change agents occurred. This rift was only to grow as the two organizations moved into Phase 4 of lean manufacturing deployment and corporate headquarters became engaged.

Phase 4: Corporate Engagement and the Next Level of Deployment

In Phase 4 of lean manufacturing deployment, both yards decided to dramatically change the focus of lean deployment from the relatively controlled environments of the back shops to the unruly beast of actual overhaul and repair on the ship itself. They were going after the big money. Our recommendation to Small Ship from the beginning was to focus on the back shops first, learn the basics of lean, and then it would become more apparent how to approach the overall submarine. The day of reckoning had come.

During the first two years of lean manufacturing deployment at both Small Ship and Big Ship, the efforts had been bottom-up, grassroots. Each organization had a similar objective, but the road map was unclear, and no guidance was being given from corporate headquarters. Seeing the positive impact that lean manufacturing was having at Small Ship, Big Ship, and other facilities, Reman established a special task force to oversee lean implementation at all sites.

In a lot of ways, the task force became the front-line battleground between the organic approach of Small Ship (represented by Liker and his team) and the mechanistic approach of Big Ship. The director of lean from Small Ship was assigned to the task force, as was the director of quality at Big Ship. This task force put out a request for proposals to contract external lean consultants based on a very formal selection process. The quality director from Big Ship used his considerable influence and aligned with the second largest shipyard to win the contract for his consultant. This led to a highly structured road map for change built around *kaizen* workshops and detailed metrics to track and control the deployment, modeled after the Big Ship formal program.

Next-Level Deployment at Small Ship

An external shock in this phase was a formal published decision by Reman to close Small Ship permanently in order to cut costs and reduce excess capacity across the corporation. It seemed like a final decision. The specter of the planned closure of Small Ship by the highest levels of Reman and, as it turned out, the nearing departure of their charismatic shipyard leader, who had been promoted to corporate, might have shut down all energy for lean deployment, but in fact it had the opposite effect. The entire workforce rallied together and decided that it needed to "take lean to another level" in order to "show what we are capable of." Fortunately the closure process took time as they were still working on submarines in process, so there was time to try to reverse the decision.

The corporate task force had little impact on lean at Small Ship during this period, as Small Ship simply ignored the corporate guidance. With the impending shipyard closure, Reman was not about to step in and mandate compliance. I facilitated a two-day offsite meeting for senior leaders to strategize about the next level of lean deployment.

The particular challenge faced by the leaders was the lack of standard and repetitive work during a ship overhaul. They had learned how to apply lean in higher-volume and lower-variety work processes in the shops, but a ship overhaul, with its low volume and high variety, presented a unique challenge. Approximately 10,000 tasks were executed on a submarine overhaul, with nearly every one of those tasks being unique. How could techniques such as process flow, pull systems, work-in-process reductions, *andon*, and visual controls work in this environment? An important revelation for the organization was that, while each of the 10,000 tasks was unique in work content and complexity, a common method and approach existed in the planning and follow-up for each individual task. A team developed a value stream map and a strategy for managing the 10,000 tasks in a systematic approach to create flow. To the surprise of many, this involved the same set of lean production tools and techniques that had been used in the ball-valve model line.

One of the key insights was that the submarine was in fact a collection of smaller physical areas, and each area could be viewed as a work cell. The team members decided to assign a cross-functional team of repair personnel to each "virtual cell" to focus on a set of overhaul and repair tasks, and support functions would bring them the needed material, tools, and information to perform those value-added tasks. A powerful lean concept that we preach is that the value-added worker should be treated like a surgeon. The surgeon needs to focus on the patient, in this case her area of the submarine, head down, with as little distraction as possible. This means getting the right tools, material, and information brought to her to allow her to do her work. Traditionally, the repair technicians would acquire their own tooling, materials, and such, often spending more time off the submarine, walking through the shipyard to retrieve tools and materials, then doing value-added work on the submarine. To reduce this tendency, the shipyard commander ordered a system to measure the actual time spent on the submarine through magnetic cards that were scanned in as repair technicians got on and off the submarine.

With a focus on keeping repair personnel on the submarine as part of a cross-trade team with a defined package of work that the team must complete from start to finish, people started to see that the goals were continuous flow and reduction in cycle time per unit. This allowed them to make tremendous strides in a short time. They established a supermarket of parts and materials for incoming work, visual communication boards, standard work instructions, significantly improved workplace organization, work-in-process inventory controls, *andon* systems, and pull systems. The deployment included work on the submarine plus all supporting production shops, and it required significant communication across multiple trades and functions. In many instances, as the strategy was being both developed and implemented, comments were made such as, "Well, we had a similar situation in the ball-valve model line; this is what we did, and this was the outcome . . . let's try that here."

The most significant cultural change occurring at Small Ship was that the employees were coming together as a single team. As one senior production manager at Small Ship put it:

> *It used to be that we would think of ourselves as one team, but we were a baseball team. We [the shipyard] would achieve success if we [each production shop] were all .400 hitters and hit a lot of home runs. Now, we still think of ourselves as a team, but more like a football team. We have blockers [support shops], running backs, and receivers [core work on submarine]. We don't care if our blockers are performing great individually, just that our running backs and receivers are moving the ball downfield for the entire team to be successful.*

The entire shipyard management team rallied around the single mission, vision, and objectives. Though progress was not always smooth or flawless, the new strategy allowed the organization to complete one of its most complex ship overhauls at a 12 percent cost reduction over a previous best and beat the scheduled completion date by one month. The huge news was that largely because of its innovation and process improvement initiatives, Small Ship was successful in being removed from the shipyard closure list, the charismatic leader was promoted to an executive level in the corporate offices, and all energy was riding high at Small Ship.

Next-Level Deployment at Big Ship

At Big Ship, energy was also riding high, as the corporate task force afforded an opportunity for it to broaden its influence in lean deployment and consolidate its efforts locally under the guidance of a corporate directive. At Big Ship, the feeling was that the organization would "take lean deployment to the next level." Big Ship now selected one of its brightest and most respected managers to oversee lean manufacturing deployment. This individual, who brought tremendous credibility to the position, proceeded to implement and oversee the rigid implementation strategy laid out by the Reman corporate office.

Quotas were established for each manager and department in terms of the number of *kaizen* events, participants, and initiatives to be achieved. All departments at Big Ship were deploying lean in order to meet their management quotas, and each was building internal examples and expertise. However, the departments at Big Ship were working independently and were not always willing to share resources; few people had an opportunity to participate in *kaizen* events outside of their own department. An additional change came at Big Ship when the Lean Six Sigma Academy was removed from the shipyard and aligned directly with the Reman task force. This resulted in a loss of control by Big Ship of the overall curriculum and vision for the academy.

Like Small Ship, Big Ship also worked to tackle the tremendous challenge of successfully applying lean to the entire ship overhaul. The approach taken at Big Ship included aligning lean deployment of the overall ship overhaul with existing accounting mechanisms and focusing its efforts on reducing the overall cost and variances of cost of major line items, with responsibility falling to the individual departments that executed the work. This strategy produced positive results, but they were largely constrained by the existing accounting measures and overall functional mindset, producing suboptimal results.

At Big Ship, the application of lean manufacturing to the entire ship overhaul was much less intense than that at Small Ship. In maintaining its "corporate and button-down" demeanor, management at Big Ship considered the task at hand to be a natural progression of the deployment strategy for training the workforce and conducting *kaizen* events throughout the entire organization. Reman, the corporate management group, pressured Big Ship to deliver significant improvement results on its next ship overhaul. Because of this, Big Ship leadership felt pressure to increase the pace of training and *kaizen* events.

Each manager was challenged to target high-cost jobs and use lean manufacturing, mostly *kaizen* events, to cut the costs. This created three significant challenges for the leaders at Big Ship: (1) each department worked independently to improve cost, thus attacking the value-added functions one at a time, yet, as Small Ship demonstrated, the most significant opportunities existed in improving the non-value-added functions, specifically the coordination between departments, (2) outside of the machine shop, few of the departments within Big Ship had any deep-rooted experiences and learning to draw upon in applying lean to the challenging applications of shipboard production, and (3) an extreme emphasis was placed on cost reduction, which made it particularly challenging for managers to achieve short-term cost objectives while enabling the needed investment in *kaizen* events.

Using the sports analogy offered by Small Ship, Big Ship was a team of individuals (departments), each working to improve its batting average and home-run-hitting prowess. As a result of these efforts, many improvements were made at Big Ship; however, the improvements were largely disconnected and potentially suboptimal. Reporting of improvement results was conducted one job order at a time, and while some costs were reduced, others were increased (with justifications provided). Minimal reductions were made in the overall schedule or cost of the next ship overhaul. Most of the learning that occurred was at the individual rather than the organizational level.

Sensei Reflection on Phases 3 and 4

For me, helping to save the 4,500 jobs of Small Ship from closure was and probably will always be the most exciting accomplishment of my career. It simply does not get much better than that!

The biggest disappointment at this time was that the competing consulting firm allied with Big Ship had won, and the corporate task force was going to push its mechanistic deployment strategy. We were convinced that this would eventually destroy the momentum of lean transformation within Reman. Big Ship was becoming even more mechanistic in response to the challenges of an expanding deployment and the alignment with the Reman task force. It was no surprise that the metrics and implementation strategy of Big Ship aligned perfectly with the mechanistic strategy and values of the corporate implementation.

At Small Ship, a clash was occurring between the mechanistic rigidity of the directives, forms, training, and accounting prescribed by the Reman task force and the flexible organic deployment that had been successful. As a result, Small Ship was ignoring corporate directions regarding deployment strategy, yet it was delivering exactly the results that the Reman task force hoped for. The organic learning that was occurring at all levels of Small Ship was very dynamic and exciting to observe. Table 6.2 summarizes both Big Ship and Small Ship in Phases 3 and 4 for characteristics of mechanistic vs. organic and for indications of success or failure.

Another critical event in this phase was that I was invited to move from Small Ship to support the corporate task force as a Reman employee. I saw an opportunity to have a greater impact on the overall deployment at Reman and accepted the job. I quickly developed strong relationships with the leaders of the task force, who saw me as their lean *sensei*. I was eventually assigned to lead the deployment efforts in all four shipyards. This meant

Table 6.2. Analysis of Big Ship and Small Ship in Phases 3 and 4

	Phase 3: "Spreading Lean Broadly"	Phase 4: "Corporate Engagement and the Next Level of Deployment"
	Illustrations of Mechanistic and Organic Deployment	
Big Ship	Widespread deployment; development of standard methodology; extensive training; shallow deployment	Organization-wide deployment; owner of the corporate training program; written implementation methodology and metrics
Small Ship	Deep-rooted model line; multiple additional pilot sites; little organizational structure in deployment	Entire management team focused on a complete submarine overhaul to learn at a new level; significant pushback to corporate deployment
	Indications of Success or Failure of Lean Deployment	
Big Ship	Big Ship is beginning to develop successful initiatives in the machine shop area; extensive change in management team and training capacity	Organization-wide deployment; owner of the corporate training program; many managers becoming trained
Small Ship	Multiple sites engaging in deep lean deployment; established models in a variety of applications; management team building deeper understanding	Primary lean initiative has become the focus of the entire management team and the cornerstone of defense against base closure

walking a very fine line between speaking the party line of the mechanistic deployment approach, working closely with the consulting group that developed it, and supporting the more rebellious elements of the shipyards who found the corporate approach too rigid and constraining. It did allow me to, in a sense, protect Small Ship from domination by the corporate mechanistic approach and to build an alliance with those at Big Ship who had developed hands-on experience and saw the corporate approach as shallow and misguided.

Phase 5: Crisis in Lean Manufacturing Deployment

Lean manufacturing deployment within the ship repair community had been growing rapidly, bolstered by an urgency to survive as budgets became tight. However, in Phase 5, each organization began to recognize growing pains in deployment. Both organizations faced tremendous, although different, challenges to the long-term success of lean deployment.

At Small Ship, the lean deployment faced five significant crises at one time. Small Ship was removed from the closure list, removing the perceived urgency for improvements. The charismatic leaders, both the shipyard commander and the head of the lean deployment team, were promoted to more prestigious positions in corporate as a result of their successes. Two of the most experienced lean change agent facilitators left within a six-month period for personal reasons, and I was transferred to corporate. Furthermore, problems were surfacing in the implementation plan established for the ship overhaul model line; some senior leaders saw this as proof that the concept of lean manufacturing in this environment was flawed. Finally, conflicts continued to grow between Small Ship and the increasingly influential corporate task force.

A five whys analysis of these specific problems would point to a single failure point: Small Ship had become overly dependent upon charismatic leadership and an unsustainable energy level for its performance. The progress of lean deployment slowed tremendously, and even regressed in certain areas. The characteristics that had helped to make Small Ship flexible and learning-oriented became the same characteristics that challenged it as it sought to continue the growth of lean deployment. The overwhelming fact was that the extraordinary energy and focus that had driven lean deployment at Small Ship was removed, and the organization had not built an infrastructure of systems, processes, and people that was capable of maintaining the deployment.

At Big Ship, the crisis was nearly the opposite. The organization became overextended in its drive to achieve the Reman quota of *kaizen* events and number of employees trained. Each manager was pushed hard to achieve his numbers. As a result, many events were poorly selected and planned, leading to a failure to deliver the expected results and value. This was not a problem during times when there were extra staff members, but resources were becoming constrained, and work was not being completed on schedule. Drawing resources away from direct labor for process improvement grew increasingly difficult.

Many managers at Big Ship were growing increasingly skeptical of the benefits being realized from the widespread, yet shallow, deployment of lean. Managers were struggling to believe the return on investment (ROI) claimed by the corporate task force, seeing this as simply "paper money." Unfortunately, the "good stories" of waste elimination were not yet quantifiable at this point. Additional pushback to lean came when Reman mandated that Big Ship deploy the same strategy and lessons learned as Small Ship on its next ship overhaul. This led to resentment of Small Ship and a strong reluctance to adopt ideas that were "not invented here."

Phase 6: Regrouping and Redefinition

Despite differences in the problems leading to the crisis, the response was strikingly similar at both shipyards. We can summarize it as a return to basics. Both organizations had pushed themselves to the point of internal crisis, and now they were both forced to rebalance themselves and their lean efforts to sustain them for the long-term.

At Small Ship, they recognized the challenges of running too far and too fast on adrenaline, only to realize that they did not have the internal strength to sustain the pace. Relying upon what had made it successful, Small Ship decided to refocus its improvement priorities in defined areas of the shipyard. At the same time, it was now requiring all senior managers to attend training and go on regular "waste walks" with the lean management team. The original charismatic leader of the lean deployment team was transferred from the corporate office back to lead the lean office of Small Ship, and I again became much more involved in the hands-on transformation. New industrial engineers were hired and trained in the corporate Lean Six Sigma Academy, but were required to spend time in each of the model-line initiatives at the shipyard. The strength at Small Ship was the pockets of deep models and illustrations of lean manufacturing. It also had a management team that had experienced the evolution and adaptation of the improvement initiatives, and now it needed to build the infrastructure of the lean organization and continue to build support among managers for long-term continuing success.

At Big Ship, a return to basics required a more significant recalibration of the fundamentals of lean manufacturing. The lessons learned thus far had largely been associated with infrastructure development and deployment, not with deep lean learning. The organization was pulling back in the number of ongoing initiatives and becoming more focused as it attempted to develop deep examples of learning. On the other hand, a growing number of black belts, supported by me, had worked on deep projects in different areas of the shipyard. They were developing relationships and coaching the supervisors and workers to take ownership of their work processes.

One deep focus of the effort at Big Ship was in the machine shop, which had been moving ahead with models of lean implementation and organic learning. It was acting largely as an independent subculture within the larger organization. Several similar production areas began using concepts from the machine shop to build lean manufacturing models throughout the organization. The organization was beginning to push back on the Reman task force by resisting pressures to continually do more and more initiatives and becoming more strategic in its selection of initiatives and deployment of resources. Its ultimate challenge was to develop an internal culture of understanding that effective lean manufacturing provides the opportunity to develop a learning organization that will achieve overall business objectives—it was not simply an issue of scattered activity and internal efficiency.

 ## *Sensei* Reflection on Phases 5 and 6

In Phases 4 and 5, Big Ship showed the weaknesses of a predominantly mechanistic deployment. In Phase 5, Big Ship focused on the "activity metrics" of number of *kaizen* events conducted and employees trained, and its overall efficiency in running those events. Ultimately it overestimated its own infrastructure and essentially outran its internal capability to support lean initiatives. It attempted to conduct too many initiatives (with a leadership team that lacked a deep understanding of lean), and the preparations and follow-up were not completed successfully. Consequently, initiatives began to fail at higher rates. In Phase 6, Big Ship became more focused on deeper deployments and models within the organization, ultimately moving in the organic direction, but drawing on the resources that it had developed in its mechanistic phases.

Unlike Big Ship, Small Ship showed the weaknesses of an overly organic deployment and ultimately became more mechanistic in nature. During the crisis stage, Small Ship lost the energy and momentum created by the potential base closure and found itself lacking the necessary infrastructure to be successful over the long run. It had been overly dependent upon dynamic personalities and the enthusiasm created by a burning platform. As it regrouped, Small Ship ultimately became more mechanistic as it built a more robust infrastructure to support continuing deployment. Table 6.3 summarizes both Big Ship and Small Ship in Phases 5 and 6 for characteristics of mechanistic vs. organic and for indications of success or failure.

Ideally, *sensei* are completely objective, carefully sifting through the facts to draw conclusions. Also, at this time I was writing my doctoral dissertation and needed to remain objective. However, to be honest, I had gone native and become emotionally involved in the transformation process. My heart was with the organic deployers at Small Ship and those at Big Ship who were rebelling against the corporate bureaucracy. As we struggled to make sense of what had happened, we had to admit that neither Small Ship nor Big Ship was a shining example of a lean

(Continued)

Table 6.3. Analysis of Big Ship and Small Ship in Phases 5 and 6

	Phase 5: "Crisis in Lean Manufacturing Deployment"	Phase 6: "Regrouping and Redefinition"
	Illustrations of Mechanistic and Organic Deployment	
Big Ship	Lean Office focused on running a particular number of events and overall efficiency of implementation; management not understanding or engaged	Big Ship is becoming more organic in its attention to deeper projects, maintaining infrastructure to support
Small Ship	When the management attention was removed, lacked a significant infrastructure to support sustained implementation	Small Ship is becoming more mechanistic, building an infrastructure to support long-term deployment
	Indications of Success or Failure of Lean Deployment	
Big Ship	Big Ship had outrun its own infrastructure, attempting to do too many initiatives; management not fully onboard and not seeing results	Big Ship backing off pace, beginning to develop deeper implementations and understanding
Small Ship	With pressure of potential base closure removed, management did not sustain energy; little infrastructure to support; recognized as being too dependent upon personalities	Small Ship building a stronger infrastructure for sustaining gains, refocusing efforts after attention had been lost to deep implementations

triumph. Both had had growing pains, and both had sustained a certain degree of momentum over eight years and were still going. That exceeds the average life expectancy of most "programs of the month." What was critical in each case was not the particular approach chosen but persevering and learning along the way. By that measure, the two organizations had ended up at a similar place and accomplished some great things along the journey.

Evaluating the Success of Small Ship and Big Ship

Many quantitative indicators were examined to evaluate the results at Big Ship and Small Ship as successes or failures. Unfortunately, the size and scope of the projects were so different that it was not possible to compare the two organizations on precise quantitative measures. Instead, the data are qualitatively summarized in Table 6.4 through the first five phases of deployment for efficiency of deployment, effectiveness of deployment, and overall success of deployment. Phase 6 was not assessed because it was too early to judge the results of the organizations' response to crisis.

The results are complex when we compare all the indicators for both shipyards during the five phases. There were some patterns of note:

1. The two organizations took very different paths. However, each began with low overall effectiveness, and both concluded with medium overall effectiveness.
2. As expected, Big Ship was more efficient across all phases compared to Small Ship. Small Ship was more effective than Big Ship in the early stages of lean deployment, but arguably Big Ship was at least as effective in the long run.
3. At Small Ship, efficiency consistently increased, but effectiveness slightly decreased (with the exception of the energetic phase of planned closure) as efforts became more widespread.
4. The highest-performing period at Small Ship was in Phase 4, largely because of charismatic leadership and the extreme sense of urgency resulting from the threat of closure. Big Ship was also most successful at this point. It was ramping up its deployment while exerting internal controls in order to proceed at an internally desired pace.

So why did Big Ship end up being just as successful overall as Small Ship if Big Ship was implementing superficial tools with little understanding? We are not suggesting that all paths to lean are equally effective. Had Big Ship continued on its initial course of textbook training

Table 6.4. Efficiency, Effectiveness, and Success at Big Ship and Small Ship

		"Early Awareness"	"Grassroots Deployment"	"Spreading Lean Broadly"	"Corporate Engagement and the Next Level of Deployment"	"Crisis in Lean Manufacturing Deployment"
Big Ship	Efficiency of Deployment	Low	Medium-High	Medium-High	High	Medium-High
	Effectiveness of Deployment	Low	Low	Medium-Low	Medium	Medium-Low
	Overall Success of Deployment	Low	Low	Medium-Low	Medium	Medium
Small Ship	Efficiency of Deployment	Low	Low	Medium	Medium-High	Medium-Low
	Effectiveness of Deployment	Low	High	Medium-High	Medium-High	Medium
	Overall Success of Deployment	Low	Medium	Medium	High	Medium

with no experienced mentors, we expect that the lean deployment would have ultimately wilted because of its being superficial, spread too thin, and lacking significant learning and results. At it turned out, some deep organic deployment seeped in, though not by design. Repeated experience by black belts at the *gemba* (where the actual work is done) in the machine shop began to transform those individual black belts and give them a level of understanding of lean way beyond that provided by the Lean Six Sigma Academy. This was reinforced by what people learned from Small Ship. These individual deployment champions began to focus on model-line projects, as Small Ship had done, and achieved the same great successes as Small Ship had achieved earlier. Ironically, as these individuals deepened their understanding, they found themselves at odds with the mechanistic strategy of the Reman task force, the textbook learning of the Lean Six Sigma Academy, and their organization's traditional mechanistic management structure on the whole. They then got additional opportunities to learn through coaching by the consulting firm that Reman hired and by me. Over the years, they, and increasingly other black belts, learned a plan–do–check–adjust (PDCA) approach to transforming people and processes They were becoming strong lean transformation coaches and had enough influence to begin to shape the culture of Big Ship. You could say that they were like an organic Trojan horse that slipped into the mechanistic culture of Big Ship and began to change it from within.

In my heart of hearts, I continue to believe that Small Ship began on a much stronger path based on its organic implementation approach. The biggest barrier for Small Ship was simply the number of people trained as lean coaches. Had it assigned numbers that were in any way comparable to those at Big Ship, I believe that Small Ship would have excelled beyond any other shipyard in Reman. It also needed some degree of infrastructure—at least some training and basic standardization of lean processes—to stabilize lean across the shipyard. This was lacking largely because there were a tiny number of people responsible for an entire shipyard.

To suggest that one methodology, mechanistic or organic deployment, is always superior would be an oversimplification. Each approach

Table 6.5. Benefits and Shortcomings of Mechanistic and
Organic Deployment

Mechanistic Deployment	Organic Deployment
Benefits:	**Benefits:**
Provides clear expectations for deployment	Provides clear examples of deployment
Builds widespread awareness throughout organization	Builds deep understanding throughout organization
Better infrastructure to support long-term sustenance	Better opportunity for long-term sustenance
Quick to engage all managers	Better enables organizational learning
Shortcomings:	**Shortcomings:**
Shallow, potentially superficial deployment	Slower, more methodical approach
Potential discontinuity between training and deployment	Slow to engage all managers
Hinders true organizational learning	Requires change agents with advanced knowledge and understanding

has benefits and shortcomings (see Table 6.5). To really evaluate a particular company, we must look at its total journey, and we suspect that in most cases, we will see ebbs and flows moving between organic and mechanistic. Ultimately, a balance is needed, and perhaps the best balance will be different in different cases. The combination of Big Ship's mechanistic infrastructure and Small Ship's organic learning led to something stronger than either the mechanistic or the organic approach by itself.

 ## *Sensei* Reflection on Bureaucracy and Leadership

Judging a complex organization is, well, complex. The standards for excellence can vary widely. Certainly by Toyota standards, Reman was far less than a glowing success. Going back to the five whys analysis in Chapter 1, Reman looks far more like a traditional Western organization than like Toyota. It suffers from senior leadership that is distant and is focused more on pleasing the shareholders and customers than on leading the drive toward operational excellence. The top leaders barely have time (or make time) to even go out to the *gemba* to understand the current condition of the shipyard firsthand. This hands-off approach led to Small Ship and Big Ship vying for ideological supremacy in deployment and seeking favoritism by corporate management. A large portion of the effort at both shipyards focused on giving the appearance to corporate management of being a model shipyard with the "right" methodology. The lean task force was much more concerned about control and reporting the right numbers upward than about real excellence in day-to-day operations in the shipyards.

In this organization, as in many, senior management moves around frequently, and the stable core of the organization is in the operational bowels. These people are struggling to do their best while tumultuous political battles are taking place above them. They really need consistent and passionate leadership from the top, and they get it only in fits and starts. So lean becomes a program that is characterized by fits and starts and by limited and disconnected successes.

Chapter 7

An Australian *Sensei* Teaches a Proud Japanese Company New Tricks: Bringing TPS to a Complex Equipment Manufacturer

(With Tony McNaughton)

Patience is the companion of wisdom.

—Saint Augustine, Christian theologian

I n this unusual case, Tony McNaughton, classically trained in the Toyota Production System (TPS) at Toyota of Australia, became the *sensei* for a Western-owned company in Japan that makes complex equipment (similar in complexity to CNC machines, commercial trucks, and robotics). The company had a culture that shared many common features with Toyota, but the production system was a traditionally scheduled, push-based system that was very weak in the main technical features of TPS. More important, the behavior was not focused on daily problem solving and *kaizen*. Over a five-year period, Tony coached the company to a new level. This is a more traditional volume manufacturing example, although it involves very large, complex equipment at a line speed that is about ⅒ that of a Toyota plant. In this case, we get an opportunity to see the orthodox coaching method of a TPS master as it was taught to Tony.

Early in 2005, Jeff Liker received a call from an executive in Japan who worked for a global equipment manufacturer (we'll call it ComplexEquip). His boss, the head of Asia-Pacific operations, had read *The Toyota Way*. ComplexEquip's business was growing rapidly in a booming Asian economy, and in particular it was adding capacity in China. The Asian head wanted to get started in applying the Toyota Production System as soon as possible. He realized that this was a golden opportunity, as the factories were relatively new and the work culture was still forming, and he wanted to get off to a good start. The value stream for the bestselling equipment started in ComplexEquip's plant in Japan, their flagship plant. The Japanese plant built the final product, but also built major modules to be assembled in China for the Chinese market. They wanted Liker to review the Japanese and Chinese plants and then present his observations at an all-managers meeting in their Asian headquarters, along with recommendations on how to proceed on the journey to TPS. ComplexEquip was developing its own version of TPS at the corporate level, but they did not want to wait and felt a need to get started in the Asia Pacific region right away.

I explained that to implement TPS seriously, the company would need a *sensei* and proposed that I be joined by Tony, a seasoned Australian TPS veteran with a decade of Toyota experience plus a decade of lean advising experience. We would map the value stream from Japan to China to make more concrete proposals for change. The result was a five-year journey in which Tony coached the Japanese plant, a journey that is still in process at the time of this writing. Thus TPS traveled from Toyota City to Melbourne, Australia, and returned to Japan, just down the road from its origins at Toyota. This chapter is written from Tony's point of view as he coached the Japanese plant that was part of the Japanese division of ComplexEquip that we will call JACO.

Background of the Japanese Company and the First Visit

I was contacted by Jeff Liker to assist with a new client, working with a Chinese plant and a Japanese plant to create lean models for the Asian region of the company. I will focus here on my experiences with the Japanese plant that was part of JACO. Before we even got started, the Japanese plants were considered to be the global benchmarks for ComplexEquip. It was clear to me on my first walkthrough that from a Toyota perspective, the plant was far from a lean model. It may be surprising to some that a mature Japanese factory was not lean to begin with—particularly since it was very familiar with the basic concepts of TPS and had even had some of the best experts from Toyota come to the plant to teach them. Even in Japan, however, TPS does not spread through simple awareness; it requires a committed effort to learn by doing. As it turned out, this was a treat, since many aspects of a *kaizen* culture were in JACO from the start; it was fertile ground for teaching and watching TPS blossom in a truly organic way.

JACO, a Japanese subsidiary of a Western industrial company, has several plants and a product development center on the same site. Plant No. 1 was for fabricating parts and assembling medium and large equipment. Plant No. 2 was for assembling small equipment. Plant No. 3 was for manufacturing components for onsite assembly and export to Asia, Europe, the United States, and South America.

Sales growth was strong from 2000 through mid-2008, but the global financial crisis had a big impact on JACO starting late in 2008. A large percentage of the company's product was being exported to North America. By the end of 2008, this demand had virtually stopped. Production volumes in 2009 were less than half of volumes in 2008. By 2010, sales were recovering, and forecasts for 2011 exceeded all previous production volumes.

My first visit accompanying Liker was scheduled for three days in Japan visiting the JACO plant, two key suppliers, and the warehouse where products were prepared for overseas shipping, then a trip to China for two days in the plant there, and finally to the Asian headquarters for the presentation of findings. We were accompanied in our visit to JACO by a former Japanese manager who had worked at the Japanese subsidiary from its beginning and was now retired, but who had been hired back as a consultant. He helped translate for us and ended up playing a critical role as he developed expertise in TPS. He had had years of manufacturing experience and had thoroughly read *The Toyota Way* in both English and Japanese. He became my collaborator and student of TPS, learning rapidly and ultimately helping to guide the transformation.

We spent most of the first day at the plant sitting in a conference room while one Japanese member after another paraded his PowerPoint slides with broken English: Dante's hell, anyone? My Toyota *sensei* would have leapt out of his seat and headed for the *gemba*, but we were mere consultants. Finally we got a chance to walk through the plant. In one sense, I could see this magnificent factory, rich with a Japanese flavor, with massive production lines and automation everywhere. The place was clean, with lots of signage and color coding like most Japanese factories. Yet, from my years of practical experience, I could also see so much opportunity:

- There was neatly piled inventory everywhere—classic indicators of independent efficiencies and processes that were not balanced.
- We witnessed slow responsiveness to abnormalities as they occurred.
- There was little evidence of root-cause analysis in problem solving.
- We noticed a changeover of a piece of equipment that we were told took about 30 minutes—it would be a 5-minute job at most Toyota plants.
- Division managers were in meetings most of every day and were not really in touch with what was occurring within their zones of control. They relied on more meetings to find out what was happening in their factories.

As we moved through the value stream, we counted inventory and measured cycle times to prepare the value stream map. Both the

Japanese plant and the Chinese plant already had value stream maps, since the parent company had required them some years back. In both plants, however, the maps were outdated and inaccurate—obviously not being used for real *kaizen*.

In preparation for the Asian headquarters' presentation, Liker took photos, as the Japanese executives cringed. As Liker was jovially taking a photograph of yet one more pile of inventory that had no apparent reason for being where it was, I recall one of the executives standing in front of it and screaming, "This is not usually here." He was correct in this particular case. The plant had had a supply-chain problem, so had built up extra inventory until the company could solve the problem at the root cause. Of course I could see through this short-term situation, and it was apparent that the plant was still very far from linked processes.

At the closing meeting of the visit, Liker proudly informed the senior management that the head of Asia-Pacific wished to have me come back and coach the company through a TPS transformation. The senior Japanese executive present politely informed Liker that the company already deeply understood TPS and had learned from the best at Toyota; they were also concerned that I did not speak Japanese. "Tony-san would have trouble on the shop floor working with our team members who do not speak English," he explained. Some members of the leadership team had convinced themselves that they were experts in TPS and that it was pretty much already in place within their company. We moved on to the Chinese plant for a similar review and then to our presentation in the Asian headquarters building.

As the *sensei* for Liker with JACO, I learned many things from the past five years of activity. The challenge of supporting this large Japanese factory was an opportunity of a lifetime for me. What better way could there be to test my own decades of TPS experience than in a mature Japanese company inside Japan that was pretty set in its own ways? Could I as an outsider really influence this proud company?

Sensei Reflection: Understanding the Current Situation

By spending sufficient time on the floor and observing what is actually happening in the working environment, you can learn a lot about the true state of the business. It also tells you what the leaders deem important. It would be very easy to be amazed at the high levels of cleanliness and workplace organization. The automation and electronic visual controls are very impressive. Yet there are other indicators that tell a different story. Looking for these indicators is important to provide appropriate direction through the consultation process.

I claim that you can tell many important things about the entire manufacturing company by simply observing how a team member goes about her work. What do I look for?

1. Is the work flow smooth and rhythmic (process engineering)?
2. Do the equipment and tools that are used function appropriately and easily (maintenance engineering)?
3. Is the work set up to maximize value-added activities (production management and engineering)?
4. Do the fixtures and jigs reflect a design that considers the team members' workability (production engineering)?
5. Are there any problems with part design and the ability to produce with good quality (quality engineering and new product engineering)?
6. What is the responsiveness to a problem like? Is there a sense of urgency (production management)?
7. Is the workload balanced, with a steady, rhythmic process operating at a discernible *takt* (production control and sales)?

What you find when you observe the plant floor is a *sum of pieces of information that roll up to tell a story.*

EXAMPLE FROM JACO

A truck with raw material components was waiting outside the receiving dock for 45 minutes to be unloaded. Raw materials were stored outside their designated locations because of excessive quantities. Processes were running with work-in-process inventory (WIP) between work centers. Visually identified material bins for damaged parts were scattered through the shop. Some parts had been in the bins for more than four weeks. Team members were clearly struggling with their processes, but no mechanism or structure existed to support them. Some team members were very busy; others not so busy. Visual indicators displayed the output schedule X and actual Y, but there was no real responsiveness to this information. And so on.

This starts to tell a story of where this company is and what is important to it. It reflects the company's current behavior.

The Power of Public Humiliation

The consolidated evaluation feedback was presented in their central Asia headquarters. The methodology was a combination of presentations by the JACO management team and the results of our intensive plant floor observations and analysis. To provide some scope or definition for the visit, a specific value stream was selected. This enabled the evaluation to be specific from both a current-state and a potential future-state viewpoint. The value stream selected we will call the *bearing plate* manufacturing process.

The value stream was analyzed with the same rigor that a Toyota supplier's value stream would be reviewed from a TPS viewpoint. In a very short period of time, Liker and I were able to demonstrate the effectiveness of shop floor fact-based evaluation and appropriate recommendations using a structured approach.

Bearing Plate Current Situation
- Scheduled push system
- Uncontrolled inventory buffers (WIP)

- No, or poor level of, visual management
- Long and uncoordinated changeovers
- Backup production lines for buffer capacity
- Poor 5S (hard to 5S in a push system)
- Poorly controlled material-handling movement
- No *andon* system
- Process imbalance
- No problem solving using the scientific method: plan–do–check–adjust (PDCA)

We objectively, and perhaps too brutally, provided the feedback on the current state to the regional leadership along with the photos of the plant, including the inventory. Actually, it was a rather standard lean prognosis. Any person with some lean training and practical experience could provide this type of list.

As part of our assessment, we had requested a future state value stream map from JACO in advance of our visit to the bearing plate line. This told much more about what the site was thinking and what was in focus. This is a good technique to get a reading on the organization's thinking. Most alarming to us was that the JACO team had defined a future state that showed little understanding of basic TPS principles:

JACO Proposed Bearing Plate Future State Vision (Two Years from Current State)

- More advanced scheduled push system
- Uncontrolled inventory buffers
- Departments still suboptimized for independent efficiencies
- No visual management systems
- Shorter but still uncoordinated changeovers
- Backup production lines for buffer capacity eliminated
- Poorly controlled material-handling movement
- No plan for *andon*
- Conservative lead-time reduction
- Waiting on a brand new heat-treatment system (technology solution) to start *kaizen* (about one year away)

In short, there was little awareness of the evident product flow and system waste. The emphasis was on expensive technical solutions. The replacement heat-treatment system was in fact required to meet future production volumes and to improve quality. There was no doubt about that. The approach was to ensure that the heat-treatment system was installed and commissioned in time to meet the projected higher customer demand rate. The future state map was the same value stream with the new heat-treatment system and a more advanced Material Requirements Planning information system inserted. In this vision flow improved and lead time was reduced because of the new, faster heat-treatment system with more capacity, but it was a classic example of throwing money at a problem with little understanding of the systems and behavior required to manage the value stream. It also provided an excuse to push off improvement.

This brief review of the value stream revealed the thinking of the JACO leadership. It was a great example of the *gemba* telling you many things about the company culture.

Liker gave the summary of the current state of JACO relative to Toyota Way principles:

- *Philosophy.* Strong history and long-term philosophy.
- *Process.* Good quality control, Total Productive Maintenance (TPM), and process improvement, but weak at overall lean material and information flow.
- *People and partners:* Strong foundation of developing excellent people and partners.
- *Problem solving:* Culture of *kaizen* at process level, but weak value stream *kaizen*.
- *Conclusion.* Build on strengths and dedicated effort with value stream or system *kaizen*!

I went through the current state map and future state recommendations for the bearing plate process, which were at a general level:

I. Develop an accurate current state map.
    A. Capture actual changeover times and frequency.
    B. Capture actual process cycle times.

    C. Capture actual machining centers capacity analysis.

    D. Capture actual inventory levels in the stream, including raw materials and finished product.

    E. Capture actual machine downtime data and causes.

    F. Capture actual quality performance and causes.

  II. Develop a future state map with the emphasis on balanced flow to *takt*.

    A. No more than 12 months from current state.

    B. Recommended a 50 percent lead-time reduction.

    C. Downtime improvement targets set based on current actual.

    D. Quality improvement targets set based on current actual.

    E. Defined system established to manage the flow and prevent overproduction.

    F. Have a method of exposing problems and responding swiftly.

 III. Break *kaizen* implementation plan into chunks or zones.

    A. Assign a process owner for achievement of each chunk.

    B. Machining processes to paint.

    C. Angle cutting and edging.

    D. Material and information flow.

 IV. Schedule regular follow-up by leadership.

    A. Floor-based reviews.

    B. A3 status summary (single A3-sized report) to reflect actual status.[1]

None of this was exceptional consulting or breakthrough thinking or methodology. It was simply how I, and other Toyota veterans, had been trained over and over within Toyota to evaluate a value stream and move forward appropriately to an improved state. The real goal was for JACO to develop a deep understanding of its current performance, capabilities, and capacity. Only then could it continue to project tangible targets and start processes to move toward those targets.

The feedback from the initial visit, including photos, was presented to the JACO leadership team in the Asia meeting in a way that was frank and perhaps even a little abrasive, given that this was the company's global benchmark facility. In retrospect, we should have realized that our calm and objective feedback was in fact humiliating for the JACO leadership team that had come to Beijing. We had both had enough experience with Japanese culture to understand the difference between public face and private discussions. We knew that *hansei* (deep reflection and accepting responsibility) meant that leaders had to take responsibility and show that they were really, really sorry. A JACO executive apologized profusely and said that he agreed with our observations and was ashamed that he had not realized it. He was particularly ashamed that there was "no flow." He then announced that he welcomed the *sensei* support of "McNaughton-san."

So, in a bizarre situation, a great Japanese factory of a global iconic company, with Toyota just down the road and sharing suppliers, was asking for help from a Toyota veteran from Australia! "Teach us how to apply the Toyota Production System." I was ready for the challenge and was very much looking forward to working in Japan once again.

The Starting Point: "Component A" TPS Pilot

As you work through this case study, you will find the approach to be reasonably standard. We started with a pilot value stream, going deep and narrow for a sufficient length of time to demonstrate both the necessary physical possibilities and also the behavioral changes required. A team of people was assigned to learn from the pilot experience so that they could transfer what they had learned to other areas. In the PDCA definition, this pilot could be described as "one cycle of learning," although there were many smaller PDCA loops embedded in it.

For the TPS pilot, we picked a common component, which we will refer to as "Component A," that was manufactured in the plant and delivered to the assembly line. It was somewhat self-contained, required both machining and assembly, and would illustrate all the key lean concepts nicely. It was also the constraint process within the component plant, and output would need to be increased in the near future. The greatest opportunity for cost reduction was in assembly, but that was an extremely complex operation, and I wanted the company to take on something more manageable that could illustrate an entire system of material and information flow. The assembly line would have mostly demonstrated part presentation and line balancing. Often you would select the biggest business opportunity as a pilot, but as pointed out earlier in the book, you need to clearly identify and balance the business purposes and the people purposes. For the people purposes of demonstrating the system and management learning, this appeared to be a better model line.

It was clear that there were skeptics within the management ranks initially. The pilot selected was also a "safe experiment" for JACO. In fact, that was an advantage in one critical way. All too often, senior management is very impatient and wants to spread lean wall to wall like peanut butter. The result is mechanistic and shallow. In this case, the management wanted us to go slowly, and that allowed us to go deep. In fact, I refused to let the company go beyond any step in the process until it had been done right so that it would be sustained.

A key success factor was that the original pilot team members were then expected to take a leading role in facilitating and working with team members from the new pilots. In support of the expansion beyond the initial pilot, the plant's senior executive did something quite special. He selected senior managers from each of the divisions (components, fabrication, and assembly) to participate in the Component A TPS activities with the TPS team on a full-time basis for 12 months and then lead deployment in their areas. They played an integral part in the pilots, as they brought explicit process knowledge, decades of experience, and credibility to the group.

Finally we got down to real work at the *gemba* in August 2005. I was working with an interpreter, the retired manager, who would himself become a lean coach, a general affairs manager, a component senior engineer, and a component engineer.

The approach to the pilot followed a pretty standard recipe:

1. Develop a current state value stream map, based on the actual situation.
2. Identify problems with the current situation from a TPS viewpoint.
3. Develop a proposal for a future state that overcomes the current problems and is aligned with the business direction.

4. Develop an action plan to manage implementation.
5. Get senior leadership support and deep understanding before proceeding.
6. Use this pilot as a showcase for further expansion of lean.

(*Note:* It was agreed that there would be no expansion until the pilot was satisfactory and stable. I will explain this later in more detail.)

The main lean concepts applied in the pilot were

1. Balance the flow of product to the customer demand rate (*takt*).
2. Reduce product "sleeping time" in the value stream.
3. Apply leveled pull-based replenishment to manage product flow.
4. Standardize *all* work.
5. Visualize the status of actual versus schedule.
6. Use reduced lead time as a catalyst for exposing all problems.
7. Use PDCA problem solving as people development opportunities.
8. Practice process *kaizen* every day. Manager to follow up daily.

The overall flow in the current state map was straightforward. Raw castings of Component A were supplied from a third-party logistic depot located close to the factory. Component A was then machined, cleaned, and deburred, and there was a finishing process. Then Component A was hand-assembled, tested, washed, painted, and palletized for shipping. The customers were different assembly plants on the same site and overseas plants.

Current to Future State Planning

There was a great deal of waste in the current state, mainly because it was a push system with unconnected flow between departments. The castings came in and "went to sleep" in inventory. There was no external logistics standardization and no strict delivery window times. Then machining was divided into two stages, with a great deal of WIP in between. A partial outsourcing process caused long lead times and more inventory. There were clear workload imbalances in the cleaning and checking areas, and that also led to WIP buildup. Overall, it was a classic push production system, with no concept of *takt*, no standardized work, and long lead times.

A well-defined current state map of the value stream makes defining the future state easier. The initial emphasis was on prioritizing those changes that could be made with little or no capital expenditure. The future state needed to deliver something that could represent a showcase for other areas, so all the bells and whistles were designed in with exceptional visual management.

The future state map had the same processing steps as the current state. The main differences were in the information flow. We shifted to pull-based replenishment, using *kanban* as the communication tool. *Kanban* came back to the pacemaker in assembly to order additional parts, and a *heijunka* (leveling) box was used to create a leveled schedule that would visually serve as a pacemaker for the process. Processes were connected through *kanban*, with minimal WIP between processes. The "preliminary future state map" was done by the team with some feedback from me. But I intentionally did not correct everything, such as letting them discover the need for *heijunka* through experience.

One of the most dramatic improvements was in the assembly process itself. It was rebalanced to *takt*, which led to a 25 percent increase in productivity. It became a visual showcase, with bright lights, signage, and the visual *heijunka* box.

Some tooling engineering was needed to create fixtures so that Component A could be completed in one cycle in one flexible machining center. There were many individual *kaizen* assaults to fix processes like changeovers and improved maintenance procedures.

Struggling to Get Follow-up on the Action Plans

The pilot activity was conducted in such a manner that each consultation visit (one week per month) would review progress, provide coaching and direction, then assign homework to be completed prior to the next visit. This was in contrast to the sometimes popular weeklong *kaizen* blitz approach. This was a marathon, not a sprint. There was no clearly defined timeline for completion of the pilot activity. Each step of the improvement process was used as an opportunity to teach Toyota's scientific method based on A3 reporting of PDCA cycles.

This case study may sound like a pretty easy application. It was actually far from smooth sailing, especially in the early stages. Some months I would arrive to find very little progress from my previous visit. Some months the operation would slide backward from the previous month. Sometimes management was not even aware that the process had slipped in some areas until I walked it with them and pointed out weaknesses. Sustaining things was proving very difficult. There were some deep-rooted, anti-lean behaviors throughout the floor.

Initially, getting the middle management to the shop floor to understand what was actually going on was really tough. On a number of occasions, I had to meet with the senior executives on-site and express my concerns that the management "was just not getting it."

We had to take action to get over these problems. There was no way I would entertain any expansion of this business improvement activity to other parts of the business while these cracks in the approach remained. It would have resulted in very shallow implementation, and we would not have gotten the desired outcomes. I had learned from my *sensei* never to leave an area until 100 percent of the objective was reached.

The most serious problem I could see was the lack of local mid-level management engagement and accountability. We were falling into the trap of a "TPS team doing it *to* them." I had to try to get the core business to own this activity.

Some things we changed to take it up a level were

1. The site consultation visit closeout with the site leadership team was shifted from the executive meeting room and a one-hour duration to the shop floor for two hours, followed by one hour to confirm the next steps.
2. The closeout meeting had previously been managed between the consultant and the pilot team members. This was changed to the department managers (such as machining, component assembly, etc.) facilitating the review.
3. The department manager would show the areas of focus. Production members from these areas would communicate

directly with the plant leadership on what we were doing and how they felt about this. They would also communicate their problems and challenges in their zones.

4. The department manager became a full-time member of the pilot team during consultation visits.

5. Explicit homework assignments between visits and follow-up mechanisms were put in place.

6. Each month's activity was summarized in a standard A3 reporting form showing trends on key metrics.

Building a Lean System—Summary of Pilot Results and Learning

The results from the pilot line were quite reasonable (see Table 7.1). There was still huge opportunity, but it was a good start, and it certainly looked impressive. In the big picture, it did not represent significant financial numbers for the plant. However, what the pilot had demonstrated to the leaders was the *size of the gap* between what they thought was an acceptable level of performance and the behavior and culture necessary to drive real business improvement.

As a result of maintaining the focus on the Component A value stream, I was able to teach and demonstrate real lean in a deep way. We spent 12 months learning from the pilot. This was a long time, and we could easily have expanded beyond this pilot sooner. However, rolling out something half-baked would have been a mistake—a common one that many lean coaches make. It seems that they see some improvement and want to leverage the gains quickly.

Table 7.1. Results Matrix: Simple, Few KPIs

KPI	Current	Target September 2006	Actual September 2006
Lead time	6.88 days	3.2 days	3.1 days
% value added	7.35%	15.8%	17%
Casting rework	7%	4%	4.5%
Casting reject	6%	3%	5%
Average unplanned downtime/day	550 minutes/day	225 minutes/day	199 minutes/day

What is required from the pilot is for the sum of the application of appropriate tools and the people working together as a system to bring to the surface and solve problems. In the pilot, we experienced problems with almost all of the tools and systems that we implemented. There were a number of PDCA cycles of learning within each focused activity.

1. *Pull system.* It was clear that there was a need to manage the flow of product within the pilot. The application of *kanban* as the tool for just in time (JIT) was appropriate. However, in order to achieve a smooth flow of *kanban* back through the stream, there had to be many adjustments.

   a. Pickups by material handlers of finished goods had to be standardized. The withdrawal window times had to be evened out in order to level the schedule at assembly and thereby level the flow of *kanban* to preceding processes.

   b. *Kanban* arriving in batches from finished goods withdrawal needed to be sorted and leveled in order to prevent *muri* (overburden of people or equipment) and *mura* (unevenness of workload) through final assembly. Introduction of the *heijunka* box to manage *kanban* was necessary to accomplish this.

   c. Team member discipline in managing the *kanban* movement needed attention. Despite creating rules for when *kanban* movements occur, if there is no sustained discipline, the system can quickly deteriorate, for example, delivering material before the *kanban* has been pulled, which basically creates a push system.

   d. Delivery of raw material castings from the outside factory consolidation center had to be standardized. Even delivery window times based on production operating times needed to be created.

2. *Standardized work.* Rebalancing the Component A assembly line took three major PDCA cycles before it was deemed stable and sustainable. What seemed a simple task of splitting the

work of four processes and rebalancing it into three processes was valuable learning for the organization.

a. The first PDCA cycle moved to three processes, but the balance was uneven, with some processes over the *takt* and others under it. It had to be undone and shifted back to four processes in order to meet customer output numbers.

b. The second cycle was a better balance across three processes, but the flow of *kanban* mix was not leveled and thus caused *muri* (overburden) and *mura* (unevenness). The *heijunka* box had to be introduced quickly to protect the standardized work of the three processes. This is a good example of the interrelationship of the tools being in place to create the system.

c. The third cycle was to standardize skill levels so that all team members could keep up. The skill levels and processing rate across the team members varied quite a bit. Although it is almost impossible to totally eliminate this variation, there are some things that can be done to mitigate this condition. The use of Job Instruction Training[2] needed to be introduced to ensure that all team members were sufficiently skilled to do their work smoothly and rhythmically.

 ## *Sensei* Reflection

I would suggest that the most important lessons taken from a pilot are the things that *do not work well* and how the team manages to overcome these issues. Managers need to be aware of these valuable "gems," as this is what is critical in expansion and sustainability. I have had experience with too many managers who review pilots from the viewpoint of "what does success look like?" There is some value to this in helping to create an awareness of what is possible, but it can lead to the incorrect conclusion that the results need to be replicated like a cookie cutter. The pilot can serve as a "showcase" to create an image of lean as a system, but what is most important is how it got to this point. Learn about the power of PDCA, not specific lean solutions.

There is one other very important point that I have learned from decades of lean application activity. I have learned not to be too prescriptive in providing direction. In fact, the less prescriptive I am, the higher the probability of sustainability and success. It would have been easy for me to calculate the number of *kanban* required. I could have provided the formulas for calculating the number of *kanban*. I could have told the team members to install the *heijunka* box to level the flow of *kanban*. I could have seen that there was too much *muda* (waste) to rebalance into three processes immediately. My role was to let the team members experience this for themselves. The method of "learning by doing" requires the *sensei* to provide the appropriate direction and allow the team to explore this direction. I see too many cases in which the consultant does the work, but when he leaves, it all caves in behind him. This is common where the motive is cost reduction or another short-term outcome.

Postscript on the Pilot

The quality of the team members selected for the initial pilot was very high. All three original team members advanced into senior management roles within the organization over five years. Two of them were promoted to department managers within the plant, while the third member advanced to become a regional *sensei* in the company's production system rollout. I continue to mentor the regional *sensei* after five years. His capability to lead deep change continues to grow.

Beyond the initial one year of intense focus and support, the Component A pilot continued to improve. The team members deepened their focus on behavior (what they call the software), as most of the hardware (reengineering the value stream) was in place.

Together we developed guidelines for focused behavior within the Components Division. I call them the Lean Benchmark Rules. I think they are self-explanatory. The emphasis was now on providing a showcase of behavior. My expectation was that the pilot group would "practice their way to a new way of behaving" using the Lean Benchmark Rules. Eventually this behavior may become their "culture."

Lean Behavior Benchmark Rules

1. We will *follow our standardized work* on all processes.
2. When we cannot, we will *expose the problems*.
3. The company will respond *immediately* and support us.
4. A system is in place for *managers to follow up* at *gemba* every day.
5. We will use our *problems as people development opportunities*.
6. We will implement process improvement *kaizen every day*.
7. We will *never* accept the current state.

Next Step beyond the Lean Pilot— Expansion Plan

The 12-month period of pilot activity was not a defined milestone. That was simply how long it took to be at a point where I could recommend expansion to other parts of the plant. Fortunately, the senior management of JACO was willing to suspend disbelief and be very patient. The managers took all my suggestions very seriously. I had the vision and experience to know where we were headed and why it was so critical that we got the pilot right, but they did not have this experience, so they needed to trust me.

I was looking for three specific indicators (beyond performance improvement) from the pilot before expansion:

1. Sufficient understanding both from within the team and from middle management of the status of the system—the gaps between actual and standard

2. Evidence of the interrelated application of tools to form a system
3. Appropriate behavioral change associated with the tools and methodologies within the pilot value stream

Once I was satisfied that this was in place—what I call "the tipping point"—we could look at expansion. I also demanded that the original three members be part of the expansion coaching activity. I say "demanded" because by now I had established trust, and senior management had seen the huge gap between the pilot area and the rest of the operation, along with the results. Management was committed to learning from me as its *sensei*. That gave me the power to be quite demanding at times.

The activity beyond the initial pilot (expanded cycles of PDCA learning) was about 15 months in duration. Expansion was a three-pronged approach to spread the activity across the site. However, the expansion was managed using a selected pilot approach once again. Department managers were requested to identify their pilots and state the business case for their selection. They needed to present their case to the plant leadership team.

As briefly detailed here, each deployment had a different focus, again based upon the needs of the business.

1. *Second pilot identified within the Components Division: "Component B."*

   Business need. This was the second significant product from within the Components Division. At baseline, it was in about the same condition as the Component A starting point. By focusing on an improved Component B value stream, the plant would achieve a critical mass of transition within the Components Division. This could then be a platform for standardizing and systematizing the production system built within the division.

   Results. The results were similar to those of the Component A pilot, with the same key performance indicators (KPIs) improving by about the same amount. Lead time was reduced by about 70 percent.

Explanation. The most significant reason for lead-time reduction was as a result of bringing the heat-treatment processes back in house and within the value stream. Recall that this was in the original future state value stream map when we first visited, and that the managers were not intending to do anything else with lean until this was in place. This reduced lead time opened up other doors of opportunity, such as the ability to build to actual sequence (and not use enterprise resource planning to schedule a forecast build plan). This, in turn, led to a much improved supply of product to both the in-plant assembly line and the export order requiremets.

2. *A pilot in the Heavy Fabrication Division: "Heavy Fabrication A."*
   Business need. Long lead time from raw materials to finished goods was cited as the need by the senior manager. Through five whys analysis, we discovered that there were some critical dimensional quality issues that created excessive amounts of rework. This rework created bottleneck processes that inhibited achieving *takt* and that clearly needed to be resolved before lead time could be challenged. This had not been clear to the production managers, who wanted to charge ahead with pull and flow. What this told me was that management within this division was clearly disconnected from the real status and issues within their operation.

   Results. Quality issues were engineered out of the process. Lead time was reduced by 40 percent.

   Explanation. The need to involve both the in-house product engineering design team and external fabrication suppliers was critical to working objectively on the quality problem. In the end, there were modifications to the process, the jigs and fixtures, and the design specification. All were necessary to overcome the issue. When this type of multicause situation arises, it is common to see finger-pointing across teams—it is the other person's fault. Staying objective and focusing on the facts is critical to work through the process logically and systematically.

3. *A pilot in the Final Assembly Division: "Frame Assembly."*

Business need. Labor productivity and rebalance. This assembly line fed into the main assembly line and was targeted to operate at the final assembly *takt.* There was a need to apply standardized work and *kaizen* to rebalance the workload appropriately. *Results.* Rebalanced work to *takt.* Implemented 156 *kaizen* points. Reduced direct staffing by about 30 percent.

Explanation. The baseline condition was very badly balanced. Some team members were overburdened, while others had very little work. The focus here was on eliminating *muri* (overburden) and *mura* (unevenness). As the *sensei*, I knew that if the team focused on reducing *muri* and *mura*, then the *muda* (the waste) would take care of itself. This proved to be so. The first attempt identified a balance requiring 14 processes (one PDCA cycle of learning). This was implemented rather quickly. Once this was done, further opportunities could be identified. Sometimes, after an improvement activity, there is a tendency to "declare victory" and freeze the focus on further *kaizen* activity. By focusing deeper, we found further adjustments and improvements that led to a further reduction of two processes—a significant lesson for the team.

The core team supporting each expansion pilot was made up of the original pilot key members as well as new members from the respective division. Each department had a second-generation TPS team. The original Component A pilot members took on a mentoring role but did not do the work for the respective pilots.

Further Expansion

In late 2007, the activity expanded to other areas, including the following:

1. Fabrication B: lead-time reduction and capacity increase
2. Main assembly line: rebalance and standardize

3. Final assembly line: rebalance and standardize
4. Shipping: product flow and problem solving

JACO now understood the approach rather well:

1. Define the appropriate area based upon the business need (as discussed earlier).
2. Clearly identify the current state performance and status.
3. Analyze the current state from a lean perspective.
4. Develop the future state vision and KPIs.
5. Create an action plan.
6. Follow up regularly and adjust with successive PDCA cycles.

The most significant lessons from this round of activity came from the main assembly line. At the time, there was little understanding within the assembly management team of the gap between its assembly line and a Toyota automotive assembly line. To be honest, I felt that there was an air of arrogance within the Assembly Department. It was a relatively new line with modern equipment and was very impressive to the untrained eye:

• Line speed interlocking installation modules
• Significant automation, including line delivery systems
• Audible and visual systems throughout

To be fair, this assembly line was building equipment larger than automobiles. Along with this, the components being assembled were heavy enough to require overhead cranes to install. This made the line less flexible and slower. The *takt* was as much as 10 times that of a typical Toyota car plant, which means the line is very slow and work cycle times are 10 times as long. This creates excessive walking as the team member walks with the assembly and walks back and forth to get parts to perform the full cycle of work and then has to return to the starting point.

The external and internal material logistics system and processes were quite good. Most products were delivered to the line side by one of the following methods:

1. In line sequence
2. In kitted form in line sequence from internal kitting stations
3. In kitted form in line sequence from a supplier or consolidator nearby
4. Replenished based on actual usage status

Unfortunately, there were many fundamental mistakes in how the line was set up and the way people worked. One of the more significant constraints on the assembly line was that materials could be supplied to only one side of the line. This made it difficult to present the materials optimally to the appropriate process. Effectively, this layout condition created a 50 percent disadvantage. (I should note that for smaller parts, it is often advantageous to work on one side of the line, the inside, and have material handlers refill parts presented from the aisle in one direction.)

When you are working with a fixed line production sequence, it is necessary to keep the planned repeatable sequence from being changed. The sequence is sometimes adjusted when there is a critical component shortage. Or it may be changed if there is a quality issue related to a certain model type or specification. I have worked with companies that have a production control group that recklessly chops and changes the production plan without realizing the significant consequence of its actions. The amount of waste that is generated when a line sequence is changed is great. Many parts are sequenced on a critical path to match the assembly line fit point. It is a well-synchronized choreography. Adjusting the plan is a relatively simple task. What that sets off, though, is incredible waste by the production department to ensure that the synchronization is maintained. Even worse is the scrambling to get the parts to the line in the time slot allocated. Huge *mura* (unevenness of workload) results. Production schedules in this plant were changing enough to create difficulties for standardized work and suppliers.

The baseline balance on the main assembly line was unique in my experience. It was a moving assembly line, and it was moving at the appropriate *takt*. However, I first observed that there were no clear workstation pitch markers. In Toyota plants, there are always big taped lines on the floor next to the assembly line. There is a big red piece of tape showing where the cycle should start. The space from where the operator should start to where the operator should finish one cycle is called the pitch. The operator should wait until the car comes to a certain fixed point (the start point) before beginning the cycle. There is then yellow tape that shows where the team member should be when she is 70 percent done with the job, to see if she is ahead or behind at that point.

On the JACO line, it was difficult to see whether a team member was working within his workstation pitch or not. Upon closer observation, it was evident that the work done by each team member had nothing to do with the line *takt*. The team members were in fact doing a series of tasks that often took them up to three workstation pitches down the line. Meanwhile, other team members would be doing the same tasks on other machines on the line. They would then gather their tools and some parts, walk back up the line, and start on the next available machine being assembled. The amount of motion waste was incredible. It was like watching on a moving line the traditional "stall build" method, in which the car sat in a stall while the worker walked around the car adding items.

I knew that we had to break this methodology if we were to be successful with the application of standardized work on the main assembly line. Without the support of the plant's senior leadership, I do not think I would have been successful in convincing the assembly management and engineers to tear up what they were doing and start again, especially at a time when customer demand was reaching all-time highs.

It was also critical to get the support of the top leaders for a change in the front-line organization structure. At Toyota, responses to *andon* calls are the responsibility of hourly team leaders, who also participate with the group leader (first-line supervisor) in *kaizen*. At JACO, team leaders existed in a sense, but they were blended into the mix as operators. This made responding to issues involving their fellow team members very slow and difficult, as they had their own work to complete. The commitment from senior management was to reinvest the gains made by the improvement activity and deploy the team leaders as an on-line support function. To have the appropriate ratio of team leader to team members (about 1:7), the *kaizen* and rebalancing activity would need to free up about 10 processes.

The first step was to mark the workstations' start and end points. This provided the clarity to see the movement of team members.

The second step was to conduct detailed time studies of all processes for all model types. This was a big job, as the cycle times were long and the product mix quite varied. (This took many months to do in total.)

To prove the methodology, the first five workstations were tackled to provide a model to continue from. The line balance (*yamazumi*) method was adopted, in which we showed on a chart the actual workload of each team member relative to the *takt*. Each piece of work was painstakingly analyzed and inserted into the appropriate process. Lineside materials were evaluated, with the target being to present the materials to the team member within his workstation pitch.

Slowly the balance planning came together. Team members were trained in standardized work using Job Instruction Training, and then trials of the new balance were conducted. After three months of intensive activity, the first five workstations were revised. The result (after a huge investment of time and effort by all involved) was that two operators became available.

Justifying the effort that went into redeploying two operators (now team leaders) would have been very difficult indeed. Fortunately, the plant leadership recognized the greater need to rethink how the work is done. Many companies I have worked with previously would have taken the head count off the books immediately in order to meet their labor and overhead targets. We were fortunate to have strong support for not only achieving process improvement but also exploring behavior change.

To make a long story short, the rebalance pilot was deemed a success, and plans were put in place to expand this to all workstations on the assembly line. The effort took almost a year in total. It was a big difference from the baseline. Ten team leader roles were created. After the changes, the way the work was being done was much better than before, but still there was too much *muda*. You do not create perfection in 12 months. Quality also improved marginally. Safety was not compromised. Not a bad effort by the team. As it turned out, the timing for this application of this methodology could not have been better.

Navigating the Global Financial Crisis

In the fall of 2008, the global economy began collapsing, like dominoes falling, and this hit ComplexEquip hard by October. In one short month, orders to the plant dropped by more than 50 percent. Production plans were immediately slashed. Management shifted into damage control in a way that none of them had experienced in their working lives.

Regular employees did not get laid off, but were encouraged to use their accrued annual leave. Suppliers were struggling to keep their heads above water financially. If ever JACO needed to test the effectiveness of its newfound production system and methodology, it was right then.

Senior plant management laid out the challenge to the departments: "Radically rebalance the entire business, without any compromise in direct labor productivity or quality!" The only way to do this was to combine all production from three assembly lines onto the one main assembly line. This made the product mix so diverse that some processes had model cycle-time variations of up to 300 percent!

Despite this, the rebalance was planned and implemented using the recently learned techniques. With such diversity, there were many changes to line-side material placement. Much of the handling equipment and devices required modification to handle the diverse mix. Rebalancing the line to such a broad mix and slower *takt* was also a huge challenge for the plant. Having a defined process to approach this in place proved very timely for the plant.

Within five weeks, the revised balance was established, the trials were conducted, and the assembly line was limping along at the adjusted speed. It happened to be between my visits, which were now every other month, so the team members did this without my help—I was very proud. When I did visit, there were problems everywhere. It was not pretty, but it was working. Every process had a problem or a *kaizen* opportunity.

The new team leader role was a huge enabler:

1. To retrain team members in their new standardized work
2. To respond to processes that were constrained because of the complex mix
3. To solve problems and perform small *kaizen* activities
4. To cover jobs when absenteeism occurred

As a result of this rough transition, the company could really understand the importance of the support departments to help production promptly when problems arose. This also raised awareness that the customers of the support departments were in fact the team members who were adding the real value day in and day out. The role of engineering, maintenance, quality, human resources, and management was to work with the team members with mutual respect and trust.

Five years is a very short time to effect sustainable change in systems, processes, and, most important, behavior. The team members in this plant were on their way, though, and the rest of their global organization began to look at JACO as the lean trailblazer.

This experience reminded me of the goals of TPS:

1. To produce the *highest quality*
2. At the *lowest cost*
3. In the shortest *lead time*

There is one more goal that we were taught in the mid-1980s:

4. To respond to change *flexibly*

Reflection on Building Lean Systems Organically

I am into my fifth year of support here in Japan and still going every other month. This has been a long-term relationship by consulting standards, but a very short period from the viewpoint of changing the DNA of a company that already was great from many perspectives. I worked with this company in the way I was taught by Toyota, which is organic transformation. The teaching was at the *gemba*, with little PowerPoint and little structure. We started with a deep pilot and spread through deep transformation of specific areas, and in five years lean has spread throughout the entire manufacturing division of the company.

The opportunities are still enormous. The senior leadership team continues to encourage the Toyota Way as an endless journey of improvement and learning. As production volumes return to the plant after the devastation of the 2008 global financial crisis, the challenges that this company will face will continue to provide fertile learning ground to develop its people and its processes.

Since the mid-1980s, I have learned a great deal about the application of the Toyota Production System in a diverse range of industries and countries. In the spirit of keeping it simple, I would like to explain my thoughts through selected pointers that I was taught many years ago:

1. *The TPS tools provide an opportunity to change behavior.* I believe the most common reason that some companies have a mediocre outcome from the application of lean is that they do not associate a very necessary change in behavior with the simple application of the tools. The language they use is "application of lean tools for business improvement." This is a common and fundamental mistake.

   To truly advance TPS, it is essential to associate distinctive behavior change with the application of the tools. This change in behavior must take place at all levels. Creating a lean value stream is not all that difficult. However, to sustain and further improve it takes resolve on the part of all involved. The concept of "never satisfied" is how I would describe this phenomenon. Simple tools such as 5S are useful to begin to build the appropriate behavior. It is about sustaining at first, then improving from the baseline. More advanced applications of standardized work or pull-based material replenishment demand a certain level of discipline and maturity. Finding the right depth of tool application to demand a change in behavior is very important. Anything less is often superficial and not sustainable.

There has been a lot of recent opinion that most companies are "stuck in the tool age." I think the more accurate diagnosis is that they did not apply the tools to the right depth to drive behavioral change. Management was oblivious.

2. *Visibility of abnormalities, with quick response and follow-up (PDCA), is needed.* One of the first lessons I learned decades ago was the necessity of being able to distinguish normal from abnormal at the *gemba*. This is elementary step number one. Programs like 5S help, but they do not go far enough. *All facets of the live work site provide the cues to drive the right behavior.* This is all about behavior—the stuff you can't see so clearly when you visit a best practice organization.

   The importance of effective standardized work to expose process abnormalities is critical at the process level. Most companies that I engage with have previously achieved mediocrity with standardized work. It is too general, and sometimes very superficial. Key points are not clearly identified and are rarely updated. The investment in Job Instruction Training to ensure that the team members have the appropriate fundamental skills is almost always missing. This prevents them from flagging problems as they occur. The problems are hidden, and the ability to investigate and solve them "live" is lost.

   What better time is there to respond to an abnormality than in real time? The evidence of the problem is right before you. Yet, too many companies fail to recognize the importance of this, and thus the response is very weak. Meeting the following morning to review yesterday's performance is OK for information sharing, but it is a little like reading yesterday's news. Instead, an organization needs to focus on the real issues, in real time.

   Creating the environment that exposes the problems is the foundation for process improvement and people development.

3. *Do the work and improve the way we do the work.* Every day at every level, the company needs to be focused on exploring better ways to do things. Continuous improvement is when all your people are solving problems every day. I have mixed

feelings about *kaizen* events and rapid-improvement workshops. Known as *jishuken* activity at Toyota, they are good for people development. They also may deliver some process improvement to the point of focus. However, I believe in this only as a complement to a core foundation of behavior as described in points 1 and 2.

4. *Go deep in the pilot.* Many years ago in Australia, we developed a couple of Toyota suppliers under the guidance of the Operations Management Consulting Division (OMCD) from Toyota Japan, a group of TPS master trainers set up originally by Ohno. It was recognized that there was a need to provide a few TPS "showcases" for other suppliers to learn from. My Toyota colleague and I each worked with a supplier. We spent more than one year in these companies before our sensei from Japan would allow anyone into the site to see our efforts. Not even the Toyota purchasing buyer was allowed on the shop floor until the OK was given. The supplier had to reach a certain level of achievement:

   a. System implementation had to demonstrate appropriate application and interconnection of the appropriate lean tools.
   b. Responsiveness of the organization to abnormalities had to be in place.
   c. Next steps had to be clearly defined, with solid plans in place.
   d. Targets for performance improvement had to be 100 percent achieved.

   From this early experience, I concluded that scattered rapid-improvement workshops merely scratch the surface. Even a one- to three-month crash-and-burn approach is not enough, not if you want your members to really think their way through the transition.

5. *Leadership must be actively involved.* A quick count of companies that I have worked with over the past 25 years exceeds 100. Without exception, the few that were truly transformed were the companies that had senior executives on site and actively involved. They were the zealots. They demanded that their direct reports be accountable for the activity. They demanded

commitment from the supporting departments: no excuses! I have seen a few attempts now in which highly capable middle management has tried valiantly to create lean systems, only to fail. For many years I was optimistic that this could be possible to achieve, but I now concede that it is futile. Senior managers attending the "monthly Lean Steering Committee meeting" is futile. It really does take a leadership team that is prepared to create the head space to be involved and drive the activity daily. They are the ones who need to develop their people through real-life work activity. Every time there is a problem, there is a perfect opportunity for a manager to develop her people.

Equally, if the approach is to set up a small lean team, then selection is important. Having the next-generation company leaders on the team not only increases the probability of good outcomes but also strengthens their resolve with practical lean application exposure—real-life people development.

6. *Emphasis on just in time and lead-time reduction.* My *sensei*, Nakayama, made clear to me many times that the pursuit of TPS without the aggressive pursuit of just in time is futile. The avalanche of recent publications seems to touch on all but this very point! Or this point melts into other information and loses the emphasis! "JIT is the relentless effort to reduce the lead time." Even half a day of finished product is deemed to be not JIT at OMCD. Nakayama would explain that JIT is not simply "the right parts at the right place at the right time." It is endless pursuit of lead-time reduction.

If we think about it, to achieve this JIT-focused improvement, it is necessary to have all parts of the TPS system in place and working correctly, such as in-station quality; stable, standardized processes; reliable equipment; robust problem solving; and so on. Otherwise you cannot survive in this "true lean" environment. The application of tools gets you to this status, but only through extensive development of your people and step changes in their behavior.

As a purist TPS practitioner, I think this very important viewpoint on JIT has been lost over the past 10 to 20 years with the "commercialization of lean." This is a very aggressive application of TPS, and it is the methodology that Toyota continues to use to this day when reengineering its Tier 1 suppliers' value streams.

In two decades with companies in many industries, the JIT focus has never failed to yield real results—if the company is up to the challenge. The learning and development along the way has been enormous by all.

The flip side is that I have had my share of failures or mediocre outcomes with some companies—short-term process improvement gains that prove to be difficult to sustain. In all cases, the JIT focus was not strong or was not understood or supported by leadership. No behavioral change was evident.

I have seen a recent suggestion that there has been too much emphasis on the tools. Maybe this is true. I think the point is that the application of the tools has been very superficial. The same goes for JIT. Too many companies install "kanban systems" that are not at all lean. They have no purpose other than to simulate the way a *kanban* circulates. This is totally missing the point of Nakayama and Toyota's OMCD.

I do not pretend to be some kind of master lean *sensei* in sharing my thoughts here in this chapter. In fact, I continue to feel like a student who is just learning. The skills and knowledge of Toyota Japan OMCD staff members leave me gasping with admiration. Their ability to evaluate any company very quickly, then immediately provide its leaders with precise feedback on the observed gaps and the way forward was truly an incredible skill. To me, they were TPS experts. Yet, they would always dismiss their status by saying that they were merely "students of TPS."

Without exception, these OMCD "students" would reinforce the need to focus on JIT and lead-time reduction. Create enough pressure within the value stream to expose the problems. The issue we found with some of our suppliers as we applied this methodology was an inability to solve the problems effectively. Many years later, while I still push for lead-time reduction in the process, I also ensure that there is sufficient problem-solving capability to react appropriately when the problems surface.

The founder of the Toyota Production System, Taiichi Ohno, was once quoted as saying, "No company will be able to successfully apply TPS unless they are facing a crisis." He believed it was this crisis that had forced Toyota to innovate and ultimately create the Toyota Production System.

I am quite honored to be accepted as a coach of JACO. Its people have been great students. Yet progress was slow for the first five years. What accelerated the process was the financial crisis. Growing quickly to keep up with demand is another type of crisis that will further stretch their abilities. Meeting challenges keeps the journey alive!

Chapter 8

Lean Iron-Ore Mining in the Pilbara Region of Western Australia

The past is the past and what is important is the current condition and what we will do next to go beyond where we are today.

—Taiichi Ohno, Toyota Motor Corporation

As a lean advisor, you quickly tire of hearing, "We're different." All work includes a variety of core processes, and at some level these are always present. All processes have waste that hides problems and presents obstacles to one-piece flow. We wish to improve the flow over time through plan–do–check–adjust (PDCA)—it's that simple and straightforward. We do have to admit, though, that every now and then we get a bit anxious when we see a new process that at first really does appear to be, well, *different*.

In this chapter, we recount the journey to lean of an iron-ore mine in Australia. Jeff Liker was asked to help it develop a Toyota Way culture, and tagged Jim Franz as the lean *sensei*. Jim and his family had previously lived in Australia when he was a lean internal advisor to Ford, so he was happy to walk down memory lane. It was a challenge to wrap his mind around such a geographically spread-out process, with the blasting of massive fields, trucks driving around, huge dig units collecting the ore, and its journey down endless kilometers of conveyor where it is crushed, sorted, and assembled into a building-sized cake that is sliced and sent by train to a port. Jim tells the story from his point of view and decided to bring it to life by writing it like a business novel, with characters and dialogue. The actual words used are based on his memory, but the essence is what he experienced over a one-year period at the mines.

How We Got Here

Jeff Liker had initially gotten involved with this particular mining company a full year before I arrived at the mine. He had been asked by its process improvement leadership in Perth to participate in an off-site session in New York, ostensibly to develop a vision for the mining company of the future. A few corporate staffers had hired a "systems consultant" who gathered experts in key fields, such as strategy, mining exploration, human resources, information technology, purchasing, and operations. Liker represented lean because they thought that lean perhaps might have a role in the actual mining.

A set of group exercises was designed to identify threats and opportunities, break down the mining company into functional areas, and "envision" what the ideal company of the future should look like. Liker pointed out that it was somewhat meaningless to envision an ideal future state when (1) we had so little understanding of the actual company and (2) few of the key stakeholders from the company were even in the room. After the meeting, the next step was to develop more detailed versions of the future vision and then visit the company in Australia (finally six months later) to discuss the findings and begin to develop "implementation" plans. Liker suggested that since lean was a process of learning by doing, he could best use his time on the trip to Australia by following the flow from the mine to the port and identifying an opportunity for a pilot lean project led by one of his colleagues, who could act as a lean *sensei*.

On a midsummer (winter in Australia) trip, Liker went traipsing around the mine and the port. There were clear opportunities everywhere. One of the obvious challenges was connecting the reality of the mine to the staffers in headquarters. The headquarters building was a 25-story steel-and-glass architectural wonder overlooking a bay. Staffers met in conference rooms and presented PowerPoints to one another while plotting how to develop the current mines to get more output and expand the company into new mines. There seemed to be little interest in how the mine actually operated at a detailed level, and few of the people had any interest in making the dirty, inconvenient trek to the *gemba*, by plane and then by car.

After the *gemba* tour, Liker presented the Toyota Way to various groups, including a one-on-one meeting with the new divisional CEO, an ex-Nissan guy. Liker emphasized that he saw a great deal of waste and very little visual management or systematic problem solving. It would take a great deal of work at the *gemba*. The CEO was enthusiastic and gushed that he wanted "Toyota's culture" at the mines and wanted to make it a top priority. After another six months of on-again, off-again communications and negotiations (*top* priority), we were informed that we had been chosen as the outside experts to assist with the mine's lean transformation. Management had agreed to the pilot mine concept after much discussion of the inch-deep, mile-wide approach (typical tools-based implementation; 5S for everybody!) versus the inch-wide, mile-deep approach we had proposed of creating a functional learning lab at one of the mines.

Liker asked me to act as the lean *sensei*, and on a second trip to Australia, we traveled around the *gemba* together, this time mapping the current state and developing a rough future state value stream map. The generally ignored blokes at the mine were delighted to be part of any effort to help them get better, and the lean concepts intrigued them.

Back at the pristine headquarters building, we presented the basic concepts of lean, our observations, and a rough plan for getting started to various staff and leadership groups. We explained that developing the process improvement teams and leadership teams was just as important as improving processes to yield more high-quality tons. We also explained that to spread the pilot, we needed direct engagement by management from headquarters at the mining site so that the managers could experience the transformation firsthand and help lead a similar transformation in other mines. There were some initial indications of a disconnect, as a number of the key directors bluntly pointed out that we lacked mining experience and questioned whether our future state vision was realistic. However, they seemed ready and willing to watch us fail.

The CEO assigned the task of driving the transformation process to his director of process improvement. This gentleman was stationed at headquarters and had "process improvement" specialists spread out among the various operations. These specialists were a young, educated group, but they were not seasoned veterans of the operation and thus had the "outsider" label firmly affixed to their name badges. This could, and would, pose a problem as we began the transformation out at the pilot site. Thankfully, the site's implementation team also included some of the mine's operational personnel, who were temporarily assigned to provide local expertise and knowledge of their particular areas. We had support from the Load and Haul group (field operations), the Fixed Plant group (crushers to train loading), and Maintenance.

 Sensei *Reflection*

We have repeatedly had the experience of advising companies that already had some sort of staff process improvement group in place. It is typical that the members of this group have advanced degrees and are well trained in some combination of Lean Six Sigma, process mapping, change management, and information technology. It is also common, from our viewpoint (since we are Toyota trained), for them to appear to be distant from the *gemba* and generally out of touch. We see our role as connecting them to the *gemba*. If the "process improvement experts" are open to learning, we are delighted to take them under our wing and teach them the Toyota Way of learning by doing. Our mission is to transfer that knowledge and understanding to the company, and these people are a core part of that. We will admit that if these bright, educated professionals have convinced themselves that they are already experts, we sometimes lack the patience to win them over. It is a lot more rewarding to go to the *gemba* and work with people who have a passion for learning. This is usually a mistake, as the internal improvement staffs represent a political interest group, and if they see the outside lean consultant as a threat, they often have more than enough influence to win the political battle.

Welcome to the Bush

I arrived in early February to begin the daunting process of transforming this mine to something resembling lean. By now it was summer in Australia, when the climate ranges from hot and dry to very hot and very dry. Welcome to the bush. My work at the mine began with the viewing of several safety videos with my counterpart, Kostas, who would run the lean effort for the mine. Afterward, we headed down to the main office to observe the leadership meeting. A few minutes before 9:00 a.m., people began trickling in, in twos and threes. By five minutes past the hour, everyone was seated, and the meeting was started by Mark, the manager responsible for all load and haul operations, including drill and blast. Chloe, his counterpart, was responsible for all of the fixed plant equipment, from the crushers through to the train load-out equipment. I learned that most of the mines were run in this manner, with a manager for the field operations and another manager for the processing of the ore once it had been dug. In a happy circumstance for me, Kostas and Chloe were a husband-and-wife team, and they even got along. Informal communication channels are never a bad thing to have.

The meeting started off with a safety briefing about the prior day's activities and feedback from the daily safety audits. The team spent almost half an hour going over its findings and what needed to be done about the more serious issues. It was obvious that these guys were fanatical about safety, which was great because that type of culture takes a long time and a lot of passion and dedication to create.

The safety checklists were quite explicit and were adhered to without deviation, for the most part—the mine had a model for standardized work, and it enforced that model. Anyone caught in a safety violation risked immediate suspension from the site and eventual termination. Typically the violators were the outside contracting crews who were brought in for specialized work. While the members of the leadership team didn't seem to have a formal PDCA-style process for dealing with issues, it was obvious that they had been exposed to formal training on the topic at some point in the past.

Once the focus of the meeting left safety and went to yesterday's production performance data, however, things quickly went downhill. It was clear that very little had gone according to plan, and the conversations were a recapping of everything that had gone wrong and the short-term firefighting that had been done to recover. For example, during the meeting, one of the workers mentioned that a *boondie* (large rock) had been dropped into the primary crusher by one of the drivers, and that it took more than an hour to clear it out. It was a complete stoppage of flow for the entire site until the blockage was cleared. When asked why it took so long to deal with this particular problem, no one could provide a satisfactory answer. The crusher was down. It is now running. Case closed. There seemed no interest in true reflection on what could be learned from these problems or ways to improve the process to avoid similar problems in the future. In other words, it sounded to me like almost every other organization I have advised since I left Toyota.

As Kostas and I left the meeting, he introduced me to the various players and told me what their functions were. As we headed back to his vehicle, I asked him for a debriefing and translation of the morning meeting. He walked me through the meeting again, talked about the players in the room, and then asked me what I thought. I noted how focused the entire team seemed to be on safety and how that was a good start. Kostas heartily agreed, commenting that strong leadership involvement and commitment, along with accountability from the entire team, had shown excellent results, with this particular mine having one of the best safety records in the region. I reluctantly pointed out that once the team moved off of the topic of safety, however, it seemed to devolve into small fiefdoms, each trying to maximize its own efficiencies regardless of the impact on the overall mine's performance. Kostas's response was a candid, "Welcome to our world."

I also found out that a boondie was a "bloody great rock" roughly the size of the SUV we were driving, and that these were sometimes an issue if the ore field that was being blasted didn't fragment properly. The oversize rocks were loaded onto trucks unbeknownst to the dig-unit operator, and they would block the crusher opening and had to be broken up with an oversize jackhammer to get the crusher running again. All very exciting.

 ## *Sensei* Reflection

It's very important to start a lean engagement by grasping the situation. In Toyota jargon, this occurs before problem solving. With even the most basic training in the seven wastes, we can look around and see opportunities to dive in and fix processes. Resist this temptation. Grasping the situation is about taking in data, unadulterated and minimally analyzed. By this point, I was beginning to understand the culture. From the example of safety, I could see that the team members had the capability of following disciplined processes, but they saw their world as an unpredictable, uncontrollable set of things that simply happened. Their job was to cleverly and adeptly respond. This is what we call firefighting. I could also see the vague outlines of flow—what should be happening in an ideal state. The team members were correct that when extracting iron ore from thousands of square kilometers of geography, there is a great deal of variability. For the operation to really flow, they needed a good plan that was updated at least every morning, and even modified as the day went on. They had spent their morning meeting reacting to known problems, and everyone had left with little shared semblance of a plan. Predictably, the team members would be spending the day fighting more fires and communicating in a reactive mode as needed.

Getting the Big Picture

After another short trip back to Kostas's office, he began explaining about both the company and the situation at the mines. The company itself was a very profitable natural resources company, with operations in industrial metals, precious metals, diamonds, uranium, coal, and just about anything else that could be dug out of the ground and sold. It had operations spanning the globe, on every inhabited continent. One of its sites had been originally mined back in the fifteenth century and had expanded throughout the centuries as technology made it feasible to dig deeper into the earth.

The global demand for the company's products was immense, as the Great Boom was well and truly underway around the world. China was consuming the entire output of the mine and had a multiyear exclusive contract with the company. At the particular mine I was assigned to support, the annual output was approximately 20 megatons of iron ore. To put this into context, one year's output of ore from this one mine would produce enough steel to build more than 200 copies of the Empire State Building. Wow! In the last year alone, the company had been able to successfully negotiate four price increases across the board, the smallest being in the low double digits. It was a good time to be in the natural resources business. The company also had expansion projects going on around the world in an attempt to try to catch up to the demand it was facing. The port operations were doubling their ship-loading facilities, the rail operations were adding capacity both to and from the mines, and the mines were acquiring new capital equipment as fast as it could be delivered. The challenge the company faced was that all expansion projects were 12- to 24-months long because of their sheer scope and scale. You don't lay down more than 200 miles of train track and signaling gear in a weekend.

Given the companywide expansion initiatives, there was also a laser-beam focus on delivering more and more tons every month. The market was there; all the company had to do was supply the product. There were quality requirements that basically specified what percentage of the pile of dirt shipped was actually iron ore and how much was pellets versus fines. This ratio had to be controlled or you risked gumming up the customer's smelting process. Even if the company had to offer a slight discount because contaminants were out of the specified tolerance (i.e., the product was of poor quality), it was quite happy to ship everything it could dig. This mantra of "get the tons" was new, but the company took to it like a duck to water. Frantic energy everywhere was focused on "moving the dirt." It was obvious from my experience in the mine's morning meeting that, except for safety, getting the ore on railcars was the main objective. The corporate measures seemed to be focused first on safety and then on volume. Everything else was low priority.

Starting by Understanding the Current State

Sitting in Kostas's office, we discussed how best we could start the process of transforming this particular mine into a showcase of lean, with efficient processes run by motivated, highly trained people churning out high-quality iron ore at low cost. Almost everyone in the company had a firm belief that he knew what was "wrong" in the operations and how best to fix it. The fixes might involve faster computers and newer software, Webcams and in-vehicle monitoring to ensure productivity, preventive maintenance software so that equipment did not continually break down, and even robo-devices that could be controlled from afar via satellite links and not require people on site. I had to confess to the team that I didn't know much about what it took to get iron ore from the ground and onto a train, so I suggested that we do a value stream map of the entire process.

Simply doing value stream mapping to get a picture was not the point. The objective was to get me and the rest of the team to start out together at the *gemba* with some good old-fashioned "go and see" to bring everyone up to speed on the *true* current state (hopefully dispelling some "common knowledge" along the way) and to give the entire team a better understanding of each of the processes, its functions and performance, and how they all interrelated with one another. The goal here was development of the implementation team itself so that it could gain a deep understanding of the processes and tools and make the transition from passive participants to the leaders of future improvements. Thus, it was important that the team members do the actual work of collecting data, developing the maps, and signing up for the action plans. My role as *sensei* was to facilitate this but as much as possible stay in the background.

The team members and I spent the next two days out at the *gemba* going through all of the processes involved in getting iron ore from the ground and onto a train. A simplified re-creation of this map can be found in Figure 8.1. It was interesting that this particular map didn't have a true supplier, other than Mother Nature. As we traveled through the processes, we were all able to gather data, or in some cases simply note the absence of *any* information whatsoever, and gain a deeper understanding of how the mine truly worked—even those among us who had worked in mines for their entire career. We were also able to arrange for the shadowing of mine personnel and ride-alongs in some of the mobile equipment.

We spent quite a bit of time initially with the various departments and groups to create the current state and got quite a download about the real, and some imagined, "problems" that kept each department from being more "efficient." We also had to dispel the myth among the mine's personnel that "lean" was simply an acronym for "Less Employees Are Needed," for the workers had recently gone through a headquarters-mandated downsizing, and emotions ran high over friends and jobs lost. Each of the major functional areas is described here, along with what we found regarding their performance, challenges, and opportunities.

Drill and Blast

Drill and Blast is really the start of the mining process. Decades ago, some geologists from Sydney went on a "walkabout" in Western Australia and found some of the richest deposits of high-quality iron ore then known to exist in the world.

The mine's geologists will identify an area that is likely to have iron ore, and the drill teams will drill a hole in the ground 10 meters deep and take numerous core samplings during the drilling process to determine whether there is anything worth getting down there. These sample holes are spaced 100 meters apart, so the process provides more of a

Current State Map

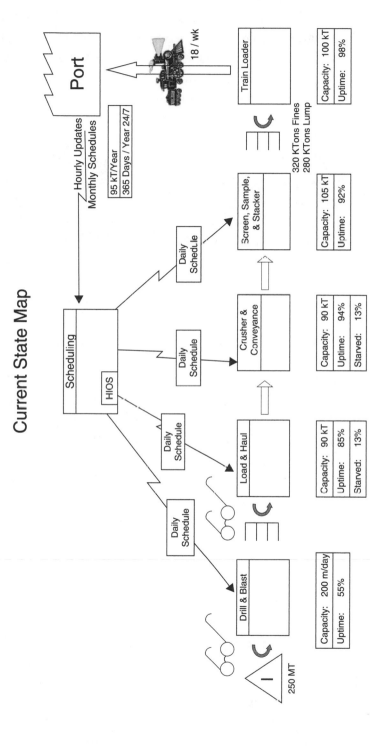

Figure 8.1. Simplified Current State Map of the Mining Process

general understanding of what's beneath their feet. If the drill-hole samples come back showing a high concentration of iron and acceptably low levels of contaminants (phosphorus, silica, and so on), the area will be added to the known reserves of the mine along with its expected properties. The lab will provide the results to the scheduling group.

The overall site plan encompassed almost a thousand square miles. Blast holes are drilled 10 meters apart (versus 100 meters for exploration) in a grid pattern over the whole site (multiple hectares), and samples are sent to the lab for analysis. The holes are filled with explosives and the site is detonated, an amazing sight. Once the site has been blasted, the survey crews will then stake out the entire area into "blocks" to be dug based on the blast-hole sample assays. Some of the marked blocks can be dug as a salable product, some can be used as blending (higher contaminants) material, and some are waste (low iron, high contaminants). A typical block diagram is shown in Figure 8.2.

As we continued to talk with the Drill and Blast teams to find out as much about their processes as we could, we discovered that the mine currently had very few "broken stocks," or material that was ready to be dug and processed. This seemed odd, as it would be very hard to allocate Load and Haul units to the right locations to keep the overall finished goods stockpile within its acceptable quality limits if there wasn't much material to choose from. We learned that this was, in fact, the current state. The stockpile had just spiked over the acceptable amount of phosphorus, and the schedulers were frantically trying to find a way to get back inside acceptable limits or risk another shutdown.

As we were driving back in from the field, we had to pull over and stop, as there was a blast scheduled that very minute. After the all-clear came over the radio, we continued our 13-mile drive back to the office area. Mines are large, did I mention that?

We rounded a bend and came face to face with a massive dig unit that was slowly climbing the roadway toward us with seven trucks in tow, like a mother goose with her chicks. The dig unit, we were told, was heading to the field that had just been blasted in an attempt to restore the finished goods stockpile to an acceptable quality level. When I commented that it seemed like a lot of work for a five-story

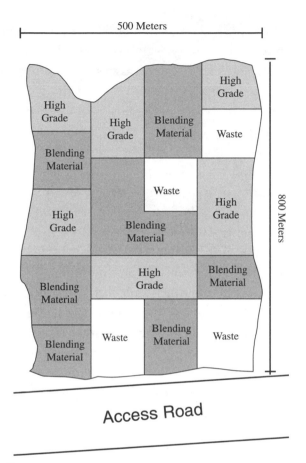

Figure 8.2. Typical Field Breakdown by Block

dig unit to slowly crawl its way around the site, I was told by Kostas that the float, a massive flatbed conveyance system that allowed the dig units to be moved from one dig site to another rapidly, had been down for a week. The Drill and Blast team had previously commented that it had had drills out of service for over a month and was currently operating only one drill when it was supposed to be using five. No wonder, then, that the broken stocks were so low.

Scheduling

Our team's stop in the Scheduling group for our first visit was reminiscent of what the planning room for the Allied invasion of Normandy looks like in old movies, though modernized with computers. There were maps pinned up on every wall, and X-Y plotters were spitting out the latest "intelligence" from the assays coming in from the field via the on-site lab. Computer monitors lined the walls, monitoring everything from the movement of trains to the progress of the lone drill that was toiling away somewhere out in the field. Front and center was the monitor showing the status of the stockpile that was currently being "built." The mine had provisions for four active stockpiles, each holding 300 kilotons of iron ore, or enough to supply the shipyards with steel plate to build a fleet of eight *Queen Mary 2*–sized vessels. The piles were roughly 100 feet wide by 1,000 feet long and were stacked more than 30 feet high.

One of the schedulers, John, was staring intently at the screen, as if through force of will alone he could bring the phosphorus levels back into the acceptable range in time to salvage the build. He quickly went to another monitor showing the current locations of the dig units and the areas they were digging. Normally the dig units would start at one end of the field and dig the field block by block until they reached the last block. Given the current quality crisis, however, the dig unit was "tunneling" through a field to get to a few particular blocks that had been shown through assay to have very low concentrations of phosphorus. Figure 8.3 shows what this process looks like.

When the unit hit a waste block, the material was tipped over the side of the nearest hill instead of in the designated area in order to save time. The Load and Haul teams needed to get the high-grade blocks on the stockpile quickly if they wanted to have a chance of getting the contaminants back into the acceptable range before the end of the build was reached. Think of this as balancing out the ingredients of a cake (the stockpile) so that each slice has an acceptable combination. So, the "quality" race was on. Could they get the "right" material on the build before the trains were scheduled to arrive to take it away? Could they get the levels of both iron and contaminants back into the acceptable range? If so, the problem was contained within the site, and only frazzled nerves and sleepless nights would be the fallout. If they missed, they would have to shut down the build until a countermeasure could be determined from the port. Though John showed little interest in us

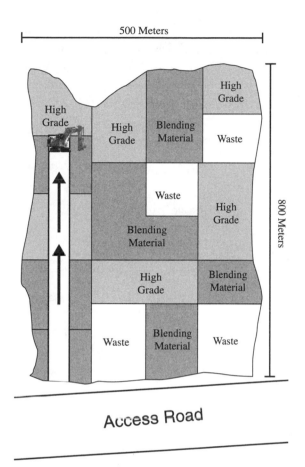

Figure 8.3. Tunneling to High-Grade Blocks

and our "study," we began to ask him questions to understand what was going on and, more important, why.

"Tell you what, mate," John began, "if you could just get the bloody dig units and the bloody trucks to follow the bloody schedule, then we wouldn't be in this bloody mess, would we?!?"

John's face grew increasingly red as he continued to heap scorn and derision on the field units' inability to simply do "what he asked." We asked him how he thought they got into this situation on this build, and we were informed that it went pretty much this way, more or less, for every build. At the beginning of the build, everything was great and all the team members were where they were supposed to be, doing what they were supposed to be doing. But as the build progressed, things got progressively worse. We were told that a build took approximately 10 days from start to finish. The mine worked 24 hours a day, 365 days a year, utilizing a rotating four-crew system, so information from all over the site was coming in nonstop. The schedulers themselves worked 12-hour shifts.

"Why do you think the dig units end up in the wrong spot?" I asked.

"Because it's easier for them to stay where they are and go for tons than it is to move the bloody dig unit and get the dirt they're supposed to," replied John.

"It's awfully tough to move the dig unit when the float's down, though, you have to admit," I challenged.

"The float's down again? Mother Mary, can't they keep that thing going for at least a week!? It's down more than it's up. We're going to be hand-marking blocks again in no time."

"You're going to be what?" I asked.

"Hand marking," said John. "It's when we go to the blocks and specifically mark the blocks that are meant to be tipped into the crusher. If you see us out there pointing out a certain block to a dig unit, you know we're in trouble."

The build had precise parameters baked into it for concentration of iron and maximum levels of contaminants in the ore. Any deviation from the acceptable ranges starts a chain reaction that has the schedulers eventually laying down the wooden stakes and marking tape themselves, on site, to ensure that the right block is dug and that the build is acceptable to the port. When the build is running well, the supervisors, dig-unit operators, and haul-truck drivers can dig a block completely before moving on to the next block.

We then asked if it was possible for the site to simply produce a product with a "standard" level of iron and contaminants. John's answer was, "Yes, in theory, because the blast-hole sampling should give the port enough data to develop a sort of 'mix' from each mine, at least for the next few weeks, depending on how much is drilled, assayed, and blasted. Mind you," he continued, "we can't sell anything straight from any one mine site; it all has to be blended at the port before final shipment. So even if four out of the five sites were kicking goals, all it would take to throw off the blend would be one site falling over. Then the rest of us would have to scramble to move dig units to new blocks and try to reblend our stockpiles to get the final blend at port back into the specs. Kind of like every day of my life."

With this, we thanked John for his valuable time and headed back to our offices to do a little reflection and regroup.

The Team Holds Its First Reflection

We sat in the small conference room near Kostas's office and began talking about what we had seen that day. As often happens, the team members skipped over understanding the problem or its cause and started firing off ideas about how they could start fixing things. The "fixes" ranged from disciplinary action against truck drivers and dig-unit operators to global positioning systems (GPS) units on each vehicle that would disable the vehicle if it strayed from its "approved and assigned" location. To the assembled team, it seemed as though the people were the problem that had to be engineered out of the equation, not part of the solution. I mentioned to the team that it seemed a bit premature to be vilifying such a large part of the organization without having even spent a day with them at the *gemba*. I also asked the team to have a bit more patience as we continued to "go and see" the rest of the operation so that we could better understand what the future state could look like. These suggestions were met with groans and eye-rolls, but we agreed to reconvene the next day to begin our ride-alongs with the truck drivers, the dig-unit operators, and their supervisors.

Load and Haul

Our morning started early on our first day with the Load and Haul gang: 5:30 a.m., to be precise. The mines operate around the clock, and this crew started at 6:00 a.m. and went until 6:00 p.m., when it would be relieved by another crew. Each crew did a three-day "day shift" rotation, then went to a three-day "night shift" rotation, and then had the next six days off. Using this rotation, each person worked a full 180 hours per month.

I was assigned to ride on an ore hauler with a young, energetic guy named Trevor. He was a recent graduate of one of the mining schools over in Queensland and was doing a developmental rotation at the mine to gain experience. He had been driving trucks for just over three months when I met him to ride along in the jump seat for a shift.

"Ready to go move some dirt?" he asked me.

I simply smiled and nodded as we began walking around the three-story monstrosity on wheels that could easily transport 220 tons of iron ore without breaking a sweat. We ran through a quality checklist before beginning; our first task was to do waste runs, as the assays had showed that the current block had little iron. We needed to dig three blocks of waste to get back to the next block of "high grade" that we could dump into the crusher and send via overland conveyor the 12 miles back to the processing plant. The waste we were hauling was slated to go into a new haul road that needed to be built to allow access to more broken stocks.

When the first load of rocks hit the truck, we rocked back and forth as more than 50 tons of material was unceremoniously dumped onto us. Once we were full, the dig unit sounded its horn twice to let us know that we were loaded and it was time to head for the dump location. The drive to the dump spot took just over 10 minutes, and Trevor called in to Control to ensure that the waste dump point hadn't been moved to a new location. Control confirmed the dump location and informed us that we would be getting retasked after lunch to a different dig unit working an area of high grade. Apparently one of its trucks had sliced a tire and had to be taken to maintenance for repair. Trevor told me that because of the massive expansion globally, there was a worldwide shortage of tires that fit our ore hauler. Apparently the manufacturer makes tires of our size (12 feet tall) on a prototyping fixture and by hand. Each mine was getting one or two tires a month and had to take extraordinary measures to try to get them to last, as an idled truck waiting for parts wasn't generating any tons.

"This is a pretty short waste run, if you're keeping track," Trevor said. "It's all pretty smick until we get behind on the tons, then we get retasked to shorter runs."

"Doesn't that mess up the planning for the rest of the build?" I asked.

"Sure does. We're supposed to be dumping waste so that the road graders and dozers can turn it into an access road so that we can access more broken stocks. If we do short runs and tip [the dirt] over the nearest ridge, the roads don't get built and we can't get at the dirt. It's all well and good for today's numbers, but we're in trouble for the next few shifts," Trevor explained.

We continued to travel the haul roads, occasionally "parking up" to let a road grader go by, for the rest of the morning. Sometimes we were the second or third truck in line, and on some runs the dig unit was waiting for us. When it came time for lunch break, Trevor called into Control to see where we should park and eat our lunches. We were informed that we should head back to the main pit as soon as we were able and check back in once we were on site. Trevor double-checked our instructions and, when they were confirmed, slammed the microphone back into the holder. He told me that the reason he was so upset was that, while the main pit had the best iron ore for nearly 100 kilometers, if they were digging from it, they were tapping into their limited supply of what would be a "sure thing" and failing to further develop the Western Ranges.

At the end of his shift, we returned to the parking pad and joined the rest of the fleet. "Thanks for the ride and the information. This was really valuable for me and the rest of the team," I said to Trevor as we walked out into the parking lot.

"Anytime. Just see what you can do to convince the bosses we should stick to the plan instead of always jumping around. It kills our numbers, even though the heavy breathers think they're doing the right thing. I'd have a few suggestions to make if I were running this site, let me tell you," Trevor offered.

Kostas picked me up in his big white and orange Toyota Prado sport utility vehicle (Toyota's were the only ones they found that would stand up to the harsh conditions). On the drive back to the offices, we exchanged stories and found a recurring theme—namely, that the dig units liked to stay in the same area for as long as possible and dig as much as possible before moving, and the trucks tended to like shorter runs to keep the dig unit busy. This was an obvious outcome from the new mantra to "move the dirt" that seemed to drive the decision-making process at the site. This was going to be a formidable challenge to address, as everyone was keen to hit the metrics and truly believed that he was doing the right thing. At least we were able to dispel the myth that the dig-unit operators, haul-truck drivers, and supervisors paid absolutely no attention to anything, but simply headed off into the wilds to do whatever they pleased. This, in fact, happened only when the build plan conflicted with the concept of maximizing tons.

Into the Crushers

As we began the next day in the administrative offices, the team members were restless to begin acting on the issues that they had found out in the field. The conference room was alive with bold assertions, unsubstantiated claims, and a general discontent with what we had been finding at the *gemba*. By now Kostas was willing to give me the benefit of the doubt and did his best to calm the team and advocate patience until we could truly understand the process from end to end. While the team members weren't very happy about waiting, they understood that it would be a bit hypocritical to ignore the very ideas, processes, and methodology that we were at some point going to be teaching to others. They also admitted that they were learning a lot more about each of the processes when we started our go-and-see exercises at the *gemba*. So, we reviewed our assignments, broke into two teams, and hit the site determined to understand what life was like at the crushers.

On a good day, the Western Ranges crusher could process more than 2,000 tons of iron ore per hour, crushing it into smaller pieces, which were then unloaded onto the seemingly endless overland conveyor system. The unit wasn't always running, as at times the dig unit was working on blocks of waste or blending material. The structure itself was built into a steep hillside, with the dump pocket at the top and the final crushed product exiting the structure seven stories below and close to 100 yards down the slope. There a short, half-mile conveyor would take the crushed ore out to the main overland conveyor, which stretched the entire length of the site, some 30 miles end to end, back to the main processing plant for sifting, sorting, and stacking.

We parked Kostas's Prado over by the office/break area and headed up the stairs to the small, dust-covered office fixed atop the crusher, right at the dump pocket. Here we met the operator, Dragan, who was able to give us a live demonstration of how any blockages that stopped the crusher were dealt with.

This prompted us to ask him about the *boondie* discussed at yesterday morning's meeting that had brought the crusher to a stop the previous evening. Dragan explained to us why it took so long to get things going again. "I was four levels down the crusher cleaning off a landing when the last truck tipped in. It was heading for waste runs, so I headed down here to get a jump on the cleaning. There must've been shin-high piles of dirt down on level three, and it took me forever to hose it off. They must've skipped the waste runs and been going after more high grade somewhere else, because the trucks were back before they were supposed to be and started queuing up because the red light was on at the dump pocket. When I got back up topside and saw the *boondie*, I tried to fire up the rock breaker, but she was broken. Every time the arm moved, it would fault out. Turned out we were low on hydraulic fluid, and it took us a bit to find the drums and get more into the reservoir. Then we were back in business." He went on to detail for us how the dust and dirt that go hand in hand with a mining operation make it impossible to see through the sight glasses to determine the fluid levels, while the dust and debris from the crusher get hosed off and fall down to the concrete pad below.

Control Room

The control room is where the entire site is monitored, with banks of computer displays showing the current status of the train load-out, stockpile status, stacking equipment status, conveyors, screen house, and the location of each truck and dig unit. The displays even showed where the actual haul roads were, thanks to the miracle of GPS. Control could monitor when a truck might not be able to see another vehicle coming up to an intersection and intervene to direct traffic or monitor if the trucks were ahead of or behind the dig unit.

The entire team had reconvened in the control room, and we crowded around as the controllers showed us how each of the systems worked. We could monitor, in real time, the speeds of all of the overland conveyors, the mechanisms inside the screen house, the conveyance systems to the stockpile stacking gantries, the massive "reclaimers" that took the ore from the stockpile and sent it along more conveyors to the train load-out, and finally the status of the equipment loading the seemingly endless string of ore-hauling cars pulled by two and pushed by four locomotives for the long run to the port. Each train was made up of about 220 wagons, good to haul about 25 kilotons—around ⅙ of the total build. Ideally, the contents of each build would be completely hauled out before a new build began, but more often than not the unpredictability of the port would result in parts of individual stockpiles being left behind. During this particular visit, we also observed further confusion and disagreement over the location of the dig units.

The Final Recap of the *Gemba* Visit

The next morning, the team reconvened in the office area and began constructing the current state map shown in simplified form earlier in Figure 8.1. The data were checked and rechecked to ensure that they were accurate, as we had a report-out scheduled with the leadership team that afternoon. Most members of the leadership team had been involved during the initial go-and-see phase as the teams visited them and were taken through the operations. There was some concern among the group that the map, which was now up on the wall on butcher's paper and stretched almost 10 feet, wasn't "tidy" and looked "sloppy." Some of the team members offered to redraw the map on the computer and get the scheduling department to plot it out for us on its massive plotters. I reassured the team that no extra points were given for computer-generated value stream maps and that the content, not the beauty, was the power of the map. We had undertaken the map to gain a deep understanding of the site and how all the pieces interrelated so that we could confidently create a future state and begin the hard work of making it a reality.

I also reminded the group that, so far, we had talked only about the processes and not about the people. I explained that it doesn't matter how wonderful a process is; if we don't have a high skill level in the workforce, we will eventually backslide to our current conditions. Given the looks I was receiving from some of the team, it was obvious that they would rather focus on the process, which wouldn't argue with them, than on the people, who definitely would if you tried to ram a change down their throats. We hadn't even begun to create development plans for the team, let alone the site, and we would be discussing this as well during the report-out to the site leadership. There were already training plans and budgets in place for the year, and we needed to be sure that this wasn't the standard "training for training's sake" approach that seems to permeate many businesses.

On to a Future State Vision and an Action Plan

After lunch, the entire site management team came down to the office conference room to begin a working session to review the team's work and to discuss how best to begin the transformation efforts. The team went over the current state map and discussed each of its findings in detail. Some of the metrics were challenged, but the team was able to support each piece of data to the satisfaction of the leadership team. It was clear that the leadership team hadn't spent a lot of time understanding the total system; instead, they were experts on their individual parts.

The conversation eventually swung back around to the pressures from headquarters to "deliver the tons," highlighted by conflicting approaches to how to deal with it. On one side, there was the call for greater output regardless of quality, noting that too often too much of what went wrong was out of everyone's control. What seemed to be behind this approach was the expressed fear that, as a group, they were "seen as being slow to respond to the market." The goal, as expressed by Mark, was simple: "We need to catch up, and the sooner the better."

On the other side of the debate was the response that a lack of quality had delayed things at the port, prompting a realization from Chloe that, as a group, they needed to "focus on getting the right tons, and not just any tons." Beyond that, Chloe also stated that, as a whole, the unit was not doing enough to address the problems at hand. "We fight fires with every build, and we don't seem to ever get out in front of it," she said. Eventually the conversation turned back to me, and the question of "what tools in the lean toolbox would help the most."

I quickly tried to draw their attention from the tools to the bigger picture: "Oh, there are lots of tools that would help in lots of places here, but I want to talk more about the operation in general. We all seem to be in violent agreement that we want to put in place systems that will highlight problems. Once we highlight the problems, we can then go to work on them, not with a work-around, but with a counter-measure. Remember, this is a specific action targeted at *that* specific problem. As we continue to identify and solve problems, we're on a continuous improvement path—continuously improving our processes and our people. I think this operation needs to focus initially on getting its processes stable."

I told the assembled group that our next step was to define our future state vision for the site. The assembled team then spent the next few hours doing just that, all the while arguing over every small detail imaginable. The arguments were good, as ideas were offered, challenged, modified, and finally accepted as feasible.

As open-cut ore mining is essentially a buffered flow operation to begin with, the future state map didn't look terribly different from the current state. In fact, the lead time from Drill and Blast to shipment to the port was longer in the future state, because the team wanted more broken stocks prior to Load and Haul. The team targeted six weeks initially as a good amount of accessible broken stocks to enable the operation to react to changes in the schedule caused by sampling error, internal issues, and changes from the port.

The team also wanted to focus on what could be done in the next few months so that it could keep its focus sharp. All of the various departments and functions had contributed to the creation of the future state map. The basic process steps had not changed. The biggest differences were in the *kaizen* bursts that littered the future state—that is, cloudburst icons that show specific focused improvements needed to achieve the future state.

"OK, so where do we start on the action plan?" asked Chloe.

"With respect to this team, I want to start with the morning meeting," I said.

"The morning meeting's going along just *fine* as it is, thank you very much. Why don't you guys do some 5S in the maintenance shops or something?" Mark asked.

"I think that we have some opportunities in the morning meeting to help the leadership team understand what's happening in the field and focus your scarce resources on issues that will give us some good gains in a number of these *kaizen* bursts," I answered.

The team wasn't totally convinced that any improvement was possible by changing around a daily meeting, but Kostas and I took the assignment to begin crafting the new morning meeting. At this point in the maturation of the team I felt I needed to be more directive to get them started on a track to some quick wins.

"We also need to work with the teams on daily management boards up at the crushers, including some basic problem solving, process confirmation by leadership, and a 5S pilot up at the Western Ranges, and we'll need to develop our overall communication and training plans for the teams. That will stretch us pretty hard, but I'm sure we can do it," I said.

"You're going to 5S the offices up at the Western Ranges, then? Good. We need to roll out 5S in all our offices like everybody else is doing," said Mark.

"No, I'd rather focus initially on the equipment, but if we can, we'll take a look at the offices as well," I replied.

"You have noticed that we're in the middle of a rather sandy area with gusty high winds on a daily basis, haven't you?" asked Mark.

"Yes, I've noticed," I replied.

"Good luck with keeping a crusher spic and span, then, mate; you're going to need it," Mark offered.

Kostas, the rest of our team, and I spent the balance of the afternoon discussing how we were going to support the various *kaizen* burst champions with things like the morning meeting, the 5S initiative, and the overall communication and development plans for the site. We agreed that we needed to communicate clearly with each of the four shifts about what was happening and what it would mean to them and their jobs. One of the managers would be present both to lend credibility to the team and to answer other questions that the team members might not be able to.

This was also our first opportunity to begin developing our internal team, as the initial assumption by the team had been that I was going to be rolling out all of the communication plans between the shifts and doing all the training and thinking. I explained one of the principles in the Toyota Way of "learn–try–reflect" and how we could use that to begin developing the team. I explained that I would lead a communication or training session or two and be supported by one of the deployment team members. After the session, we would discuss the material, and I would answer any questions the deployment team member had until I was confident that she could lead a communication session. She would then lead a communication session, and I would support her. After one or two communication sessions, if it was apparent that the team member had a deep understanding of the material and was communicating the concepts effectively (versus reading from slides), we would "qualify" her to be able to run this particular communication/training on her own.

To track who got qualified and in what, we developed a versatility matrix for each of the team members, as shown in Figure 8.4. Given that all team members had to, at a minimum, attend a training session, support a training session, lead a training session, and finally lead

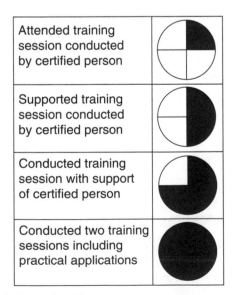

Figure 8.4. Sample Versatility Matrix

the exercise at the *gemba* at least twice, there was considerable pushback against the time it would take them to gain their "certification." Why couldn't they, for instance, just observe a training session, then lead one and be certified? Some of the material was pretty basic, after all. They asked how hard could it be to lead a discussion around why the site was undertaking this lean transformation initiative? Since the old proverb goes something like "A trial is worth a thousand opinions," I invited them all to attend the first communication session with the site teams, and we would conduct a reflection activity after the session.

 ## *Sensei* Reflection

When you've completed the initial go-and-see activities and planning for a project, it's important to get whatever implementation team you're working with deeply familiar with the material and comfortable in the role of teacher. Too often, team members are willing to act only in the "support" role and aren't comfortable standing at the front of the room leading the effort. It's the *sensei's* job to give them the experience and confidence to eventually lead the efforts.

It's very apparent when someone is simply parroting from a slide deck rather than actually teaching a group. Presentations tend to be generic, but questions and concerns tend to be very specific. You have to be comfortable with taking the general principle or philosophy and applying it directly to a problem. If you don't, you'll lose the confidence of the people you're working with in a real hurry.

In this specific case, I threw a broad net, capturing both the front-line operators and the leadership team. This was because if we didn't align the leadership team with the efforts in the field, the probability was high that entropy would creep in when our focus shifted. The teams needed experience conducting workshops at the working level, and the leadership team needed to

(Continued)

think and act more systemically. Even though we emphasize letting the teams struggle, at times early on I find I need to be relatively directive. I laid out the plan fairly concretely, as I wasn't confident that we would have arrived at it through general discussion, since we were just getting started, but later I would allow the team members to struggle more in developing the plan.

Communicating across the Site

The first communication session was with a team of dig-unit operators and haul-truck drivers from the Western Ranges and their supervisors. They were a rowdy bunch and had quite a few questions regarding the entire deployment plan. The questions ranged from impacts on job security to the entire rationale for undertaking a lean initiative at a mine. While the group certainly seemed a bit rough around the edges, the questions were quite thoughtful at times and usually stemmed from a lack of understanding of what we were trying to accomplish and, more important, an undercurrent of generally poor communication throughout the site. The members of the deployment team jumped in where they could to offer insights and information when they had a clear answer. The 15-minute "overview" presentation stretched to more than 30 minutes by the time the group members had gotten enough information to satisfy them. After the group left, we gathered around one of the larger tables and talked about how the first session went.

"So, anybody want to be certified right now to lead the next one?" I asked.

A chorus of "no way" and "not me" ensued.

By exercising a little "go and see" the team was able to gain a better understanding of what was involved in developing enough knowledge and experience to credibly deliver something as benign as an introductory presentation. It was obviously much more than just what to say. The biggest risk with sending someone to deliver a message that he is not capable of delivering is that the credibility of the team and the entire initiative is at risk. Like it or not, perception is reality, and we have to deal with that all the time and in every circumstance. The team better understood that if we were going to jointly develop people and processes, it was going to take time.

It took 12 days to reach all four of the operating shifts, and, given vacations and the availability of some key personnel, it took a second 12-day cycle before we had been able to communicate the initiative to all of the people at the site. During this time, we were busy reengineering the morning meeting and attacking the operations out at the Western Ranges.

Planning for the Morning Meeting

Make no mistake, it's difficult to try to change long-entrenched behaviors, so when you finally have a chance to do so, you need to take every opportunity to make it stick. Missteps and mistakes will be amplified and will make it harder to proceed. With that in mind, I sat down with the deployment team to discuss our plan of attack with the site managers and the morning meeting.

The debate raged around how the team was going to convince the managers not to focus on the daily tonnage numbers (the output) but to pay attention to other items that involved the process itself. After about 10 heated minutes of a team member writing on the whiteboard, wiping it off, handing the dry-erase pen to another team member, and repeating the process, Kostas looked at me with an arched eyebrow, as if to ask, "Are you going to contribute something here, mate?" so I asked the team if we could do a little exercise to see if we could make some headway before the next morning meeting.

"What is the problem here that we're trying to develop a countermeasure for?" I asked.

"The problem is that we're focusing only on delivering tons to the customer."

"Why is that a problem? Isn't that how we all get paid?" I asked.

"OK, yes, delivering tons to the customer *is* how we get paid, but it's the way we go about it that gets us in trouble," Kostas offered.

"Go on," I prodded.

"You know as well as I do that the only thing, after safety, that gets anybody's attention is how many tons we moved yesterday. I doubt if anybody could tell you how many drills we've got up at the moment, and very few could tell you what we've got in broken stocks. The information is there, but it's not being used. Maintenance gets a hiding if its overall utilization numbers for the equipment drop, so it keeps as many pieces of gear up and running as possible, regardless of whether it actually helps the build or not," Kostas said.

"How do you mean?" I asked.

"If you're a maintenance scheduler and you've got to decide whether to have your guys work on dig units, trucks, road graders, water trucks, drills, or anything else, what do you think you're going to focus on? Dig units and haul trucks. You already know that the drills are low priority. If we have dig units and trucks running around and no equipment, or not enough equipment, to keep the roads maintained, then we risk damaging tires or stopping the flow of dirt until a road can be fixed up. All I'm saying is that the measures in place are too generic to be useful or even have a good conversation around. Maintenance can have an overall utilization of over 90 percent, meeting our corporate target, but every dig unit could theoretically be down. This doesn't happen with dig units, but you get my point," said Kostas.

"Yes, I do. It sounds as if we've got interconnected systems here that currently seem capable of sending up only a single piece of information: tons. But I also remember that Chloe also used the phrase 'the right tons' when she and Mark were debating the issue. We need to use that," I said.

"That's exactly right. If we don't focus on more than just what happened last night and how and why it happened, then we're never going to do anything more than firefight," Kostas replied.

This exchange got the team more focused on understanding the mine as a highly integrated system and identifying areas where it was important to be able to highlight abnormalities. Currently, the site was focused only on the very end of the process: the stockpile build's quantity and quality. It wasn't important at present *how* that outcome was achieved, only that it *was* achieved. It was our challenge to put in place ways to monitor the entire system and then be able to develop countermeasures when problems occurred up and down the entire extended value stream. Problems that occurred months ago could, and did, have a negative impact on what we were trying to accomplish today, and what we do today will affect outcomes that are months away.

"So why don't we start with broken stocks?" a team member offered.

"I agree that's important, but in order to get broken stocks, we need the drills working out in the fields," Kostas countered.

Everyone agreed that drilling and blasting started the value stream and were major contributors to instability, so we should focus on these processes first. We also agreed that it was important to identify some process metrics so that we could understand the current state and develop specific targets for improvement. A basic measure of "availability" was considered for a while, but was then abandoned as being a bit too generic. There were five drill rigs on the site, and each was a different make and model, with different performance characteristics. Apparently, when they were purchased, over time, the corporate procurement department had gone for the lowest-cost units that were then available on the market. Two of the drill rigs were newer and had a much higher capacity than the other three, so a basic availability metric could be misleading, since if the two newer units were out of commission, the older units, while working, would not be drilling as much as was needed to guarantee a certain amount of broken stocks. After much discussion, the team finally settled on "meters drilled" for the prior day. Each blast hole was approximately 10 meters deep, so using "meters drilled" would filter out machine types. We could use each machine's capacity and availability numbers to arrive at a baseline "meters drilled" target number. Normally we would want to compare this to the customer demand rate for meters drilled, but the reality was that demand exceeded capacity anyway. I reassured the team that as time went by, we would all be revisiting these metrics to ensure that they maintained their relevance and were still effective at highlighting issues in the field.

The next measure we talked about was broken stocks, the amount of material that was available to be dug. The site was currently showing more than three weeks' worth of material ready to be dug.

"There's no way we've got three weeks' worth of broken stocks if the dig unit is crawling itself into a freshly blasted field. Absolutely no way," a team member said.

"Sure there is," Kostas countered. "A field can be blasted and counted as 'broken stocks,' but that doesn't mean that the trucks and dig units can get to it. The drills are pretty mobile compared to the dig units and trucks, and they're not confined to the haul roads. I'll bet that if we looked at the site plan, we'd find that there actually *are* three weeks' worth of blasted material, but we can probably get to only a small portion of that because we haven't pushed any of the roads into them yet."

"So when we take shorter runs and tip waste over the sides of hills instead of driving the extra 10 minutes to get to where the roads are being built, we hurt ourselves, eh?" I asked.

"Exactly. Having broken stocks doesn't do us any good unless we can get to them. I'd propose that we change the metric from broken stocks to *accessible* broken stocks," Kostas said.

"Who puts together the broken stocks report?" I asked.

"Scheduling puts together the reports. But I know John would be keen to change it. He's all over those roads every day anyway doing his site surveys, so he'd be able to tell straightaway which blocks are accessible and which aren't," Kostas said.

And so it went through the rest of the value stream; we would look at the process and, if possible, identify the one key metric that would help us highlight any problems in that area. Given the extensive use of computer monitoring of processes and geological databases of the site, it was relatively simple to set up the leadership's "dashboard" for the site. The final metrics we settled on for launch were:

I. Meters drilled
II. Accessible broken stocks
III. Load and haul (tons)
    A. High grade (actual vs. schedule)
    B. Low grade (actual vs. schedule)
    C. Waste (actual vs. schedule)
IV. Crushers
    A. Uptime (by individual location)
    B. Tons processed (actual vs. schedule)
V. Fixed plant
    A. Uptime
    B. Tons processed (actual vs. schedule)
VI. Maintenance
    A. Availability by asset class (drills, dig units, trucks, and so on)

With this simple breakdown, each manager's metrics were tied back into the entire production system. It was our intent to design alignment with the goals of the site into the morning meeting process. The metrics would help people to acknowledge the existence of, and start talking about, *problems*.

We took a few more days to plan how we would use the metrics and how the meeting would run. Initially, the deployment team wanted to use the miracle of IT to create an automatically updated A3-style report that would, every morning, go out and "fetch" the data from each of the respective databases so that at the touch of a button, voila! instant report. It took more discussion around the topic of "go and see" to convince the team that there was more merit initially in having each of the managers bring in his own data and update the metrics by hand. The team agreed to try this method and created a 48- × 96-inch board for the purpose of displaying the site metrics on the wall of the large conference room for all to see. Each function in the mine had its distinct section of the wall to keep up to date.

 ## *Sensei* Reflection

One thing I've found over the years is that conversations among team members usually need to run their course. Everyone has her own experiences and brings them everywhere she goes. As part of the learning process, a lot of ground needs to be covered during these initial discussions to ensure that everyone understands the "what," the "how," and, most important, the "why" of what we're attempting. This doesn't mean that you spend endless hours in pointless debate trying to build consensus; rather, it means that you keep asking the team questions to ensure understanding. As far as the initial metrics for the morning meeting went, I wasn't too worried if they were modified even after all of our planning and consensus building. The PDCA process views all initial ideas as provisional until they are actually tested.

The First Morning Meeting

Fifteen minutes prior to the start of the morning meeting, Chloe and one of her superintendants, Ben, came in and began updating their metrics on the dry-erase board. The performance of each of the crushers was noted, giving the uptime of the systems and the tons processed versus the schedule. One of the crushers had processed more tons than scheduled, and Ben was happily marking the overage with a green marker when Chloe asked him whether processing more tons than scheduled was actually a good thing. Ben was taken aback by the question and responded that it was *absolutely* a good thing. Chloe pressed him further and asked where those tons might have come from. Was it possible that instead of digging the blocks in accordance with the schedule, including low-grade ore and waste, perhaps other blocks might have been dug instead? After a few seconds of thoughtful chin-scratching, Ben simply replied, "Most likely." It was gratifying to see that Chloe and her team understood that abnormalities caused by overproduction of the wrong stuff can be as wasteful as underproduction.

Maintenance came in next, led by the manager, Paul, and trailed by his supervisor of heavy mechanics, Allan. They were in an animated discussion about the merits of the new series of ore haulers versus the older models. Apparently the newer series of haulers required much more maintenance when they came in from the field and were giving the guys fits and starting to have a negative impact on the operating budget. After wishing us all a "G-Day," Paul proceeded to update each of the categories of asset class: dig units, trucks, ancillary equipment, and drills. As expected, the availability numbers were best for the dig units and worst for the drills. This was apparently normal, so no notice was taken.

Right behind Maintenance was John, the harried scheduler, and he updated the "meters drilled" and "accessible broken stocks" metrics with the red marker and a shake of his head. He stood in front of the board for a few minutes looking at all of the metrics and consulting some paperwork he had on his clipboard. He then gave us a hearty "G-Day" and a handshake and took his seat, obviously anxious to get started.

Last into the meeting was Mark, followed by Ryan, one of his supervisors. Mark took his seat while Ryan walked to the dry-erase board and wrote down yesterday's production data. John kept a close eye on Ryan as he filled out each of the boxes on the dry-erase board showing total tons dug of high grade, low grade, and waste. He double-checked each of the figures with a piece of paper he had on his clipboard and was apparently satisfied as he sat back in his seat.

Chloe kicked off the meeting by asking the Safety group to take the team through yesterday's events and review each of the managers' audit findings. It soon became apparent that it wasn't possible for everyone to see the board while they were ensconced in their padded chairs, so following Chloe and Mark's example, they all got up and gathered around the board. John spoke to the next metric, meters drilled, and reported that they had planned to drill 850 meters but had managed to drill only just over 200 meters for the day. Chloe asked John why the large discrepancy between plan and actual, and John informed the group that only one of the high-capacity drills was out working the fields. Paul double-checked his numbers and verified that the other four drill rigs were down for various reasons; two were wait-ing for replacement parts from the coast, and two were in the shop waiting for personnel to work on them. Mark asked Paul if he could cannibalize any parts for the two that were waiting and was told no; all of the drill rigs were unique and shared no critical parts. Chloe pressed further and asked how long the units had been in the shop. Paul responded that it varied; the two big units waiting for parts had come into the shop in the last two weeks, and the smaller units had been there since just before the start of the month but weren't listed as a high priority. After a few minutes more discussion about the need to get the drill rigs prioritized, the team moved on to the next metric, accessible blasted stocks.

John reported to the group that using the new metric of accessible blasted stocks, the site was sitting on just over seven days' worth of material. This took the room by surprise, and Chloe asked him to verify the figures. John double-checked his figures and confirmed that the entire site had the equivalent of 14 shifts of work ahead of it, and then it would be idle.

"What have the bloody Drill and Blast boys been doing all month?" thundered Mark.

"Just throttle back a bit, Mark; we've got closer to six weeks' worth of broken stocks, but the metric we're using says *accessible* broken stocks. They're no good to us if we can't get to them," John replied.

"We've been tipping waste into the roads every shift; how come the roads aren't being built?" continued Mark.

"We've been tipping waste all right, but obviously it's not all going into the roads. Some of my site checks show that we're tipping in alternative locations, closer to the dig units," said John.

"Are you saying my boys have been tipping where they shouldn't be, then?" asked Mark.

"You know they have. We preach 'tons, tons, and tons' every day to every crew, and now we're surprised that's what they're doing?" asked John.

"All right, this is good stuff and really gets to the heart of at least some of our issues, but we need to keep moving here. Let's the three of us take the discussion around tons and roads offline, shall we?" said Chloe.

The team moved to the performance measures of the Load and Haul group. As expected, the total tons for the day achieved target. This normally would garner a "good job, boys" from Mark, but he was staring closely at the breakdown of the high-grade, blending, and waste numbers. It was obvious from the data that the previous shift had focused more on the high grade than on the other categories. The numbers for waste weren't awful, but after the discussion about *where* the material was actually going, the team wondered aloud whether the tons moved actually got dumped in the right spots to make roads.

The leadership team spent the rest of the meeting finishing a review of the fixed plant equipment and discussing the train schedule when Chloe asked the room how they thought the meeting had gone. The first response was "long." True, the normally 60-minute meeting had lasted just over two hours, but Chloe and Mark agreed that they had uncovered a fair number of issues that would need to be dealt with by the members of the management team going forward if they hoped to meet their yearly goals. As the team got more comfortable with this new system, the meetings would return to their normal durations,

I assured them. They all agreed that this would not be an opportunity to point fingers and cast blame, but rather a chance to find and fix problems. As the meeting finally ended, each of the managers swung by our assembled team and asked us to stop by their offices when we could. Apparently the new morning meeting had opened some eyes as to the true health of the organization. Mark and Chloe were the last to leave and asked us to stop by Mark's office for a debriefing of the morning's events.

They appraised the meeting as a success—albeit an eye-opening one—before moving on to addressing what would be our next step. "We're going to have to start capturing these problems," Chloe declared.

"Later this week, we're going to be bringing in problem/counter-measure strips that the guys came up with. They're about 2 inches high and 18 inches long. They slide into magnetic holders and will stick to the whiteboards so we can move them around from 'active' to 'monitor' to 'closed' status. They're not back from the printer in Perth just yet," Kostas said.

"Good; we'll tell whoever gets one to have it in the 'monitor' status by lunch, *or else*," Mark said with a devilish grin.

"Actually, that's probably not a real good idea," I said.

"Why not? We need to get moving on these issues, don't we?" Mark pressed.

"True, but do you think somebody can really identify an effective countermeasure to a problem that probably hasn't even been well defined yet? Let's be honest, what we think is a problem might be only a symptom of the true root cause. I don't want people thinking that they can pencil-whip a piece of paper and call it problem solving. This is one area where we need to be very supportive of the team," I said. "And patient."

"Fine; let's just get started and see where it takes us. Right, Jimbo?" asked Mark with a smile and a wink.

Daily Production Boards

With the challenges of the morning meeting firmly in hand, the team turned its attention to the task of implementing daily production boards out at the major sites. An area was found to install a whiteboard on which the critical data could be captured. Along with the key performance indicators (KPIs) of safety, uptime, and high-grade/low-grade/waste numbers, there was a designated space to capture issues in real time as they happened. As we took each of the supervisors through the boards and explained each section to them, we encouraged them to highlight the issues on a daily basis, as they happened. Up until now, a weekly summary report was written on the computer, e-mailed site-wide, and usually archived after it was distributed. Anything that was highlighted was soon relegated to the historical record of the site and wasn't acted on. Major issues were worked on, but usually because they created a huge amount of immediate pain in the organization. This inability to highlight issues, prioritize them, and then go to work on them was limiting the effectiveness of the individual groups and the site in general.

The deployment teams got serious pushback from the operational teams when it came to capturing issues that happened during each shift. They were worried that if they said that something was wrong, they'd get beaten up for it. Or they might look incompetent. Also, they argued, what was the point of writing something on a whiteboard if nobody was going to do anything about it? This highlighted to the deployment team that we had a lot of work to do to build a true problem-solving culture here, and that it had to start with trust. In the beginning, we could only reassure the teams that highlighting issues was important and that we were putting systems in place to capture these issues, prioritize them, and get them resolved. Again we were met with more than a little skepticism. It would be up to us and the leadership team to show that this was more than window dressing to impress people down in headquarters.

5S at the Western Ranges Crusher

The deployment team's next action was to take a look at what was happening on the jaw crusher that was requiring the operators to spend so much time keeping the area clean. The seven-story piece of equipment had multiple staircases and landings that needed to be hosed off at regular intervals to ensure that the machinery would continue to function properly and that they were safe to use. This was done by means of garden hoses located at each of the landings. The operator would start at the top and work down the landings until he either got to the bottom or ran out of time and had to return to the control room. When the team arrived at the crusher, it was just after lunch break, and we made our way to the top. Each of the team members took turns hosing off the guardrails, machine covers, grates, structure, and other areas. The team found that for the most part, the "dirt" was the fine dust that continually blew across the Pilbara and wasn't that difficult to remove. We could completely wash down a landing in just a few minutes and inspect any parts of the equipment that needed it. There were some smaller piles of dirt that were actually smaller pieces of ore that had fallen out of the crusher at the various connection points. These took a bit longer to knock down to the ground. The team was also identifying anything on each deck that would be important to clean, such as sight glasses on reservoirs, oil levels, air pressures, and so on. If an operator couldn't do the entire cleaning circuit as a result of issues that arose during the shift, we wanted to give her a "critical-to-do" list to complete regardless of what might occur. We made our way down to the fourth level of the unit, the place where Dragan had spent too much time cleaning earlier, and found a massive amount of dirt and ore scattered around the place. The team immediately began getting to work clearing out the mess and trying to figure out where it was all coming from.

"Man, now I see why Dragan was down here so long. This is ridiculous," a team member commented.

"Yeah, I don't remember seeing it this bad down here before," added Kostas.

"So, what do we know, team?" I asked.

"We know that crushers are very dirty," offered one of our team.

"Yes, I can see that. Is this normal?" I continued.

"No, not really. The other levels are what I'd call 'normal,' with a coating of dust and a little bit of dirt that's fallen off the bottom of the conveyors," another responded.

"I can't get over the amount of fines that are lying on this level," Kostas said.

"Fines?" I asked.

"Yeah, fines are one of two ore types we sell. Lumps are the bigger rocks and fines are the smaller stuff," Kostas answered.

"There has to be a leak somewhere that we're missing," a team member offered. "Let's find it."

With that, the team began inspecting the awesome piece of machinery that was the jaw crusher. The deployment team member that was on loan from the fixed plant crew was very familiar with the crushers and identified the source of contamination. He called us all over/up to take a look. There was a small gap between the side walls of the conveyor down into the unit that sorted lumps from fines and the side walls of the screen structure, and ore was falling through the gap onto the structure, and eventually down onto the landings and below. Nothing appeared to be broken; it was simply designed with a gap.

"So, let me get this straight. We've got this small gap here that's raining ore onto the landing, and we lost more than an hour's production recently because we were down here cleaning it up instead of clearing blockages at the top," a team member said.

"Yep. And at just over a dollar a ton for this dirt, we essentially flushed $2,500 on that one incident alone. And who knows how many times we've had smaller stoppages," Kostas said.

"The boys up in the welding shop in the main maintenance area can get this fixed up pretty quick if we give them a call," another team member offered.

"Good idea. We'll also take this into tomorrow's morning meeting as an example of how to use the problem-solving part of the KPI board," Kostas added.

Coaching Problem Solving

We now had the second 48- × 96-inch board attached to the wall in the main conference room next to the original KPI board. We had the board divided into sections labeled "active," "monitor," and "closed." At the conclusion of the KPI review, the managers would lead a discussion of which problems needed to be prioritized and worked on first. Our biggest challenge was to slow the team down enough to truly define the problem.

At first, champions of the problem would simply fill in all the information on the problem definition, current condition, gap, root-cause identification, countermeasure selection, and implementation. We spent some time coaching the team that this wasn't something that got done in a day; it involved a fair amount of investigative work at the *gemba*. Initially we were met with eye-rolls and complaints of lack of time and resources, but eventually the team members discovered that if they truly put an effective countermeasure in place, the problem didn't recur. If they were solving high-priority problems in this manner, then gradually the operation was getting better and they had more control over their time and resources. At the start of the process, we encouraged the managers to take on the high-level issues first, and we would be there to coach and support them through the process. Later, as the problems and countermeasures strips filtered down through their subordinates, they would be in a better position to offer coaching and help their team members succeed and develop.

The specific problem concerning the excess ore falling out of the crusher up at the Western Ranges was championed by the supervisor of the fixed plant maintenance group. The welders went up to the crusher to review the situation and welded on an extension plate that would carry the ore further out onto the screening deck before dropping it. This countermeasure worked at eliminating the ore falling out of the crusher, but it was only a short-term countermeasure. After a week in service, the welds failed because of the extreme vibrations, and the extension piece fell onto the screen decking and shut down the crusher. The maintenance team then had to wait for a longer shutdown to do a more thorough structural refit of the equipment.

Process Confirmation

Our next challenge was to prevent backsliding on the work we were doing in the field. We knew that we needed a countermeasure against "industrial entropy." We also knew that we didn't have too big a window of opportunity out at the sites to breathe life into the daily management boards that the supervisors were now using. We worked with Mark and Chloe to set up a simple process confirmation board near their offices so that we could review what we were finding in the field on a daily basis. Each manager was out at the *gemba* every day anyway, so it wasn't too hard to launch the process. Each respective manager would pull his card(s) for the day and perform the tasks listed on the card. This could be a simple 5S review of a maintenance area, a review of a daily production board, or whatever process had been put in place to help improve the stability of the operation.

Once the team members in the field saw that their supervisors and managers were looking at the details of the operations and were actively addressing issues, there was an increased respect for what we were trying to accomplish. Not every problem could be addressed immediately because of budget and people constraints, but the effort that was being put forth both in the attempt to identify the root causes of long-standing issues and in trying out countermeasures to deal with them was definitely a morale booster out at the *gemba*.

 ## *Sensei* Reflection

Experience has shown that companies are weak on the "check" and "adjust" parts of the PDCA cycle. Current "realities" and daily pressures for performance tend to keep leadership teams from spending time observing the results of improvements and reflecting on how things could be done better next time. Process confirmation provides a method for engaging the leadership team at the *gemba* in reviewing the results that their current processes are delivering. It is far more powerful for a manager to observe something firsthand than to read it on a report or in an e-mail. In a quote attributed to Taiichi Ohno, he acknowledges the value of data but says that he "prefer[s] facts," which he defines as those things that he observes directly. Likewise, I have found that the simple act of taking a card out of a rack, performing the tasks listed on it, and observing abnormalities at the source has opened many a manager's eyes as to what is truly happening in her operations. This understanding can then be leveraged into PDCA thinking.

Early Deployment Challenges

This company, like most others, had many initiatives running concurrently that required scarce resources to launch and sustain. The divisional CEO was very supportive, but his subordinates lacked his passion for the concepts of lean and the Toyota Way. This initiative was seen as one among many and, as such, was competing for the same scarce resources as the others. The overall responsibility for the deployment was delegated to the process improvement group, which fostered an "it's their job" mentality among the operational people. This led to a lot of unproductive discussions surrounding the deployment efforts.

We also discovered early on that the alignment of the various groups was very poor and that some groups could, and did, succeed at the expense of others and of the company in general. If a manager did not have accountability for the work that was being done in his particular area, his support was lukewarm at best. Issues tended to be cherry-picked for their impact on the bottom line and the specific manager's results.

We also ran into quite a bit of organizational inertia when it came to change. Certain topics were considered off limits if it was perceived that they would cause any short-term pain in the department or organization. Many times, when root causes were uncovered, they were dismissed because they ran counter to tribal knowledge or "years of experience." The power of the status quo in an organization cannot be underestimated when you are in the middle of a lean transformation. People don't have to be actively campaigning against the improvements being made in the organization; they only need to quietly withhold their support and/or resources. We found ourselves spending a lot of time in conversations with individuals such as these trying to show, through logic, facts, and data, how this initiative was truly going to benefit the organization and their particular department and lobbying for the chance to run a pilot activity to demonstrate our position. Fear of change and the unknown can be a big demotivator for people, and we found that there is no shortcut in deployment; rather, the problems need to be explicitly named and dealt with one by one.

The entire organization had a bit of psychosis built into it, as it had expanded and contracted over the years to match the overall market demand. Just three years prior to the start of our transformation efforts, the company had undergone a head-count reduction under the banner of "lean." In truth, it was simply a mass involuntary separation, lacking any coherent framework or process. The company wasn't "going lean"; it was "going without." Given this, when the new initiative was announced, the people in the operations were justifiably concerned that this was a precursor to another downsizing, even though the company globally was on a massive expansion kick.

Lessons Learned at Start-Up

The initiatives got off to a strong start, with a focused deployment in one of the operations and good local support from both line and staff leadership. A true cross-functional team was created, and each of the departments made resources available to support the deployment. The value stream map provided an anchor point for all of the improvement work that was undertaken and allowed the management team to have a broader understanding of the entire site. This also helped the deployment team when it came to getting additional resources, albeit temporarily, whenever the need arose. Even though the map wasn't a typical batch-to-flow exercise, it allowed the team to prioritize the work based on the key leverage points for the site, ensuring that the leadership team would be in alignment with our efforts.

The visual management system set up in the main conference room also helped the leadership team constantly reinforce to its subordinates what the goals were and how the teams were progressing toward those goals. Gaps in performance were visible and were highlighted immediately so that they could be prioritized and worked on. There was a learning curve for the teams, and the metrics and ways in which information was displayed were refined over time.

Once the initial target areas were established and the teams went to work on the transformation, it was essential to keep the rest of the site engaged in the effort, even though we weren't directly affecting their areas. The deployment team would regularly update the site on the various teams' progress and shared the communication across all four of the operating shifts. As the efforts gained first traction and then momentum, it became less difficult to challenge the status quo and slaughter the sacred cows at the site.

The teams were able to register some early wins during the transformation, which gave credibility to the effort and allowed for gradual expansion beyond the initial application areas. By about six months into the effort, there were enough improvements that results could be seen. All the metrics were trending upward, and the mine achieved a record number of tons of iron ore. And much more of the right ore was being mined. Other mines were taking notice, and some of the lessons learned were being replicated by some of the sister sites.

Expanding the Efforts

After roughly six months of work at the site, the implementation team began to stabilize and standardize some of the communication and training on the various tools. It was able to take the generic material and improve it to help make it more relevant to open-cut ore mining. Each of the site deployment personnel had also been progressing through the versatility matrices and adding depth when the opportunities presented themselves. In the beginning, there was a fear that we would run out of things to do before all of the team members had a chance to make the transition from spectator to teacher in the various areas of deployment. This fear was unfounded, as there were more and more demands for their time than their schedules allowed.

For the overview training, a two-day offsite session was created that covered the basics of the lean transformation. A universal complaint was that the "simulations" that we used were too analogous to an automotive manufacturing system, and participants couldn't easily relate what they were learning to their jobs. So, the team and I created a custom-designed mining simulation, from Drill and Blast through to Train Load-Out, to show the various aspects of the mine and how the different applications of lean tools would look in that environment. The various team members were able to continue to refine the simulation based on their own backgrounds and expertise. As the deployment teams gained in experience and knowledge, we were able to step back into a coaching role and continue the development of the site personnel.

The emphasis remained on improving the processes through problem solving and expanding the capabilities of the people in the system.

PDCA as a Key Driver

The key leverage point for the transformation effort was the adoption of and adherence to PDCA thinking. While it was typical for the organization to resist this type of structure in the beginning, the leadership team was firm in its conviction that the process would be implemented as designed and that deviations and shortcuts would not be allowed. The use of the PDCA "strips" in the morning meeting to identify, prioritize, and assign the relevant issues served as a focal point, allowing the team members to understand the power and relevance of a structured problem-solving process. Their willingness to understand that problems are complex and can't be solved in a single day was a key enabler that let the various teams and people engage in true problem solving. Having metrics in place that would track the effectiveness of a particular countermeasure also allowed the leadership team to know when to move a problem from "monitor" to "closed." It became a source of recognition and pride for the various personnel to be able to move one of their countermeasure strips over into the "closed" column.

The biggest mindset change at the site concerning PDCA was understanding that the PDCA process included planning, checking, and adjusting, not simply doing. It is very easy for an organization to sit in a firefighting mode and celebrate and promote those who do whatever it takes to achieve a goal. In these situations, processes are scorned as "bureaucratic" and "too slow" to be useful, and shortcuts and work-arounds are seen as the only solution. Like any effort to change a corporate culture, instilling PDCA thinking is a huge challenge, and it takes commitment from everybody involved.

The End for Us

The end of our journey with this company came rather abruptly. Kostas and I had just finished an introductory training session at a sister mine site and were driving the hundred kilometers or so through the wilds of the Pilbara on the main road that connected the two sites and eventually terminated at the coast. We were discussing how the training had gone, as this was our first attempt at expanding our efforts beyond the initial pilot mine, when his mobile phone rang. He looked at the caller ID on the display and said, "It's headquarters. I wonder what they want."

I listened to the conversation from our end as Kostas talked with the bosses down at headquarters. The conversation went from a description of our results at the mine to our expansion to the closest sister site, with Kostas explaining the progress that the teams had made. He listened for a few moments, and his expression went from neutral to shocked.

After he ended the call, he shook his head, looked at me, and simply said that our contract was being terminated. The business process improvement director at headquarters was moving to sales and marketing and was being replaced by the manager of the rail offices. The rail manager had decided to replace us with another lean consulting firm that had worked with the aluminum division. This incoming manager was a strong supporter of the broad, shallow deployment model, with layered audits and complex scoring tools, and didn't agree, conceptually, with the pilot line approach. He was unhappy that we had not developed generic tools that could be deployed in a standardized way across the company. The other firm had all of this. The site successfully fought to keep us for the rest of the year, offering to pay us out of its budget, and we did our best to stabilize the processes that were in place and teach the team members all we could to keep the effort going. Ultimately we wound down our efforts, packed up our things, said our good-byes to the team, and returned home. The head of the mine and her husband, our best students at the mine and the only ones who went through all the training, did a great job at keeping lean moving for another two years. During that period, the mine enjoyed two record years of output and became a corporate benchmark in maintenance. Then the powerhouse couple was transferred to headquarters in business planning. Some of what we had started at the site stuck, but it was gradually weakening. Eventually this couple would get back out to a mine and have an opportunity to use what they had learned as they continued their own lean journeys.

Sensei Reflection

At the end of an engagement with a company, even one that ends as abruptly as this one did, it's always good to reflect on what you've learned throughout the process. While it would be easy to blame a company's leadership, that wouldn't be very instructive. In retrospect, the part of the business that we neglected was the headquarters building. We always preach about engaging the leadership in the effort to ensure alignment and support, but we were focused only on the pilot site's leadership. While it was very difficult to get anyone from headquarters to "go and see" what was happening, that is a poor excuse on our part. We needed to keep the headquarters leadership team engaged and using the same type of information centers that the sites were using with success, but we didn't. We neglected a key stakeholder in the transformation process, and it ended our efforts at the site. Lacking this support and understanding, we had built our castles on sand.

Chapter 9

Bringing Ford's Ideas Alive at Henry Ford Health System Labs through PDCA Leadership

(With Dr. Richard Zarbo)

Quality is doing it right when no one is looking.

—Henry Ford,
American industrialist and pioneer of
the assembly-line production method

Since lean became a broad movement, it seems that about every five years another industry pops up as the hot one. It started in automotive, then spread to other heavy manufacturing companies, then to small- to medium-sized manufacturing companies, then to the U.S. defense bases that repaired and overhauled weapon systems. By about 2005, it had spread very broadly to banking, call centers, government, mining, public utilities, warehousing, retail, and many others on a global scale. But the big prize for the lean movement was health care.

By some estimates, health care in the United States costs 16 percent of the gross national product annually. President Obama put through the most sweeping transformation of health-care insurance since social security, and central to the promise is reduced health-care costs. So it is quite natural that lean health care would catch fire as the new frontier to conquer. The question is what lean health care means and what success looks like. Is it a slash-and-burn cost-reduction program? Is it a clinical application of tools by experts, with shallow penetration and little ability to sustain it? Or is it the broad and deep growing of a continuous improvement culture that we have been advocating in this book? Certainly the concept of organic development should fit in health care, if it fits anyplace. Quality of health care and patient lead time must be critical concerns. In one part (pathology and lab medicine) of one major health system, the foundation is being established for a true plan–do–check–adjust (PDCA) culture. And it starts with leadership.

Dr. Richard Zarbo, chairman and senior vice president of pathology and laboratory medicine at the Henry Ford Health System, literally transformed his own leadership style on the road to becoming a lean leader of his organization. We'll follow his perspective as he details that journey for us.

The Motivation for Change Started with Quality

I run the laboratories of the Henry Ford Health System (HFHS), a $565 million–a–year business with 785 employees out of 23,000 in the Ford system. At this point in 2010, we are organized as a hub-and-spoke delivery model for laboratory services. As senior vice president, I am the single point of responsibility and accountability for all the laboratories in six acute-care hospitals and 30 additional medical clinics, some of them large 24/7 ambulatory clinics with freestanding emergency rooms, and some of them smaller clinics. Downtown Detroit is the core laboratory, the hub, and we send a lot of things from the spokes to the core for testing, with 44 courier runs a day. We perform about 6.5 of the 11 million overall tests per year in the hub, which means that there are many opportunities to fail, and a single failure can have catastrophic results for a patient.

What I am going to share with you is five years of our journey adapting manufacturing-based principles, tools, and culture to a health-care environment. We have emulated the successful Deming-based management principles as they evolved at Toyota Motor Corporation to develop an empowered workforce using defined work rules that drive standardization, a knowledge of in-process variation and waste, and a scientific basis for hundreds of annual process improvements. I often quote Henry Ford, not only because he founded us, but because all the lean principles can be found somewhere in his writings.

Our business case for change lies in Deming's Quality Chain Reaction. While quality seems like a worthy goal in itself, Deming showed that it was the path to much more. Internally, doing it right the first time increases productivity and decreases costs, which both lowers prices and feeds profits. Externally, quality increases customer satisfaction, which increases market share, again feeding back to increased profits. In my business, quality can be the difference between satisfied customers and controllable costs, on the one hand, and mis-takes that could ultimately drive us out of business, on the other. I became convinced that lean is a holistic path to high quality.

What gets me up in the morning to continue on this quest for excellence is a simple vision. It has been my goal in my lifetime to improve and control this behemoth of a laboratory so that it can serve hundreds of thousands of patients with excellence. Not much decision making gets done in medicine without a lab test, and our goals are first and foremost accurate and timely results, followed by cost effectiveness for the system. As Deming would say, my internal direct customers are the thousands of physicians who send me samples and specimens every day, and they are overworked and impatient, and have a huge impact on the health and safety of our real customers, the patients.

Life would be simpler if satisfying customers was my only assign-ment. Like everyone else, I have CFOs who tell me they want it cheaper, so I have to reduce my costs. They want more and immedi-ate productivity, so they take out full-time equivalents (FTEs) every year. I have promised my people that participating in improvement will not get them fired. So my challenge is to remove FTEs without laying anybody off. Of course everyone wants better quality, but unless I drive profit as well, then nobody gets a bonus, and then I have a lot of senior staff members who get upset with me. I have to play the same game as leaders of other businesses, only I have a different product. I have been a leader and involved with quality for more than 20 years, and I have always led from the top down. As leaders, that was all we knew. So this was an opportunity to do something different, to create an organization that is constantly learning and improving on its own, creating ownership for problem resolution and developing people. So as I'm writing this chapter, the folks back there at the laboratory continue to improve the shop every day. What can be better?

We Wanted It, but We Did Not Understand It

I started at Henry Ford Health System in Detroit as a surgical pathologist in 1987. By 1990, I was division head of surgical pathology, and in 1995 I was named vice chair of anatomic pathology. In 2001 I was made chair of pathology and senior vice president for the Henry Ford Health System laboratories. For most of my career, I was a top-down manager and fit most of Jeff Liker's descriptions in his books of the traditional manager. I was autocratic and dictated the improvements from my personal view. I checked and audited and set goals, and for the most part it worked reasonably well.

I may speak critically of our past before lean, but in reality we had a decent foundation for quality in the philosophy of W. Edwards Deming. In 1989–1990 I was trained in Deming. I got to hear him talk when he was an old guy. So we trained in PDCA, and supposedly we were all focused on PDCA. In fact, we called it Focus-PDCA. Unfortunately, we didn't have a clue about what we were doing. We had been given a book on Deming's principles, but basically all we had learned was how to run meetings more efficiently and use a few quality tools; we had no idea how to lead to become a Deming culture. Then the managed-care culture of the 1990s caused us to violate all the Deming principles in an effort to survive. The focus wasn't on quality, but on immediate low cost. We failed because we didn't change our culture, our internal politics, our alignment, none of that. We didn't do Total Quality Management (TQM) well. I don't know of anyone in health care who did TQM well back then, frankly. Our culture defeated us. I knew I had to change because we had an angry culture, with people blaming each other instead of solving problems. As Drucker said: "The only things that evolve by themselves in an organization are disorder, friction, and poor performance." And we had those in spades.

On any given day, I could walk through the labs and see highly skilled technicians conducting tests using state-of-the-art equipment and marvel at their level of skill and commitment. But during this walk, I would have to navigate around carts and containers piled everywhere with blood and tissue samples to be tested. Figure 9.1 is an example of the wasteful ugliness that surrounded us. Every one of the samples in these large coolers came from a patient who was waiting to know his fate and a doctor who was waiting to decide how to treat the patient. There was no real rhythm or flow to the process.

It was also difficult to know how well the process was running other than looking at some very general statistics in the computer that reflected what had happened over the last month or so. Our accreditation renewal requires a quality management plan and indicators of quality, and we had them, but in the past I felt we were largely giving

Large specimen deliveries translated into potential hours of "wait" time before they were "received"

Time Waste

Figure 9.1. Large Batches = Time Delay

lip service to it. Once a month I went through the reports on these quality measures, so I knew that some number of cases went wrong, but it was too late. I could yell and scream and put generic policies in place, but did we really understand the root cause? Now I want the indicators right away so that we can fix the defects that same day based on understanding the root cause of that specific problem. It took us five years of sometimes gut-wrenching change to get to that point. I had to fix the crushing weight of all the big problems to get to that level.

Basically, I had to do some soul searching and ask whether we were simply enamored by Deming's philosophy or really living it. What would it look like to really live the philosophy? Lean consultants that I encountered could not tell me that. They were too focused on tools, projects, and return on investment.

Four Rules of Toyota's DNA

I started by simply reading everything I could get my hands on. I came upon lean, and I was intrigued that its roots were in Toyota following what that company had learned from Deming. From what I read, Toyota was the best example in the world of a company that was actually living the Deming philosophy, which had penetrated into the culture at a deep level. What made the biggest immediate impact on me was an article by Steven Spear and H. Kent Bowen on the rules of work in a lean system, published in the *Harvard Business Review*.[1] I bought *HBR* reprints for all my managers and made it mandatory to read it and hold discussion groups. They reduced the DNA of the Toyota Production System to four simple rules:[2]

1. *Specify all work as to content, sequence, timing, and outcome.* Previously, our work had been specified by the skilled technicians who were doing the work. We called it "trusting their abilities," but it really meant that no one was learning from anyone else, and improvements were largely in the head of the one person doing the job.
2. *Every customer-supplier connection must be direct, and there must be an unambiguous yes-or-no way to send requests and receive*

responses. This simple principle probably led to our greatest breakthroughs. Everyone was doing their assigned job, but no one was thinking about the next customer in the line. By clearly identifying customer-supplier relationships and figuring out how to signal what was up next and when it should be delivered, we probably took out half the lead time.

3. *The pathway for every product and service must be simple and direct.* Like many other organizations, we did some spaghetti diagrams to look at how the samples flowed through the labs. It was a great way to lighten the mood by making fun of ourselves for being so foolish, but it was pretty depressing at the same time. I cannot tell you how many process maps we have developed over the years to continue to refine and simplify the flow.

4. *Any improvement must be made in accordance with the scientific method, under the guidance of a teacher, at the lowest possible level in the organization.* We were already supposed to be a research and teaching hospital in addition to serving patients. Teaching and the scientific method should already have been in our DNA. Unfortunately, this was not part of our daily work. None of the managers wanted to be dictators, including me. Yet we were always micromanaging about three levels down instead of trusting the people who did the work to understand how to solve their own problems. The scientific method is something I use in my publications, but it was a huge cultural change to start to apply this to daily problems rather than simply jumping to solutions.

Spear and Bowen went on to warn that "all the rules require that activities, connections, and flow paths have built-in tests to signal problems automatically. It is the continual response to problems that makes this seemingly rigid system so flexible and adaptable to changing circumstances." What fascinated me was the concept of developing a standardized system that is extremely flexible and continually improving. Standards abound in medical labs. We had notebooks full of standards. Unfortunately, that was often as far as the standards got—onto pages in notebooks. We needed to bring the standards into daily use and then develop visual systems to make deviations from the standards visible. Then we could address the deviations by either solving the problem or changing the standards if they were out of date or overly rigid.

Beginning the Lean Journey: Every Breakthrough Starts with a Failed Experiment

The start of the story goes something like this. I had the opportunity to become exposed to the Toyota Production System (TPS) in early 2004 at Pittsburgh Regional Health Initiative's (PRHI's) five-day course to teach us how to apply Toyota principles to health care. As there was no model for its implementation in laboratories, I wondered for some time whether this would be successful, and it took me a while to come around to the idea. I had to sell this to my own leadership team first. Later in 2004, I obtained funding from PRHI to take four leaders to Pittsburgh for the same course I had already taken, and I wined and dined them every night. Over a couple of bottles of wine, I kept prodding them: "Don't you think this will work for us?" "Won't this work in our production?" "Aren't we like a production system?" They all went, "Yeah, yeah," and I took that as my approval to go ahead and just change the culture. This would be such a big change, potentially destabilizing, that I needed to bring along the existing leaders first or they would stop what I wanted to do.

Several months later, in 2005, I did the usual top-down leader approach to change. I gathered the workers of one laboratory that I had led for many years as a young man, illustrated the principles of work flow and rules of work, and then proceeded to write and post standard work for the first workstation. I thought the workers were as excited about these ideas as I was, and I instructed them to follow the standard. Well, when I returned one week later, no one was following it. It was a total failure. But I walked away with a big lesson: this one would require a new approach to my own leadership and how we approached work.

A Little Help from a Friend

I would never claim that I did all this myself. I figured out early on that I needed a lot of help, but I also chose to hire talent instead of relying on outside consultants. I knew I had to take the responsibility for leading the change, and I wanted people by my side who were going to live with the changes and be committed for the long term. Early on I hired Rita D'Angelo, who had an excellent background in Deming and quality, but no background in lean. What I saw in Rita was her people skills, tenacity, and commitment to learning and improving.

I was able to get a grant from my CEO, so Rita and all our quality facilitators are grant funded. Formally, the system won't pay for quality. I can't include it in my budget, as the CFO would tell me to take it out because it provides "no direct value." So maybe this is better, because I spend one-third of a million dollars a year on quality in the laboratories, much of it grant funded. Most comes from my endowed chair grants. Instead of using it for "research," I use it for process improvement. But to me this is research, research into the science of how to do the work better. Henry Ford once said, "It's the work, not the man that manages." Now we live and learn that lesson daily.

It took us several months to sit down and think about how we would design a culture and the structures that would mirror and function like Toyota's. We decided to focus on a pilot area to have a real go-and-see example. To gather leadership support and create the sense of team, in January 2006 I again accompanied individuals from a planned pilot area in one division of surgical pathology to Pittsburgh for the same five-day training. Maybe I'm a slow learner.

Based on that course, Rita created our own on-site training modules for our pilot area workforce of 77, who would subsequently receive eight hours of basic training. And then we started. We attempted to truly listen to the workers. We trained, trained, trained. Then we immediately implemented—learning by doing. Remarkably, we obtained 70 process improvements in the first seven months. This already radically changed the way we worked . . . and the way I thought.

Surgical Pathology as Our Learning Laboratory

Let's start with our model line, surgical pathology, or analyzing tissue samples, which continued to be our learning laboratory for four years. Starting at the beginning, the specimen intake process was a chronic bottleneck, as very large batches of disorganized specimens would accumulate from the previous afternoon to be tackled by several employees at 5 a.m. each day. Their work consisted of eight steps of sorting and resorting, opening and closing brown paper shipping bags of various sizes sent by couriers from 26 regional medical centers and numerous hospital campus operating and procedure rooms. These workers had no control over the incoming volumes of specimens or the specimen types. They weren't armed with any ability to suggest or make significant changes. Once we began lean, in less than seven months, through numerous worker-informed changes, we reduced the intake steps by 60 percent and created defined, color-coded specimen streams by case priority and diagnostic specialty. Eventually, brown paper bags gave way to clear plastic bags to enhance workers' ability to identify specimens for triage at first encounter and assign them to specific work streams. Simple changes to reduce batch size gradually reduced turnaround time, like reducing the size of the racks used to transport specimens. A year later, this intake process was only two quality-controlled steps, directing the specimen directly into a specific work stream queue.

I realize that value stream mapping has become a popular tool for driving value stream improvement, and it is a great tool, but at first we chose not to use it. The big-picture vision that it provides seemed to us to be too abstract to get real engagement at the worker level. Instead, we focused on direct supplier-customer relationships. As Spear and Bowen suggested, we looked ahead to the next customer. Our technicians could understand the simple questions: "What does my direct customer want?" and "How am I doing it?" Is there a clear and direct connection? Is there a clear, unambiguous signal on what is needed, when, and how much? What problems prevent me from satisfying the customer every time? In this way, process by process, we began to get stability, flow, and pull.

Our goal when we started the pilot was for all teams to report all pathology specimens within two days and most simple biopsies within one day. This seemed reasonable, but even with all the process improvements in the first year, we had not achieved it. Since specimens from remote sites would always be delivered after the end of the 8 a.m. to 5 p.m. shift, I suggested a second shift. This was resisted by the manager. I spoke directly to the workers to acknowledge their ownership of the work and to describe the goal that would make us more efficient, competitive, and able to deliver what our customers wanted. I asked for volunteers, and for the first time in my career, I was able to staff the second shift. Amazingly, I did this without assigning a single worker to these hours against his will. The three strongest supporters of the new culture stepped forward to lead their respective work cells on the new second shift.

This change allowed for work-flow smoothing, greatly reducing the large morning batch. Because the workers who dissected the specimens could not complete the evening work by the hour they had set for themselves, 10 p.m., they took it upon themselves to extend their own hours until all the work was finished. We now had ownership and accountability by a strong second team. I requested that the turnaround time results and workload of each shift be posted weekly. Another metric that I requested was work left over (or in process) between shifts. An internal competitiveness between days and evenings was now apparent. This was a good thing, and it allowed more staff members to take on team leadership roles. Before long, the manager became a convert to the second-shift concept, especially as the workload leveling of the routine work made the work of the day shift much easier, so that the workers could tackle other special procedures and tasks that they had previously groused about. Informed by the metrics and no longer resistant, the manager now saw additional opportunity. We are now staffed around the clock by three shifts. The 5 a.m. work bottleneck no longer exists.

Once this culture became mature, we were able to work on frontloading our processes, from specimen intake through gross examination and subsequent tissue and glass slide production. We did this by challenging all current ways of doing the work, eliminating processes that were of no real value, like dictating (into a Dictaphone) descriptions of examined tissues, instead designing standardized text templates to replace the function of transcription; repurposing the personnel involved to the new front-loaded aspect of work; and aligning new bar-code technology that we had been developing with a corporate partner that reinforced the lean work rules and specimen standards at each work cell.

Overall, the number of process steps from specimen intake to diagnostic report was reduced by 31 percent, from 35 to 24 steps. Front loading increased the number of steps in the first work cell, specimen intake, by 80 percent, but reduced the work of the second work cell, gross tissue examination and dissection, by 33 percent; eliminated the work of the third work cell (transcription); and decreased the work of the histology laboratory by 33 percent and the work of the pathologists by 50 percent. The work became safer as well. The use of bar codes to link work cells, standardize work according to predefined protocols, and maintain specimen and part identity resulted in a 62 percent overall reduction in potential misidentified parts and a 95 percent reduction in glass slide tissue misidentifications. The savings in human effort to correct defects, elimination of non-value-added tasks, and increased throughput amounted to the workload equivalent of 5.7 full-time workers, or roughly $250,000 per year. As you can see from some photos of the surgical pathology labs, you can get an impression of a well-organized process with flow (see Figure 9.2).

Of course with all this "leaning out" of processes, you might imagine that the workforce was now stretched to the limit and grossly dissatisfied. You would be wrong. After three years in surgical pathology, the responses to our employee survey had never been more positive. As you can see in Table 9.1, assessments of many aspects of work life and the labs improved incredibly from 2003 to 2006.

Was it easy? No, it was not easy. There was a lot of resistance and cantankerousness, and it has taken years and constant diligence on my part. But eventually we got to a point of stability, and that's just the way we work. Hopefully, you can see that this was an ongoing daily

Figure 9.2. Photos of Surgical Pathology Labs

leadership struggle, not something that I could delegate to staff members or outside consultants. As we progressed through PDCA, I was learning to PDCA my own leadership approach. I had learned to be a physician, I had learned to be a manager, and now I was learning to be a lean leader. It has been the most exhilarating phase of my career.

Table 9.1. Technical Staff Satisfaction in Surgical Pathology

		Percent favorable by Surgical Pathology workers
		> 15% = significant
2003	**2006**	
64%	94%	There is a strong emphasis on customer service.
71%	94%	Customer problems get corrected quickly.
56%	91%	Where I work, we are continually improving the quality of our products and services.
79%	91%	My job makes good use of my skills and abilities.
65%	91%	The people I work with cooperate to get the job done.
47%	84%	Where I work, day to day decisions demonstrate that quality and improvement are top priorities.
27%	75%	The overall physical environment is safe and pleasant.

Our Henry Ford Production System

As we gained experience in surgical pathology and refined the training, we were also developing the Henry Ford Production System (HFPS). The principles will not be new to anyone with lean experience. We tried to keep them extremely basic. You can think of this as creating a lean work flow to bring problems to the surface and allow engaged people supported by technology to solve them.

Lean Work Flow and Building in Quality

During the identification phase of a defective process, little is known about in-process variation that leads to waste and poor quality. As part of the learning process, defective handoffs need to be observed to identify (1) whether a process is in place, (2) the customers and suppliers involved, and (3) defects in the process (see Figure 9.3). We defined a defect as a deviation from a predetermined outcome in specimen processing that leads to work being delayed, stopped, or returned to the sender.

A lean work flow is a continual flow process composed of smaller, evenly paced batches, introducing raw materials and utilizing workers at the right time and place with the right tools to produce a finished product that can be distributed quickly. This can be challenging, as a lab cannot schedule deliveries but must accept uneven batches of specimens from different locations, perform multiple analytical

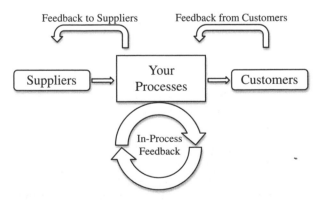

Figure 9.3. Sources of Feedback to Reduce Variation

Color-Coded Racks

Low-Cost Process Improvement

Smaller Racks Move Samples Faster

Large specimen racks were a time waster and bottleneck creator. Lab assistants tended to wait until the rack was filled before any delivery occurred.

Small racks allowed for a much more rapid movement of specimens— instrumental in the improvement of turnaround times.

Figure 9.4. Tools to Reduce Batch Size

processes, and report results to a diverse group of customers, each with its own set of expectations. The key was not to create a lean work flow, but to move closer to the ideal a step at a time. As we take each step, waste is eliminated and time is compressed. Lean moves away from batch-mode production, where defects are addressed at the end of a production cycle, to a continuous mode in which each step detects and resolves defects in real time, minimizing downtime and rework. Many of the changes to get to a leaner work flow were very simple, like reducing the sizes of specimen racks in order to reduce the batch size (see Figure 9.4).

Standard work output is a goal that depends upon having a standardized way of doing the task. This is, of course, easier said than done, as workers can get creative when carrying out tasks. Standard work output also requires a production cycle with predefined connections between customers and suppliers and a predefined pathway for products and services.

HFPS encourages the use of simple and prominent visual cues in the workplace that identify predefined work streams and guide the movement of a specimen (or its derivative) as it moves through the laboratory. Wall posters and whiteboards at the workbench give instructions and record defects. A pull system for replenishment uses *kanban* to define, locate, and reorder supplies. Multiple staff members are trained to pull a card at predetermined order points and pass it to inventory staff, reducing the time lost as a result of unavailable resources. Inventory stock is kept to a minimum, and former stockroom space has been reclaimed for other use.

Engaged People

Ironically, we used a very top-down approach to move the culture toward bottom-up engagement. For problem resolution, HFPS depends on a worker-driven, bottom-up approach rather than a management-driven, top-down approach. Our approach is not a slave to data collection and statistical analysis; rather, it uses data and direct observation for root-cause analysis and to assess interventions. You will see A3 reports throughout the lab, but at first we were not orthodox about using them in a rigid format. We were afraid that in the early stages we would discourage ideas and initiative if we tried to force team members to use a structured method and reporting format. After five years, we started to evolve a standard problem-solving process and A3 reporting format and began training the workers in this more rigorous approach.

The closer we get to one-by-one problem identification and resolution, the less we need to rely on high-level statistical analysis. We have created a quality improvement organizational structure by aligning lab personnel with team leaders in work cells of three to five people that identify the nature and scope of defects, stimulate and guide discussion of possible solutions, and implement and test a solution until it addresses the scope of a defect. Customer teams are encouraged to document defects and communicate them during customer-supplier meetings. The supplier team is expected to understand the customer's expectation and reevaluate and improve its processes to satisfy that requirement. It is through improving these direct connections that we get to flow and pull. This cooperative approach hinges on a no-blame-but-all-accountable sense of process ownership. The work expectation is to never pass along a defect.

Supportive Information Systems

HFPS reinforces its high standards, work rules, and quality tools through its information systems infrastructure by introducing technologies such as bar-code-driven histology work flow and digital photography. We have also launched systemwide online availability of ISO-compliant manuals, policy/procedure documents, and work guidelines that support our paperless operations. We have one common laboratory information system to map the movement and processing of specimens and electronically deliver standardized reports across locations and physician offices. These reports use synoptic menus to eliminate the omission of essential diagnostic information and facilitate clarity for the end user. Note that we still find high value in whiteboards for presenting data relative to targets and for problem solving—paperless does not mean everything is on a computer screen.

Spreading beyond the Pilot Line

Over the years, the one surgical pathology laboratory was joined by other labs as we extended this initiative to other lab leaders and their workers. Many of these labs are composed of 50 to 75 to 100 people. We have discovered the power of just-in-time training—training followed immediately by application. That is why we did this in a sequential fashion, locking down the culture with progressive successes (see Figure 9.5).

After one year of success in the surgical pathology laboratories, we introduced lean management to the more highly regimented and automated clinical core laboratory in 2007. The core lab deals with blood samples using sophisticated chemical analysis. I used the same approach, bringing the whole team of lab leaders to the weeklong lean training in Pittsburgh. By this time, I personally had weeks of repetitive training under my belt! We have since developed our own condensed two-day training program for leaders.

The core lab is highly automated and, perhaps because of its highly technical nature, tends to have leaders that are highly analytic in personality and border on micromanagement. Therefore, their

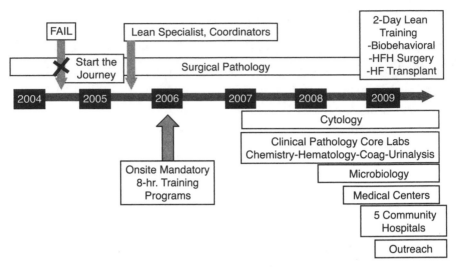

Figure 9.5. Henry Ford Lean Lab Progression

initial stance of "containment" meant that they would do a few select projects and drag them out through the year because they were too busy to do more. And that's exactly what they did. I tolerated this; however, I gave my vice chair, who oversees that laboratory, feedback in his end-of-year performance review that his leaders would have to change in order for the workforce to evolve to empowered work cells. He needed to buy into this model, with his own management style going through his own PDCA growth. And with my support and coaching, he did this.

Looking back, it is easy to forget what is was like in our core lab five years ago, but I will try to keep it real simple. The workers in general did not like each other or work together well—and they did not like us leaders very much, either. I try to blank out these memories, but when we would put them in a room to hold a customer-supplier meeting to describe each other's work requirements, they would yell at each other and get angry and blame people. Then the quality facilitators would have to call me in as the arbiter to cool everyone down and get back to focusing on the process. That was how angry a shop it was. Because of all the rework and the kind of nonsense we experienced, it was difficult, and there was a lot of blaming of everyone. That was the condition that we started with.

Once again, I had to go through the process of teaching managers to look at their processes scientifically and understand the waste. We had to start at the beginning of stabilizing the process. The workers appreciated being listened to and seeing their ideas implemented. The middle managers were the toughest. The aha! for me was the uphill battle that was required to train the leaders that they had a new job. They had been leaders for 20-some years, and now I was telling them that their new job was to work on the system every day. Do you walk around to check the processes first hand? How do you know your system is stable? How do you know how you are doing today? You have to make sure that the work system that you're responsible for is consistent and reliable. You have to know what your variation is. The system has to be operating within a certain limit. We were so far from that goal that we couldn't even imagine it at that time. If you're a micromanager, then you have to let go. You have to empower your team members. Your experience should be their experience as you continue to share and train them. So this was the uphill battle for my existing staff.

I made the effort to spend time with these folks every day, but they still did not get it. Recalcitrant micromanagers had to tinker. I put lean management behaviors in their performance appraisals. It was a cheap version of *hoshin kanri*. We reviewed daily variation reports. If they did a poor job of listening to workers, they were dinged. If they were not making process improvements, it hurt their appraisal. I brought in my vice president of labs to teach lean. And even with consistent top-down pressure, it took years for them to understand that this was not going to go away. As this went on, everyone else in health care around the country wanted to do the same thing, and my group began to appreciate that it was ahead of the curve. It was a long journey to understanding.

At the time we renewed our efforts to transform the management style of leaders in the core lab, a fortunate change in leadership took place. The previously resistant, negative, and micromanaging core lab manager departed voluntarily. I replaced her with a manager who had experienced several months of lean work facilitated by our quality specialists in our largest satellite medical clinic in a very difficult human resource environment. We agreed on how she should lead the core lab, and I was encouraged. Nevertheless, the culture was so entrenched and she was so new that nothing changed for months.

Then I had a brainstorm. What if I took my managers on a "field trip" to illustrate the design of another lean core lab? I had met a group from a lab in Nebraska that was developing a reputation as the best in applying lean methods in a core lab. They ran it with very few people, reorganized into work cells. In 2008, I invested $10,000 and took these 10 managers to Nebraska, and indeed the lab was impressive and quite a cut above the HFHS labs—at least on the surface. The lab was well organized, and there was visible flow in the processes from one step to another. Standardized work sheets were posted. It had 5S audits, and the place was spic and span. There was color coding galore and impressive statistics showing macro-level improvement. We took pictures and asked questions for one solid day. At lunch, the workers described their culture, and we described ours. Their lab had hired a major lean consulting firm for a significant sum and did not involve its employees. It was a top-down process and a tight ship—if an employee made two errors, he was fired.

In a debrief afterwards my entire management team agreed that it was an impressive sight but that there was something missing in the feel of the place. It was a purchased lean culture, and we wanted the same efficiency, but we also wanted worker engagement. The lab in Nebraska had 70 percent turnover, and we had many loyal employees for life. We jointly agreed on a vision to get the same efficiency but to design the system from the perspective of the worker.

Let me preface the story of how we did this by saying that many of the macro-level changes have been and continue to be proposed by myself and Rita. The workers and their team leaders accomplish all the micro-level changes that bring the structural changes to life, such as details in the standardized work. When we returned from the trip, I shared photos of the physical changes aligned with lean that could be adopted in our labs. I call this macro-lean, or changing the physical layout of workstations, drop zones, proximities, visual enhancements, and so on. The one major change that I wanted was to relocate the Laboratory Support Services (LSS) group, which was located across the hall in a separate room from testing activities, to the middle of the core lab, adjacent to the testing equipment. LSS's role is to accept, register, track, process, and deliver all outpatient specimens to the numerous specialty laboratories of the main hospital. The bulk of its work was directed to the core lab. These workers toiled behind a closed door, tackled large coolers (like the ones you take on a picnic) of transported specimens sorted and racked the blood tubes, then delivered them to the appropriate testing lab. As they say, out of sight, out of mind. There was no sense of immediacy, no real organization to the work except for the perpetuation of large batches of specimens, and the general sense of the hardworking technologists in the core lab was that LSS wasted a lot of time.

The relocation concept had been developed one year earlier by Rita when she was teaching a community college process-improvement class. The students had developed the concept and the new layout and presented them to the lab leadership (see Figure 9.6).

The move required the demolition of a wall dividing two sides of the core lab to open up this potential relocation space. Once the wall was removed, the resulting space filled up in the same random manner in which a gas fills a container. That was going to change, but I did not specify how, only the goal that LSS would be relocated into that space in the middle of the core lab. I allowed the workers to choose a new name for the entity, Central Receipt, as it was centrally located within the core lab. The manager and supervisor began this change in an iterative way. First, there was a delay because they needed to order new workbenches. This took six weeks. Initially, they moved only several functions from LSS onto one relocated bench. It took almost a year and six redesigns of structure and function, but at the end, four benches for the entire function of LSS sat in 725 square feet of Central Receipt. Roughly 1,548 square feet of former LSS space has been repurposed to support the inventory of a new outreach business and a new cytology testing lab.

The other innovation that Rita devised was to eliminate LSS work steps by front-loading the blood tube sorting work process at the point of supply at the regional medical centers into color-coded, clear plastic bags designed to track directly to specific testing analyzers. In

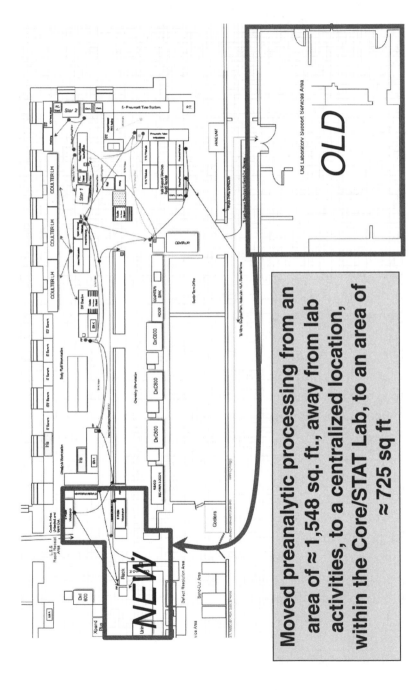

Moved preanalytic processing from an area of ≈1,548 sq. ft., away from lab activities, to a centralized location, within the Core/STAT Lab, to an area of ≈725 sq ft

Figure 9.6. Core/STAT Laboratory Relocation of Preanalytic Activities into Lab

conjunction with batch-size reductions made possible by tweaking courier pickup times, the turnaround times for the most common blood count and chemistry tests were reduced by 50 percent.

To fill the additional capacity that we would free up through lean, we established a new outreach strategy to bring more work to our lab from other hospitals and clinics. To create urgency for change, I repeatedly communicated that the new outreach business would deliver thousands more specimens to the core lab, which would need to be processed efficiently with no increase in staff. We had dedicated time to changing gradually by driving change from the bottom; now it was catch-up time.

Our consistent performance from the core lab, which we were quite proud of, was that all specimens submitted that day from throughout the health system outpatient clinics were analyzed and the results in the electronic medical record by 6 a.m. the next morning. Unfortunately, accomplishing this feat meant that the midnight shift, an unpopular one, was the busiest of the day's three shifts. Our physician customers at least could count on the test results on that day's patients waiting for them bright and early the next morning, but they were not so happy when they received 3 a.m. phone calls from tech nologists warning of critical test values on specimens that had been drawn much earlier in the day.

So we decided on our next stretch goal, which was to complete all tests submitted by 5 p.m. that day by midnight of that same day, and all subsequent process improvements focused on achieving this overarching goal. We had already done some work to support this, including leveling of courier deliveries of blood samples from all sites to the Central Receipt. This change had significantly reduced lead time. The power of a stretch goal that the team agrees to cannot be overstated. Our baseline in January 2008 was 74 percent of the day's test results reported by midnight. One year later, the core lab was consistently reporting 98 percent of those tests by midnight. But we could do better. The percentage of tests reported by 10 p.m. increased from 54 percent to 94 percent, and the percentage reported by 8 p.m. went from 40 percent to 78 percent. We then adopted a new stretch goal of completing all tests by 8 p.m.

As you can see, there is no need for external benchmarks in a true lean culture. You are your own benchmark, and what you did yesterday can be done better tomorrow. This is not unlike Henry Ford's admonition: "We know from the changes that have already been brought about that far greater changes are to come, and that therefore we are not performing a single operation as well as it ought to be performed."

Deepening Ownership by Work Groups

Management can control structure, resources, formal education, rewards, and punishments. These are the levers that can get the lean journey started. We can establish the cells, teach the tools, provide coaching support, support the investments in improvement that are needed, put lean into performance appraisals, and develop recognition events. As leaders, we can go to the *gemba* and take every opportunity we see for firsthand coaching. However, at some point, the work groups have to take ownership of and responsibility for their own work.

Driving Quality through Employee Engagement

One of the most powerful "lean tools" that we used to encourage daily problem solving and improvement was the whiteboard. Early on, we took a first pass at identifying in-process waste by asking all employees to participate in an environmental survey of commonly encountered work defects. This resulted in 100 specific defect types, which we organized by work cell along the path of the work flow. Then, based on these data, we stationed a whiteboard at each work cell to collect information in real time and establish a baseline of current efficiency and targets of waste. Across the top of the board we wrote down the different types of errors they commonly face, and along the bottom we created a menu of generic root causes. The teams then wrote down the case number and the type and cause of each defect as it was detected. This board filled up every four hours. The workers had to erase it every four hours because the pathologist, the doctor at the end of the work path, had that many defects passed to him or her. Eventually we had to put up two of these whiteboards to collect data. These eventually became standard whiteboards for each work cell, so we can now see what is going on in the shop.

From two weeks of data collection, our baseline, we learned that 28 percent, or roughly 1 in 3 cases (a case may consist of one or more tissue specimens), had a defect that caused the worker to stop his work, reject the specimen, and either return it to the sender or fix it himself. In any case, it caused a major delay. Essentially, these data were granular measures of variation that could now be targeted by specific teams. Based on the annual volume, this translated to 50 case defects per day encountered throughout the division. Without a problem solving culture and a defined methodology for change, we were the proverbial drowning person. All that the workers could do, from technicians to pathologists, was get angry and either accept the frustration and inefficiency or blame others. My leadership role at the top was that of chief apologist to our clinician customers and occasionally irate patients. We rarely got feedback, so it was again out of sight, out of mind.

Starting to build our new lean culture, targeting specific opportunities defined by data, we drove rapid process improvements, the no-brainers, that didn't take much analysis and could just be done, as well as projects involving numerous customer-suppliers over many months. After one year and approximately 100 process improvements, the defect rate was reduced by 55 percent to 30 defects per day, or a case defect frequency of 1 in 8 cases. Remarkably, by examining our own condition with the use of work-cell-specific whiteboards, we could see that we were our own worst enemy, creating 89 percent of the defects or rework ourselves! Some defective processes experienced waste reductions of 97 percent over that first year, speeding the delivery of product and final report turnaround times, while freeing up valuable worker time to continue work on process improvements. By the third year, the in-process waste had been reduced to roughly 5 case defects per day, or a case defect rate of 1 in 40 cases. This is a 91 percent reduction in waste from the baseline three years earlier. Now, in reality, if I had pushed this harder top-down and Rita did a lot of the work herself, we could have gotten those improvements in far less time than one year. But we were investing in developing a new culture, and it was evident in morale and the way people worked day by day.

The New Leadership Model

It is all about leadership. We court and develop our own people and promote from within. I like to simplify the world into two basic leadership models: you can be an egocentric leader or a humanistic leader. An egocentric leader is self-promoting, competes and builds silos, finds fault, is suspicious of others, is focused on what's in it for *me*, thinks she's always right, and craves the spotlight. In a Deming-lean culture, it's the humanistic leaders who succeed. It's about praising and coaching others, building teams, sharing knowledge, supporting and teaching, being open to new ideas, apologizing when you get it wrong, and sharing the stage. I can understand why Toyota brings its own people up from within. When you bring in a big figure from the outside, he often wants to set up his own culture. I would not accept that, and as the culture matures, the workers would not accept it either.

The pivotal and most important role in the system is that of the team leader. This individual, at the interface between the value-added workers and the managers, is the key to success, and every work cell must have an identified team leader (see Figure 9.7). We are often asked what our definition is of a work cell. This is a more difficult concept in clinical medicine. Here's our definition: it's a semiautonomous and multiskilled work team that contributes to a task, service, or product that is used by or serves another group in the workplace. You can identify a work cell by asking a few questions. Who does what for whom (customer-supplier)? Who passes you your work (supplier)? Who requests work from you (customer)? Are they inside or outside your department (internal or external suppliers and customers)? It has been important to identify the team leaders in work cells along the path of work flow so that there are no gaps in the connections between workers. Team leaders can be identified by ability, by passion for quality, or even by vote of the work cell members. I don't care as long as a work cell has someone who is effective and whom the members respect.

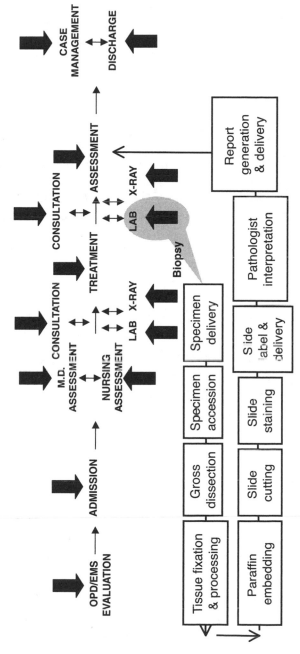

Figure 9.7. Team Leaders along the Path of Workflow in Pathology Labs

The team leader's role is complex. These leaders are the most important, as they do the heavy lifting. They must manage people and processes where the actual work is done. They do their share of fire fighting as the day goes on, but their principle role is to lead continuous improvement, which includes:

- Identifying, selecting, and prioritizing projects
- Constantly focusing on problems and process, not personalities
- Understanding and adhering to the work rules and principles
- Using the tools effectively
- Selecting team members
- Defining the project's scope and measures
- Ensuring the appropriate customer-supplier connections
- Reality-testing proposed interventions, as not all ideas are good ideas
- Tracking the projects
- Constantly pushing for continual problem identification in the work cell and seeking ideas for change based on data-driven knowledge of the defects
- Communicating with and recognizing, coaching, developing, and encouraging team members
- Dealing with failures as the team progresses toward a goal
- Celebrating the team's success

We ask each work cell team to have three initiatives on the whiteboard so that everyone can see what has gone wrong and what needs to be tackled next. If it sounds like I'm a slave driver, you're absolutely right! The leader sets the pace of change. I want the team members to learn from these defects in the work and to learn from their proposed fixes. I want them to fail occasionally so that they won't be content and won't do it again.

We also have a role assigned to support the teams called quality facilitators. People usually think that these folks are in charge of quality, but they are not. Every hospital has silo support people. These people can't possibly be responsible for quality. Quality takes place at the level of the work! The facilitators can't keep track of these hundreds of process improvements, let alone understand what took place. What they can do is help in many ways: educate workers in the appropriate use of process improvement work rules and tools; assist in study design and statistical data analysis; assist in scheduling meetings; follow up on team progress; remove communication roadblocks, especially between people who don't like each other; facilitate cross-departmental meetings; facilitate presentations and worker recognition; facilitate group learning from failures; spread knowledge of best practices as lessons learned across sites; and especially maintain a positive attitude in confronting problems. This takes a special personality. These folks can never go negative on you and must deal with malfunctioning processes and frustrated people all day long.

What about the rest of the workforce? These are the team members. We ask them to identify defects daily, cluster around whiteboards, form groups to share and brainstorm problems, join teams to address interventions, assist in the design of measurement tools, collect data, assist in root-cause analysis, use the five whys, communicate with customers and suppliers, communicate with managers and leaders, keep track of process improvements, continually seek better ways of performing the work, present the results of their improvement work, present their successes, and learn from their failures. We are not satisfied with the status quo.

With these leadership roles we now have 82 champions for lean in the main campus labs. Each one of these individuals leads a team. That's how you get to 536 improvements in one year.

An Empowered Culture and Teamwork

The goal is to convert from a present culture to a future culture, from renters to owners, by developing a culture that leads, manages, and drives quality and patient safety every day and by engaging the entire workforce. We want people to own their work.

Empowering the worker has taken on a different meaning. I used to have a suggestion box on the wall in the 1990s. The first week, I got a handful of suggestions, then they stopped coming. That wasn't really empowerment. We want the workers to be comfortable with having, in the words of Juran, the "knowledge, skills, authority, and desire to decide and act within prescribed limits." Then we want them to "take responsibility for the consequences of their actions and for contribution to the success of the enterprise." Workers must learn to see their daily work in the context of continually learning based on what they are doing as defects are fed back to them using the PDCA cycle. By doing this, we are creating a culture, a new culture.

Early on, we used to feature a "Spotlight Team of the Month." We would put the team members' pictures up on a poster with the many process improvements that the team had accomplished. This was okay as a starting point, but we improved on it considerably.

In the new process, all teams present monthly in departmental meetings called "Share the Gain." Because we are so large, we meet with 75 people or so at a time; we hold two of these meetings each month. The second group meeting we hold twice in one day so that we can catch the workers on two shifts as they overlap. These monthly "Share the Gain" meetings really set the continuous expectation and pace of monthly process improvements—one process improvement per work cell per month. They also spark enthusiasm for sharing successes, expose failures, and really develop the staff members. This is like your second-grade teacher, where there was an expectation of one book report a month. Didn't you just hate that year? But eventually you knocked them off, didn't you? And you learned something, too! Well, this is the same thing; they all have a book report to do for me each month.

The other thing we do is have the team members recognize each other. This is an idea that we borrowed and improved upon from one of our site visits. We call it the "Well Done" form. If a worker is really indebted to a colleague who went the extra mile for her in her work, she recognizes that colleague by writing a brief narrative about him and about the event. People get a real kick out of reading these narratives posted on the board. At the end of the month, the manager pulls two cards out of a hat, and two employees receive a token gift card. So if you're really helpful to your fellows, you've got a better chance of winning. But it's not really about winning. It's the recognition of your peers, and it models best behaviors.

Use of Metrics and Performance Evaluations

We build effectiveness in lean management into the performance evaluation of leaders. I know that one of Deming's principles was to eliminate annual performance appraisals, but we are not that mature, and we still need them. Our performance appraisal focuses on developing people who are truly our assets. I know who my next supervisors are. They feed on this, they enjoy this, and this is the way they work. If they are totally indoctrinated in working in this fashion, I won't have to train them to be leaders; they are leaders.

We acknowledge that the worker is the expert. This allows you to get the hundreds of process improvements, again and again. Leaders also promote the goal. In the past, we had been doing benchmarking, pursuing a median performance level—oh, isn't that great! Half of the people are better and half are worse than you are. Isn't that reassuring? When you go out to dinner and spend your precious dollars, do you want to be served by a median waiter or have the best experience? We tell our people that we are striving for perfection. We may never reach it, but that's the goal.

I focus our leaders on their metrics. Every week they focus on their metrics. In some sections, the metrics are posted every morning after a day's efforts by three shifts. Then the supervisor has to chase down the special cause variation. We do not want this to degenerate into pointing fingers at the guilty. People always want to blame someone else for their ills. We reiterate that it's the process, not the people. This is something that a leader must constantly neutralize. Finger-pointing is not as frequent as it used to be, but every once in a while it rears its head.

Metrics can be used as a management control tool to reward and punish, or as a tool to aid the work groups in identifying and solving problems—a tool for continuous improvement. We didn't get to managing by metrics as a continuous improvement tool for four years. It requires an awful lot of work to get to the point where you actually have daily metrics of system performance. We always had quality indicators, but not daily; they were shared at the end of the month. How do you know what actually happened 30 days ago that led to the defect? Like good detectives, we want to at least identify the cause (and ideally the solution) within the day, each and every day.

It took us four years to get to this point where there is a defined pathway of daily defect identification and resolution from the doctors or pathologists to the corrective action. The pathologist fills out a form; the lab now makes use of it, and it becomes a visual part of the defect resolution board, where the workers post their solution. The workers cluster around the metrics board. Every week, one worker in the lab is assigned to the board for oversight. Now they own the defects that are identified to them, and they fix those defects in real time. Now we have enough people with time on their hands because we aren't burdened with rework and we can recognize the quality control person of the day. Her picture is on the wall. Now we know exactly whom the defect gets communicated to.

Lessons Learned

Our single objective in the five-year period was to create and sustain the foundation of a lean management system. We have come a long way toward lean management in the central laboratories of the main hospital. In the Detroit labs, we have the Toyota work rules operational in all work groups. It is a workplace that is visible, with blameless identification of defects on whiteboards by workers. All laboratories have metrics in place. Workers are responsible for taking a PDCA approach to resolving defects. Now we are at the point where we can fix defects in real time. As I write this chapter, our effort this year is spreading it across the five suburban hospitals of the system.

I am loyal to my people, and to get this level of participation in improvement they must have trust that I will fight for full employment—job security. I tell them that as long as I am around I will use all my power and resources to provide them a job with us; workers might not park in the same place and might not have the same job, but we are large enough that I am confident they will always have jobs with us. There are certain job classifications that have disappeared, but we have repurposed these folks to do more meaningful value-added work. In the early stages, I intentionally kept a low profile within the broader health-care system, keeping the details of cost savings hidden from corporate finance, because I knew that if I revealed them, I would be asked for headcount reductions. To me these are valuable human resources I have worked hard to develop, not heads to hunt.

Our respect for people through this process is showing positively in measures of employee engagement, which has never been higher. Gallup does an employee engagement survey and we had it done in 2008 and 2010 with all measures improving. On a 5-point scale, most of the measures went from about 3.5 to about 4.5. Even bonds of friendship have strengthened. Here are a few examples from the initial histology lab in which we piloted the lean culture:

- Overall satisfaction (3.6 to 4.5)
- In the last 7 days, I have received recognition or praise for doing good work (2.8 to 4.1)
- At work, my opinions seem to count (3.4 to 4.2)
- I have a best friend at work (3.7 to 4.4)
- This last year, I have had opportunities to learn and grow (3.6 to 4.4)

Lean is the continual driver of better quality, higher productivity, and worker satisfaction. We have achieved significant national and international recognition for our success in lean management and culture because we invest time in publishing our experiences in the peer-reviewed literature, present abstracts of our quality work at numerous national forums, teach national courses at major societies, and offer our own intensive lean training to the world five times each year. The outside professionals who attend our lean training pay a fee that helps fund our lean program. And more important, it provides remarkable recognition for the team members. We regularly have people touring our labs, and that is the best sustainer of 5S we have. Pride is a powerful motivator.

Besides my passion for quality, the only way I could effect a culture change was to have internal, dedicated quality professionals embedded within this department. I created a Quality Systems Division composed of five staff members who facilitate the Henry

Ford Production System at all of our laboratory sites. Other health-care institutions do versions of lean, and they often have a corporate quality division within the hospital (which we also have). These are folks who report to the senior leadership of the hospital or the broader health-care system. They are Lean- and usually Six Sigma–trained professionals or quality engineers to whom senior leadership gives the task of selecting and conducting projects. These folks are often a frustrated lot. When you give them tasks for projects in this fashion, disconnected from the front-line workers, they can come up with great ideas, but somehow they have to get other people to follow them. They run *kaizen* events and then walk away from the process. Since they are not around except when they are doing the projects, the new standard operating procedures quickly disintegrate, and there is no continuous improvement. Only a leader with some span of control can change the culture of work, so we developed our own embedded quality professionals to facilitate lean transformation daily.

Henry Ford founded our organization, and in many ways he is our central role model. The biggest criticism I can make of Henry in his role as leader of Ford Motor Company is that he didn't have a good succession plan. So a lot of his great ideas were lost for decades as the company grew and eventually had to relearn the lessons from Toyota. That is another thing on my to-do list, to make sure the culture is sustained. In other words, who will replace me and be equally passionate about quality? Am I going to turn this over to a search committee led by an external nonpathologist physician who has no appreciation of this culture and other goals for the department? That would destroy my life's work.

Ironically, while we were getting recognized in many parts of the world as the laboratory leaders of lean, there was little interest by our leaders in the rest of the Henry Ford Health System for following our lead and changing to a true Deming culture. I can't blame them. This is hard work to change culture within a culture. As we enter our sixth year of progressing toward a Deming style of management in health care, I now have more stability within my piece of the Henry Ford Health System, affording me the knowledge base and practical experience to extend my influence to other parts of the system. In Toyota, they call this managing horizontally when you do not have formal authority. Fortunately a new CEO of our largest hospital and the CEO of our newest hospital understand the importance of culture for success in worker-empowered continuous improvement and are working with my group to begin the long journey of change in their hospitals. I am increasingly optimistic that our approach of focusing first on what we controlled, demonstrating leadership, and then waiting for a pull from other parts of the enterprise will prove effective in the long term.

Chapter 10

Teaching Individuals to Fly by the Numbers: Transforming Health-Care Processes

(With Steve Hoeft)

I don't care how much power, brilliance or energy you have, if you don't harness it and focus it on a specific target, and hold it there, you're never going to accomplish as much as your ability warrants.

—Zig Ziglar, motivational speaker

Steve Hoeft worked with us for about 10 years before he left to join what would become Altarum and founded its lean health-care practice. He was trained by some of the best TPS experts from Japan while working in a Japanese seat supplier and then an American seat supplier to Toyota. Steve is tenacious and has boundless energy for improvement. He has the *sensei* instinct for seeing the actual situation at the *gemba* very clearly and getting teams of novices turned on and engaged by solving real problems. It is no real surprise that he adapted quickly to applying lean in health care and became a leader in this area.

Chapter 9 by Dr. Zarbo was a detailed case study in health care, but some would say that labs are more like a repetitive industrial process and are different from core health-care processes. Steve has been able to apply the basic concepts of TPS using a plan–do–check–adjust (PDCA) approach to coaching in virtually every type of process in health care, with great results. In this chapter, he focuses on two arenas—an insurance company and a long-term care facility. It could just have easily have been an emergency room or an operating room or a CT scanning facility, and the lessons would have been the same. The use of tools like value stream mapping, in which we envision flow and pull, and elaborate *andon* systems is never enough. Steve highlights the essence of lean—PDCA thinking. The elements we need to bring lean to life as a problem-solving and people development process are a teacher-coach, a real problem, a problem-solving process, and a mechanism for visualizing the problem and progress in solving it. The visualization tool that Steve focuses on is the results board—a whiteboard. Steve understates his own role as teacher, coach, and motivator a bit in order to bring daily huddles around the whiteboard to life as dynamic learning experiences.

The Problem

"It can't work here!" "But, we're different!" Back in the mid-1990s, I started keeping a "quote count," partly for my own amusement, tallying every expression of resistance to lean management that crossed my path. In the two decades since I learned the simple, effective Toyota Production System (TPS) principles, I had the privilege of working with many firms in industries of all kinds. As each new industry considered TPS, the quote count continued to climb. From the factory floor to business processes to boardrooms, the reaction to the application of these timeless and unchanging principles follows a path from disbelief to skepticism to (for some) embracing a powerful new reality. But, it's not easy. And, a different way of thinking is needed to make it stick.

My company, the Altarum Institute, is a nonprofit health systems research and consulting institute with more than 350 employees in five states and the District of Columbia. Altarum's mission is to serve the public good by solving complex systems problems—integrating research, technology, analysis, and consulting skills. Most of the organization focuses on improving human health by solving technical issues and using best practices and technology better. I helped start Altarum's Lean Six Sigma for Healthcare practice. We call it "Lean Six Sigma," but I first learned TPS on the shop floor of a seat supplier to a Mazda plant and then at a Toyota plant, with some tenacious Japanese *sensei* admonishing me to "keep looking and keep asking why five times." They would have found it amusing that I was now calling it "Lean Six Sigma." The tools of statistics and flow were clearly secondary, and what I was taught was PDCA by working on real problems with a real impact on the business. That is what I have dedicated my career to teaching others.

I had 19 years of experience applying lean in manufacturing and some service processes, but never in health care. Interestingly, the closest I came to this was some Shingo-winning work for the U.S. Air Force overhauling and maintaining aircraft. We used health-care analogies in repair, since we were disassembling and diagnosing the aircraft, fixing it, and then "closing it up."

As we approached our first health-care clients, we wrestled with many questions. How would lean principles apply in health care? How would the process be the same? How would the improvement methodologies and thinking be different? How could we apply the unchanging TPS principles to health care, and use the PDCA thinking process that I learned from Toyota? This chapter focuses on two unrelated organizations and how PDCA thinking was applied to their unique health-care support processes.

We use the entire gamut of TPS methods in our work, but in this chapter I want to focus on one very powerful, but often underutilized tool—the lowly *results board*, which is sometimes called an "attainment board" in manufacturing. We also called it an *SQDCM* (safety, quality, delivery, cost, and morale) visual metrics board, since these were the key categories of metrics that Toyota and other world-class manufacturers use to give daily feedback in operations. It has come up in many of the chapters in this book as a key tool, for example, by Charlie Baker talking about product development (see Chapter 11) and Dr. Zarbo using it in his labs (see Chapter 9). Why would something is simple as a blank, erasable board be such a powerful tool? I will focus on this because, if used properly, it can transform a dead-end tools approach to lean into an opportunity for real PDCA and ultimately culture change. In other words, it brings lean to life at the basic work group level.

In the two cases that follow, results boards, posted and updated in the area where team members were making changes, greatly increased the pace of change and the ability to sustain it. Both organizations were struggling in their implementation of value stream mapping (VSM) action plans until we developed simple results boards. Value stream mapping is a great tool to get a team focused on a shared future state vision, but the map is not the reality. It is the beginning of a plan. The future state map then has to be broken down into actionable steps in order to execute, or else we will simply have a map with no action. The action plan serves as the invaluable step-by-step driving directions to get from where you are now to your future state. Unfortunately, even a great action plan is not enough. I have seen many cases where the action plan is poorly implemented and the lean effort degenerates into a program in name only.

As a countermeasure to the implementation struggles I was witnessing, I began the practice of visibly tracking progress on action items and posting targets versus actual data on key outcome tracking charts. The team members started conducting brief daily "huddles" around the boards. Rather suddenly, action items were completed, checked, and made part of people's daily work, completing the PDCA cycle. It seemed to be a missing link.

Background

The most common and successful intervention tool I have used to transform end-to-end processes was leader-led, cross-functional team-based value stream mapping. As I covered the project room walls, I marveled at how similar these end-to-end maps looked when they were completed—even in different industries. As with all tools, it was not the resulting map that greased the skids toward implementation, it was the work done in studying a process. It was the *aha*! moments of understanding when people really *see* waste and also begin to respect what others do. *Yoi kangae, yoi shina*! Or, "good thinking means good products," goes the early Toyota motto.

After a brief foray into finding waste in government operations, I started to look for an untouched (unruined) area in which to focus lean principles. To my curious eye, one "industry" that seemed to be lacking Toyota-style thinking to an unusual degree was health care. Something was keeping health-care systems from adopting a *process* focus. As a user of several key parts of the system, I marveled that *incredibly smart* professionals were impeded daily by even more *incredibly broken* processes. So, I helped to start up a lean health-care effort. Within my first few weeks of health-care change activities, my "quote count" reached 21.

Case 1: Insurem (Insurance Company)

This historic insurance company helped control health-care costs by using good business and clinical support processes. We will refer to it here as Insurem. Its main value-add was getting providers paid, while controlling costs. Balancing these goals is not an easy task. But consistent growth and good financial results over decades seemed to have created an environment in which continuous improvement was neither continuous nor an important focus for the giant organization. As the metal industries in the Midwest dwindled and its clients were reduced, Insurem had to become responsive to rebuild its customer base. It found itself to be bloated and slow, and thus uncompetitive. Customers complained about poor response times for every key process. Enrollments dropped precipitously, costs rose, complaints continued, and then leaders sought solutions.

The First Change Event

I was brought in to set up and facilitate a leader-led, team-based value stream mapping workshop for a key process. I used our standardized setup checklist and took great care to get good baseline data, set good goals, and assemble a strong team that was ready for the change event. The team members bemoaned the endless waste as they drew the current state of a simple customer benefit change request. Each request seemed to be "aged like a fine wine or cheese." They created an excellent ideal state vision and then painted an excellent future state representing how lean they thought the process could be 12 months from today. I led them through developing an action plan of step-by-step directions that would take them from their current to their future state. I always preached that value stream mapping was not whole until a good action plan was developed. Action items were assigned, due dates were set, and the team members were motivated as they presented their plan to management. We had completed the plan, or P, part of PDCA. And it felt great. I thought I had hit a home run and could notch another successful lean event on my belt.

I returned 30 days later for a follow-up visit and audit. Not one item on their surefire action plan had been completed! The lean project team leader and the supervisors in the area admitted that they had not spent much time asking others about how they were doing on their action items or working on their own. Daily work pressures and lack of focus had pushed important action items to the bottom of to-do lists. Several team members thought that they had implemented some small changes, but when pressed, they admitted that they had "only sent an e-mail to everyone about needing to get to work on the list."

So, there was no check or adjust, either. I got the team together to reflect. My question to the team and its leaders was, "So, how is this deployment strategy working?" I took responsibility for failing at the proper care and feeding of this team. We had good goals. The team members knew and believed in the action items that they had defined. They all agreed that the current situation was unacceptable and that they needed to greatly improve. They were committed to lean. I needed a method to keep them focused on day-by-day progress, which I began to call "flying by the numbers."

We Cannot Improve without Feedback

Few people in organizations have the word *change* in their titles. Reaching back into my memory bank of what I had been taught by my *sensei* at Toyota and at Delta Kogyo, I could see one key difference between this health-care support process and my experience in seat factories. When a seat worker implemented an improvement action item or made a small change, there was always some sort of measurement board or physical indicator in the workplace that gave him quick, visible feedback. What was that for Insurem? I stood in a (Ohno) circle with a key leader for quite some time. What could we see? I asked several team members how they would *know* whether completing their action items had caused them to move closer to their goals or not. They said, "We have no clue." Could a missing ingredient be a simple results board?

I returned the next morning and worked feverishly with the team leader on a combination results and communication board. We displayed our *case for change*, posted updated tracking charts for all four of the project's major goals, and even posted pictures of the process improvement team.

After a week, I returned to find that the team had still not completed a single lean action item. As the team leader and I removed "Item for Sale" posters and pictures of cats from our board, we came up with an age-old idea. Why don't we implement a "daily huddle" around the results board? The department already had weekly meetings. But, no focus was placed on the change action items and reasons for doing them. The charts were updated, the team was assembled at 8:00 a.m., and there were some great discussions centered on key action items. Team members seemed pleased that their struggles were being heard. Leaders were impressed that the team members really wanted to deploy their ideas. Somehow, both the huddle (to-do list prioritizing) and the results board (feedback) were needed for this team to implement change. Do–check–adjust cycles swirled slowly, then faster, then faster. Within a few months, the majority of the action items were completed, and the team members celebrated hitting all four goals!

Owner/Updater for Each Huddle

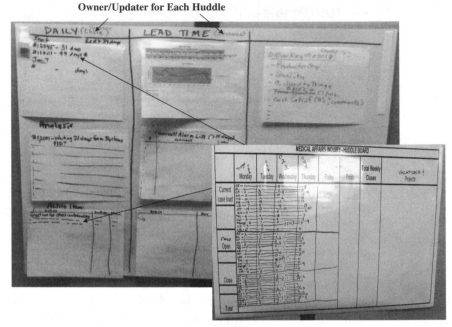

Figure 10.1. Team Leader's Update of Our First-Pass Results Board

Figure 10.1 shows an update of the team leader's initial results board. Notice how primitive the board is. No fancy software was used. There were no printed-out graphics. We actually wrote stuff on pieces of paper. I am not suggesting that making charts with software and posting them is a bad thing. I am suggesting that the board needs to be posted in a visible area, gaps between target and actual must be highlighted, and the updating and activity must take place daily if improvements are to take root.

When I worked for a Japanese company, the mood was frankly rather somber. My *sensei* was great, and I will be forever grateful for his profound teaching. But just occasionally, I would have liked to hear, "Attaboy, Steve!" As an American, I like a little praise now and then. In fact, most of the people I have worked with feel the same way. Figure 10.2 shows the team celebrating several straight weeks of meeting *all* its goals. Immediately after this celebration, this team made plans to recast its lean value stream vision. Even higher goals were established. Customer complaints were reduced dramatically. Team members expressed their enthusiasm for both their jobs and the lean process.

Figure 10.2. Celebrating Achieving Goals

Case 2: T-City Care Homes

T-City provides long-term care (LTC) in a dozen sites or homes across a large metropolitan city. Its main value-add was providing round-the-clock care and programs for elderly residents. The staff members were well trained, and small leadership teams at each home focused on the quality of the care systems. But every process seemed to become bogged down in paperwork, and each new regulation created additional work for staff members. Residents had to wait lengthy periods before being allowed into one of the homes, even when beds were available. Worse, residents occupied space in local hospitals while waiting to be moved to the LTC. This was a job for lean!

T-City Change Event

We were brought in to set up and facilitate a leader-led, team-based value stream mapping workshop for T-City at one of its better LTCs. We again used our standardized setup checklist, set good goals, and prepared the team for the change event. The team members quickly saw waste in their current state. They also painted an excellent future state representing how lean they thought their new admissions process could be 12 months from today. We developed an action plan of step-by-step directions and assigned them. The team presented its plan to management. We had once again completed the plan, or P, part of PDCA. And again, the team felt great about it.

I returned a few weeks later for a follow-up visit and audit. Not again! Not one item on the action plan had been completed! I guess I am a slow learner . . . or a hopeless optimist. Daily firefighting and lack of focus had once again plagued this team and its leaders. Important change items were pushed to the bottom of to-do lists on days where there was more work than staff—which proved to be just about every day. Several team members checked off action items as complete when in reality someone had merely said, "We don't think that action item will work."

Again, Simple Feedback to Motivate Do–Check–Adjust

During our scheduled 30-day audit meeting, my reflection question to this well-meaning health-care team was, "So, how is this deployment strategy working?" As their *sensei*, I took responsibility again. Team members knew and believed in their own action items. I needed to teach this team to "fly by the numbers" as well.

What was the visible measurement board or indicator that would give these team members quick feedback? I asked a few how they would know if their action items were successful or caused them to creep closer to their goals. The missing ingredient again appeared to be a simple results board.

I returned the next morning and worked with the LTC team leader and a few team members on a results board. We found a conspicuous spot and posted tracking charts with the project's major goals. But, in attempting to produce the tracking charts, we found that most of the data either were not available (needed to be collected manually) or had no "owner" assigned to continue collecting it. We stapled up a few hand-drawn charts to hold the place where the updated charts would eventually go. We "sliced" our improvement items, aligned them directly under each of the goal charts that we expected to affect, then stepped back to view our work (see Figure 10.3). This intervention was

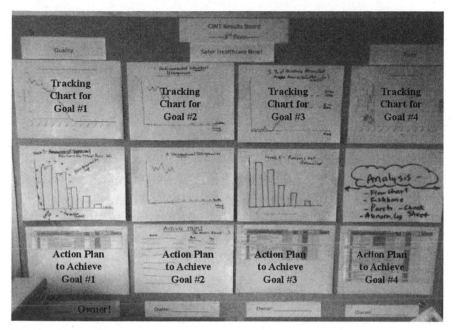

Figure 10.3. Tracking Charts for Long-Term Care Team

going to take much more shoe leather than the other health-care projects required.

It took several weeks, but we finally created a "rallying place" where the team members could come for quick meetings and quick feedback. The hardest part was getting individuals to "own" each metric or goal chart. This was not because of a lack of desire. The LTCs just did not have the type of IT or even administrative support that we were used to receiving in larger health-care operations. We applied lean principles to the collection and posting of goal charts. A simple results board was created, with ownership of the data and the charts.

We implemented a "daily huddle" around the results board to focus on the improvement items. Many excuses dropped away as the multifunctional team met around this board each day. Do–check–adjust cycles swirled slowly, then faster, then faster. Again, both the huddle (to-do list prioritizing) and the results board (feedback) were needed for this team to implement change.

After the first successful audit, the LTC and team leaders asked me, "When should we recast our VSM [value stream mapping] visions?"

I told them, "When you have implemented most of your action items, or when your main results charts start to flat-line."

As the team slowly earned success, it became apparent that some goals had been set too high, and a few had been set too low. However, the results board created a way to harness and focus the organization's power, brilliance, and energy on a specific target and hold it there to accomplish what its ability warranted. Just like the opening quote predicted.

After another successful audit, we scheduled a team celebration and also made plans for a VSM mini-workshop to *recast* the lean value stream vision. Even higher goals were established. Lead time was reduced, and capacity in the LTCs was freed up, which will eventually free up capacity in the hospitals. And the most important part: team members in the LTCs had renewed enthusiasm for their jobs and their ability to solve daily problems using the lean process and simple PDCA tools.

 ## *Sensei* Reflection: What Did We Learn?

I started the journey of lean health care a bit apprehensive. For years, I had improved manufacturing processes, and I could walk into any factory with confidence, knowing that I could make a big difference. Who was I to think that I could teach highly trained professionals, even doctors, a thing or two about improving their processes? After all, I am not Dr. Steve. What I discovered once again was the power of PDCA thinking. That is what I learned from all of my years of tutelage by Japanese *sensei* and years of experience working with teams to improve processes. I learned how to lead others to focus attention on the right problems and a repeatable problem-solving process. Frankly, I also learned the meaning of "in your face" problem solving. Unless the problems are "in your face," they tend to get ignored or pushed out to another day.

A Final Reflection

Admittedly, the two organizations in this chapter are not in the core of medicine. On the other hand, they are very different from each other, and yet the same philosophy and approach worked in both cases. In both cases, we saw a fundamental weakness in PDCA thinking that prevented the organization from understanding the root causes of its problems and taking appropriate corrective action. The answer was to shorten the PDCA *loops* and make the process visible and public.

One health-care employee told me, "These action items must be important because we are tracking them." Another said, "It is hard for me to find time to do these action items, but I can see every morning that my actions are getting our team closer to the goal." The results boards showed respect for the team members who were making changes by giving them feedback, and also gave each team member instant gratification by letting her see the impact of her changes. Another key factor in the success of these tools was that they caused staff members to see the gap between target and actual, and then kept that gap in front of the group. It was like seeing a chair out of place in a long row of chairs. Team members wanted it back in the right spot.

It seems that the continuous improvement cycle never gets beyond P until we install a management tool or "forcing" function like a results board and daily huddles. It changed these two health-care improvement efforts from meaningless plans to something that they really needed to do. Then, the boards gave the team members instant gratification for making and sustaining changes. They changed P to PDCA.

Another piece of the puzzle in these cases and others that I have worked on is the role of the coach and the business unit manager. I worked closely with the manager of each focus area in designing the results board, and the manager led the daily huddles, with me watching like a fly on the wall. I then coached the manager and provided encouragement to maintain the energy level. I was teaching a problem-solving process through ongoing activity and coaching—the only way it really sticks. The results board and huddles provided the opportunity for the learning process. The experience and results created a positive cycle that began to be self-reinforcing as individuals learned the power of PDCA and saw the power of their own actions.

I have since learned that one-off value stream mapping workshops are never enough. I do not want to give the impression that a value stream mapping event is a bad idea. In fact, in both cases, the VSM workshop was critical in getting the group to see the waste and develop a shared big-picture view of what the process should look like. I am not even sure that giving the team members some time to struggle and fail was a bad idea. It opened them up to the countermeasure of a daily huddle. In the final analysis, health-care processes are *people* processes, and human behavior is neither linear nor ideal. What keeps me coming back for more is watching the lightbulbs go on as teams of people come alive and solve their own problems.

Chapter 11

Transforming How Products Are Engineered at North American Automotive Supplier

(With Charlie Baker)

The best way to predict the future is to create it.

—Peter Drucker, management author and teacher

How do you "lean out" an engineering process? Engineering is a messy process and is intensely knowledge-based. There are frequent iterative loops. Each workstation is a person. Cycle times for a piece of work can range from seconds to months. There is very little to observe with a stopwatch. Even the definition of waste is unclear. If we generate an engineering concept, test it, and it fails, that is a defect, and it seems like waste. Yet from this experiment, we now know one thing that does not work, so in that sense it was value-added work. Some argue that we learn as much from failure as we do from success—any learning adds value. The reality is that these gray areas of defining waste are trivial compared to the remarkable amount of waste that comes from handoffs across the many departments that touch product development, including sales, marketing, finance, quality, different production engineering specialists, tooling engineering, manufacturing engineering, parts suppliers, tooling suppliers, equipment suppliers, and more. And then there is the noise created by those in senior management, who often feel that they have the prerogative to change design requirements at a whim late in the development cycle—leading to huge amounts of rework.

At companies like Toyota and Honda, part of the solution for dealing with this complexity is to give one person, a chief engineer, the ultimate authority to run the development project. Charlie Baker was the first American chief engineer for Honda. He learned from the ground up a different, leaner way of developing cars that made sense. Then he had the opportunity to teach what he had learned to an American company, in this case a supplier of major systems that are part of the automobile. Charlie chronicles his history, the transformation process of North American Automotive Supplier (NAAS), and what he learned along the way.

Who Am I?

I admit it—I am an automobile development junkie. I love it. Starting in a "one-horse" garage in St. Paul, Minnesota, I dreamed of developing cars 24/7. Somehow I convinced the registrar at General Motors Institute (now Kettering University) to admit me to school to become a mechanical engineer. I talked my way into a cooperative engineering work experience leading to a job in product engineering at Pontiac Motor Division of General Motors, and for seven years I was convinced that I had the dream job of all dream jobs. Then I woke up one day to find that there was no more Pontiac Motor Division.

I went on to Saturn at its inception, and thanks to a former boss at Pontiac, I was in on the ground floor of product development—literally the ground floor, since I was the third hire in Saturn product engineering and found a job as a working-level engine design engineer. Saturn spent more than $2 billion on the development of a product and another $2 billion on the factory and equipment to produce 240,000 vehicles (a huge investment for that volume). We were asked to benchmark the Japanese—and I benchmarked obsessively. One company stood out: Honda. It had far higher technology in its engines compared to the rest of the world, but the price was the same, and it made the engines in America. How could this be?

I wrote a letter to the then president of Honda of America Manufacturing, a Mr. Irimajiri. In the letter, I explained that I was a Honda motorcycle owner and an engine design engineer at Saturn, and that I was obsessed with Honda engine design. The letter ended with a request to come down to speak with him.

I could not imagine a reason in the world why he would take my letter seriously, but a week later his administrative assistant called to set up an appointment. I rode down on my 1983 Honda Interceptor motorcycle and had half an hour to talk about engine design. Every question I asked about engine design he answered by talking about Honda philosophy—especially the company principles and how they guided the quest for the highest efficiency and quality at a reasonable price. It rocked my world.

About this time, the book *The Machine That Changed the World* came out—a groundbreaking book that discussed lean practices based on the Japanese model in all areas of the enterprise. The example for product development was Honda—the development of the 1986 Honda Accord. Clearly there was a very different way to develop great products from what I had experienced to date. I realized that for the same investment as Saturn, Honda had facilitated well over double the production capacity that Saturn had—in the United States—and had created many fantastic automobiles.

By chance I received a call from a headhunter in 1990 asking if I was interested in new opportunities. I said the only company I would be interested in working for was Honda. He said we should talk. I was hired into Honda R&D Americas and started December 1, 1990. At the time, there were a total of about 50 associates working in automotive R&D in Ohio.

When I think back to my years at Honda, what first comes to mind is sweat and struggle. The Japanese were a bit reluctant to trust Americans with development responsibility, so they started us on smaller projects, specialized versions of vehicles engineered in Japan like the 1993 Civic coupe and the 1994 Honda Accord station wagon. Through this process, we were developing a team of warriors. Honda's Japanese management had done a great job of identifying hands-on engineers like me who loved automobiles. Of course, we made plenty of mistakes, but Honda management expected as much and asked only that we learn from the mistakes and not repeat them. We had great Japanese teachers, and we had to learn at intense speed. I was learning lean development by doing it and getting promoted as my learning deepened. Things like plan–do–check–adjust (PDCA) were not corporate programs but rather philosophies that were deeply engrained in everything we did. My first job as a Honda large project leader, the ultimate in responsibility at Honda and the equivalent of a Toyota chief engineer, was the relatively low volume 1996 Acura CL. I later discovered that the only reason that Honda management had developed the CL for Acura was to train the American development team. On reflection, I now appreciate that it is quite an honor that Honda would invest the money to develop a new product as a training program for us.

Several years later, I led the development of the 2001 Acura MDX sport utility vehicle in Honda R&D Americas. We won every major automobile award possible—*Motor Trend* Truck of the Year, *Car and Driver* 5 Best Trucks, North American Truck of the Year—everything. It was developed using a lean methodology unimaginable to U.S. industry at the time, and it required about 40 percent of the resources of a nonlean methodology.

I was then off to Japan to lead the development of the 2003 Accord, the first American to lead an all-Japanese team as a large project leader. For me, this was a significant bookend to reading about the development of the 1986 Accord in *The Machine That Changed the World*.

I then returned to the United States to become vice president of R&D for several years, during which time we introduced the Honda Element, the Acura TL, the Honda Ridgeline, the Civic coupe, and others. I took great pride in helping to shape a capable lean development organization that produced great engineers who created great products in the finest Honda tradition—the best technology and quality at a reasonable price for world-class customer satisfaction.

It became clear that I had done what I could at Honda, and my dream morphed to aspiring to teach others in U.S. industry what I had learned. Consulting was not my first choice. I knew that to transform product development, I needed to be responsible for it, so I joined a large-scale firm, which I'll call North American Automotive Supplier, as vice president of engineering. I was part of a management team that was motivated to dramatically improve the cost, quality, and timing of the company's product development.

This chapter is the story of what we did and what I learned over a three-year period, focusing primarily on our development activities in North America. Consider it the first generation of learning for me—one large PDCA cycle. It worked in the sense that we achieved or exceeded all of our goals and set North American Automotive Supplier on a positive course toward becoming a lean product development organization. What I have discovered so far is that lean development can be transferred to a traditional organization, with dramatic effect. What I learned also reinforced the idea that lean transformation is first and foremost a process of transforming people.

In the early stages, I focused on basic PDCA. The problem-solving culture was weak, and I had to teach good problem-solving practices in the trenches. Another major focus was on understanding customer requirements at a level of detail that few in the organization had ever experienced. As we stabilized the process, we began to bring in other lean tools. I was aided in this by people who reported to me who had worked for Toyota. We added A3 reporting, which formalized the PDCA process. We set up *obeya*—the big-room meeting process that gets cross-functional teams together in the same room, with visual displays of key data on the walls. We strengthened the project management system. We implemented the methodology of cost tables and designing to aggressive cost targets. We formalized the role of subject-matter experts to reinforce technical depth, which had been weakened over the years. We took out a great deal of waste and rework. None of this would have been possible without my intense involvement at the *gemba*—in this case, working directly with customers, engineering, purchasing, finance, and manufacturing. I would like to convey how these concepts apply and how to approach lean in an intensely knowledge-based process like product development.

Case Background

North American Automotive Supplier (NAAS) is the leader in supplying a complex system for the automotive industry, with more than $5 billion in sales. It serves every major automobile manufacturer, including Japanese and Korean transplants. Each system is custom-engineered for the vehicle manufacturer's brand and to its specifications. The system is an integral part of the vehicle's safety systems, with challenging functional requirements for performance in front, side, and rear crashes. Standards for craftsmanship, although specific to every vehicle manufacturer, are high. Pressure for cost reduction is intense. The number of product variations can exceed thousands. The supply chain is exceedingly complex, integrating commodity-type products and proprietary products with high technology, and utilizes both low-cost country manufacturing (China, Mexico) for parts and JIT (just-in-time) manufacturing. Finally, pressure to reduce development time has been relentless for the last several decades, driven primarily by Japanese and Korean customers.

The Problem

The situation at the start of the lean product development transformation in late 2005 was typical of the state of many North American companies that develop new products—as the organization grew, a great deal of waste had crept into the process. Business was strong—about 600 people were employed in the North American engineering organization, with outside contract resources frequently being called in to manage work overflow. Seven major development programs were in process, with launch dates from one to two years out. There were many medium and smaller development programs as well. Morale was not good because the company had had several RIFs (reductions in force) over the last several years as the auto industry had started to shrink, and people at every level were feeling overworked. In general, many people were talented and technically experienced, and many of them had worked in engineering for one of the Detroit Big Three automakers. A couple of key leaders and staff members had a Toyota product development background. Firefighting, however, was valued and was regarded as the primary engineering skill.

Within the NAAS organization, each automotive customer (Toyota, GM, Ford, and so on) had a separate customer business unit (CBU) facing it, with dedicated program management and staffs for engineering and manufacturing (although these staffs had to interface with core engineering and manufacturing resources in the course of a development project). In an effort to improve efficiency, a "front office/back office" organizational structure had been implemented. This was an attempt at combining a customer product structure (CBU-focused) with a functional specialty structure, but responsibilities and leadership were unclear, and this created further stress and some confusion.

The CBUs had a great deal of autonomy in managing development projects, although they followed a similar process at a high level. The process was based on a popular "phase-gate" model, in which phases are defined (e.g., concept development, detailed design, prototyping, and so on) and gate reviews between the phases check the attainment of functionality, cost, quality, and timing targets. The program management systems were somewhat loose, with virtually every program reported to be in distress based on these phase-gate metrics. The distressed program status typically did not prompt management attention until budget overages occurred, and unfortunately, overages were significant and regular (mid-eight figures in U.S. dollars per annum for the top seven programs)—an immediate and obvious waste stream to concentrate on with lean. Quality as measured by scrap and rework in the plants was not particularly good. J.D. Power IQS (Initial Quality Study) results trailed the industry. Another waste stream was the amount of tooling changes required late in development because of test failures or manufacturability oversights. This in itself was also in the mid-eight-figure U.S. dollar range per annum for the top seven programs, and it was not reimbursed by the customer—it was simply written off against the original business plan for the development.

On the positive side, some very good work had been done to create a product standardization strategy on some of the capital-intensive products. There had been earlier attempts at lean transformation that had not gone far, but at least provided some basic awareness. It was also clear that there was real depth of talent and knowledge for each individual engineering function.

Grasping the Situation at the *Gemba*

NAAS realized that the situation was not good, and hired me as vice president for North American engineering. I did not have a background in lean transformation, but I had learned from Honda how to lead within a lean organization, and I had learned problem solving based on PDCA. I knew that applying lean tools in and of itself was not going to eliminate the malaise that was evident in this organization, so I had to start by engaging people at the grassroots level and at least stabilizing the basic engineering design process.

The starting point for me was to understand the actual situation at the *gemba*, where the engineering work is done. To accomplish this, I asked to attend design reviews for each of the projects. Even this was a struggle; the report back was that there was no time to do design reviews because of administrative tasks and customer meetings. Undaunted, I initiated evening design reviews—once-a-week meetings called in the evening to enable the teams to get together as a team, both for a general project meeting and to review the design in depth. These were not popular, and there was not a consensus that meetings with the entire team were even required, but I sent the message as loudly and clearly as I could that working as a team was foundational and required.

As I attended these early design reviews, it was immediately clear to me that the building blocks of lean were absent. There was a program manager (PM) for each program, but in many cases the PM did not have a technical background and was clearly relying on the engineers to self-manage anything that had to do with engineering. Communication in many cases was not good, and in some cases the evening design reviews were the first time the entire team had assembled for a meeting. As a result, even understanding what problems the team was facing was difficult, and in several cases the initial meeting was devoted to consolidating multiple problem lists, each being maintained by a separate team member, into one team problem list with appropriate prioritization.

Teamwork was good in some cases and lacking in others, depending on the leadership style of the program manager. Within engineering, there was confusion regarding the "front office/back office" structure. Engineering leadership was unclear. System integration responsibility was unclear. How to resolve functional issues was unclear. The end result was that either everyone viewed himself as responsible, or no one viewed himself as responsible (both conditions existed).

Methodical problem solving was very rare, with a great deal of "shotgun" or "try and test" problem solving in evidence. The program management tool used for follow-up of any action was the "who-what-when" list. An informal survey of dozens of team members revealed that historically, only about 20 percent of the actions listed on this tool were ever completed on time—an indication of both gross overload and an inability to create, understand, and execute detailed tactical plans. In many cases, teams were struggling with finding a solution for problems involving basic requirements that had been promised to the customer at the start of the development but had not been considered when the design was created.

As mentioned before, management did not have good visibility into the actual status of development. The phase-gate system had been revised to focus on a general assessment of in-process activity, not completed deliverables, and thus was not helpful when trying to understand project status. Even with this, every program was reported to be in distress, and without a consolidated and ranked list of problems, risk assessment was not possible. Interestingly, nobody seemed overly concerned about all of the "red" conditions, as everyone thought that this was "normal for a complex program like this."

In addition to the *gemba* of the development teams, I also visited actual customers and their factories. In some cases, relationships with customers were excellent—this correlated directly with the leadership and teamwork in the development teams. In other cases, relationships were very tense, with weekly meetings between customer and NAAS top management to report out in minute detail, since trust had been lost.

In manufacturing, three totally new manufacturing plants with a variety of new processes were being launched. Manufacturing was struggling with new plants, new processes, and new people at every level, and it was clear that there were missed opportunities to optimize the product to the process. Certainly, manufacturing had little time to spend on the critical top seven product development programs, especially as manufacturing engineering expertise was weak compared to my experience at Honda.

An Overall Vision for Transformation

To start the transformation, both a tactical and a strategic approach were created. This was not done and set in stone, but both approaches morphed over time through many, many PDCA loops. The tactical approach was designed to address the most critical issues at the time in the teams and with the actual developments. The key here was to make the issues actionable, simple, of limited scope, and demonstrating PDCA "quick wins" so that the organization's confidence could grow. The strategic approach built upon the tactical approach as the foundation but outlined a three-year transformation that combined a long-term vision with a short-term set of manageable PDCA steps. The three-year vision for NAAS North American engineering is represented in the model in Figure 11.1. Below this were detailed plans and a timeline for execution. The expectation was not that people would completely understand lean but simply that they would

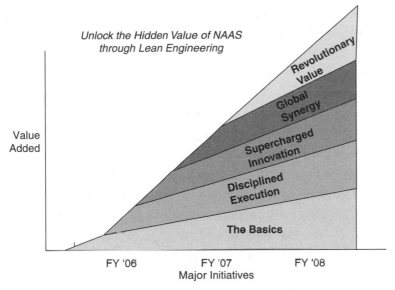

Figure 11.1. Three-Year North American Engineering Strategy

get a sense that this was part of a larger plan and not the "initiative of the week."

Getting Started on People Engagement and Stability

The first step in the creation of the plan was the engagement of engineering leadership at a director level to rank and prioritize the issues, and to get to the root causes using lean methods. This was done in a series of offsite meetings in late 2005 and early 2006. The overall umbrella term used was creation of "the development factory." The concept of a factory processing designs helped bring to life the image of a smooth flow without waste. As part of this, the responsibility of line managers as trainers and coaches for lean was clarified. At this time, we were very lucky to have a person with many years of Toyota development experience to serve as a staff coach for lean, and to create much of the methodology for these initiatives. However, it was critical that the line managers understand their responsibility for the implementation of lean—this cannot be a "staff person's job."

Key initiatives that were created by the team as part of the tactical approach to starting lean were

- *Revising the organization structure of engineering to clarify system integration responsibility.* We needed a single person who could lead the technical project and take business responsibility at the same time, similar to the very powerful chief engineer at Toyota, but at a more elementary level to begin with. We also needed strong leadership of functional engineering specialists to drive standardization and implementation of best practices. The new matrix organization structure was implemented starting in January 2006.
- *Revising the phase-gate development system to eliminate a lot of the bureaucratic waste yet give a far more detailed picture of the value-added steps of development.* The revised system was designed to align with customer deliverables, promote teamwork, give clear risk assessments, rotate lessons learned through "teaching audits," and escalate through appropriate management if the project was in distress.
- *Creation of and training on the "basic engineering process."* This was a 10-step methodology for problem solving based on PDCA and using the whiteboard in real time and A3s to capture and report knowledge. Often companies ask how much capital investment is needed for lean. One of my biggest expenses for lean implementation was whiteboards. They are an indispensable tool for lean engineering because they enable visualizing and problem solving by teams in a way that current computer systems cannot.
- *Cross-functional creation of detailed tactical plans for all activity.* This was part of the problem-solving methodology, but it quickly expanded beyond this. The future state in value stream mapping provides a high-level plan, but we wanted each functional group to provide rolling five-day plans in great detail and to have the skills to continually update these for course corrections as the inevitable deviations occur. These were done by whiteboard or through simple graphic programs like Excel and PowerPoint. We avoided project management packages for this purpose because they tend to be overly complex.

- *Introduction of a requirements engineering function, with dedicated staff members to methodically collect all customer requirements, assess the design by formal audit, and clarify technical risk.* Many firms have some kind of requirements engineering process, often rooted in software, but it does not get translated into the level of detail required for actual product and process design. We had each functional group break down the requirements to that detailed level and compare the actual design to the requirements in every review meeting. The gaps that the groups found were the basis for problem solving, and they also formed a basis for our know-how database for future designs.
- *Training and driving best practices in design and project reviews, including coaching and implementing all the previous initiatives.* As an escalation, when teams were in distress, cross-functional project reviews were initiated on Friday afternoons, with the intent being for upper management to understand the team's challenges and assist with appropriate resources and support (more on this later).

This "suite" of initiatives directly maps to the top concerns as understood by the detailed assessment made at the *gemba*, and each uses PDCA as the foundation for the approach.

 ### *Sensei* Reflection on Challenges to Lean

Challenges to lean at this time were myriad. At the core, the company had become very successful by promoting an intense entrepreneurial ethic. It is said that this, in fact, is a virtue of American innovativeness. Creative engineers, if left to their own devices, can develop brilliant new ideas, as well as fight fires in the trenches when a crisis breaks out. This may be a virtue if the primary task is to brainstorm and mock up breakthrough ideas, but not when developing a complex system with hundreds of parts that must

(Continued)

work together in harmony to meet extremely challenging targets for timing, cost, quality, and safety.

Upper management above me had recognized the need to change to react to competitive and customer pressure, and was promoting systems to push best practices across the company. The key word here is *push*. There was natural resistance to this at the middle and lower levels of the company, and not complete alignment at the executive levels. Lean was different from either of these approaches, although it did lead to best practice promotion. Repeatedly, the first reaction to any lean initiative or process was to ignore it.

One of the biggest problems I needed to solve was that in many cases, follow-up and accountability had been lost. Time after time I came back to teams and individuals that had agreed to take an action, to find that the action had not been completed. I eventually learned that for many, this was the first time they had seen an executive consistently follow up on a plan or a promise. Often they had never experienced an executive coming to the *gemba* and drilling down to understand what was really happening—to understand the detail of the actual situation. This was the flip side to the entrepreneurial strength of the culture: many entrepreneurs have strength in spontaneous creativity and can quickly generate a list of countermeasures, but do not necessarily demonstrate consistent follow-up. Historically, the organization had grown accustomed to this behavior. Certainly this was never tolerable at Honda.

A final challenge was termed "malicious compliance." Once they understood that lean was not the "initiative of the week," people resigned themselves to compliance but wanted to be told exactly how to do lean in a rote way. It required education and steady pressure to explain that lean is not rote, and that the most important thing is that people understand their responsibility for thinking and continuous improvement—of themselves, of the product, of the tools, and of the process. If done right, lean is also empowering—a way to avoid issues being decided by title. All this was somewhat foreign to the existing culture.

When there are identified problems, we need countermeasures. The typical response is, "Tell them they have to do it or else." I will admit that part of the message was that participating in lean was mandatory, not optional. This was not a participative, consensus-based process in the early going. On the other hand, simply ordering compliance gets only compliance—perfunctory execution of lean tools to say that they did it and get their boxes checked.

Fortunately, I was able to assemble a team of people who could see deeper than superficial application of lean tools. With my background at Honda, and several people from Toyota, we could participate actively in design reviews and problem-solving meetings and coach the way to a far deeper approach. This required being at the *gemba* all the time to put steady, persistent pressure on the middle management and the working level. I cannot emphasize enough how central this was to actually changing behavior and the culture.

Metrics the Lean Way—Making Flow, Waste, and Value Visible

The curse of modern industry is metrics—scorecards with red, yellow, and green rankings. The more the better—there can be dozens, even hundreds of metrics. When in doubt, invent another metric, create an official procedure (that no one uses), and make another scorecard. After a short time, people become understandably numb, and management loses credibility because workers cannot possibly react to the myriad of metrics that are created.

Another concern is the "tyranny of the red-green present," or the tendency of traditional organizations to focus on the "high-level snapshot" of the current situation, summarized by "red–yellow–green" metrics. This drives a firefighting culture in which management charges at the reds like a raging bull to micromanage the issue at hand, while not having any information on the details, trend, or systemic issue behind the metric. In the worst case, teams feel that they do not have the power to control their destiny but are simply "going through the motions"; their true job is simply to bring problems to the surface so that management will solve them. This is anathema to lean.

Creation of true lean metrics is quite critical and requires resetting everyone's expectations of what metrics should do. At a top level, metrics should make flow, waste, and value visible, and facilitate not only tactical execution but also systemic improvement of development. Metrics should also facilitate the team's self-assessment and tactical countermeasures. Fewer, more powerful metrics are preferred over vast numbers of metrics. Metrics can and should be cascading and embedded, with the detailed metrics supporting and illuminating the metrics for the general situation. Metrics should be variable and should be tracked over time to allow an understanding of trends and to facilitate continuous improvement. For this reason, key metrics for lean development include the following:

1. *Days late to schedule* (phase gates). In a lean system, the development or phase-gate system should consist of tracking the activities that add value and knowledge to the product. If the teams are late to the schedule, this is critically important information to study, both tactically to understand why the team is struggling and to provide assistance, and also strategically to prioritize (Pareto) and address the systemic problems that the entire organization is struggling with. Days late, as opposed to "red or green," allows specific systemic improvements and trends over time to be analyzed in some detail. This analysis typically brings to the surface areas where systems need to be created to drive knowledge and best practices and areas that have non-value-added or unwieldy systems or processes—both should be addressed. This is the primary metric for tracking flow.
2. *Project-based cost of development.* This is typically broken down into parts, labor, and testing. This absolutely needs to be tracked by project, and a good managerial accounting system allowing

real-time visibility and control is a key prerequisite. Projects need to be "normalized" for content and compared to understand best practices and benchmarks. Part of a good lean system is driving the right kinds of entrepreneurial behavior and empowering the chief engineer of a particular project to spend resources and money appropriately, but having very clear "best practice" targets that the chief engineer is held accountable for. Lean tools and initiatives are the methods by which the chief engineer can achieve the development deliverables at a competitive "best practice" cost. With normalized project content, best practices can be harvested and institutionalized, and the effect of lean initiatives can be understood almost immediately. Key here is a balance between the entrepreneurial behavior of teams and the implementation of lean "best practices" establishing ever-lower benchmarks for development cost. Note that this is incredibly powerful—with this system, in the first two years of lean implementation, a 40 percent reduction in "apples-to-apples" cost of product development was realized in NAAS programs.

3. *Tooling waste.* In any capital-intensive industry, maturing the design so that tooling can be released is a critical midterm goal of development. A less obvious but very illuminating metric for waste is money spent on production tooling changes or, in the worst case, production tooling that has to be discarded because of late design changes. This provides relatively short-term goals and gives a clear picture of the ability of the development organization to mature the design to a schedule. This metric is dependent on good teamwork among purchasing, suppliers, engineering, and manufacturing in the development team, but more importantly is an indicator of technical capability and the ability of the technical groups to connect with teams effectively. Bringing this waste to the surface and tracking it drives great team behavior and systemic improvements. As mentioned, tool waste at the start at NAAS reached well into eight figures annually, and this was reduced by more than 80 percent after three years of systemic improvement.

4. *First-time pass rate for testing of parts from production tools.* Another great short-term metric to illuminate waste is tracking

the first-time pass rate for tests from production tools. This again gives an excellent understanding of team performance, but the power behind the metric is analyzing the systemic reasons for test failure. This was an existing and traditional metric, but in the traditional system no one had done the "why-why-why-why-why" analysis to understand the systemic issues and take appropriate countermeasures. This metric had hovered in the 80 percent range for years. Doing the five whys analysis revealed that the reason for these failures was overwhelmingly not understanding customer requirements and specifications at the start of design, with a secondary reason being poor problem solving that allowed the recurrence of issues late in development. With a lean mindset, this led directly to the creation of the requirements engineering functional group, methodology, and audit discipline as well as the A3 problem-solving method and training. Within two years, the first-time pass rate increased to virtually 100 percent. At this time, because of other lean initiatives, product costs were decreasing. This result was viewed as virtually unbelievable by the broader organization and did much to establish the credibility of lean in many people's minds.

Other metrics were created and tracked, but the clear lessons I have learned are that

- Fewer and common metrics are better.
- Metrics should illuminate flow, value, and waste.
- There should be a few critical, overarching metrics that are standardized to allow the recognition of trends and tracking of overall improvement.
- Detailed metrics at the process level should be directly mapped to the few critical overall metrics and be used as diagnostic tools.
- Metrics are most powerfully used not only for tactical status but also for systemic analysis and improvement.
- Interpreting metrics requires managers at the *gemba* who understand the actual situation so that they can judge what changes in the metrics mean, both positive and negative.

Teaching Problem Solving: A Case Example

An example can illustrate the situation. In one of the critical and complex product developments, a very complex mechanism was designed. Unfortunately, a very basic requirement was not considered in the design until the design had been fully detailed and released for production tooling. In addition, this requirement was critical for safety—it was absolutely essential that countermeasures for this concern be included in the design.

One of the most important methods and ways of thinking that I introduced was problem solving as it had been taught to me at Honda. I later confirmed with a former Toyota chief engineer we hired that it is very similar to Toyota practice. At NAAS we called it BEP (basic engineering process), a 10-step problem-solving methodology based on PDCA. The steps are summarized in Figure 11.2.

The first step is to define the problem statement, which sounds simple, but in so many cases people simply jump past this critical step. Step 2 is to clarify what "good" looks like by establishing clear targets. This leads to determining how we would measure "good," and how much "goodness" is required. This again seems like common sense, but it leads to clarity about what exactly should be measured, what variation we should expect, and what exactly the final target should be. The

Basic Engineering Process

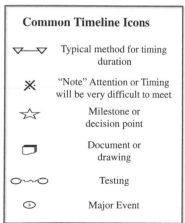

Plan Work as a team, use the whiteboard
1) **Define** Problem or Objective
2) Establish **Targets**
3) Understand the **Physics**
4) **Brainstorm** Alternatives
5) **Analyze** and Rank Alternatives
6) Evaluate **Impact** in all Areas
7) Create Visual, Detailed, Double-ended **Schedule**

Do
8) **Execute** Solution

Check
9) **Confirm** Results

Act
10) **Reflect** and Transfer to Knowledge Base

Common Timeline Icons

▽—▽	Typical method for timing duration
✳	"Note" Attention or Timing will be very difficult to meet
☆	Milestone or decision point
▱	Document or drawing
O—O	Testing
☉	Major Event

Figure 11.2. The Basic Engineering Process

third step is to "understand the physics." This is the Achilles' heel for most traditional organizations' problem solving. Most of the time people are so interested in action that they completely jump past a robust root-cause investigation, which is what "understand the physics" really means. In addition, much of the time the physics is not correctly summarized and then becomes opaque. For some time I offered a reward if a problem could be found where the physics could not be summarized into one graph. It was months before an example could be found that legitimately was complex enough to require more than one graph, yet these were problems that were costing us tens of millions of dollars.

The fourth step is "brainstorming alternatives" with the emphasis on team behavior—drawing the best ideas out from every member with the idea that in problem solving, titles are irrelevent. Analysis and ranking of ideas by Pugh analysis is the next step, again as a team. The Pugh analysis simply looks at a number of criteria (e.g., weight, cost, functionality), rates the idea on each, and calculates a total score. Through this step, team buy-in is achieved as well as utilization of the combined expertise of a number of smart people, rather than one or two.

Next is "evaluate impact in all areas," which essentially means "anticipate unintended consequences." Often a problem is solved and several more are created simply because the approach and solution are not well thought through. This step is intended to specifically play "devil's advocate" to probe the intended direction to discover the weak areas before the team plunges ahead. I learned this as I observed my Japanese *sensei* stare at a whiteboard for what seemed like an hour as they made absolutely sure they considered every possible impact of a proposed approach or plan. The final "planning" step—seven in all—is creation of a visual, detailed schedule by the entire team for implementation. The remaining three steps of the BEP are essentially "do," "check," and "adjust."

The purpose of the BEP was to define what a great plan looks like, because the inclination of almost every conventional engineering organization is to skip one or all of the planning steps just described. In any case, the team was familiar with something similar to the BEP but had not used it on a real problem. The team's "common sense" at the time was to use the traditional problem-solving methodology—that is, try and test, without working as a total team. The problem was complex, with manufacturing, tooling, supply chain, safety, function, timing, and other facets being impacted. The team was struggling and had not made progress. Everyone had a pet opinion on how to solve the problem and what to do.

I personally engaged the team in several meetings to start the BEP process, and got the team's agreement to use the BEP. The first steps were to define the problem statement; to establish a clear, quantifiable target, including allowances for variation; and to understand the physics of the problem. The natural and traditional behavior of the organization at this time was to skip all these steps and simply come up with ideas to solve the problem; this happened in several meetings. Although the team members had a great sense of urgency, they did not realize that skipping the initial steps in the BEP meant that any apparent progress was illusory.

Finally in the third meeting, the team again presented ideas without defining the problem, setting targets, or understanding the physics. At this point, I became very directive. It happened to be a Friday evening, and given the urgency of the situation, I asked the entire team to stop all other activity (including personal plans) and focus on this issue. Several hours of looking at the parts (*gemba*) and graphing the appropriate physics started to reveal the essence of the problem and suggested further steps and analysis that were needed to understand the physics in depth. Once this was done, brainstorming ideas (Step 4 of the BEP) became far more fruitful, since the ideas started to address the physics of the problem. The team at this time was cross-functional, with manufacturing and assembly staff involved, and this helped the ideas become more creative and effective. Use of the whiteboard to drive visibility of the data and thinking, and to allow everyone to participate and contribute, is absolutely essential to the BEP or any lean problem-solving process, and the team finally embraced this. Still no clear solution presented itself, but as a result of the Friday night session, the team had a clear understanding of the physics and the target, and ideas began to flow from around the company, including overseas engineering support facilities. I contributed several ideas as well.

At the end of a couple of weeks, more than 20 ideas had been generated. Most of them could be eliminated as not solving the problem, impossible to manufacture, or very poor based on timing, cost, investment, or other criteria. The methodology used to evaluate ideas was Pugh analysis (ranking alternatives on a number of dimensions), again with the whiteboard, with the entire team agreeing on rankings for each criterion, but yielding to expert judgment where appropriate. The team started to become energized and started to understand the power of the BEP approach. It contributed greatly to simply acting as a team.

At the end, two approaches were "in the finals." I had contributed one of the final ideas (which I was proud of), while the other had been contributed by an overseas engineering center. The team assessed both. My idea was simple, low cost, and easy to implement; required minimum tooling modification; worked on mocked-up parts; and could meet the required timing. The idea from overseas was considerably more complex, required significant tooling changes, worked on mocked-up parts, and would be a struggle to meet timing.

To my surprise at the time, the team chose the overseas idea, and I ended up agreeing to its direction. Why? Actually it was an outgrowth of Step 6 of the BEP process, which is "consider all consequences." Car bodies traditionally have a good deal of variability, and this forced the system to be mounted in an out-of-plane position for some number of vehicles. The team, as a result of considering all criteria, had established "robustness against mounting variation" as a key criterion, and mocked-up parts showed that my idea, while simple and easy to implement, was not robust against this variation. The overseas idea was considerably better.

A key culture change here was to force the team to make this decision based on facts, not based on organizational position. Traditional management behavior is to require information so that the manager can "make the call," and this is anathema to lean. This case was even more sensitive with my idea "in the finals" because it was less expensive and less risky to implement. The team expected me first to make the call, then, when I refused to do this and the team was pressed to make the call, to reverse the decision that the team had decided upon.

Critical leadership behavior here is to thread the needle. The true lean leader cannot arbitrarily reverse the team's decision—but she can challenge it to ensure that the team has "done its homework" and thought through every facet of implementation. In this case, I sent the team back several times to get more technical data and to flesh out the implementation plan and schedule in great detail. The team members, who were used to traditional "quick decisions" that were reversed later, repeatedly pushed back that it was out of time and needed an immediate decision. Again I was trying to model correct lean behavior. Plan thoroughly, then decide, and avoid changing decisions if at all possible.

A side benefit was that the team became stronger and stronger, and was forced to demonstrate exceptional collaborative behavior to rise to the challenge. The team's emotional commitment to success, and specifically to the solution it chose, became hardened.

The final result was completely successful. The critical technical issue was resolved, the team met timing and cost targets, quality was good, and the product was a great commercial success, both for the customer and for our company.

The Need for Emotional as Well as Intellectual Engagement

Although there were individual bright spots, and one by one people were starting to first consider, then try, then become proficient with and embrace the first lean tools, progress was excruciatingly slow. The enterprise was still struggling with many technical problems, and this had a direct impact on budget and customer satisfaction. Firefighting was still the primary mode of behavior. The urgency to implement lean and see results increased. I had several offsite meetings with my team to come up with ways to reinforce the lean message.

One effective tool was an all-employee meeting to review the current situation and ask for people's renewed commitment to lean. The goal was to break through the "blah blah blah" of traditional meetings and reach people on a more visceral level. For this reason, the meeting was started by showing the "drill till you throw up" scene from *Miracle on Ice*. In this scene, the coach of the 1980 U.S. Olympic hockey team is so exasperated with his team members' lack of teamwork that he makes them drill until they collapse.

The meeting started with this clip, without comment, and then a summary of the engineering budget, product quality, and program timing of current programs was presented. All metrics were miserable. The next slide was the simple question "Do we have a problem?" This was followed by a review of lean strategy and lean tools and a request for support, and finally a team that had demonstrated great BEP problem solving was honored. The meeting concluded with the scene from *Miracle on Ice* showing the U.S. team winning over the Russians in the Olympics. As can be imagined, this was a unique approach to an "all hands" meeting and stirred up a lot of comment. It was intended to be dramatic and "in your face." Implementing lean is not just a rational exercise; the real challenge is to overcome apathy, inertia, "not invented here," and "wait and see" to engage people emotionally as well as intellectually.

The all-employee meeting is not the only tool, and it may not be the most effective tool, but to really change an organization, the message and the actions have to be multiple, aligned, and relentlessly promoted and communicated. Other methods included recognition of teams that effectively used lean, A3 of the month recognition, and so on. Emotional engagement at every level is at least as critical as intellectual engagement. It is impossible to do too much.

Another Win as a Result of Lean

Another great example of bringing problems to the surface and turning them into opportunities was creating a system to minimize test properties. At the start, each individual team made a determination of how many test properties were required, based on its "common sense" and customer input. Typically, because of bill of materials (BOM) system limitations, all properties were built to a full system BOM, an entire product, even if the test in question did not require the full system. Many expensive parts were thrown away and wasted. In many cases, expensive prototype parts could be reused, but teams overlooked this opportunity. Analysis of best practices across many teams revealed many great ideas to minimize test properties and expense. Just as important was the combination of these individual practices into an overall methodology based on sound statistics, which allowed further improvements. The final methodology incorporated an expert to coach the team (and eventually approve the test plan) to

- Understand the statistics concerning minimum sample size and tests required to gain the required reliability and confidence for the system.
- Specify the minimum bill of materials required for each test.
- Take advantage of recycling parts and properties when appropriate.
- Appropriately challenge customers when their requirements lead to excessive test samples when compared to best practice.

As a result of excellence in this area, test cost was dramatically reduced, while reliability of and confidence in the testing that was conducted actually improved. Customers respected the clear methodology and deep expertise that was demonstrated. PDCA was continually advanced. Knowledge was captured and effectively reused.

The Importance of Tactical Planning by Whiteboard

The ability of teams to make cross-functional plans and schedules using a whiteboard is absolutely essential to lean, but at the start, this skill did not really exist. This is important not just to create a plan to be able to cycle through PDCA loops but also to drive cross-functional teamwork and finally to empower teams. Teaching and constant reinforcement of whiteboard-based tactical planning was driven from the start. Within the first month, I had ordered $60,000 worth of whiteboards to be installed in every conference room and team meeting place. I bought the fancy kind in which you can print what is on the board. Why was this so critical?

One foundation of lean is flow, and this is where any number of consultants start when implementing lean in product development. This is the correct approach, but in the worst case it can morph into statically applying the resultant value stream map to all future situations, regardless of changing circumstances. In some cases, the value stream map cannot have adequate detail for all activities. At its core, teaching whiteboard tactical planning is teaching the organization real-time value stream mapping—but it is even more powerful.

Whiteboard tactical planning (WTP), when properly done, drives the true team-based planning that is the foundation of PDCA. The key is that a common "language" of symbols is developed, so that everyone understands how to contribute to the plan. A whiteboard inherently allows everyone to participate in planning (pick up a marker!) and gives instant visibility to detail and commitment. Note that the popular commercial project management programs are much less common in a true lean organization because they require one person (the "program manager") to create and maintain the schedule. All too frequently, the formats driven by the program are obscure and uncommunicative. In the worst case, charts of 500 "blue bars" with unintelligible task labeling are offered as the "plan." These programs never produce the desired results because by their nature they prevent participation, collaboration, visual management, and real-time visibility for task dependency. As a result, there is a suboptimized plan and no real team buy-in. This is inevitably a complete disaster for lean. True buy-in for a plan can be accomplished only when the plan is created by the team and individuals take responsibility for specific subtasks.

Contrast whiteboard creation of tactical plans. Someone on the team (generally the junior member of the team is the default scribe for training) draws the appropriate scale for time across the top of the board (column headings). Work streams for major functional activities are listed down the left side of the board (row headings). Key events known from the current situation and key milestones where future deliverables are required are added. The entire team participates in determining how to connect both ends (the beginning and the end) of this "double-ended schedule" with the detailed tasks required for success. Creativity and extraordinary effort are frequently required, but the team can work together creatively to optimize the schedule.

A focus is to ensure that each member clearly defines what is required for his success—clear responsibility for each task; what information, parts, or other deliverables are required at the start of a task; and what precisely the output of each task is. This may require nested plans, where one part of a higher-level plan, such as prototyping, gets blown up into a separate, more detailed plan. Notes and diagrams can and should be included. The plan should be updated periodically as conditions change. When consensus is achieved, the "print" button is hit, and the plan becomes a promise. There is no need for any further documentation; the plan is simply scanned and e-mailed virtually in real time. By creating the plan together, all the team members can rotate PDCA loops on their personal development and rapidly learn to be excellent planners—at every level and within every function of the organization. All activity can be critically evaluated with a value stream mapping mindset by the people who understand the value best—the people who are actually doing the work.

Definition of Lean Management Philosophy: ORPMAR

Although this was not identified as an initial initiative, it quickly became clear that I was confusing the organization with my expectations for management behavior. Management behavior at the start ran the gamut from micromanagement of every detail to complete hands off ("I trust my people"). Both are incompatible with true lean management.

After reflection I created an acronym, ORPMAR, to describe management by PDCA.

1. Define the *objective*. Ideally, the objective should have a clear target, but at a minimum, it should be written down and correlated with the other projects and objectives of the organization.
2. Assign *responsibility*. This starts with ensuring that there is a capable leader, but it goes beyond this to ensure that the proper team makeup is in place. This includes dedicated resources where applicable, and also resources that are drawn upon as needed. Correlation with other functional groups to ensure proper support is key.
3. Review the *plan*. This is the magic of empowering the team. The first responsibility of the team is to collaboratively create a detailed plan to achieve the objective. The term *collaborative*

brings to mind the Japanese concept of *nemawashi*, which means that the person responsible brings a draft of the plan around the organization for feedback and to build consensus. Then the document serves as the "contract" between the sponsoring executive and the team. The plan defines the team's tactical approach and proposed schedule of deliverables. It allows the executive to add value by questioning and coaching, but not by micromanaging the detailed activity.

4. *Monitor* the team. As part of the plan, the team and the executive can agree on what kind of engagement and coaching are needed at what intervals. Clarification of what is expected in midterm and final deliverables should be part of the plan.

5. Drive *accountability*. This is the accountability of the executive to the team as well as the accountability of the team to the executive. All too often in traditional management, the objective is unclear, responsibility is confused, adequate resources are not provided, and there is no clear plan or prospect for success, yet accountability is "driven." This is not reasonable, to say the least. On the other hand, it is essential to hold the team accountable for working hard and following the lean methods when the executive has made a good-faith effort to provide good oversight.

6. Conduct *reflections* after each project. This is essential for rotating PDCA loops toward continuous improvement. The emphasis is on collecting knowledge and embedding lessons learned into the fundamental engineering systems.

With this system, a virtuous cycle of empowerment, responsibility, control, coaching, and achievement can be established. On the other hand, consider the monthly meeting for project reporting that is typical in many organizations. Teams and leaders are typically in the middle of activity and simply try to give confidence to management that things are progressing—but frequently they do not clearly understand the status of the project themselves. Often there is no clear objective, responsibility is confused, and a clear plan may not be in place. The team and the leader are trying to assure top executives of the project's progress, or in difficult situations are asking for help. With a chronic state of, at best, opacity and, at worst, confusion, most executives either give some light coaching or, if they sense that the project is struggling, cannot help but instead delve into micromanagement. Neither is consistent with lean, and both can be avoided by using ORPMAR.

 ### *Sensei* Reflections on the Initial Implementation of Lean

Although there were significant successes, and the organization was starting to "turn," several lean initiatives and ideas had unintended consequences. An example was the implementation of a cross-functional top management project review meeting. Teams were accustomed to struggling without help from or visibility by upper management until they had "made it through" the development or "blew up" because of a missed budget or schedule, or because of customer complaints. The middle layers of management were engaged somewhat sporadically, and in some cases not effectively. To combat this, the concept of "layered audits" was introduced, and specifically the responsibility of each layer of management to help the team and add value through coaching and knocking down barriers. If the team was still struggling, the issues should be elevated—finally, if necessary, to the top management project review meeting. The objective was open communication and transparency to enable management to understand the actual situation and help the teams, which was not always the case in the existing organization.

While this concept was true to lean and was the right thing to implement, it had unintended consequences. It was discussed in a general staff meeting, but deep *nemawashi* to gain agreement on this approach with each of the existing customer business unit (CBU) vice presidents and throughout the management organization was not done adequately. As a result, the CBU vice presidents

(Continued)

and other key members of management did not understand the philosophy behind this approach, and did not understand their role in it—to them it felt like "policing" or "second-guessing" their responsibility as general managers.

Cooperation at the top management project reviews by other functional groups was sporadic, and in general the idea that layered audits would be done was not understood or embraced. The traditional attitude by top management, cascaded through the organization, was that "this is what I pay 'my people' for—to keep the developments under control." In reality, this attitude was simply translated into no encouragement to report bad news and no visibility for systemic issues that confronted many teams.

Finally, my behavior as the lean leader at these audits was not always positive. When the true struggles that the teams were having became evident, the situation was often miserable. While I had the highest intentions to help, in too many cases I showed frustration. On reflection, this was the first time that this level of detail had been exposed, and many individuals and teams had concluded that management did not care about excellence in development. In some cases, skills and training were inadequate. In other cases, clearly people had poor attitudes, lacked experience, or lacked leadership skills. The point for the lean leader is that when bad news is brought up, you cannot react negatively, or you will inevitably lose the trust of people when it comes to bringing up any further bad news. Of course, if there are deep-rooted problems in the team, including attitude, leadership, or competence problems, they will need to be addressed after investigation and at a separate time.

With proper *nemawashi*, the top management project review meeting should have been very positive and have had the potential to dramatically move the organization forward; instead, it was resisted and ultimately killed. Teams continued to struggle in the organization in the short term until other methods were put into place to improve the situation.

In a larger sense, the top management project review meetings point out the need for alignment, alignment, alignment around lean at a top management level at the very start. At the very beginning, there was almost no discussion of lean development with other functions, such as program management, manufacturing, purchasing, and finance, before it was launched within engineering. Part of this was due to the intense ethic driven into me at Honda to "look to your own problems first" and to address the issues within engineering before pointing out where other functions could improve. Part resulted from the belief within the organization that the issues within product development were simply a result of engineering being "messed up." Part was the resistance to change by other functions and by the CBU general managers. Part was the belief by the general manager of the region that there was no need for a systemic transformation to lean—simple management "common sense" was all that was required. In any case, the final result was that engineering made early gains, but the systemic transformation of the organization to lean product development was slow once the "low-hanging fruit" had been harvested.

Another pitfall was not understanding the impact of criticism on the organization. A foundation of lean in Honda and Toyota is to relentlessly self-criticize—to focus on what needs to be fixed and improved, not to simply spend time on the positive news. At Honda, there were 99 critical comments for every positive comment—this was simply part of the culture. When I used this same method and behavior, I was surprised to find that I was considered to be a negative person. In fact, I was intensely proud of the organization's progress and accomplishments; I was simply trained never to dwell on this. I now believe that lean is best adapted to Western companies through a positive approach, with a rule of thumb to give several positive comments for every critical, but constructive one.

The Second Stage: Sustaining and Expanding Lean

After approximately 18 months, the first building blocks described here had taken hold, and the organization was able to see progress in driving engineering excellence through lean. Engineering had a budget reduction task that was well into seven figures—and we had overachieved this financial task by 50 percent. Technical execution had significantly improved. Customers saw improvement. Some teams had been converted emotionally as well as intellectually and were now evangelizing the benefits of lean. It was time to continue PDCA on the existing initiatives and take the next step. After assessing the organization's condition, the leadership team put the following in place:

- *Establishment of a Lean Champion executive staff position.* I appointed the executive director with the most energy and intellectual horsepower to this position. He was an individual with deep development experience in the organization and was widely respected, and he became a key evangelist for lean. Although he had no staff "reporting" to him directly, he became the project leader for all the lean initiatives that follow, and he assembled teams of appropriate people to accomplish the objectives of each initiative. It was critical that the organization understood that this was a key position and that it had my full support in terms of budget and resources.

- *Implementation of Lean Skill Set Assessment.* Expected lean skills were clarified, and every staff member was assessed. This not only was important for each staff member's personal development but also allowed reflection on what was "taking hold" and what needed further reinforcement.

- *Intense communication of lean resources, tools, and best practices.* This was done through newsletters, an extensive Web site, designated Lean Subject Matter Champions, training programs, recognition of lean accomplishments, and other methods.

- *Designation of subject matter technical experts (SMTEs).* The SMTEs had specific responsibility for developing the deepest technical expertise in each product group.
- *Design for cost.* This entailed making cost an engineering variable through the creation and correlation of basic cost tables for all major commodities in collaboration with the cost group. After cost tables were established, this allowed reverse engineering of all competitors' products for cost as well as performance.

These initiatives were not introduced on all projects, but instead were targeted for 2010 programs. This allowed a controlled introduction with good focus.

Identification of Subject Matter Technical Experts

Critical to lean is the development of profound technical expertise in all engineers (called "towering technical competence" by Morgan and Liker).[1] This is easy to say but difficult to execute. One reason is that most organizations have no clear expectations for or ways to measure technical expertise or value added. An individual's worth in a traditional organization is typically determined by how many people report to her. This system makes it almost impossible to develop deep technical expertise, since technical expertise is simply not valued.

As a management team, we resolved to recognize and reward deep technical expertise, and this starts by identifying the leaders who can show the value added by deep technical expertise. Fortunately, experts in each major functional area were already in the company, although few of them had been appropriately recognized and rewarded. These experts became the SMTE organization. They had no staff members reporting to them, but instead were charged with adding value through knowledge. This started with gathering all the accumulated knowledge of the organization, to be formed into design checklists. With these, the SMTEs were empowered to engage teams at the start of design to share the checklists and come to agreement on design concepts. After this, they would engage the teams throughout development, using the checklists to coach and ensure that knowledge was correctly embedded in the drawings and specifications. SMTEs were empowered to approve all designs before they could be released, giving them veto power. This required coaching of both teams and SMTEs to ensure good collaborative behavior—the teams needed to heed the SMTE's guidance in technical matters, but the SMTE had to respect the cost, timing, and integration challenges that teams needed to address that might have prevented the ideal technical solution.

Beyond the creation of checklists and engagement of teams, many SMTEs quickly found additional ways to add profound value to the organization, including

- Creation of labor-saving tools and methodologies for product design and optimization
- Management of part number deproliferation and creation of an optimized product portfolio
- Technology prospecting and innovation
- Long-term technology road mapping
- Maintenance and improvement of cost tables (discussed later)
- Deep competitive benchmarking, including a profound understanding of cost

As individual SMTEs created more and more ways to add value to the organization, it was obvious that an overall strategy combining best practices from each SMTE was needed. This was accomplished by creating a "stage model" for SMTE activity that incorporated the best of each SMTE's value-added technical activity so that this could be uniformly implemented and tracked.

Implementing Design for Cost

One of the most frustrating rework loops in traditional product design is "value engineering" and "value analysis" (VE/VA). In principle, value engineering should take place as part of the initial development process to design to cost targets, and value analysis should be continuous improvement to drive out costs after the start of production. In a conventional organization, engineers frequently have no access to or understanding of cost information. Although they have good intentions with regard to minimizing cost and maximizing value, without information, their designs are inevitably suboptimized for cost. This becomes evident only after the initial design is finished and cost has been "rolled up" by the finance staff or purchasing. At this point, everyone looks accusingly at the engineers as the people who designed something too expensively. Even at this point, it is not clear what "too expensively" means, since true design cost drivers often are obscured by inconsistent or overly complex calculation rules, reflect commercial gaming by suppliers, or simply are opaque.

The end result is that the call goes out for value engineering and/or value analysis activity, in which the product is redesigned using some rules of thumb and previous experience to "reduce cost." The cost drivers are still opaque. The cost estimators are again engaged to calculate cost and come back with different numbers—which are not always better and not always understandable. Typically this process requires a significant amount of time, and the cost estimators are often overloaded, so that the VE/VA design is completed just as test results for the initial design are available, at which point everyone concludes that it is too risky to substantially change the design.

Believe it or not, this is the traditional design cycle of industry. It generates incredible amounts of waste and a rework loop so profound and embedded in the process that the design is often never optimized for cost.

A true lean approach is profoundly different. The rework loop for cost is completely eliminated. Cost is treated as a design variable, no different from calculating stress, strain, or weight. To accomplish this, several things need to be put into place.

The first is the creation of simple cost tables based on "best practice" material costs, machine rates, labor rates, tooling costs, and SGA&P. The objective for each commodity is to create a simple economic model for a well-run shop using best practices to generate optimized cost and quality. This is not so different from traditional cost estimating, but in some cases, traditional cost estimating attempts to model the specific machine, factory, burden rate, commercial agreement, or other detail. Attempting to chase this detail will prevent the design from being optimized, ensure that cost is the exclusive responsibility of the full-time estimator, and allow commercial gaming by those who would benefit from cost confusion (in many cases, this is the supply chain). On the other hand, having simple cost models allows engineers to calculate cost. The true drivers of cost can be highlighted. Alternative constructions and solutions can quickly be compared, and the design can be optimized.

Importantly, the simple design cost calculated by the engineer should be used as the base by the cost estimator, who remains responsible for the creation of the "official" cost, which in many cases must include specific exemptions for machine rate, labor rate, logistics, SGA&P, or other details. The power of the simplified calculation is profound, however. Since it is based on a "best practice" or idealized cost model, it can serve as a very effective cost target for internal manufacturing operations or for the supply chain. There is magic when the design engineer teams up with the purchasing agent to review a supplier's quote together—to compare what the supplier states is needed to process the design with what has been calculated based on a best practice model. Properly done, it is very fair and gives suppliers a clear road map to a sustainable business model—and where they have gaps from that model.

In a yearlong effort, the finance staff was engaged, agreed to collaboratively create cost tables, agreed to the operational model in which the "official" cost was built up from the engineering cost as a base, and helped train engineers in cost estimating. Eventually, hundreds of engineers were capable of doing cost calculations for the key commodities. The results were immediate and dramatic. The cost estimating department was immediately unloaded from the crushing burden of calculating hundreds of "VE/VA" ideas—most of which were not worthwhile anyway, since they were created without understanding the cost drivers. Instead, far fewer ideas were submitted, but almost all of them were clear "winners." Optimization of design was accomplished far more quickly. Purchasing and engineering effectively teamed up to help suppliers understand and achieve optimum cost. Suppliers appreciated the rational approach to ensuring a sustainable business model. Finally, NAAS was able for the first time to convince Japanese customers that the organization understood and could optimize cost, leading to additional business. Cost tables gave a "common language" throughout the supply chain, from customer (at least Japanese customers) to supplier. Designs could be optimized from the start, and cost transparency promoted a sustainable business model for all.

Reverse Engineering to Gain Overwhelming Competitive Advantage

Once cost tables began to get embedded in the culture and engineers had been trained to calculate cost, the next step could be taken. A massive competitive benchmarking exercise was started—but in a new way. Every competitor's system was methodically broken down into like subsystems and "reverse engineered" for cost—in other words, its cost was calculated using the NAAS cost tables. We could use our cost tables, which related different design features to best-in-class manufacturing processes and what it would cost to make the product, and thus predict our competitor's costs (assuming that it was using the best manufacturing process). This required a large amount of work, but the results were extremely interesting. For the first time, real clarity concerning the cost-effectiveness of competitors' designs was achieved. In particular, comparisons could be made between the cost of the NAAS design and that of competitors' designs, and in most cases the NAAS design was at a significant disadvantage.

The next step was to establish a "Frankenstein target." We had calculated our competitors' costs by subsystem, and we knew who had the lowest cost for each subsystem—each structural characteristic, methods of fastening, and design of stamped and welded parts. Of course, nobody was the lowest cost at everything. We cobbled together all the lowest-cost subsystems from different automakers as if we were building a Frankenstein product from a variety of separate parts and rolled these up to set a system target. We challenged our development teams to "copy it or beat it." This was inherently unfair, since a system could not be built from disparate subsystems, but after some grumbling, the team members engaged with a positive attitude and became very innovative about creating new solutions. They created a system either from the most effective competitors' ideas or from original ideas that proved to be more cost-effective than the competitors' best subsystem.

The final result was a system that achieved roughly a 30 percent reduction in total cost from that of the previous system. This technique drove the creation of a new generation of products that allowed NAAS to win business from an extremely demanding Japanese customer for the first time. It appeared that this methodology created a "world beater" product for value, which it logically should if the fundamental manufacturing cost base is competitive.

If we consider what we were doing here in terms of the some of the concepts from earlier in the book, it was mainly a target-setting and problem-solving process. As in the model in Figure 4.1 (page 70), we had a clear business purpose for the exercise—we set a challenging and concrete target based on a clear rationale (cost target from Frankenstein model). It was not clear at the outset how to go about achieving it, but teams were motivated to be creative and to find solutions step by step through PDCA, which they had been trained in. It had taken time to move the culture to this level of maturity, but it worked!

The Change Process—the Underestimated Critical Variable

I have described what we did at NAAS, and while it may appear to be difficult, the mechanics are pretty straightforward. It also may appear that I had the clout, so I just "made them do it." There is a grain of truth in this, as I could not have done it without the clout of the executive office, but it is far more than this. I cannot overstate the importance of positive emotional engagement (or the flip side, resistance to change). At the end of the day, when the organization looked back after several years, it for the most part could understand the logic of lean product development and was glad to have made the journey. During the actual process, there was battle after battle.

In many cases, people's emotional reactions were patterned after the emotions of grieving—from denial through anger, bargaining, depression, then acceptance—but finally many people were able to embrace the new way of operating. For the most part, I believe that the transformation is sustainable and that it had the profound effect on the business that NAAS management had hoped for. The limiting factor in every case was resistance to change and the ability to have positive emotional engagement, which required patience, many one-on-one conversations, and a human side that many engineering executives will have to work hard to cultivate. As an engineer at heart who wants to "get it done now," it was certainly my greatest challenge.

At NAAS, we managed the change process with champions for lean; targeted teams for initiatives; extensive peer-led training; celebration of successes; communication by town hall meeting, Web communications, and newsletters; and many other methods. Some of them worked and some were difficult to judge in terms of effect, but we were constantly looking for ways to reinforce the need for change and the expectations for new behaviors and ways of operation. The actual mechanics, as in lean manufacturing, are becoming well defined and almost "cookbook." What moves lean from a static set of tools to a powerful tactical and strategic weapon is passionate, committed leadership that can unleash the creative energies of working people throughout the organization.

Chapter 12

Going Nuclear with Lean

(With John Drogosz)

The opposite of every great idea is another great idea.

—Niels Bohr, physicist

Nuclear Corporation develops and manufactures nuclear fuel assemblies that go into many nuclear power plants that supply power throughout the United States. We began working with Nuclear in 1998 as it began its lean journey in a small assembly operation in the eastern United States and had seen the tangible benefits of applying lean. In the meantime, its parent company had purchased a competing manufacturing site on the West Coast in 2001. Nuclear's vice president of operations was convinced of the benefits of lean and wanted to start the recently acquired West Coast site on its lean transformation as soon as possible.

John Drogosz was the consultant on this effort and has followed Nuclear's lean journey over nearly a decade. This chapter takes John's perspective as he facilitated the West Coast site's lean journey, including the benefits that it experienced and the challenges that it faced in changing its culture.

Background on Lean at Nuclear

Nuclear's vice president of operations had read Jeff Liker's book, *Becoming Lean*, and was convinced that lean could be applied to the highly regulated nuclear industry. As a result, he hired Liker and his associates to come to his East Coast facility beginning in October 1998. The facility had about 120 employees and was primarily an assembly operation that stuffed uranium pellets into nuclear fuel rods and then assembled them into "bundles" that are the fuel for power plants. Over the next year, an external lean coach was sent in full-time for six months, followed by several one-week *kaizen* events leading to the typical savings in lead time, productivity, and quality. Some of the managers were starting to see and understand the changes, while others were still on the fence. After two years on the lean journey, the parent company decided to expand its presence in the industry by acquiring a competing facility on the West Coast that made the uranium pellets as well as assembling them.

The newly acquired site was much larger than the East Coast site. It had more than 650 employees and many more value streams. In fact, the new site had the total value stream (see Figure 12.1), from raw materials (gas), conversion to powder, transformation to pellets, and rod and bundle assembly. It also had "side streams" for machined components (tie plates and end caps for the bundle assembly) and waste reprocessing.

The site was clearly a traditional manufacturer, full of excess inventory and every other type of waste. The process was very much batch and queue between departments, and metrics were focused on the performance of the individual departments. The company was a very quality-conscious organization, but it was focused on inspection and oversight. Lead time and cost were not particularly emphasized, and consequently the site was losing a lot of money. The vice president of operations was convinced that the company could get large improvements in lead time and productivity while maintaining its quality levels by implementing lean, and he again asked Liker for a full-time external coach for the first year. That was where I came in, starting as the *sensei* for Nuclear in May 2002 and working with the company for eight years.

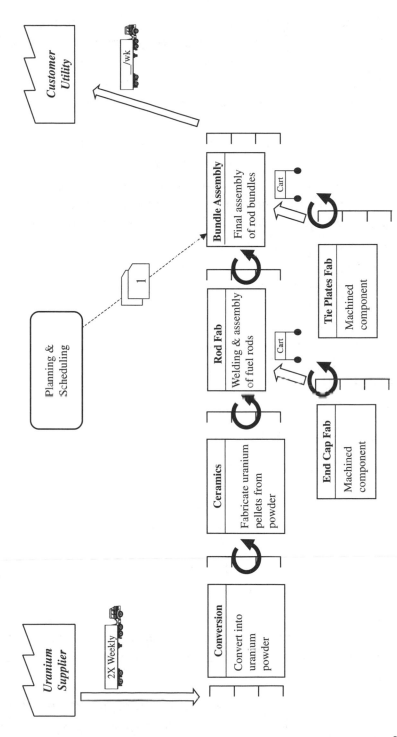

Figure 12.1. Nuclear High-Level Value Stream after Lean Transformation

The nuclear industry is highly regulated, and hence many procedures and audits are in place to ensure safe operating conditions. The challenge in production is that there are different designs of the product for each customer. Every order (contract) is different from the last one because of changes in the operating conditions of the electric utility and thus the nuclear power plant. Customers' expectation in terms of quality is "zero tolerance for failure." From a production viewpoint, many of the processes in the plant are automated continuous processing and consequently are not easily changed because of the technology, cost, and regulatory requirements. The regulatory requirements also include very detailed traceability of all components throughout the value stream, which implies that the company must process voluminous amounts of information in addition to fabricating the parts and assemblies. Of course, at the outset, the managers, all veterans of the nuclear fuel industry, were skeptical that lean could be applied to this highly regulated industry, and they had to be convinced through years of direct experience with actual improvements in their processes. As the *sensei*, I could not envision at the beginning exactly what changes would be made or how, and I learned with them along the way.

Phases of Deployment

Looking back on the deployment of lean manufacturing at Nuclear, we categorized what happened into five distinct phases:

Phase 0: Structural changes in preparation for lean deployment. A preliminary assessment, organizational changes, and adjustments in workforce levels were conducted that were not directly focused on lean but did set the stage with a right-sized workforce.

Phase 1: Lean awareness and value stream vision. The site was introduced to the concepts of lean manufacturing through training, definition of value streams, value stream mapping, and the first set of *kaizen* events led by consultants.

Phase 2: Implementation of lean pilots. The container refurbishment and machined tie plates value streams were selected as pilots to develop more depth in the understanding of lean and provide models from which others could learn.

Phase 3: Spreading the implementation across the other value streams. We then spread implementation to the larger "fuel" value stream. The pilot had moved beyond initial deployment and continued to deepen, while the site manager sought to spread lean manufacturing more broadly within the organization.

Phase 4: Management learning and the start of continuous improvement. It took a full six years for the management team to really start to understand its role in managing the change and the teams on the floor and to deeply understand the nature of continuous improvement.

Phase 0: Structural Changes in Preparation for Lean Deployment

Before he even introduced the word *lean* at the new site, the vice president of operations conducted a preliminary assessment of the site that included both the operations and the organization's strengths and weaknesses. He wanted to "clean up the place" before even starting the lean journey. These changes took place over a four-month period.

First, some of the managers, including the plant manager, needed to be changed out, as they clearly had an entrenched mindset of the traditional manufacturing that was prevalent in the nuclear industry. However, most of the managers were replaced initially by managers from other departments at the same site. For example, the new plant manager came from the engineering department. While he had no preconceived notions about mass production versus lean production, he also did not have much production experience and did not have credibility with the production supervisors.

Second, on the operations side, preliminary analyses of the number of people relative to the production volume indicated that there were significantly too many workers and managers. Given that the nuclear industry is not a growth industry and that contracts tend to be long-term, the company could not bank on growing sales enough to redeploy so many operators and managers. This led to the difficult decision to downsize both the blue-collar and the white-collar workforce by approximately 20 percent. Senior management agreed to apply the hatchet in one fell swoop before introducing lean so that the change to lean would not be associated with the downsizing.

Third, an internal Site Lean Leader (referred to in other chapters as an internal coach) was selected who would learn the principles and the transformation process from the lean consultant. Ultimately, he would become the site expert who would continue to develop more lean leaders in each department. The person selected was a manager from the site who had been with the prior company for more than 25 years. The idea was that if the site had "one of its own" leading the change, this would accelerate the acceptance of lean principles.

While the strategy outlined in Phase 0 was a good idea and was necessary, in retrospect the senior management team underestimated how entrenched the old culture was and the level of resistance and resentment that the corporate takeover and the subsequent restructuring would create. Putting long-term employees into new management roles rearranged the pieces but did not significantly change the culture.

Phase 1: Lean Awareness and Value Stream Vision

A few weeks after the dust had settled from the restructuring, the vice president of operations held a formal kickoff event for lean at the new site. The kickoff included a "state of the union" address about the current financials and the need to become more competitive in order to survive. His message was that the company needed to use lean techniques to better satisfy its customers' high quality needs *and* make a profit. Reducing waste in its processes was the key to operating at the same sales volume with the recently reduced workforce. It turned out to be a rocky start.

All managers went through a basic introduction to lean principles. During the training, we were continually told that the nuclear industry was "different," which wasn't news to us, and it was clear that the managers were having difficulty visualizing lean in their environment.

To help them translate the lean principles to their situation, each manager and his team participated in a value stream mapping workshop facilitated by the consultant and the internal Site Lean Leader to help them identify waste in their process and see how they could apply the lean principles to their areas. Most areas saw opportunities to reduce lead times by 20 to 50 percent. This helped turn on the lightbulb for some of the managers, but others still remained skeptical. However, as we all know, the best way to learn lean is by applying it on the shop floor, at the *gemba*. Based on the future state from the value stream mapping sessions, *kaizen* events were conducted in targeted pilot areas of the value stream.

 ***Sensei* Reflection on Phases 0 and I**

The restructuring of the company was a painful but necessary step to enable a clean start for lean at the facility. The lean training and value stream mapping sessions were valuable in getting managers engaged in understanding the fundamentals of lean and seeing opportunities for improvement in their respective areas. In retrospect, while it was great to have all the managers go through the activities at the same time, it also caused several challenges. First, not all managers were at the same level of readiness for change. Some of them were still learning their new jobs and getting to know the capabilities of the people in their departments. Consequently, several managers were distracted, did not really take the time to absorb the learnings from the training and the value stream mapping activity, and did nothing to expand their learning afterward. In addition, the internal Site Lean Leader was just starting to learn the job from the consultant, and hence the bandwidth to coach and follow up with the managers was limited. Most of the value stream mapping results sat idle as we focused on two lean pilots. Experiences of this type have led us to recommend against wall-to-wall value stream mapping in the early stages of lean.

Phase 2: Implementation of Lean Pilots

Based on the value stream analysis and the size of the site, two pilot areas were identified to show quick results and to gain implementation experience for the people at the site. The pilots, each with its own challenges, were

1. Container refurbishment
2. Machine shop—tie plates value stream

Container Refurbishment Pilot

The container refurbishment value stream takes the large containers that hold the nuclear fuel assemblies returned by the customer, verifies and fixes them, and certifies that the containers are ready to be loaded with new nuclear bundles and sent to the nuclear power plants. In a one-week *kaizen* event, under the guidance of the consultants, the team of 12 workers was able to clean up the workspace and organize tools, rebalance work to *takt* time, implement one-piece flow, and create initial standard work. The results exceeded the team members' expectations. They reduced their work-in-process inventory by more than 75 percent and improved productivity by more than 110 percent! Clearly, the team members felt very energized by their accomplishments that week, and the plant manager recognized them for their great work. All managers were encouraged to attend the *kaizen* report out and to visit the area to see firsthand how lean could be applied in their facility. Most managers were shocked by the level of transformation of the area and went back to their departments to "think about what it meant for their area."

After several months, the container team had more or less maintained its area, and the metrics continued to show that it was meeting its *takt* time. However, the team had not really pursued any of the other ideas that had come out of the *kaizen*. The manager of the area was pleased with the results that the team had already achieved and did not encourage or support the team's other ideas for improvement. Consequently, the team continued to coast along, showing off as a "model" of lean. In retrospect, it was clear that the manager felt that she had punched her ticket and had finished "doing lean." The plant manager lost interest after the big gains were achieved and was content to let the team be, as he was more interested in the big wins to come from the next *kaizen* events.

Machine Shop—Tie Plates Value Stream

The tie plates are the upper and lower portions that hold the fuel bundle assembly together. They are made of expensive casting material; they are complex in design, and hence require several machining steps at very tight tolerances. The machine shop had grouped similar types of machines in a process-oriented layout, with highly experienced machinists at each machine. Machinists would process entire campaigns of customer products (batches of 200 or more parts) and push them into inventory awaiting the next machining step. Overall, the machine shop was viewed as a poor performer in terms of cost and lead time and was frequently part of outsourcing studies. The machine shop manager was relatively new to the job but had extensive experience in machine shops at other companies. After the lean training, he practically pushed his way to the top of the list to be a pilot area.

The culture in the machine shop could easily be characterized as traditional manufacturing. Most machinists had more than 10 years of experience at their specific jobs and hence were quite fixed in their ways. The machine shop was also very cramped, with some shared pieces of equipment, so moving equipment around would be a series of chess moves.

Given the initial circumstances, the machine shop manager wanted to tread more slowly than the container refurbishment pilot. He felt that before any big moves were made or tasks redistributed, there was a lot of low-hanging fruit that would not only improve the performance of the machine shop but also help the lives of the machinists. Thus, the workshops conducted on the tie plate value stream were limited to tools for stability and flexibility. *Kaizen* events were held around 5S, Total Productive Maintenance (TPM), error proofing, and quick changeover.

The first few workshops were really meant to "get the stones out of the operators' shoes" by improving their workplace and the reliability of their machines. After this initial round of workshops, the machinists (with some prodding by the manager) started talking about the layout of the shop and how it really did not help them process the tie plates effectively. The team then started looking at alternatives, using a spaghetti diagram to see how they could reduce their material movement and walking distances.

The team came up with a great "ideal" layout for the best possible flow, and implemented what was realistically possible. As part of this activity, the team also reduced its batch sizes by more than 75 percent! Productivity also improved by more than 30 percent in the first year. After the first round of workshops, the machine shop manager continued holding meetings with the team every other week to come up with other areas for improvement. Shortly after, he started the same process with the bundle end caps value stream, which was housed in the same building.

Other Value Streams

While the selected pilots were in progress, the other value streams were focused on the elements of "stability" in their value streams. Most areas were conducting workshops on 5S, error proofing, and standard work. The idea was to keep the other teams gradually moving forward on their lean journey while the two pilots developed deeper learning that could then be passed along to the other groups.

 ### *Sensei* Reflection on Phase 2

The pilots were a great learning experience for the teams, and the results achieved were impressive. In addition, they helped develop the expertise of the internal Site Lean Leader and gave the manager of the machine shop a strategy for spreading lean to the other areas of the machine shop.

While the learning was great for those involved, the pilots did not yield as much benefit as expected in providing a learning experience for the other departments. In retrospect, the pilots chosen were great candidates in terms of size, scope, and management willingness. However, they were not the best choices in terms of acceptance by other groups. Namely, the two pilots were considered side streams of the core flow, as they were not in "hot zones" where nuclear materials were being handled.

Another challenge in this phase was keeping the other areas engaged in the process. The internal Site Lean Leader wanted to make sure that all areas received some coverage to keep the momentum going from the initial value stream mapping sessions. Since the lean team resources were focused on the pilots, limited time was allocated to the other areas. There was not much time available for coaching these managers, and some of them felt that *kaizen* events were pushed onto them (and they could hardly say no, given that the vice president of operations was promoting lean). As a result, most of the *kaizen* events in these areas were limited to 5S, standard work, and error proofing. While these were important lean building blocks, they did not always lead to noticeable savings, unlike the savings being seen in the pilots, leading some managers to question the value of implementing lean in their areas. All of this led to some interesting and unexpected outcomes in Phase 3.

Phase 3: Spreading the Implementation across the Other Value Streams

By now, Nuclear was well into its second year on its lean journey. So far, the implementation of the pilots had had a few bumps in the road, but overall they were seen as successes by the vice president of operations and the plant manager. They now felt that it was time to start spreading the implementation to the larger value streams of conversion (fabrication of nuclear powder), ceramics (fabrication of the nuclear pellets that go into nuclear fuel rods), fuel rod assembly, and bundle assembly (final assembly of fuel rods into a predetermined array held together by a fuel cage, tie plates, and end caps). Some of these areas had already begun trying out lean methods, for better or for worse, based on what they had directly seen from the pilots or at the prodding of the internal Site Lean Leader, who was trying to spread lean faster through the *kaizen* events mentioned in Phase 2. It was at this point that the implementation approaches and results started to diverge.

Several issues started to surface as the deployment was spread that led to high variation of outcomes (some good and some not so good):

1. Tools-based implementation versus a value stream focus
2. *Kaizen* events being perceived as the endgame of lean
3. Shortage of internal lean leaders to support and coach the expanding number of teams
4. Delegation of lean implementation by some managers
5. Resistance by supervisors to changes in their areas and their roles
6. Changes in the management team
7. Changes in the lean team

Tools-Based Implementation versus Value Stream Focus

While the pilots were progressing, some of the managers took it upon themselves to start "implementing" what they had seen. In fact, this was encouraged, as it was felt that this approach would help the individual managers and teams learn and take ownership of the lean system. Unfortunately, sometimes the best intentions led to unexpected outcomes.

For example, while the lean team was focused on making the pilots a success, some managers were busy copying 5S in their areas. In fact, the Site Lean Leader of Nuclear was so happy that the areas were actively implementing this tool that he started doing 5S workshops for anyone who asked, then started doing assessments and giving out awards for 5S. This did create a lot of buzz about lean and good competition between the groups to strive to improve their workplace organization. However, it also planted the seed in the minds of many operators and supervisors that lean was a collection of tools to be applied to each area in a checklist fashion.

Kaizen Events Being Perceived as the Endgame of Lean

As the implementation spread, a new round of *kaizen* events was planned for each value stream with the support of consultants. Some groups embraced the *kaizen* events, while others tried to stonewall, claiming that they "did not have time" to do events. For several months, weekly *kaizen* events were being held, and some were leading to strong initial results like those experienced by the pilot teams. Ultimately, each team, either willingly or by management push, had taken part in at least one *kaizen* event. The plant manager and the Site Lean Leader actually kept metrics on the number of *kaizen* events and the results so that they could report back to the vice president of operations how much they had done with lean. However, after approximately six months, it became apparent that the level at which lean was being sustained was not what had been seen in the initial pilots. It was clear that the teams were doing the plan and do phases of the workshops, but that the check and adjust phases were not very consistent. In many cases, this was not the fault of the teams but rather stemmed from a lack of coaching by the Site Lean Leader and the management team.

Shortage of Internal Lean Leaders to Support and Coach the Expanding Number of Teams

During this hectic phase, the focus on *kaizen* events across so many areas led to a critical shortage of internal lean leaders. The consultants did as much coaching as they could while they were onsite, but they were not there day after day to follow up with the teams. It also became apparent during this phase that the internal Site Lean Leader was changing his role from being a *kaizen* facilitator and shop-floor coach to being a manager. He got sucked into tracking implementation plans, conducting assessments, doing tours, and creating progress reports. As a result, the teams started perceiving him more as an administrator than as a coach who could help them with the implementation issues that they were facing. The plant manager did not step up to identify other potential candidates who could become internal lean leaders. This was also the time when senior management started to reduce outside lean support (i.e., me), as the managers felt that the internal Site Lean Leader must have learned well over the past year, since they were seeing such great "results."

Delegation of Lean Implementation by Some Managers

This was one of the biggest barriers to spreading the lean implementation. It became clear early on which managers were truly "on the bus," which were on the fence, and which were passive-aggressive when it came to lean implementation. Most were fine with doing workshops as long as the disruption to their operations was minimal. Feeding the *kaizen* event machine was the perception by some managers that lean was to be led by the internal Site Lean Leader with the support of the consultants. Consequently, they would call the lean team whenever they needed to improve a process or solve a problem. While this "pull" was a good sign that these managers saw value in the lean approach, it also highlighted that they did not view their jobs as including driving improvement. They saw results during the events, but they had the perception that the lean team and the supervisors were responsible for following up with the shop-floor actions. Consequently, the Monday after a workshop, everyone went back to work, and a lot of the action items went into the red. Over time, this started to affect the perception and credibility of the lean deployment.

Resistance by Supervisors to Changes in Their Areas and Their Roles

One of the toughest nuts to crack during the spreading of lean on the site was resistance by the first-line supervisors in each area. While there had been changes in the management during the reorganization, the first-line supervisors had remained essentially in the same positions.

As lean came their way, most of them were unsure of what was in it for them. Their new managers were telling them that they should participate in *kaizen* events and that they should support the changes. However, they received very little coaching from their managers or the lean team. The managers saw sustaining lean as being the supervisors' job, even though they did not do much of it, and the lean team was already being stretched thin, so its only coaching opportunities came during the *kaizen* events.

Over time, as the number of *kaizen* events grew and the corresponding action lists grew, the supervisors started viewing lean as giving them more work. In addition, most of the supervisors had many years of experience and felt that the changes being proposed by their team members were naïve or simplistic. "There is a reason we do things the way we do, and here you are changing what has worked for us for so many years," said one supervisor. We also saw that while the managers and the lean team were preaching lean, the supervisors were still being measured by traditional metrics. For example, *kaizen* events were highlighting the evils of large batch production, yet the supervisors were being driven by number of units produced per person, and inventory did not even show up on their scorecards. Consequently, supervisors were tacitly encouraged by their managers to run big batches so that they could make their numbers and leave the changeovers to the next shift. Clearly, this caused supervisors within the department to be competitors, and their downstream customer departments would at times suffer from parts shortages; those departments would then have to run overtime to get caught up.

Changes in the Management Team

During the spreading of lean, it became clear that some of the management changes that had been made during Phase 0 had not panned out as expected.

First, the plant manager who had been assigned in Phase 0 did not work out and ultimately was moved to another position. While he was not opposed to lean, he also would not confront the managers below him who were clearly not exhibiting the right lean behaviors. As he was not originally from operations, he did not want to rock the boat too much with his direct reports, but consequently, he was also not able to move the ship forward as much as was needed.

The new plant manager came from another company where he had had some experience with lean. He was a clear proponent of flow, and he saw early on that while progress had been made on parts of the value stream in some departments, the focus needed to be on tying all the pieces of the value stream together.

Some of the department managers also moved on to other positions during this phase. Not all of this was due to lean implementation issues, as other opportunities had presented themselves to some managers. This did lead to some slowdowns in implementation in some departments, but for the most part the leadership changes at this point in the implementation helped breathe new life into the efforts in the departments that had been plodding along. In retrospect, it was clear that the senior management was learning to identify the true leadership characteristics needed to drive and sustain lean improvements. While the first round of management changes appeared to be more focused on selecting people with technical competence, this second round of changes tended to put in place managers who had not only technical competence but also better "soft" skills at managing people and change.

Changes in the Lean Team

With the changes in management, there also came changes to the lean team. The original Site Lean Leader was replaced by someone who had more shop-floor experience and credibility with the operators. Approximately six months afterward a Lean Manager was also appointed to help coach the managers and push those managers who had been sitting on the fence. This two-pronged approach worked very well, as there were now coaches in the lean team that both management and the operators could feel more comfortable working with during the ongoing implementation.

Continuing the Deep Pilot in the Machine Shop

While the implementation efforts were spreading to other areas in Phase 3, the machine shop continued quietly along its lean journey.

With the pilot phase complete, the manager had gleaned several learning points that helped him spread implementation throughout his machine shop more effectively, namely

1. *The need for a long-term vision for flow.* As mentioned earlier, the machine shop had a very process-oriented layout and hence tended to work in large batches. From the pilot, it became clear to everyone that improving flow was the key. In addition to the value stream maps, the team created a spaghetti diagram of all the value streams crossing through the machine shop. After this exercise, the goal of the machine shop was to "untangle the spaghetti." Given the need to keep production going and the number of crossed streams and amount of shared equipment, it became clear that this would need to be done in a series of steps. The team created a set of "future states 1, 2, and 3" to guide the implementation through phases. The first future state was the largest, where all support machining was separated from production machining. The team moved more than 50 percent of the equipment in one weekend! Needless to say, come Monday, the operators and managers of the other departments were shocked by the change and the subsequent improvements in flow and reduction in batch sizes. For example, the team had now gone from doing batches of two to three weeks of production down to one- to two-day batches!

2. *Teaching and coaching supervisors and operators.* The machine shop manager realized that he needed to get his supervisors on board with the current and future changes. He started by giving his supervisors reading assignments and having weekly sessions with them on how they could apply their learning to help "untangle the spaghetti" as they moved forward with their vision. Each supervisor had projects assigned and would report out on the shop floor to her colleagues on her progress. The manager was there to coach supervisors, ensure that their ideas were aligned with the overall vision, and provide assistance (e.g., tooling engineering, purchasing) to help them implement their team's ideas. The manager said that he wanted to retire in the

coming years, and his ultimate goal was to make sure that he left his team with the right tools and mindset to sustain a lean machine shop.

3. *Continuous improvement—small improvements really add up!* Once the flow started to improve after the first series of machine moves, the teams started seeing many other opportunities. At first, the teams were a bit hesitant to make the changes, as they were viewed as small relative to the big changes that had taken place so far. However, the manager and his supervisors canvassed the machinists to help them identify the waste and frustrations that they still had on the shop floor. They then prioritized the list and started chipping away at these issues. Many were low-cost ideas related to error proofing, quick changeover, ergonomics, and flow. As the first round of small changes started to be implemented, operators and supervisors started asking more questions like, "Why am I walking these parts all the way over there to this shared washer?" and, "Why are we sending parts to the back of the shop to be inspected?"

With all the changes in both management and processes, Nuclear ultimately made great progress along the overall value stream during Phase 3. For example, with the new plant manager's focus on improving flow, Nuclear was able to reduce lead time by almost 50 percent and work-in-process inventory by 40 percent by introducing a pull system and paying better attention to buffer management.

 ## Sensei Reflection on Phase 3

Looking back, this was the most exciting yet challenging phase of Nuclear's lean journey. The teams achieved great reductions in lead time along the core value stream and many other improvements in each area. However, the journey was quite bumpy at times in terms of achieving sustainable results, changing the mindsets of managers and supervisors, and maintaining the morale of the lean team. For many groups, this phase was truly where they figured out how lean applied to their areas and how to start driving change.

It was also the phase in which the lean team learned where its gaps were in terms of capability and capacity to support the lean transformation. While experience has shown that a value stream approach and creating deep learning pilots are key elements in driving sustainable improvements, it is also clear that each group will still learn at its own pace, and part of this learning process is allowing the group to make its own implementation mistakes (such as taking a tools approach). The lean leader needs to accept that each group will want to take its own implementation path. While it may be frustrating for the lean leader to see his counsel and the learnings from the pilots not being implemented to the fullest extent, it is important for managers and their teams to learn in their own way. The lean leader needs to take the time to coach the managers through this learning phase and must have the patience and persistence to guide them through the twists and turns of their individual lean journeys.

Phase 4: Management Learning and the Start of Continuous Improvement

After three and a half years of implementation, the teams had gone through many *kaizen* events and shop-floor rearrangements. The key metrics of lead time, quality, and productivity were trending well. The teams on the shop floor, however, were getting "*kaizen*ed out." While there were still opportunities, the teams were resisting doing more *kaizen* workshops, as most of their ideas were now smaller in scope. In addition, the lean team again found itself stretched thin, since the entire site, including the support teams (purchasing, labs, engineering), was now practicing lean, and the lean team could not support facilitating all improvement activities. It was at this point that the lean team saw that while the *kaizen* workshops and small shop-floor activities were good catalysts for deploying lean on the site and getting measurable results, they also led to the groups becoming dependent on the lean team to run lean activities. Supervisors and manufacturing engineers did not feel comfortable facilitating events in their respective areas, and most managers now had the expectation that the lean team was the service provider for lean activities.

It was at this point that the lean team, senior management, and the *sensei* (me) did a "check" and stepped back to assess where Nuclear was on its lean journey and how to keep the momentum going.

It became clear that while at this point, virtually everyone understood the benefits of lean in their respective areas, the managers and supervisors still had not taken ownership of the process. From the lean team's viewpoint, it had not really worked with the managers and teams to create the infrastructure in each area that would enable that area to be self-sustaining on its lean journey. Specifically, lean leaders in each area who were responsible for growing their knowledge of lean and then spreading it to their colleagues had not been identified, and managers did not have clear expectations set by senior management that they were to drive the ongoing improvements. It was thought throughout the deployment phase that as people participated and learned, they would grow organically into taking ownership of the process and continue to spread it into their groups. Clearly, some people in some areas took it upon themselves to do so, but this was not consistent, and the depth of knowledge was also highly variable. It was also clear that some teams had started to make shop-floor improvements on their own (good!), but these were not always aligned with the value stream vision.

This was a very challenging time for management and for the lean team. While it was felt that implementation had been a bumpy road, the site was moving overall in the right direction. It was good to see some people taking the initiative to make improvements on their own, but it was also disheartening to see others standing still. The varying maturity of the teams was taking its toll on sustaining the gains in some areas. The different levels of maturity in the teams along the value stream also led to some friction between the teams. For example, one of the downstream teams had continued to improve its machine uptime to the point where it was now able to consistently pull at the required *takt*. It had done great work through a cross-functional team of manufacturing, maintenance, and engineering to improve the overall equipment effectiveness (OEE) on the loader from a low of 46 percent to a consistent 79 percent. A perfect OEE of 100 percent means that the equipment is running at its full rate, making only quality parts, with no unplanned downtime. However, the team's upstream supplier department still had challenges meeting *takt* consistently. It was called out on the team's value stream map, but since that team had not "matured," it had been somewhat complacent in continuing to improve its processes, as it had been comfortably able to keep up to its downstream customer in the past. As a result, while the downstream department was actually doing better on its implementation of lean, it was sometimes forced to run more overtime because of parts shortages from the upstream department and could not get its OEE up past 79 percent. Clearly, the supervisors and operators started to question why they were working so hard on lean, only to be thwarted by a complacent upstream team!

The management team and the lean team agreed that there was a need for a more standardized process for sustaining and continued implementation. Leaving the teams to their own devices was not going to lead to the consistent results that the company needed. However, there was also agreement that they did not want to create a large bureaucratic reporting process that would turn off the teams. As a result, each department along the site's value streams established "sustaining and continuous improvement teams" (SCI). Each SCI was coached by a member of the lean team.

The SCIs were made up of the manager, supervisors, a manufacturing engineer, maintenance, and selected operators. One of the members was also identified as the Lean Coordinator. This person's role was to ultimately become the internal lean expert for that area. The SCIs started by reviewing their future state maps to see how close they were to the stated goal and what other opportunities for improvement still existed. They also canvassed the operators on the shop floor for other improvement ideas. The team then prioritized the items and started working on the top three. The teams met weekly among themselves and biweekly with the lean team to review progress. As each team completed an item, it would pull the next one in the queue onto the team's agenda. To monitor progress, each team set up a board in its area to communicate the activities and to display the key metrics. The establishment of the SCIs, with the coaching from the lean team, quickly led to more consistent deployment of lean across the site, more focused problem solving, and better tracking of results. Most important, the teams started to take ownership of the process, as they were the ones selecting the projects and were now having to do more of the implementation on their own (with assistance from the lean team as needed).

The teams became more self-sustaining, driving a larger quantity of smaller improvements. Internally, supervisors were coming around slowly, and operators were continuing to submit ideas to the SCIs for consideration, many of which were being implemented based on the set priorities.

And yet, below the surface, there was still some inconsistency in making the improvements stick. More learning was to come when it came to sustaining the process and the true nature of continuous improvement.

Standard Work—the "Adjust" Phase of PDCA

As the lean team walked the floor and observed the operations, it was clear when we looked at the standard work that there were many "little" inconsistencies in methods and that several of the improvements that were being made through *kaizen* events were not finding their way into the standard work instructions (SWIs). Digging deeper, we found that while ideas were being implemented by those involved in the *kaizen* event, the teams were not always taking the time to update the SWIs, and consequently operators on other shifts were not all using the best practices identified during the improvement activities.

In addition, supervisors were not very engaged in the SWI process. They had been trained in SWI implementation and had participated in creating the original SWIs with their teams during the past years of implementation, but they did not clearly understand that SWIs were

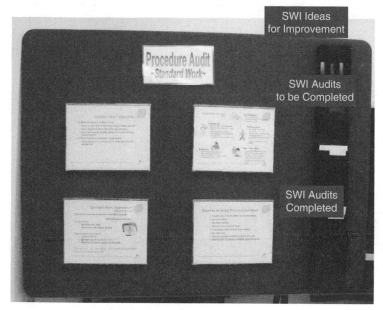

Figure 12.2. Standard Work Board

the mechanism for sharing best practices and driving continuous improvement with their operators.

As a result, the lean team went back to basics with the supervisors and their teams and spent more time training, updating, and continuously improving standard work. A daily audit system was put in place where supervisors reviewed operators' use of standard work and solicited their feedback on changes. A board (see Figure 12.2) was set up in each area to show the audit status and also to provide operators with an area where they could post ideas for improvements in the standard work. The supervisors would periodically review certain SWIs to monitor how the operators were using standard work, using a SWI review card (see Figure 12.3) that allowed them to review and comment on the operators' application of the SWI and to solicit their feedback for changes that they thought should be made.

It took the supervisors a while to settle in with this new process, as they did not want to become the policemen for standard work, and they also needed to rebalance their workload so that they could dedicate more time to retraining their teams and assessing improvement

Standard Work Audit Card

Applies to: SWIs, SOPs, MCPs and Aids

Update Document ☐

(Review training for workstations)

Date: _____ Workstation: _____
Operator: _____ Doc # _____
Auditor: _____

	Yes	No	N/A	Comments/Corrective Actions to Notes
1. Is the document at the workstation?	☐	☐	☐	_____
2. Is the document the most current revision?	☐	☐	☐	_____
3. Can work elements be performed as written?	☐	☐	☐	_____
4. Are standard times included per work element?	☐	☐	☐	_____
5. Are key points and symbols relevant to work elements?	☐	☐	☐	_____
6. Do the pictures match the instructions?	☐	☐	☐	_____
7. Is the operator trained and current for the workstation?	☐	☐	☐	_____
8. Are work elements and key points performed correctly?	☐	☐	☐	_____
9. Were steps performed in correct order?	☐	☐	☐	_____
10. Are all tasks performed included in document?	☐	☐	☐	_____
11. Have any critical steps been identified?	☐	☐	☐	_____

Other Comments:

_____

Rev 2.0   Date: 12/22/09

Figure 12.3. Standard Work Card Used by Supervisors to Audit

ideas than they were used to doing. However, after approximately six months, it became clear that operators and supervisors alike were seeing the benefits in the form of less firefighting of errors on the floor and improved communication between operators and supervisors on how to identify and evaluate improvement ideas.

 ## *Sensei* Reflection on Phase 4

This phase was a critical point in Nuclear's journey from deployment and implementation to sustenance and continuous improvement. The challenges mentioned in Phase 3 regarding the ability of the lean team to support the implementation became even more acute in Phase 4. It was clear that while lean was progressing at the site, it was limited by the lean team and the managers' reliance on it to drive improvements. While most of the areas achieved good results during Phase 3, it was clear that lean expertise and, more important, the ownership of sustaining and continuous improvement were not embedded in many of the areas.

The lesson learned during this phase was that growing expertise and ownership during the implementation phase is just as important as driving the results. The system can sustainably grow only as fast as its people grow. There is also a need for some infrastructure to support teams that are going forward on their lean journey into the continuous improvement phase. Implementation teams similar to the SCIs mentioned here provide good structure and discipline to identify, prioritize, and drive long-term improvements. Most important, the first-line shift supervisors and their teams must take the lead in implementing and sustaining improvements in their own areas. The use of standard work is at the foundation of this effort. While this is easy to say, as the Nuclear case shows, it may take several years for teams to develop enough depth of understanding of lean to truly move toward a culture of continuous improvement.

Final Reflection

As I write this, Nuclear still has a long way to go on its lean journey, but it has clearly made good progress over the past few years and, most important, it has learned what it really takes to implement and sustain those improvements.

We began the lean journey with Phase 0 in May 2002. If you were to walk through the plant in 2010, you would see the following:

- Visual factory was quite good.
- Inventory levels were significantly lower.
- Product flows were simpler and clearer to see.
- Machines were running much more consistently.
- Operators were not idle.

This was a long and rocky journey with many starts and stops, but at no point did the company quit on lean. The original executive in charge who championed lean stayed with the company for the entire time, getting promotions, but maintaining responsibility for manufacturing and continually insisting that lean was the company culture. While the teams still had a lot more opportunities for improvement, there was no denying that they had made some great progress, particularly in the last five years. On the wide-aisle tour of lean, they looked very good. Many of their customers had noticed the changes on their visits to the facility and had commented as much. Their lead times also continued to improve, reducing inventory, freeing up valuable space, and allowing problems to surface more quickly. It also helped to ensure on-time delivery to customers, which was critical for the complex task of refueling a power plant planned years in advance. Figure 12.4 summarizes the improvements in lead times over the various phases.

The story of Nuclear has many similarities to other cases I have experienced over the years. Some key elements to keep in mind during your lean journey are

- Do drive the implementation along the value stream. This is a well-known, proven methodology that has been validated by

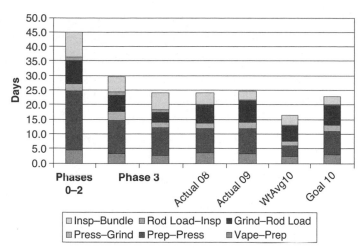

Figure 12.4. Nuclear's Fuel Stream Lead Time

many lean practitioners. However, be prepared for uneven implementation along the value streams.

- Use lean pilots to gain depth of understanding of lean principles and implementation experience in a given facility. However, do not expect that you will simply be able to "cut and paste" what is learned from the pilot into other areas. People who were not involved can gain some basic appreciation and awareness of lean from the pilots, but their real change in thinking and behaving will come from their own experience, and this takes time.

- The lean transformation is just as much about developing lean expertise and ownership in the area as it is about implementing the future state.

- The lean leader (internal coach) needs to accept that teams will want to chart their own way on their lean journey. Even though the leader may have more knowledge and has seen many best practices, she needs to be patient and to persevere in guiding the teams along the path (even if it is not always the path she wants them to take). Even letting them fail occasionally can be valuable for their learning. The goal is to get the teams to start the journey and then coach them through the twists and turns in the road to keep them going in the right direction.

- Changes in management (some for the best and others for the worst) will always occur during the lean journey, and this will lead to uneven progress. The lean leader needs to coach management newcomers as they enter the process so that they can engage their areas. In addition, the lean leader needs to work most closely with the first-line supervisors and their teams, as they tend to be the more stable entities in most companies, and they are the ones who ultimately have to take ownership of sustaining and growing lean in their areas.

Since the start of its lean journey, over a seven-year period, Nuclear's lead time has dropped by 63 percent and total process costs per unit have declined by 19 percent, and this is not adjusted for inflation. During the writing of this chapter, the site has been doing so well that headquarters decided that the West Coast site could handle all of the work in North America, and that there was no need for the East Coast site. This was viewed as a large vindication by the West Coast site, which always felt that it was the underdog on its lean journey relative to its sister facility. This will clearly signal the start of a new chapter in the company's lean journey.

Section Three

Making Your
Vision a Reality

Learning never exhausts the mind.

—Leonardo da Vinci, Italian Renaissance architect,
musician, anatomist, inventor, and engineer

Where do we start on our lean journey? There's only one place—at the *gemba*. When we start working with companies we always move as quickly as possible to a pilot, or what Toyota calls a model line. The model line is an area where we can experiment, demonstrate, teach, and plant the seeds for growing a lean culture. The model line can be a physical place, such as an assembly line in manufacturing, or a virtual line, as in the product development program for one new model in an engineering organization. In all of the cases in Section Two a model line approach was used early in the process, but we never really went into great detail about what happened.

We decided that the best way to give a visceral feel for this pilot learning experience is through a model line short story. The story in Chapter 13 was written by Jim Franz as a composite of many experiences he has had leading model line efforts as an outside *sensei*. It could be any organization in any industry. There are common themes. We'll revisit those in Chapter 14, where we reflect on the case and what we've learned from it and move on to how to spread lean both broadly and deeply in your organization. Chapter 15 focuses on lean leadership and the corporate philosophy, starting with the CEO, that can turn lean into a sustainable culture.

Chapter 13

One Time around the Plan–Do–Check–Adjust (PDCA) Loop: A Lean Short Story at Alte Schule[1]

A journey of a thousand miles begins with a single step.

—Lao-tzu, Chinese philosopher

A key success factor for all of the real-world cases in Section Two was developing a lean model someplace in the company. The purpose is to demonstrate success and teach what deep implementation of lean means—something that goes beyond the superficial application of lean tools and penetrates to the culture. To give a visceral feel of what this process is like, we visit a fictitious company, Alte Schule, as it is starting its journey to lean with the kind of teaching *sensei* that we recommend. We join our implementation team on a Monday morning, having just gotten approval the prior Friday from the local leadership to start working on a lean pilot project—the "model line," in Toyota terminology.

The First Pilot Team Meeting

The new external *sensei*, Tim, had been brought in by the company to lead the transformation effort. He walked into the meeting room, right on the shop floor, that had been cleaned up to become the command central for the project to address for the first time the team he had helped to hand-pick. The room itself was pretty unremarkable, with a door to the factory floor, a large, newly installed wire-reinforced window that effectively christened the room "the fish tank," a significant amount of wall space, and large enough capacity to hold the five-person team. The team had earlier filed through the door, which was being held by Jesse as he was bowing deeply and making grand sweeping gestures toward the team's new home. They took their respective seats around the conference table, waiting for their contracted leader.

"Morning, all," Tim said to no one in particular. "Sorry to be the last one here. I didn't expect the Spanish Inquisition when I was checking in at the front gate. Please give me some background on the line that we're going to be working on."

"I can run you through the technical aspects of the line," offered Jesse.

"Sounds like as good a place to start as any. Go ahead," said Tim.

"Well, let's see. The line produces about 50 different products, all auxiliary drive units of some sort, for customers ranging from OEMs in transportation to OEMs and Tier 1 in heavy agriculture. We make some products for large excavators and some other low-volume stuff," explained Jesse.

"God bless Sales and Marketing," quipped Trish.

"Jesse, don't forget about aftermarket," said Sarah.

"Oh, yeah, that's right. We also have to run a ton of old junk that gums up the line to keep fossilized fleets running somewhere out in the hinterlands," said Jesse with an exaggerated eye roll.

"Be nice, Jesse; that 'old junk' has a nice margin on it," said Nguyen.

Jesse proceeded to run down the technical specifications on the line. It was a basic arrangement of workstations and assembly and test equipment. "There are," began Nguyen, "anywhere from 13 to 16 operators on the line, depending on how the schedule looks for the week. Most of the operators have less than five years with the company, but there are a few of us 'old-timers' out there. The line runs one full shift with a small skeleton crew that stays over, mainly to make up any shortfall caused by part shortages, downtime, a high mix of aftermarket, or what have you."

"How's the quality of the finished products?" asked Tim.

"I can take that one," said Trish. "Overall the quality is good, with a very low defect rate at the customer. Our internal fallout rates are a bit higher, of course, but we keep that off of our customer's radar. Some products, especially the newer ones, run very well. Some of the older products and aftermarket—mostly the aftermarket, come to think of it—tend to give us most of our problems. Overall the line runs reasonably well and is generally profitable for the plant. The overtime eats into the margin, but the product is still a moneymaker. During high-volume months, or months with a high aftermarket mix, I think we generate almost 20 percent of the revenue for the entire place."

"So will somebody please tell me why we're on this line again?" asked Jesse. "It's running fine, the quality is good, or at least reasonable, and it's printing money for the bosses."

"Jesse, we talked about this at length," started Sarah. "We needed a pilot line that we could use as a showcase for the rest of the plant. Tim called it our 'lean laboratory.' It had to have important business consequences. And need I remind you that our goals and objectives for this year on this particular line are pretty aggressive? The same-old, same-old wasn't going to get it done."

"What do *you* think we should do, Jesse?" asked Tim.

"Isn't that why you're here and getting the big bucks? To tell us what to do?" countered Jesse.

"Am I?" asked Tim.

"Now stop answering questions with questions, Tim; it's rude," said Jesse.

"Well, I can tell you beyond a shadow of a doubt, I am definitely *not* here to tell you what to do. That would be a waste of your money and my time," said Tim.

"Its about the *gemba*," said Nguyen, looking at Jesse.

"Exactly, Nguyen," said Tim. "Everything starts with deeply understanding the *gemba*. Okay, team, let's go and see if the real world matches the one you so patiently described to me," said Tim as he stood up from the conference table, put on his safety glasses, and put in his earplugs.

Getting Started on the Deep-Dive Pilot

The team members filed out of the office and headed toward the pilot area. Tim was lost in thought about the composition of his new implementation team. He had found that without full-time support, any initial improvements were quickly squandered as "industrial entropy" took hold. If the team was going to have any credibility out of the gate, it needed to be staffed with people who were well respected by the organization and seen as having high potential. It didn't hurt that Kate Drayton, the CEO, had dropped in at the last two executive meetings discussing the team composition as an "observer," either. She was able to ensure that the implementation team, while maybe not perfect in everybody's eyes, was the best they could do right now.

The team was an interesting mix of people, and Tim was grateful that he had worked as hard as he had up front to get them, even if they would never know it. Sarah, the new Lean Coordinator, was the prototypical up-and-coming manager. She came out of the engineering department, had a couple of engineering degrees, and was a natural leader. She didn't bowl you over with the power of her personality, but she had a quiet confidence that sort of filled whatever room she was in.

If Sarah was the quiet leader, then Trish would definitely be the even quieter technical whiz. She was incredibly sharp, seemed to have total recall, and could do any task after having seen it performed just once. On the other side of the ledger, she was painfully shy and seemed to feel awkward in just about any situation. This was going to be a challenge, thought Tim, because he first and foremost wanted to develop his team into the leader/teacher mold, and Trish would probably end up being his crown jewel if he was successful.

Jesse, on the other hand, was anything but shy. He was "loud and proud," as he liked to say. He was one of the highest-seniority people here at Alte Schule, having started back when the current CEO's uncle had started the business. Jesse had the title of "senior technician" and was, according to his manager, a very, very sharp cookie. He was comfortable around all things mechanical, electrical, controls—you name it.

Nguyen, the final team member, was the natural-born teacher in the group. He had almost as much seniority as Jesse did and had spent his entire career out on the shop floor. Tim had learned that different managers had tried to promote Nguyen into different departments throughout his career, but he had politely refused each offer. For reasons known only to Nguyen, he had remained out on the shop floor as the most senior production associate in the company.

Grasping the Situation at the *Gemba*

At first glance, the pilot area was a beehive of activity. Operators were busy at workstations, and more than a few were scurrying about, either carrying parts or looking for parts to carry from one station to the next. All of the workstations, occupied or unoccupied, had parts scattered around them. Raw materials were stacked on the right side of the tables, and semifinished goods were on the left. There were numerous small carts with material on them around the area. Operators would run all of the parts on their stations through a machine, like a bearing press, load them onto a cart, and either take them to the next station or leave the cart where it was as they went looking for more parts to run through.

Sarah and Trish were standing back by the measuring equipment, peering intently at the display screen as an operator cycled a cart full of parts through. True to Trish's word, there wasn't a single reject in that bunch.

Tim was watching Nguyen, who was standing next to a workstation watching an operator align the splines on a gear. After watching a few cycles, Nguyen asked the operator if he was doing OK. The operator responded with a shrug and pointed to the alignment tool with an "I guess so" look on his face. Nguyen stepped around the work table and ran a few cycles much more quickly and smoothly than the operator had done. Nguyen showed the operator how to use the alignment tool properly to ensure that none of the delicate gears were damaged. After a few more cycles, the operator was starting to get the hang of the "new" method and thanked Nguyen with a smile.

Tim said nothing in response, and he and Nguyen moved to the front of the line to meet up with the rest of the group. Tim asked the group members if they had anything else they wanted to see before heading back to the office. No one could think of anything, so they proceeded to walk back to the conference room to do a debriefing.

"Right, team, so what did you see?" asked Tim.

"It looked a bit cluttered, didn't it?" offered Sarah.

"A few of the people were struggling a bit, but mostly it was folks who had rotated in from other areas," said Nguyen. "The line has a few high-content models in the schedule coming up and an aftermarket part that's always been a pain. A high-paying pain, but still a pain."

"Fine. What else did you see?" asked Tim.

"We had a fair amount of material around the line," said Sarah, "but when I asked one of the operators if that was unusual, he said it's always been like that."

"Some of the flow racks were empty," said Jesse, "and the operators were just running either right out of the bins on the table or off of the small carts. Maybe we should start by rearranging the material and the workstation layout." Immediately the others started chiming in with ideas for improvement.

"Hold on, hold on! I appreciate your enthusiasm and your great ideas, " said Tim, "but before we start firing off solutions and tinkering with workstations, we need to understand where the problems are."

"But they're everywhere," said Jesse. "We saw them with our own eyes."

"I agree that we saw things that weren't right, Jesse," continued Tim patiently, "but I'm not sure, personally, what the true problems are. What were the symptoms and what were the causes? We spent less than two hours out in the area, so I truly doubt that we know what goes on out there and why."

"OK, Einstein, then what do you suggest we do?" asked Jesse.

"First, I want to run this team through the short training modules that I use when I get started with a new implementation team," said Tim.

Basic Level-Setting Lean Training

"We're going to handle the training here just in time," began Tim. "If we're going to be focusing on an area or a specific countermeasure, then we'll spend the time just prior to doing so learning about the theory and then applying it on the floor. We'll then circle back and reflect a bit on what we did and what happened. This is sometimes called the learn-try-reflect method of learning. But first we will start by running this team through a one-day lean overview module that I think will help us. Then, once you understand, you're going to help me train the team members out on the line."

The overview training for the implementation team and a few key individuals from the pilot area was a mixture of short, focused lectures and hands-on simulation exercises using popular children's building blocks. The participants would learn about the theory of the different parts of a lean system and then immediately try them out in the simulation to cement the learning.

The simulation exercises were, by design, loud and crazy. Jesse was the hit of the session, insisting on acting as his team's "burgermeister-meisterburger," generally serving as the butt of numerous jokes and pranks, and obviously enjoying himself immensely. A small factory was set up to build a product using batch and push. Inventory was everywhere. At first it was all one factory with departments of subassemblies leading to final assembly leading to final inspection. Some people could work faster than others, so inventory built up in front of the slower processes. Defects were hidden in piles of inventory until they were discovered in inspection. The process was chaotic, and very few good units were produced. As the various rounds progressed, the overall factory was reorganized into smaller teams with better flow; all the teams' performance improved, as they were able to apply different countermeasures to problems that they faced. As Tim had warned them a day earlier, the final round of the simulation pitted the teams against one another to see how efficiently they could run their simulations and how much profit they could generate. By now they were in one-piece flow cells that they had designed, with far fewer workers needed. After the final round, Tim called the room to order and took the teams through a debriefing of the day's events. They discussed the various topics, how they interrelated to form a production system, and the obvious need to have high-quality people running the processes. All in all, the day went as expected, and the line team members were able to go back to the line with a basic understanding of what they were going to be involved with going forward. They now needed to convert this into a common view of the principles that would guide the transformation to a lean model line.

Building a Common True North Vision

The next morning, the team gathered in the conference room.

"OK, team," began Tim, "any further thoughts from yesterday?"

"Nope," said Jesse. "Let's get to implementing those tools. Yee-haw!"

"Let's talk about that concept for a minute," said Tim. "There's a huge distinction between simply implementing tools and developing a true lean system."

"Please explain," said Jesse.

"Fine," said Tim. "What we're going to be working on out on the floor is the development, implementation, and sustaining of a lean system. Typically we tend to think only of processes and material, like so." Tim drew a simple process box and inventory icon, as shown in Figure 13.1.

Figure 13.1. Basic Process and Material

"And, if I continue to draw the rest of the process equipment and material, I end up with something that fairly closely represents what we see out in our pilot area. There are lots of processes with lots of associated inventory arrayed out on the floor." (See Figure 13.2.)

"If we look at this, it screams, 'Batch-push,' and indeed that's what it is. If we take a tools-based approach to this, we'll want to implement some kind of flow, if we can, and pull if we must. Just for simplicity, let's draw some of these processes linked via marketplaces. The preceding process will replenish what the next customer process takes away, just like a supermarket." Tim erased the multiple processes and inventory

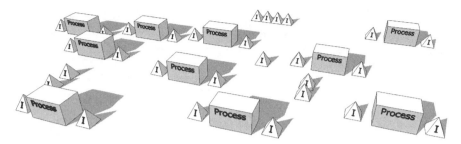

Figure 13.2. Rough Sketch of the Auxiliary Drive Area

and drew a few processes linked via marketplaces utilizing a pull signal. (See Figure 13.3.)

Figure 13.3. Basic Processes Linked to Marketplaces

"If we're not careful," said Tim, "and we're focusing only on tool implementation, we would look at this new process, declare ourselves lean, and move to begin replicating these pull systems and triggers throughout the plant. However, while we have implemented a tool, we haven't done much to highlight problems in these new processes. Remember, we implement tools as countermeasures to problems, but we want our entire system to be effective at showing us *all* of the problems. They can be big, small, or somewhere in between." Tim then added "trouble bubbles" to the drawing to represent the problems, as shown in Figure 13.4.

Figure 13.4. Small, Medium, and Large Problems Bubbling Up

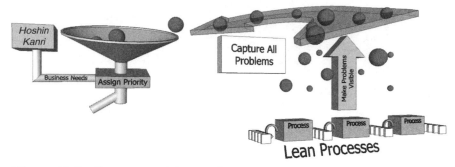

Figure 13.5. Capturing and Sorting Problems

"Once we bring these problems to the surface, we need a method for catching them and then prioritizing them based on the business's needs. We use our *hoshin kanri* process, a very simple version at first, to help us prioritize the issues because we don't have enough resources to work on all of them at once." Tim continued to develop his drawing, shown in Figure 13.5.

"Once we've got the problems sorted and prioritized, we can go about solving them, one by one. It will look something like this." Tim added more detail to his sketch until it looked like Figure 13.6.

"But," interrupted Jesse, "we're not going to be able to make a ton of headway, given that it's just us waving the flag out there. Plus, we're going to be spending all of our time baby-sitting the line."

"When I said 'we,'" said Tim, "I meant 'we' as in both this team and the team out in the area. You're right that there are only a few of us, Jesse. That's why this team is going to get experience in PDCA and

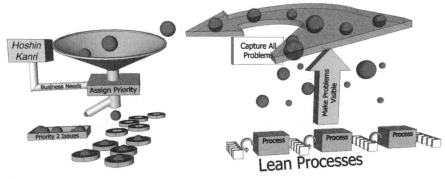

Figure 13.6. Sorting Problems and Starting PDCA

then work with and develop the team on the floor. That way, the team gets stronger and the processes get better. We'll work as coaches to the team members to help them solve their own problems. Here, let me finish my artwork."

"That make more sense," said Jesse.

Tim continued to add to his drawing until it looked like Figure 13.7.

Analyzing the Current State

As a starting point, Tim organized a value stream mapping session to better understand the current state. He conducted a short training session with the implementation team to understand the value stream mapping tool, then immediately went with the team to the auxiliary drive unit assembly area. The implementation team was there to discover the true current state, or "actually is," as opposed to the often-quoted "should be" that plagues so many mapping efforts. Tim assured the assembled group of operators that amnesty would be enjoyed by all, and that if there was something wrong that wasn't easily visible, they should point it out to the implementation team.

The implementation team hit the production area just after lunch and began the value stream mapping exercise. The team members recorded inventory levels, cycle times, quality rates, and machine uptime numbers where available, and talked with the operators as they worked at the various stations. In accordance with Tim's request, a representative from the material control department met them out in the finished goods area to explain to the team how the lines were scheduled and how changeovers were determined. The team then headed back to the conference room to begin the task of creating the value stream map of the current state.

"I must admit," said Trish, "that I was a bit skeptical about your claim that none of the engineering cycle times would match what we found on the floor."

"And," asked Tim, "what did you find?"

"Well," said Trish, looking at her clipboard, "they were closer than you thought they'd be, but about a third of them were way off. I mean *way* off. A couple of them were off by more than 70 percent."

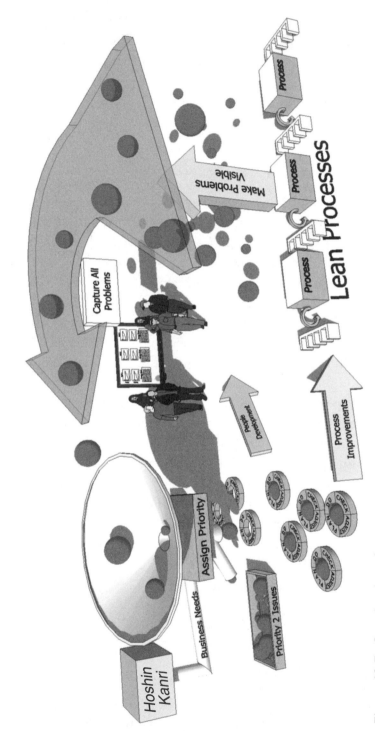

Figure 13.7. Complete Lean System

"And," added Jesse, "I was surprised to see how little information was being collected on those machines. Those new controllers can identify and track a lot more information than they're set up to catch. Some of the machines don't even record the last cycle time."

"OK, team," said Tim. "Now, who wants to volunteer to draw the current state map?"

"Jesse!" yelled everyone on the implementation team, except for Jesse.

"Wonderful," said Jesse as he walked to the butcher's paper that was taped to one wall of the conference room. "OK, who's got the customer requirements data?"

The team members spent the next couple of hours creating the current state map up on the wall, using sticky notes. They began moving through the processes and recording the key process data in the data boxes. As they finished the overall material flow, they moved on to the overall scheduling process. A number of heated discussions ensued as the team struggled to make sense of the notes they had taken during the interview with the material control department representative. Tim watched the discussions for a bit and then suggested to the team members that they call it a day and pick up the information flow mapping in the morning.

The next morning, the team reassembled in the conference room and began mapping the information flow for the area. Jesse looked amused as he warned Tim, "I'm sure you're going to get a kick out of this Rube Goldberg system we have running here."

"Why don't you draw it up on the value stream map and then we'll talk about it," suggested Tim.

"OK, fasten your seatbelts," said Jesse. He began to describe how the customer demands began as a long-range forecast, changed to a medium-range release forecast, and then finally morphed into a this week/next week schedule. All of the customers and suppliers were tied together using a relatively new material requirements planning (MRP) system that supposedly integrated the whole process so that everyone had the same system and data. The demand for each of the almost 50 unique end items varied greatly from part to part. Jesse explained that almost half of the parts had monthly demands requiring that they be run every day, while the rest required anywhere from two to ten days of production to make the monthly volume. Some parts weren't required at all in some months. There were also special builds that the line had to produce because Sales and Marketing allowed customers to order products that weren't regularly available.

"So there are some parts that you run every day (runners), some parts that you run every month (repeaters), and some parts that you rarely run but still have to, and then you have some crazy stuff come through occasionally, thanks to your eager Sales and Marketing people (rogues)," Tim summarized.

Jesse went on to explain that the MRP system provided a printed monthly schedule along with the this week/next week schedule. Component parts were ordered by the MRP system, taking into account shipped and scrap quantities, using the preprogrammed lead times (i.e., guesses) that had been loaded into the system. Daily stock checking was done on components that were deemed "critical to schedule" by the material control department, and parts were ordered or expedited if required. Daily production numbers were entered into the system at the end of the day, and the MRP system would forecast any required overtime.

"Seems pretty straightforward," said Tim.

"Yeah, but here's where it gets good," said Jesse. "Once the schedule is set and the line starts building, things start happening that drive the line crazy."

"Such as?" asked Tim.

"Lots of things," said Jesse. "Part shortages, downtime, high reject rates, and variation in line productivity, to name a few. We can't keep up with all the changes, and it adds up to pandemonium."

"MRP systems," said Tim, "can fail to account for most of those items you listed. They assume a perfect world—a nice dream. Or they need a ton of input and human intervention. Tell me a bit more about the changeovers and new model tryouts."

"The changeovers aren't really a problem," said Nguyen, "until we start doing short runs because we don't have enough of the component parts to complete the order. A box of gears might be only half full, but somehow it shows up as a full box on the system, and then we run short, causing us to change over to the next part. After a few of these, we're basically running around looking for the parts we need to complete an order, or we leave carts of partially built orders parked around the area. You saw a lot of those carts during our current state walk yesterday. The schedulers and stock checkers continually monitor those partially built orders and work with Material Control to get in the missing parts. Once the missing parts arrive, they're brought out to the area, and the order is reinserted into the schedule."

The team began filling out the sticky notes with all of the different information flows to and from the floor, including the schedules issued to the floor, the daily stock checks done by the line, the demands from the customers, and the orders issued to the suppliers. Although it wasn't pretty, the map conveyed the current state of the auxiliary drive unit area clearly, and, as is usual with a plant that is just starting out on lean, that state was not good.

Fully 40 percent of the products had fairly stable volumes from month to month and represented the majority of the work. The long tail of low-volume and aftermarket parts made up a minuscule portion of the volume but seemed to cause a majority of the issues on the line. Unfortunately, when all of these issues were jumbled together throughout the month as the line struggled to meet customer demand, nothing ever got resolved, as the next part would provide a new set of issues. Firefighting was a way of life, and the operators would serve as pseudo-material handlers instead of being able to focus on adding value. A lot of this waste would turn into cost that was difficult, if not impossible, to measure beyond vague terms like "efficiency."

Creating the Future State Map

The team got up from the conference table amid a scraping of chairs on the linoleum flooring. Tim had dismissed the team for a short break to grab a quick coffee and bio-break. When they returned he covered a few standard topics on developing the future state, such as *takt* time, shipping from marketplaces, flow, pull, pacemakers, leveling, and pitch. He then said: "OK, let's get started by calculating the *takt* time."

Immediately the team seemed to run into a Gordian knot. Simply taking the available time and dividing by the customer demand is fine and dandy as a concept, but when you have large variations in product demand and many different part numbers, the waters get a bit murky. The team members talked about this issue for the better part of an hour, analyzing the situation from every angle they could think of. Their solution to this seemingly complex problem, they would later find out, would dramatically change the way the area went about its daily business.

"Why don't we carve out the low-volume and service parts?" suggested Trish.

"What do you mean?" asked Nguyen.

"I mean don't run them down the same line," answered Trish.

"No way, Trish," said Jesse. "Engineering has invested a lot of money and political capital in the current concept of 'agile,' or 'flexible,' or whatever they call it. They beat their chests and proclaim the virtues of being able to run any part through the line without any issues. Don't you remember when they were featured in that industry magazine?"

"The status quo," said Tim, "can be a formidable foe. At this point, let's develop a good future state and worry about political issues later. Trish, why don't you want to run the low-volume and service parts through the same line?"

"Well," said Trish, "for one thing, the low-volume parts tend to have a huge increase in build content. The same goes for service because we don't have any of the original production tools. Some of those jobs take the better part of an hour to get a single part through the line. Why can't we just dedicate one or two of the workstations to running the low-volume and service parts? In fact, why don't we just break that area into three different lines?"

"For one thing," said Jesse, "we don't have enough leak testers and some of the other big machines, including the quality stations. So we'd need to ask the bosses to get out their checkbooks straightaway, and I thought we were going to be able to avoid that, right, Tim?"

"Yep," said Tim. "We're going to start by focusing on what we can do without writing checks to machine vendors. But I don't disagree with Trish, either. How would we draw that?"

"With three value streams," said Jesse. "We can calculate *takt* time on what I'll call the 'main line,' and we could also calculate some kind of average on the 'low-volume' and 'service' lines, but I don't see the point there. Those are all make-to-order jobs, especially service, and we'd spend more time recalculating the numbers each month than we'd spend building the parts."

"I agree, Jesse," said Tim. "After all, there's no law that says that every product you make must conform blindly to some 'rule of lean.' If those parts are make-to-order and have massive swings in work content and demand, I don't have any problems with calculating only the main-line *takt* for our future state. We'll need to calculate overall capacity on the lower-volume parts and service jobs instead of using *takt*. Remember, team, this future state is only to pilot for the next 60 or 90 days, not for the rest of our lives."

"OK," said Sarah, "now we've got our *takt* time for the high-volume line. What's next?"

Tim led the team members through the rest of the future state mapping exercise for the area. By the end of the day, they had come up with a vision that the team believed was achievable and a few more "stretch targets" that Tim offered as a challenge to the team.

Developing the Action Plan for the Future State

Tim discussed how they would develop a plan for implementation. They would start by identifying bundles of activity that would be called "*kaizen* bursts." Some of those could best be handled in structured *kaizen* workshops to get all the right people involved in a defined period of time, while others were things that the team would do outside of workshops. One by one, the *kaizen* bursts went up on the map. A rough timing chart was then worked and reworked, checking with other departments, until the team was confident that it could deliver the future state in the next 90 days. Some aggressive commitments had to be made by Scheduling, Maintenance, Purchasing, and Production. The team members then transferred all the information to a master schedule for the implementation, and one of the team members was identified as the champion for each particular task. Eventually all of the tasks required were captured on the master schedule, and each of the implementation team members had volunteered to take a share of the workload.

"Whoops," said Trish. "We forgot one."

"Which one?" asked Jesse as he stared at the map. "We've got every process identified out there. Man, look at all this work!"

"Guess," said Trish.

"Training," said Jesse with a self-satisfied smile. "We need to include all of the training that will need to be done as we launch the 'new and improved' area. When I said 'process' a second ago, I remembered how we talked about the two value streams, people and process."

"I'm impressed," said Tim. "I usually work with groups that only want to move machinery around, declare victory, and proclaim, 'We're lean.' The line gets effectively 'blown up' over the weekend, and come Monday you have a lot of confused people. But let's stick to 'just-in-time training.' We'll also need to circle back and check the process on a regular basis and do a bit of reflection with the operators to ensure that they're fully capable and to see if there's anything in the training itself that we can improve upon."

"Cool," said Jesse.

"I'm still confused about the future state map," said Nguyen. "It seems that all we did was move some of the problems to a new area. We didn't solve a single problem; we just rearranged the deck chairs a bit."

"I agree, Nguyen, that we haven't solved the problems yet," said Tim. "Remember that what we're really trying to do with this future state map is to create a process that brings problems to the surface. Solving the problems will be the job of the work groups after we put the basic tools in place. We'll be training them on basic problem-solving methods." With that, the team members went back to their respective desks to begin scheduling the time with the affected areas to go over their implementation plans.

Doing It!

The overall implementation plan involved a basic area rearrangement that introduced flow to the higher-volume components and created smaller work areas for the low-volume and service materials. The low-volume line had only three workstations, and the team had agreed to also develop a separate service area that had two workstations. The biggest challenge for the team was how to deal with the shared resources, such as the leak test machines and the final rolling resistance test. Every part had to go through them, but now there were multiple places that parts could come from. The team had to answer the question of how the operator knows what to do next. In the early stages, it had no answer; so this went up on a problem-tracking matrix.

Tim had been relentless in demanding that the team use simple visual controls so that the operators knew what they had to do without referring to a computer, a scheduler, or a stock checker. In some cases, this was as simple as designating areas on the floor for raw material, and in some cases it was a bigger challenge, such as removing the dedicated, standardized flow racks that were on each workstation and instead making smaller, portable racks that could be right-sized to a number of jobs and moved in and out of the line easily. This way, the material handlers could set up the "next job" rack and have it ready to move into position when the "current job" had been run (called *sequential pull*).

By far the biggest initial improvement to the area was the introduction of the high-volume line. Changing the production method from batch-push to flow allowed the operators to focus on production and reduced distractions. That allowed the team members to work with them on developing standardized work for each job. The material control department was able to put in a rudimentary pull system for all of the high-volume parts and keep the line well supplied with all of the common parts. It is often missed that pull systems depend on stable, leveled production schedules to really function at maximum efficiency. With this newfound stability, all of the existing problems on the line now showed themselves very quickly.

Tim had the team install a line management board in the area so that the various team members could identify problems as they happened. They also tracked simple measures such as safety, defect rates, labor hours/order, scrap rates, and attendance. Tim knew that the visuals themselves were not the answer. If they responded quickly to problems as they arose, the team members in the production area would come to value the board and make it an important part of the area. Otherwise, it would just become another list of problems that were ignored.

After the newly rearranged line was launched, the implementation team spent its days out on the floor, observing and helping the area adjust to the new way of operating. As problems were discovered, the team would try to fix them immediately, or at least dutifully log them. At lunchtime and also at the end of the shift, the implementation team would meet with the various departments to both clarify and prioritize the issues and assign a champion for each issue. As was to be expected, the issues were legion. There were basic operating issues, such as repairing faulty equipment and worn and damaged fixtures; there were part shortages and wrong component deliveries; there were unscheduled changeovers caused by late orders and "favors" to Sales and Marketing; and there were a whole host of other small annoyances that kept the team from achieving its daily production goals regularly. About half of the time, the high-volume line was able to hit the target in regular hours. The low-volume and service lines were still a bit of a basket case.

Tim emphasized that finding and fixing these problems was not a failure of the new lean systems but a sign of the system's success. This *kaizen* process was the true essence of lean, and the part missed when lean experts rush in and do one-week *kaizen* events and then rush out leaving all the real problems behind.

Tim was out in the area standing by the line management board looking at the various charts and graphs when Jesse and Nguyen walked up. Jesse tapped his ear and pointed to the conference room, indicating that they had something that they wanted to talk about away from the harsh sounds of the line. The three of them then headed to the conference room, where Trish and Sarah were already standing next to the implementation team's countermeasure board and master schedule.

"Morning, fearless leader," said Sarah. "We think we have a countermeasure to the low-volume and service parts getting through the leak tester and quality machines during the shift. As you know, we've been keeping somebody on overtime for over for an hour every day to finish running those parts."

"Yep," said Tim. "Not a great countermeasure, but definitely a step in the right direction."

"Anyway," continued Sarah, "we were meeting with a few team members at lunch, and Tina suggested that we set up a second 'inbound' lane to the leak tester and run parts through while the line is changing over. That way they won't have to stay over to run the low-volume and service parts."

"Only one problem," said Jesse. "The leak tester and quality machine need to be changed over to run those parts. Isn't that going to interfere with the line?"

"It's a seal kit for the leak testers," said Trish, "and a program change. The rolling resistance test is just a program change."

"Yeah, but we still have to change all the programs," Jesse began. He then stopped for a minute and stared at the table in front of him. He suddenly shot to his feet, walked over to the whiteboard, and began drawing quickly. "It's ugly," said Jesse, "but I think we can do this without major surgery."

"Jesse," began Tim, "do you want to explain what we're looking at?"

"No worries," said Jesse. "You see, the basic problem is that whenever you want to run a part through a machine, a leak tester or the rolling resistance unit, you need to call up the correct program for each machine. When the area was first set up by our all-knowing engineers, the assumption was that each machine was 'infinitely flexible,' so that all you needed to do was swap the seals and call the right program, and you could run one part or a thousand parts through that machine. One of the problems is getting the right seals to the machine. Because they're easily damaged and ridiculously expensive, the maintenance department keeps them under lock and key in the equipment crib. Plus, the controls on each of the machines are different. Some of these machines are 10 years old. But I think we can daisy-chain the machine controllers together so that you only need to change the first machine's program and it will 'handshake' the data down the line through the quality machines. The programs are messy, and they're all in different machine languages, but I think we can make it seamless. If we can get the seals out of the maintenance crib and have them delivered to the line with the parts, all we need to do is write down the right program number and we'll be in business. Maybe we can make some laminated cards or something to include with the parts so that the operators know what program to run."

"Or," added Nguyen, "we can put it right on the seals themselves."

"Even better," said Jesse. "That will really speed up getting those parts through."

"Excellent work, team," said Tim. "Sarah, let's go talk to Tina and let her know what we're planning to do. We'll need to talk to the supervisor as well."

The implementation team spent the next few weeks working with the production team to implement the new quick-change process and inbound lane system, and it worked beautifully. As the area continued to run, more and more problems were brought to the surface. By now, the team was comfortable with using PDCA to attack the problems as they arose. And, in the weeks following the initial launch of the future state implementation plan, there were encouraging signs from the floor teams that they were both understanding and using the tools that they had been trained in. It was now that Tim called the team members together one last time before they had to report to the CEO and her executive team.

One Last *Hansei* before the Executive Presentation

The team had gathered around the conference room table and sat quietly. Tim noticed that Jesse looked rather depressed and asked him, "Why so glum, Jesse?"

"He didn't get all of his *kaizen* bursts implemented," offered Nguyen.

"Oh, I wouldn't worry too much about that, Jesse," said Tim. "The work this team has gotten done has been remarkable. Having a few open items doesn't mean that the implementation wasn't successful."

"I agree," said Sarah. "Have you looked at the 'before' and 'after' pictures from that area? They're incredible. I'd almost forgotten how the area used to run, but looking at those pictures really blew me away. I can't believe the amount of change."

"I suppose," added Trish, "that because we've been so deeply involved in the day-to-day work and the changes were incremental, we didn't notice the bigger picture."

"Exactly," said Tim. "The reason we took all of those pictures before we got started was to remind ourselves how much we have progressed. Remember, only your relatives can tell you how much your kids have grown. You see them every day and don't notice the change. So, team, what have we learned, and what can we do better?"

"I was surprised," said Sarah, "at the amount of planning that went into a 90-day future state implementation. I know that it's the first step in PDCA and all that, but once you sit down and truly try to make a comprehensive plan, well, it was a lot of work."

"Not to mention," added Trish, "that you needed to spend a lot of time with other functions working on the plan. Otherwise, if one person wasn't aware of what was going on or what to do, you'd be back at square one and have to start again."

Sarah added, "Look at the key performance indicators for the area. Safety has never been better, our internal defect rate is at the year-end target level, our labor minutes per order is dropping, changeover times are down, and the area looks incredible."

"I think," said Trish, "that we've cut well over $80,000 in inventory from the high-volume line and almost that in the low-volume and service lines. Finance owed me the numbers yesterday, but has promised to have them to me today so that we can include them for Monday's meeting."

"Great!" said Tim. "So, team, what are we going to do differently next time?"

"Definitely get reps from the other departments from the beginning," said Sarah. "That will chop out a lot of lead time bringing them all up to speed and having to argue each point individually with each department."

"I think we can be a bit more regimented in the training phase the next time, based on what we learned this time," said Nguyen. "We spent a lot of time training people that would be transferred to other areas, and then we'd have to start over again with the new person. The temps were even worse. By the time we got one trained to a level where he didn't need support or cause disruptions in the line, the agency would send us new people. Can't we get the same people back?"

"I talked to Human Resources about that," said Sarah, "and they said they'd look into it. Overall, they want to play a bigger part in the delivery of the training and get the records of who was trained into their system."

"Good," said Tim. "What else?"

"I'm not sure if it's going to be possible," began Nguyen, "but is there some way to get the supporting departments more aligned with what we're doing? In some cases, we were trying to implement changes that conflicted directly with other departments' goals for the year. Like, remember when we wanted to get the parts delivered right into the flow racks instead of having full pallets dropped in the area? We now had room on the line-side racks, so all they had to do was to load the racks and pull the empties, but they said it would decrease their 'efficiency,' which was measured by 'moves per shift.' They were trying to reduce their 'moves per shift,' but it was hard for the line to keep running when somebody had to run around and load up the line."

"Alignment," said Tim, "is usually a big problem wherever I go. That's a problem that we need to attack at the executive level, and one that I plan to bring up at Monday's meeting."

"So, fearless leader," said Sarah, "are we ready for Monday?"

"Absolutely," said Tim, "but I want us to be ready for what comes after Monday."

"Which is?" asked Nguyen.

"Don't say it," said Jesse. "Don't you dare say it."

"Our next future state," said Tim, looking right at Jesse, who by now had his head buried in his arms and was mock crying.

"OK, then, if that's it," said Trish, "I'm out of here. See you all Monday."

The Executive Report

The executive conference room was located on the second floor, directly adjacent to the CEO's office. It had a long mahogany table with so many coats of varnish on it that you felt as though you could fall right into it. The conference room door swung open as Kate, the CEO, followed closely by Lyle, her vice president of finance, came into the room. Tim and the implementation team came through next, followed by the rest of the executive team. Kate called the meeting to order, and everyone took their seats around the enormous conference room table.

"Everybody comfortable?" she asked. "Good, let's get started, then. First, I want to thank you all for the huge amount of work you've accomplished these last few months. I walked through the area, I guess we now call it the *gemba*, late last week with Tim to review the progress. I was very impressed with the improvements in the area. I talked to some of the people on the line, and I was excited by the level of engagement that was evident in their enthusiastic explanations. Tim, you and your team have really opened my eyes to what's possible out there on our floor."

"Lyle," asked Bob Mays, the vice president of engineering, "what was the bottom line for that project out there?"

"Ahem," began Lyle. "The overall productivity of the line, as measured in labor minutes per order, has improved by almost 30 percent. We had no customer returns, and our in-process inventory, according to the data, is down by almost $200,000. Unfortunately, that means I'm going to have to prepare the board members for a drop in profitability for the products in the area."

"Why?" asked Bob. "What's the problem? Cash is king, right?"

"Because, Robert," said Lyle, "the in-process inventory is counted as valued assets used in our profit and loss calculations, and as a result, such a reduction will show up as a similar reduction in profit, even though our cash balance will increase by that amount. If you don't follow the numbers from the P&L sheet over to the balance sheet, you might mistakenly think that this project reduced our overall profitability. It's only for the reporting period in which the inventory reduction happens, but it has to be accounted for this way. I'll be able to explain it to them so that they understand that it is not a real loss."

"What else?" asked Kate.

"Well," said Rachel Taylor, the vice president of human resources, "we had one trip to Medical for a laceration, which is down from an average of five per month. We started a new measure out in the auxiliary drive unit called 'near misses' as a way for the associates to identify things that might lead to accidents. We've had a total of 23 near misses reported, and we've closed 20 of them. The other three issues involve separating powered vehicles from people, and that's going to take a bit longer."

"I have a comment on the temporary employees," said Nguyen as he nervously looked up and down the table.

"Go ahead, Nguyen," said Kate.

"Well, I think that we're wasting a lot of money on our temporary employees," Nguyen started.

"We need those temps to account for our volume peaks," said Bob.

"I know," said Nguyen. "I'm not trying to say that we don't need temps; I'm just saying that it would be nice to get the same temps back. We spend time training these folks and get them to a basic level of skill, and then we get new faces the next month. The new lean system we set up is even more dependent on highly skilled and trained team members. Can't we ask for the same people back?"

"I'm already looking into that," said Rachel. "I wasn't aware that was happening before the lean pilot. I'm hoping to work out a deal where we get the temps back as long as they're still working through the agency. If we have openings, it'd be nice to pick from people that we've already been exposed to and who know our systems. It would save a lot on the initial training as well."

"How much do you think it would save, Ms. Taylor?" asked Lyle.

"Well, that's tough to say exactly," began Rachel, "but at least two weeks of orientation and training and maybe another week or two of specific process training, depending on the area. And that's for each employee. We've got almost 200 employees working on direct labor jobs, and we have an annual turnover of around 9 or 10 percent."

"Hmm," said Lyle as he stared at the ceiling. "That is a fair amount of savings. It's interesting also that the training costs are currently either aggregated into plant overhead or charged to HR directly. In general, those costs tend to be hidden."

"One other thing I've noticed," continued Rachel, "is that the turnover from the pilot area is basically zero, and I've gotten more than a dozen requests from people wanting to transfer into that area."

"They did seem pretty energetic out there," observed Kate. "It reminded me of when my uncle first started the business. It was more like a family back then."

"We had a few problems initially," said Vic, the material control manager. "When we put in the basic pull system, our people still wanted to use the MRP schedules and reports. Tim gave me a heart attack when he told me to unplug the MRP for the line. Once I picked myself up from the floor and we talked it through, it made sense to still use it for forecasting and supplier look-aheads. It also made sense when you think that they're replenishing the line every hour, but MRP only updates every night at three in the morning or so. It's not running perfectly in the area yet, but the reduction in work-in-process inventory has been pretty dramatic."

"So when are we rolling this through the rest of the plant?" asked Bob. "Since so much efficiency can be gained by going back to the technological dark ages, we should begin rolling this out immediately. I can send my engineers and managers down for training as soon as you want, and they can continue rolling out the changes."

"I'm not sure that will work," said Tim warily, sensing an ambush.

"Why not?" asked Bob with a little heat in his voice. "Certainly my engineers can grasp your simple lean concepts and rules and continue to rearrange the plant."

"I say I'm not sure," said Tim, "because I don't know that the specific countermeasures we put in place in the pilot area will still be valid in other areas. Plus, the rearrangement was only a small portion of the actual improvements."

"Why do you say, Tim," asked Rachel, "that it was only a small portion of the project?"

"Because most of the actual improvements happened because the team members became aware of, and fixed, problems in the area. Moving the workstations from their original 'cluster' layout into three separate areas dedicated to product families simply separated the problems that were unique to each product family and concentrated them in each area. The key performance indicator boards showed how the team members were doing hour by hour. Then all the wastes became visible. It wasn't until the team members tackled the reasons *why* the line was shutting down and they were missing their production targets that we began to move the metrics toward the goals. Our job as an implementation team was to work with the members of the operating team and coach them through the problem-solving process, a time-consuming job requiring exceptional people skills. Our team learned a tremendous amount from the experience, but we still only scratched the surface, gathering up the low-hanging fruit. No offense, but your managers and engineers don't yet have that experience. Another concern I have is that the teams still need support. You don't change a culture in 90 days. As you all noted, we've come a long way, but we've only just gotten off the launch pad. As I told my team when we got started, we're trying to change to a culture of PDCA problem solving, with everyone involved and capable. After all of this work, we've managed to get around the PDCA cycle for the first time. As you know, doing anything just one time does not make you an expert."

The discussion continued until late in the afternoon and swirled around the topics of expansion, resources, benefits, in-sourcing, temps, capital expenditures, and the overall workforce. The implementation team members talked about how they had modified and updated their plans along the way as they got further into the different *kaizen* burst projects, essentially putting to rest the theory that there is a 'one size fits all' approach to a lean transformation.

The team members were very excited and animated in discussing the changes out in the area, both the changes in the processes and the major investment in the operators themselves. They eagerly outlined what their next steps would be in the area, with a focus on trying to level the production on the high-volume lines, expanding the pull systems back to the suppliers, focusing more closely on the capital equipment, and trying to develop team leaders out in the area.

Earlier, Kate had talked to the production leadership team and the area supervisor involved in the implementation about the team leader topic. The supervisor was practically begging for help. The amount of work he had to do to keep the line running and also drive some of the implementation work was pushing him over the edge. Run the line. Coordinate with Material Control. Coordinate with Maintenance. Staff the line when training was happening. Follow up on missing *kanban*. Follow up on training records. Add to that a thousand other things throughout the day to make sure that the line runs as it should. The concept of team leaders wasn't new to Kate, but there hadn't been an opportunity before now to seriously consider it. After all, the team leaders could be "funded" out of the existing improvements that the teams were realizing.

As the discussions wound down, Kate thanked the team members for their time and gave them the rest of the afternoon off. She also briefly talked with her executive team about what they were going to do next. Kate thanked the members of her executive team for their support and advice, and they headed back to their respective offices to get caught up on the work that had no doubt piled up in their absence.

Kate's Reflections on What She Learned

Kate was alone in the conference room now, with rain quietly hitting the huge windows that her uncle had once been so proud of. She looked around the conference room at the ridiculously large table that she couldn't bring herself to get rid of. There were still burn marks in some places from her uncle's cigars. He was so passionate about this company, she remembered, and he always talked about the responsibilities of leadership. Plan for the long term, he had admonished her, and remember whose work pays the bills. He was referring to the people out on the floor, all of whom he knew by name. It seemed like such a long time ago. She stood for a while looking out at the rain as she pondered everything that had happened in the last few months.

She had been worried at first about committing both the people and money to the lean pilot, and she had gotten pushback right away from Engineering and Material Control; they were confident that everything was going along great, thank you very much. Lyle, in finance, would always side with whatever helped the company's financial position, but he had a serious blind spot when it came to the people on the floor. He saw them as a cost that was to be reduced, and now, here was the pilot team, trying to show him that the improvements in the pilot area mostly came from the people, not the equipment. She definitely sided with the pilot team, and what she saw convinced her this may have been one of the best investments she ever authorized, but convincing others of it was going to take some work. Ah, well, Kate thought, if leadership were easy, everybody would be doing it. One simple pilot area had seriously shaken up the status quo.

She stared out at the rain for a few more minutes, quietly contemplating the past, present, and future before turning to leave the room. She took a last look around the room, her gaze lingering on the massive conference table; she smiled, and then she left. The door slowly closed and clicked shut behind her. A few minutes later, the motion sensor dutifully turned out the conference room lights, and all was still except for the rain outside, still falling softly against the windows.

Chapter 14

Sustaining, Spreading, Deepening: Continuing Turns of the PDCA Wheel

Learning is not attained by chance; it must be sought for with ardor and attended to with diligence.

—Abigail Adams, second first lady of the United States

I n Chapter 13, we had an opportunity to go deep into the transformation process and experience it through the eyes of the team of internal prospective lean coaches and their fearless lean *sensei*, Tim. Alte Schule, Inc., made a remarkable transformation in one of its core processes. The team members mapped the value stream, created a lean layout, and eliminated waste. "Are we lean yet?" We can imagine what Tim's response might be if one of his team members asked this naïve question:

Congratulations, team. We have successfully completed one turn around the plan–do–check–adjust (PDCA) wheel in one small part of Alte Schule, Inc. We have learned some powerful tools and opened our eyes to the tremendous opportunity we have to improve our processes. On the journey of understanding PDCA and improvement skills, we have taken our first steps, like a toddler finally stumbling across the room into its waiting mother's arms. Now let's go through our second turn of the PDCA wheel and continue to learn to walk. We will be 'lean' only when there is nothing left for us to learn.

The Alte Schule case is fictional, yet every aspect of it reflects our experiences in actual companies, including the disappointing response of some of the senior executives. The machine paradigm so dominates that it is a natural way of thinking in most companies. The machine-thinking executives, other than the CEO, lacked the vision to see the game-changing potential of lean and thought about the pilot in simple cost-benefit terms: what will I get for that project, and what will it cost me? Unlike the lean implementation team, the executives did not experience the process and change their way of thinking.

As the pilot line progressed, the members of the implementation team went through dramatic personal changes in the way they thought about work, waste, team member development, standardized work, and, first and foremost, how to achieve challenging objectives. By the end of the pilot, they showed the beginnings of understanding PDCA as a way of thinking and learning. They began to understand the intimate connection between process improvement and people development. They could now start to understand the meaning of operational excellence. They also understood the many bureaucratic obstacles to excellence in the current organization and got a little experience in navigating around them. This naturally made them feel a bit like converts who were now expected to become evangelists in selling their new discovery to the doubters. It's an exhilarating experience, but it's also frustrating and sometimes overwhelming.

The production supervisors and workers in the model area also went through a transformation, although not nearly as deep as the one that the implementation team experienced. When the lean team engaged the production team members by asking what their problems were and helping to solve them, it got overwhelmingly positive reactions. Apparently, listening to the people who do the work is not a widespread skill in traditional organizations.

Over time, the model area was transformed in remarkable ways to perform at a level that the organization had never experienced before. To the outside observer, the before and after were like night and day. Interestingly, the members of the lean implementation team were so engaged in day-to-day transformation that they did not even notice how profound the changes actually were; they were able to see the many flaws and continuing opportunities for improvement in a more detailed way. Think of the proud parents (executives) marveling over the musical skills of their child who is learning to play an instrument and the self-critical child (implementation team) who grimaces at every mistake.

The results of the lean pilot were so positive that one would expect the senior executives to jump out of their seats, run to the floor to drink in this incredible transformation, congratulate the team, and commit to lean as a way of life on the spot. Unfortunately, that did not happen, and in our experience, it rarely does. Instead, the executives sat around the boardroom and wanted data to show the return on investment so that they could decide whether to continue the "program."

Fortunately, in the case of Alte Schule, the executives got the black-and-white data that they hoped for, convincing them that there was a great return on investment, so their next response was let's go, go, go and "train up" the engineers to transform the rest of the plant. This put the members of the lean team in a challenging position because they knew what they had learned and they knew that it takes time and a deep experience to learn it. They could not simply communicate what they had learned and experienced to the machine-thinking senior executives.

We get a ray of hope at the end of the story that the CEO, Kate, was getting it. She reminisces about her uncle's original dedication to the company and how he tried to teach her to think long-term and focus on the people doing the real work. In the words of Jim Collins, he was trying to create an organization that was "built to last,"[1] and he had passed that responsibility on to Kate. Kate was beginning to understand how what Tim had started in the pilot area was a road to excellence and innovation that would allow her company to become truly great. She was touched by the engagement of her production associates and their pride in making real improvements. She also understood that one of her key leadership roles was to protect the process from some of the more narrow-minded executives.

The most important results of the lean pilot for Alte Schule were not financial but in learning. The CEO learned, the production employees learned, and some of the support staff learned, but the deepest learning was in the implementation team. Now imagine that the implementation team had not been recognized, its members had been moved to other positions where they could not use what they had learned, and they ultimately became so frustrated that they left the company. You are imagining our experiences in a large number of organizations we have worked with, such as the iron-ore mining company in Chapter 8. When this happens, most of the learning from the pilot stays with the individuals involved and does not translate into organizational learning.

The good news and the bad news is that learning resides only in people. This is good news because we can develop people to very high levels and then use their unique human capabilities of reasoning and imagination to transform our organizations to greater and greater levels. It is bad news because people, unlike machines, need recognition and nurturing. They are much more than an entry in an Excel spreadsheet. Developing and nurturing the people and the process is more like raising a family than replacing defective parts in machines.

In this chapter, we will build on some of the lessons in Chapter 13 about getting started on the lean journey. In the process, we will extend the lessons of the Alte Schule case to consider where we might go next to spread lean, while continuing to deepen the learning that began with the pilot.

The Role of the Lean *Sensei*

The starting point for any company that wants to either start the journey, restart the journey, or move to a new phase on the journey is to find a *sensei*. You do not change your golf game, learn a musical instrument, or become a master chef solely by reading books or going through online tutorials. Reading can get you oriented, teach you some basic concepts, and help you chart your path, but you still need a teacher with experience, knowledge, and ability to develop real skill. The *sensei* can be either internal or external.

Charlie Baker (Chapter 11) acted as an internal *sensei* for product development at the automotive supplier. He had acquired deep knowledge and understanding at Honda through increasingly challenging assignments that developed him as an engineer, a leader, and a person. He had had many guides along the way. He did not simply live in the Honda organization, but helped to build Honda's engineering culture in the United States. This gave him some important experience in translating the Honda culture into an American environment and in developing people with very diverse backgrounds. As vice president of engineering at NAAS, he was given line authority and an organization in crisis, and now he had a learning laboratory. He was self-aware enough to realize that moving this established organization with strong learned routines for getting work done and an entrenched bureaucracy required a different skill set from that needed for building the Honda engineering organization in the United States. He needed deep technical expertise, a strong intuitive understanding of lean, leadership ability, and change management skills. Charlie had a good deal of success at the seating company, and he was helped by the lean coaches reporting to him who came out of Toyota. As the vice president, he could motivate, lead, and, as a last resort, use his authority to make it happen.

For organizations that do not have a veteran lean expert as a key executive and choose to go outside for help, the *sensei* should have certain characteristics that we saw in Tim in our lean short story. Here are a few key points to keep in mind when seeking *sensei* support.

The *Sensei* Is a Teacher, Not a Process Improvement Engineer

The role of the process improvement engineer is to come in and do it for you: reengineer the process, propose changes, perhaps help implement the changes, help you do a check to confirm the results, report on the results, and collect his check—see you later, pal! The role of a teacher is to guide, coach, and develop others. The old master-apprentice relationship in the craftwork era is the model at Toyota. In fact, Toyota still uses the terminology "master trainers," and managers are considered "masters" at developing their subordinates, who are apprentices.

Eventually, any organization that is going to sustain the journey will need its own internal "masters" who can coach others. The Six

Sigma process is based on that model, with the "master black belt" developing "black belts." It comes from the martial arts tradition and can be highly effective in creating an organization of black belts, who usually work in staff positions. Some companies have effectively moved these staff black belts into line management, with great results. The lean philosophy tends to favor working directly within the line organization and developing all managers as teachers. The core skill set of the manager is PDCA—the ability to understand the situation, develop a vision for the ideal process, take steps toward that vision, reflect, learn, and start the next PDCA loop. That's the core skill set that the *sensei* is working to develop in others.

The *Sensei* Must Be a Skilled and Passionate Problem Solver

If PDCA is the core skill set, the *sensei* had better be really good at it. We describe PDCA as a passion rather than a scripted procedure. The person who goes through the PDCA procedure in rote form will not engender passion in others, and will generally leave a lot of waste on the table. Part of what has made the great Toyota leaders so special is that they believed they could accomplish remarkable things. They learned over time that the seemingly impossible is possible when you take one step at a time. This great confidence and excitement about achieving ever greater levels of performance made them inspiring leaders. When a Toyota Production System (TPS) master says of someone, "He lacks the passion for really solving the problem," she is making a pretty damning statement. Since TPS is such a passionate part of the company, people who lack the passion are generally sent out to pasture. You can develop someone who has the passion, but it is hard to put the passion into the person who is simply going through the motions.

The *Sensei* Must Be a Respected Mentor at All Levels, from the CEO to the Production Team Members

This is one place where we can argue that Tim in the Alte Schule case was weak. We got no sense that he was a trusted advisor to Kate, or even on the road to becoming one. Ideally, Tim would have personally met with Kate weekly during the model line project, brought her to the floor to see what was happening as the model was progressing, and perhaps even involved her in *kaizen*. If that had happened, there would have been no surprises for Kate at the conference room presentation, and after the meeting she probably would have wanted to meet with Tim immediately for reflection. After all, this was shaking up her entire company, her family heritage. In that particular company, Kate should be leading the transformation with passion. The model line project was starting to get her to warm up, but it's not clear that Tim was the type of *sensei* who would seize the opportunity to win Kate's confidence and work his way into becoming her trusted advisor.

We have personally experienced cases where we are brought in by an operations manager or the head of quality at the request of a vice president, and the middle managers "administer our contract." Without a connection to the top of the house as trusted advisors, there are usually limits to how far we can go.

Hiring a *Sensei* Is More Like Finding a Life Coach than Like Hiring an Electrician

We have spent way too much of our time filling out proposals and making formal presentations to large bureaucratic organizations that put out a call for proposals by lean consultants: "Give us a presentation of your capabilities." If we were really being true to our values, our answer should probably be: "We don't think you're serious about learning."

Generally, these companies treat the process of hiring lean consultants as if they were purchasing a machine or contracting with an electrician to install it. Presumably a machine is effective if it performs the intended function. If you can find a reputable electrician who charges a reasonable price, you step out of the way, assume that he will fix the problem, and give him his pay as he walks out the door. Hiring a lean consultant in this way makes the assumption that the consultant is a skilled technician who is coming in to repair your processes, then puts his tools back in the toolbox, leaving you with a lean process.

Consider the folly of hiring any of the following in this way: a marriage counselor, a music teacher for your gifted child, a coach for your high school team, or a golf instructor for a budding PGA professional. In each of these cases, you are making a long-term commitment to someone who can inspire, teach, and help shape lives. You wouldn't find a few candidates from a phone book, ask for a written quote, and then make a selection on that basis. You should view a *sensei* as an organizational transformation coach who will be developing the most precious thing in your life—the organization that will be your legacy.

The Role of the *Sensei*

Sensei means "highly respected teacher." Every lean transformation needs a *sensei*. The *sensei* must have deep personal experience with lean. The *sensei* must be able to move up to the top of the organization and down to the working level, gaining respect across the organization and becoming a valued coach. The *sensei* is not there to be the technical expert making design decisions or the architect of the transformation but rather to work through others by teaching and guiding them. Asking the right questions is often her most valuable role. Two of her most important tasks are developing the top executives and developing the lean coaches who act as evangelists for change.

Developing Internal Coaches as Lean Evangelists

One of the most important roles of the *sensei*, whether he is an external consultant or an employee, is to develop internal lean coaches as champions for change. We say *coaches* rather than *sensei* because a *sensei* should have a minimum of 10 years of experience with lean and generally more. The Toyota *sensei*, sometimes in the role of "master trainers," typically have 25 or more years of experience. Another term we have seen used in place of *lean coach* is *lean evangelist*. This is an odd corporate title, but it does give a feeling for the true role of these people. They are selling the new way of thinking and culture every day.

Should you hire your lean coaches or grow them from within? We have had mixed experiences with hired lean coaches. What often happens is that the organization starts to hire people one by one. They will be hired at various levels in the organization and will often be hired by different parts of the organization, e.g., different divisions. People who call themselves lean experts may have many different backgrounds and many different philosophies. A hodgepodge of lean coaches with different, perhaps conflicting, views of lean can be devastating to progress. For example, do they take a mechanistic, tools-based approach or an organic, people-development approach? Is their main implementation tool of choice *kaizen* events, or do they develop deeper model lines for learning? We are not looking for cookie-cutter lean, but we do want some coherence in the principles that are being taught.

Another issue, as indicated in the story in the last chapter, is experience and credibility within your culture. This is not a showstopper, but hiring a collection of lean coaches from the outside who lack the internal credibility, and in addition have different views of what lean is, often has very bad results. We tend to favor growing lean coaches from within. Then they will have a common learning experience from the *sensei* and learning by doing at your *gemba*. There is an exception, however: if you hire a *sensei*, like Charlie Baker, as an internal high-level manager, we suggest that you let him hire several outside experts. An effective *sensei* should be able to spot talent and judge whether people have compatible philosophies and high levels of skill. The *sensei* will lead the team to develop a common philosophy, build relationships, and establish credibility.

Like the *sensei*, your lean coaches should have the right temperament and interpersonal skills to manage change, including[2]

- The basic technical ability to understand the processes and lean tools
- Natural curiosity

- A strong desire for learning and personal growth
- Basic presentation skills
- The ability to relate to many different types of people, at all levels of the organization
- Great listening skills
- The respect of her peers
- A passion for improving the organization

We could go on, but you get the idea. These people have to go into the workplace, understand the problems, work with teams to develop future state visions, learn how to apply the lean tools, learn PDCA thinking, engage others, challenge leaders to work toward challenging objectives, overcome resistance and skepticism, and more. As we saw in the Alte Schule case, there are many different types of people who can thrive as lean coaches. In our experience, the most challenging problem after you identify and develop strong coaches is holding onto them. The more skills they develop, the more opportunities they have to get another job outside the company.

You will need a stable core of people who learn lean over many years, so finding stable employees who are likely to stick around helps a great deal. There are many ways to move these people around between staff lean positions and operational management positions. Our only warning is that once you find the type of person who thrives on leading organizational transformation, he or she is likely to love the lean coaching job and may not want to go back to a routine supervisory position.

How Do We Learn Complex Skills Like Lean Coaching?

Think of your lean coaches as going through multiple PDCA loops of their own to learn. A useful model of how people learn complex skills was developed by Dreyfus and Dreyfus,[3] who argue that skills that require a great deal of judgment, such as playing chess, advance through five stages: (1) novice, (2) advanced beginner, (3) competent, (4) proficient, and (5) expert. As the learner progresses, she is moving from rigid adherence to a set of rules provided by the teacher to the freedom to use the rules fluidly and innovate:

1. *Novice.* A novice must rigidly adhere to the teacher's rules without deviation. The teacher breaks down the task into individual basic elements that are taught one at a time.
2. *Advanced beginner.* Someone at this level can begin to string together the elements into combinations of steps that make up a routine, but each element is still treated separately. The student cannot adapt the routines to the situation.
3. *Competent.* This person can perform routines comfortably without focusing intensively on them and can begin to see longer-term goals, as well as adapt routines to different situations.
4. *Proficient.* Someone who is proficient has a holistic view of the situation and can apply appropriate routines to solve the problems at hand. She follows basic rules of application as guidelines.
5. *Expert.* The expert no longer needs rules of application to check off and can intuitively adapt routines to each situation. She has a deep understanding of the tools and principles, how they apply, and the reasons for specific courses of action.

If we go back to the Alte Schule case, after the pilot experience, at what level of lean expertise would we place the implementation team? Despite their having completed an ambitious model line project with great results, we would put them at the novice level. They have used a variety of individual tools, like value stream mapping, once. And they did so under the watchful guidance of their *sensei*, Tim. How can you be more than a novice when you have tried some complex skills only once? Yet, the senior executives were ready to roll out the training and have engineers with even less than novice skill "deploy lean." What does that say about the respect we give to skill acquisition, or to the importance of lean transformation, for that matter?

At the very minimum, to get "lean coaches" to the advanced beginner stage, they should see a tool in use once, participate in using it under the watchful eyes of a teacher, and then try it, with a teacher observing and judging their performance until they have some basic level of competence with the tool at an advanced beginner level. Does that seem like overkill on teaching? Can you think of any complex skill in music, sports, or medicine that can be learned simply by watching someone do it or trying it yourself only once? Yet, we rarely see organizations go even this far. Too often we see what Liker and Meier in *The Toyota Way Fieldbook* refer to as "microwaved lean coaches."[4] Send someone to an expensive five- or ten-day program at a prestigious university where he can get a certificate saying that he is a lean coach. This is great for padding the résumé, but it is not the way to develop real skills and capability.

There are a number of books about how people develop high levels of skill that have become quite popular, including those by Colvin and Coyle.[5] Both books discuss the central role of "deep practice," which they attribute to Anders Ericsson, who studied how people become high performers. According to Colvin, deep practice has core characteristics: it is specifically focused on activities to improve performance, often with a teacher's help; these activities are repeated a lot; feedback on results is continuously available; it is highly demanding mentally, even if it is physical activity; and it is not much fun. In the terms of the Dreyfus model, we have to begin at the novice level by breaking the task into small elements and repeating those elements with feedback until we can perform them exactly; then we can move on to more challenging individual routines. At each stage, we practice with a purpose, and we must have feedback so that we can make corrections. As we move along to higher levels of skill, we can begin to deviate from the prescribed method, that is, improvise. Mike Rother[6] has done an excellent job of breaking down the process of developing others in PDCA thinking, which he calls the "coaching *kata*." It is broken down to a level where we can begin to teach it systematically based on deep practice.

Studies have found that experts in various fields take 10 years to reach a high level of performance, with thousands of hours of deep practice in that time. Interestingly, when Gary Convis, who rose through the manufacturing hierarchy at Toyota to one of the highest levels reached by an American, was asked how long it takes for an American to learn to be a strong Toyota leader, he said 10 years. He had not read these books, but through his experience, he had come to a similar conclusion.

Unfortunately, it is rare in our experience for companies to devote 10 years to developing lean coaches or lean leaders. Few companies have been on the journey that long themselves, and most will have moved on to a different program before they reach their 10-year anniversary.

Training World-Class Performers

Instead of thinking of lean as a process improvement methodology, think of it as a journey of developing world-class performers—an Olympic athlete, a virtuoso musician, a master chef. How would you train and develop young budding talent? The Dreyfus model gives us a useful road map for moving from novice to expert. In the early stages, the coach focuses on basic exercises and drills to build up fundamental skills, and as these become natural, the student builds up to repertoires of skills strung together and eventually can innovate. Just as the world-class performer is never done learning, there is no expert in lean who has finished learning and developing. Despite years of intensive, mind-boggling discipline and development, an Olympic athlete can get out of shape in weeks. There is nothing self-sustaining about peak condition; in fact, the higher your body rises in conditioning, the farther and faster you can fall out of it. When you assess your lean systems, do not ask how well the tools are in place. Instead, ask whether the people in each area are being developed as world-class performers in PDCA.

The Dangers of Creating a Mechanistic Lean Bureaucracy

We definitely recommend having a dedicated group that is responsible for becoming the internal lean coaches, but whenever bureaucracies add a department, it will tend to become another bureaucracy.

Then we have the irony of a lean bureaucracy—an organization that is supposedly there to coach and teach organic lean growth, but ends up using coercive methods to control the tools and methods that people use. Often these lean bureaucracies are led by "microwaved" lean coaches. We saw in Chapter 6 the rift that developed at Big Ship between the seasoned Lean Six Sigma black belts who had deep experience and those coming out of the academy who thought they were experts. A mechanistic organization will typically be attracted to the idea of lean looking the same everywhere and will fear allowing too many different business units to have the freedom to do things their way. Experimenting challenges the control and is put down like a rebel uprising. The key features of a lean bureaucracy are

1. A detailed recipe for deployment (some use life-cycle models to display tool implementation at different stages)
2. Extensive training modules
3. Certification for internal experts (like black belt programs)
4. Lean metrics to measure deployment and outcomes and audit the programs
5. Executive support for holding business units accountable (e.g., bonuses tied to achieving lean metrics)

Companies with an organic culture are more likely to let individual business units experiment. They want ownership within the business units, with any corporate support being "pulled" by a need and desire for help. Customization of the process is considered positive because it demonstrates initiative. Organic organizations often fear bureaucracy and will want to keep a corporate group small and in an advisory capacity. Toyota's master trainers of TPS are in huge demand and devote their lives to training and developing others wherever they go—staff and line personnel. They are interested in control only in the sense of insisting that basic TPS principles are followed, not in the sense of restricting the particular solutions that a group develops. Table 14.1 summarizes the differences between

Table 14.1 Bureaucratization of Lean Deployment

	Mechanistic Deployment	Organic Deployment
Formalization of lean support structure	High	Low
Autonomy to customize process	Low	High
Source of lean expertise	Mostly lean group	Mostly line organization
Strategy for deployment of lessons learned	Audited compliance	Knowledge sharing
Process to address organizational entropy	Rules and regulations	Continuous improvement

mechanistic deployment by lean bureaucracies and lean deployment facilitated by a group of lean coaches.

We discussed the problem of entropy in Chapter 5. These two types of organizations have different approaches to this problem. A mechanistic bureaucracy will try to combat evidence of decay of lean methods with more rules and increasing control. In some companies, we have seen auditing processes grow to several-inch binders as the lean bureaucracy adds more and more metrics to respond to signs that the lean process is not being followed as specified.

Organic organizations are more willing to be patient and will resonate with advice that the real goal is continuous improvement. If the processes are decaying, it is because they are not owned by the work group, and we need to work harder to teach the group members how important it is to follow the process until they come up with a better way. Gaps in following the process are actually indicators of problems, and we are seeking to bring those problems to the surface. The reaction should be renewed commitment to teaching how standardized work and continuous improvement go hand in hand.

We will revisit this issue of mechanistic deployment versus organic growing later in the chapter and suggest that it is not an either-or proposition. In fact, a healthy balance between the two is needed in most cases. For example, the early stages of Dreyfus learning are very mechanical by design.

Sustaining the Gains

One of the most common questions we are asked is how to sustain the gains once we have improved the process. A lot of work went into getting the process right in that carefully planned *kaizen* workshop, and it is certainly wasteful to see it slip back to where it was before the change. Unfortunately, the most common outcome of process improvements is slipping backward. Why does this occur?

The problem is actually a fundamental misunderstanding of what it means to sustain the gains. It goes back to our old friend: machine thinking. When you make an improvement to a machine, you expect it to operate in the new improved state for some time, as long as some basic maintenance is done. For example, you do not expect to make a change that improves an engine's output and then have it creep back to the lower level of output within weeks. On the other hand, when you improve a socio-technical system, it is not just a physical thing that you are changing. Let's consider three examples of lean improvements that are often made by staff experts:

1. *Line rebalance.* Rebalance the work on the line to a given *takt* in order to increase productivity.
2. *Standardized work.* Develop new standardized work, emphasizing quality key points, to reduce variability in order to improve quality.
3. *Pull system.* Organize a supermarket area with defined minimum and maximum inventory levels and a *kanban* system in order to reduce inventory.

In each case, the improvement project may be great technically, with superior visuals and precisely calculated quantities, yet still fail in the long run. There are two problems. First, each of these projects is based on the set of conditions at the time of the project, which in reality will change over time. Second, each of these projects assumes a set of behaviors by the people working in the area, which may in fact not occur.

One assumption of each of these lean projects is a certain rate of customer demand—the *takt*. What if the customer demand changes? Then you need to rebalance the work to a new *takt*, you need to revise the standardized work based on a new *takt*, and you need to identify the quantities in the supermarket based on the new *takt*. Many other things can also change—the mix of products may vary, there may be engineering changes to the product, parts may come and go, customers may use different containers, and so on. Each of these changes requires some adjustments. Unless the expert who set up the system stays around indefinitely to make these adjustments, the system will degrade. And unless the expert stays around to continually retrain the workers and to monitor their behavior and provide feedback when they stray from the standards, the system will degrade.

A Systems View of Sustaining the Gains

If we shift from machine thinking to systems thinking, we get a very different perspective. It is well known in systems thinking that systems are always changing, even when it appears that they are staying the same. To maintain consistent output, one must continually adjust the system to changing environmental conditions. This is called *dynamic homeostasis* in systems thinking, or running to stay in place. Think of the hamster madly running on a wheel and simply staying in one place. If the hamster stops running, it will be carried backward by the momentum of the wheel.

So asking how to sustain the gains is equivalent to asking what the dynamics are that will keep the system in homeostasis. There are two parts to the answer: (1) dynamic adjustment to changing conditions, and (2) people being checked and coached on how well they follow the standard process.

The dynamic adjustment needed to keep the system stable is what Toyota calls "maintenance *kaizen*."[7] It is well recognized at Toyota that it takes a lot of work to maintain a system. And the dirty little secret is that the more waste you take out of a system, the more work it takes to maintain the system at that high level of performance. Maintenance comes from having clearly defined standards, observing carefully for deviations from those standards, and then developing and implementing countermeasures to eliminate the deviations. Sometimes a new standard is needed simply to maintain the quality or safety or productivity because conditions have changed. It is really

hard work, and it can be done only on a continuous basis by someone who is continually in the process so that he can closely monitor
it, which in most cases means the team members, team leaders, or
group leaders.

Machine thinking assumes centralized control of processes. One
company that brought in Jeff Liker to advise it was very proud of its
Deming heritage. The company made roof shingles, and it had automated every process possible. Since people tend to be variable, it
worked to design processes so that they were people-proof. For example, all processes were run by computer, and the computers themselves
used secure passwords; even the technicians monitoring the processes
did not have the password and could not change the programs. Not sur-
prisingly, there was no evidence of continuous improvement. When a
process broke down, like building poor-quality shingles, the company
would simply run off the bad parts into a big pile until someone came
to fix the process. It then did nothing to try to understand the cause of
the problem and put in effective countermeasures.

Lean processes are based on decentralized control, with centralized
checking of the process and the leadership. We have defined a lean system as one that brings problems (gaps between standard and actual) to
the surface, has a clear way of prioritizing the problems based on business objectives, and has people who are highly skilled and motivated
to solve the problems using complete PDCA cycles. If we have such a
system in place, it will be self-correcting, and the minimum expectation should be that it will be sustained. An expectation of continually
improved performance is better. We need to emphasize that this is not
the same as "autonomous" work groups. The leaders at higher levels
need to be very cognizant of what is going on at the *gemba*, actively
checking and leading on a daily basis. That is why it is referred to as
gemba management.

It is through a combination of top-down leadership and instilling
a level of pride in every team member that TPS begins to take shape as
a system. Notice that after top-down, we said *leadership*, not management. Once TPS is in place as a *system*, it actually starts to become
self-sustaining, to a point. In Chapter 5, we pointed out that entropy
is a law of the universe, so a self-sustaining system is impossible, just

as a perpetual motion machine is impossible. What we mean by self-sustaining is that when you get the right combination of technical and people systems in place, the following happens continuously in every work group every day:

1. The expectations for performance, the targets, become crystal clear. Some of these targets are to maintain the system, and others are the expected next level of improvement.
2. The methods for achieving the expected performance are carefully designed and well taught.
3. Deviations from standard, the gaps, surface quickly, and the problems are visible to the work group and to outside observers.
4. Leaders, from the boss to the boss's boss and on up, visit regularly, seeing the actual state of the process with their own eyes and wanting to know what the problems are so that they can help in achieving the targets.
5. There are clearly defined roles and responsibilities, so that when something does not go according to plan, it is clear who should lead the action to fix the problem.
6. Team members, and certainly leaders, are well trained in problem solving and know how to react based on facts and a complete PDCA process.

Now, is this organic or mechanistic? We would argue that it includes elements of both. Is it employee empowerment? If employee empowerment means that employees are on their own to do whatever they think is right, then it is far from empowerment. There are too many rules and too many leaders coming around. If empowerment means that you have clear expectations for performance, and that the company will provide the tools and leadership needed to help you meet or exceed them, then it is empowerment.

A Lean Façade or Evolution to Continuous Improvement?

We are often asked to visit a "lean plant" to offer our opinions and advice, and one of the most common questions is: how can we sustain our lean improvements? More often than not, it is clear why the company is having problems with sustaining the changes because what we see is a "lean façade." Façades are often used in movie sets to make fake buildings look like authentic originals. The façades may make the set look like an old New England town, but behind the façade may be scaffolding or trailers. Sustaining a façade can be done by bringing in a maintenance crew to pretty things up and make minor repairs. This is very different from the challenge of maintaining the right thinking and behaviors to keep the process operating at a level of excellence.

The lean façade usually includes 5S (in reality, only 3S, without the standardizing and sustaining), various signs and labels, standardized worksheets posted, a well-labeled supermarket, and other indications of lean tools. If we talk to a few supervisors, we hear about the "lean program" or what "they" (the lean experts) did in a *kaizen* event six months ago. Further questioning indicates that the supervisor does not really understand the tools or use them correctly. Data posted on visual boards are often out of date. The tools are lifeless, driven externally by management or by the lean office, providing only a record that there once was some lean activity. If the model line at Alte Schule were to be ignored while the lean team spread lean to other areas, it could easily become a lean façade.

In reality, virtually all lean transformations begin with tools and projects led by internal or external lean *sensei* and coaches (see Figure 14.1). This is a normal Phase 1 of lean deployment. We have to learn the basics before we can advance to a deeper understanding of lean as a system. It is only when this first phase becomes the last phase—in other words, when evolution stops—that we are stuck with a lean façade with nothing on the inside.

In companies that advance into the next phase, managers take a serious interest in learning lean and begin to lead it. The manager of an area (e.g., the area superintendent) and the supervisors are deeply involved and will proudly talk about the lean tools and how they are being used to improve the process. If the supervisors are coached and developed, they will in turn become lean coaches for their individual work groups (ideally, 20 to 25 people). Now, instead of having a few

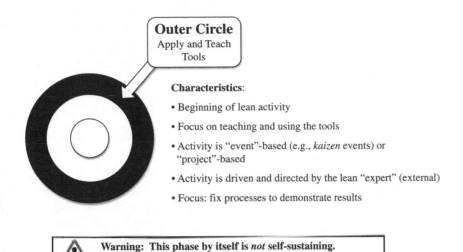

Characteristics:

• Beginning of lean activity

• Focus on teaching and using the tools

• Activity is "event"-based (e.g., *kaizen* events) or "project"-based

• Activity is driven and directed by the lean "expert" (external)

• Focus: fix processes to demonstrate results

> **Warning: This phase by itself is *not* self-sustaining. Entropy will set in, degrading to a lean facade!**

Figure 14.1. Lean Deployment Phase 1—Applying and Teaching Tools

coaches for an entire organization, we have lean coaches whose full-time job is leading a particular work group. An effective supervisor as coach will be checking the process throughout the day, thinking about how to improve elements of the process, engaging team members, continuously coaching people, and adjusting the process. If the supervisor is going it alone at this stage, with minimal engagement of the team members, she will generally still be splitting her time between firefighting and improvement. The improvements are likely to be episodic, not continuous improvement, but in this phase at least the tools that are in place will be kept up, data will be kept up, and entropy will be significantly arrested (see Figure 14.2).

Companies that continue beyond Phase 2 will progress toward the ideal of a complete lean system, aligned from top to bottom. When we penetrate the inner core, we have won the hearts and minds of the team members. Organizations at this level will have team leaders who are more advanced in problem solving than the typical team member and have become part of the improvement staff of the group leader. Now we have a lean leader for every five to seven team members and regular engagement of the team members. At this point, we are very close to true continuous improvement, and the improvements will be

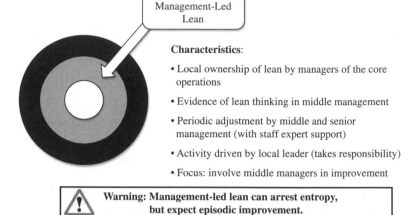

Middle Circle
Management-Led
Lean

Characteristics:

• Local ownership of lean by managers of the core operations

• Evidence of lean thinking in middle management

• Periodic adjustment by middle and senior management (with staff expert support)

• Activity driven by local leader (takes responsibility)

• Focus: involve middle managers in improvement

> ⚠ **Warning: Management-led lean can arrest entropy, but expect episodic improvement.**

Figure 14.2. Lean Deployment Phase 2—Management-Led Lean

at a very detailed level process by process (see Figure 14.3). It would take the pilot area at Alte Schule at least three to five years to get to this point with very intensive coaching. The Henry Ford Health System pathology labs got to this point in some of their work groups through Richard Zarbo's passionate leadership (see Chapter 9), but even

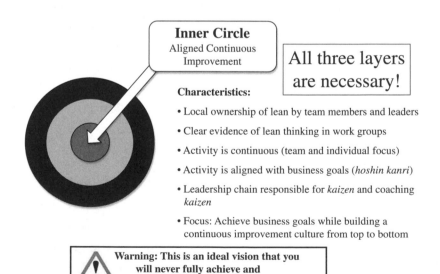

Inner Circle
Aligned Continuous
Improvement

> **All three layers are necessary!**

Characteristics:

• Local ownership of lean by team members and leaders

• Clear evidence of lean thinking in work groups

• Activity is continuous (team and individual focus)

• Activity is aligned with business goals (*hoshin kanri*)

• Leadership chain responsible for *kaizen* and coaching *kaizen*

• Focus: Achieve business goals while building a continuous improvement culture from top to bottom

> ⚠ **Warning: This is an ideal vision that you will never fully achieve and requires a lifelong commitment!**

Figure 14.3. Lean Deployment Phase 3—Aligned Continuous Improvement

after five years, Richard concluded that lean could go backward if he left and the wrong leader replaced him. Maybe Gary Convis's 10-year rule applies here as well.

Use of Process Checks and Feedback

"You get what you measure" is a common refrain, and indeed, an advanced lean organization seems measurement-crazy. There are boards with measures posted everywhere. Again, we warn that it is dangerous to confuse the surface "façade" level with the deeper reality of behavior and thinking. Differences in how measures are used can be like night and day.

One tool that has become popular in lean is sometimes called a "layered audit." We explained in Chapter 4 the concept of *hoshin kanri*, which sets measurable objectives at each level of the organization that are aligned from top to bottom. This is a plan. A layered audit is a way to check the progress being made toward those objectives at every level. It supports the C and A in PDCA. Indeed, if we look carefully at the boards with metrics in a Toyota plant, we will see that they are aligned based on the *hoshin kanri*, and that there are various audits from top to bottom. Toyota calls this "process confirmation." The underlying thinking behind these checks is very different from what some companies do with layered audits.

The difference can be understood through Adler's distinction between coercive and enabling bureaucracies, discussed in Chapter 5. In a coercive bureaucracy, the layered audit is a means of control: check, punish the failures, and reward the achievers. In an enabling bureaucracy, process confirmation is a means by which managers can go to the *gemba*, understand its condition in detail, find weak points, and coach the teams on how to improve. In other words, it is part of PDCA as a process of learning (see Table 14.2). Whatever you call it, this process of checking, giving feedback, and checking some more is one of the keys to sustaining the process and continuous improvement, with the right philosophy. It is understandable why companies in the "lean façade" stage use the layered audit as a means of control. In fact, there is nothing behind the façade that enables the

Table 14.2 Layered Audits for Control versus Process Checks for Learning

	Layered Audits for Control	Process Checks for Learning
Purpose	Compliance	Skill development
Method	Rewards and punishments tied to results	Feedback and engagement
Who drives the audits?	Mostly lean group	Mostly line organization
Assumption about people's motivation	"You get what you measure and reward"	People need feedback and coaching to learn
Skills required	Measurement and interpreting data	Giving and receiving feedback

organization to respond positively to feedback. This is likely to frustrate managers who have only the carrot and the stick as tools. As management and workers mature, the feedback can actually be used for learning and development, and the process checks are valued by the teacher and the student.

Spreading While Deepening

Let's go back to Alte Schule, Inc., and assume that the lean implementation team spent enough time and effort training and coaching the leadership in the pilot area that its improved performance is sustained and the area is continuing to improve. Now what?

Spreading Best Practices or Learning?

We already learned in the executive presentation that several key decision makers were anxious to spread lean quickly in order to get similar results everywhere in the company. These decision makers appreciated the results and wanted more, everywhere, as quickly as possible. Bob, the vice president of engineering, said that he would "send my engineers and managers down for training as soon as you want, and they can continue rolling out the changes." Tim gasped at the thought.

Imagine if Bob had had a more sophisticated understanding and had said something thoughtful like this:

I can see that the implementation team learned a great deal in three months," observed Bob. "How can we build on that learning so that they can continue to deepen their knowledge and increase the exposure to others through similar learning by doing projects? I would like to have a few of my engineers involved in the next one so that they can learn along with the team.

This would have been heaven to a *sensei* like Tim. As it was, Bob was completely missing what the implementation team had learned and what people in the pilot area were starting to learn. To Bob, with his mechanistic engineering mind, it all seemed very simple. He thought, "My engineers can grasp your lean concepts and rules and continue to rearrange the plant." He clearly missed the cultural transformation that was just at the very beginning, starting to take hold in the pilot area. Sending his engineers to run around rearranging the furniture in the plant would absolutely kill that culture change, and the transformation effort would be dead in its tracks.

The most important things to recognize are

1. *The pilot area is never done.* It will not progress on its own, and entropy will kick in if it is not supported by the *sensei* until the local leadership has the skills to arrest that entropy. It is also the advance guard of learning for the coaches and senior management, so it needs to stay ahead of the other areas. Continue tending to the pilot area and going deeper and deeper, step by step, and the rewards will be great. Going deeper means solving problems one by one as they arise, turning the resulting improvements into the way we do things through standardized work, refining metrics, advancing local leadership in problem-solving skills down to the team members, and increasing the challenge of the targets for safety, quality, cost, delivery, and morale.
2. *You are spreading learning and understanding, not simply replicating solutions through tools.* We often hear the term *replicate*, and our

blood runs cold. You can replicate the tools or the look and feel of a process in a mechanistic way, but what we want to replicate is the learning process and people development. This means that as you spread lean to other areas, you have to go through a learning process like the one the pilot team went through. As you can see, this is much more time-consuming and requires a great deal of patience compared to simply replicating the physical systems.

Is Becoming Lean Fun for All?

OK, so now you're convinced that the real goal of lean is excellence, which means creating a flexible, adaptable learning organization of people and processes that can achieve ever more challenging business goals. People must be empowered to do this. Organic organizations are more flexible than mechanistic ones, and patience is required to allow the organic seeds of lean transformation to germinate throughout the organization, with careful tending by lean coaches. Given the opportunity, people will come into their own if you give them the resources, space, and sage guidance. Throw out the mechanistic thinking and bring in the organic.

Unfortunately, the world is not that simple. The old wives' tale that people resist change is true. You can teach an old dog new tricks, but the dogs may not enthusiastically line up to learn them. Research in the neurosciences has given us rare insight into the working of the brain, and not everything we are learning is good news for those who are zealots of change. With sophisticated imaging technology, brain researchers can monitor brain activity and see how various activities activate the pain centers and the pleasure centers. It turns out that change hurts.

When we perform routine behaviors that have developed well-worn neural pathways, we use the basal ganglia, the "habit center," whereas learning something new uses active working memory in the prefrontal cortex. Using the habit center for well-learned behavior is comforting and feels good, while taxing the working memory is, well, work, and causes discomfort.[8]

We are certainly not claiming to be experts on the brain. What we have been able to decipher is overwhelming evidence that resistance to change has a real chemical-physical base. It is not just stubborn people who need to adjust their attitudes. It is how we are wired, and rewiring is difficult and painful. As we develop well-worn neural pathways, following known methods is comforting, and we prefer it. Change means burning new neural pathways and is arduous, painful, and something that we would rather avoid. In describing how world-class performers develop themselves, Colvin writes[9]

> *It isn't much fun. . . . Instead of doing what we are good at, we insistently seek out what we're not good at. Then we identify the painful, difficult activities that will make us better and do those things over and over. After each repetition, we force ourselves to see—or get others to tell us—exactly what still isn't right so we can repeat the most painful and difficult parts of what we've just done. We continue that process until we are mentally exhausted.*

The good news is that we can overcome the pain of change through giving the new behavior highly focused attention and then repeatedly practicing it to reroute our neural pathways. In fact, when we do manage to learn something new, it is exhilarating and leads to great pleasure. And the more vigorously we practice learning new skills, the easier it becomes. This requires deep practice. The process of creating new neural pathways seems to seize up when we do not do it often and gets more facile with use, kind of like our muscles in physical activity. So there is hope, but us old dogs are not going to volunteer for painful change if we don't have to. This is the role of leadership—to cajole and encourage us, and sometimes to forcefully push us out of our comfort zone, to take steps that may not feel great in the short term, but that will benefit us and the organization in the long term.

Top-Down, Bottom-Up, or Both?

We must admit that we have never seen lean get very far from the bottom up. On the other hand, we have also made it clear that the top telling Lean Six Sigma staff to lean out the operations will not work in the long term. So the tricky balancing act is for the top to lead the bottom to "voluntarily" cycle through PDCA loops, painfully learning better ways so that people can feel good when it succeeds.

Fortunately, the people at the top don't have to do it alone. First, they themselves can benefit from a coach to help them learn new problem-solving skills. Second, they can access the power of the hierarchy. The hierarchy can be an ugly thing when it becomes a chain of command of managers who are mindlessly executing the boss's instructions. It is a beautiful thing when it's a chain of leaders who are teaching and coaching small groups of people to become leaders so that they can teach and coach other small groups of people to bring problems to the surface, challenge assumptions, and innovate. It's awesome when that problem solving is aligned toward positive organizational goals. Unfortunately, it is also really hard work to develop the individual, then the group, and then the organizational capability to do this regularly, and then continually tune, refresh, and update our high-performing organization.

There is a conventional wisdom that organizational transformation requires a "burning platform." We will not jump off while the platform is safe and cozy. However, a crisis like this is rarely positive. For example, big jumps in sales do not mobilize the organization to change as much as major drops in sales do. A jump in sales often means that we just do more of what we are already doing, usually with more people. A crisis that threatens the future of the organization and the livelihood of its members can aid lean transformation in a number of ways. It legitimizes the top leaders' decisions to push hard. Fear motivates people to push themselves out of their comfort zone. It provides an occasion for organizational restructuring. In extreme cases, it may force the hard decisions about who can really perform and who needs to be moved aside or even pushed out.

On the other hand, top-down forced change in a crisis does not automatically mean that the organization will emerge stronger and poised to become a learning organization. It can just as well lead to weakening of capability and degrading of the trust that binds members to the organization. It depends on what the leaders do with the crisis. Also, crises are periodic events and hard to plan. So, after the crisis, people can begin to settle right back into using their well-worn neural pathways, with a few new ones that they picked up, leading to a new level of static, mechanistic routines.

Both Charlie Baker in transforming product development at NAAS and Richard Zarbo at the Henry Ford Health System labs led the transformations aggressively from the top down, but engaged people from the bottom up. Charlie came into NAAS when it was in a crisis that had led to downsizing and aggressive cost reduction, while Richard had to transform an organization that was relatively healthy by making it clear that participation in lean was a requirement of the job. Neither leader waited patiently for people to come to the conclusion that lean was the right thing to do. They made the decision for the organization.

If pushing and rewarding and threatening by the top were the only force for lean, it would be extremely difficult to sustain. Fortunately, we do have something in our lean bag of tricks that will help. Recall that concept of lean systems bringing problems to the surface? If we truly develop a system that brings problems to the surface, along with systems to sort through and prioritize the problems that are revealed and work groups that have the leadership and skills to solve the problems, then we have something approaching self-sustaining without the need for constant vigilance from the top. At least it's as close as we will get to locally self-sustaining. It is still very vulnerable and depends on the skill level and continuous motivation of the group leaders, team leaders, and team members. But the system itself is signaling what the problems are, not senior managers or engineers who come around to point out problems. There is a great power to this. People will respond much more positively when they can see the problems directly as they do the work every day. This is the bottom-up part, but in the early stages, the top leaders have to get the system in place to start this self-regulating process going, which is the top-down part.

Narrow and Deep or Wide and Shallow?

This is another balancing act. We have no doubt that drilling down deep into specific model areas and achieving specific objectives for critical business processes is the best way to develop people and processes. We often wince when we hear people describe how they are value stream mapping all of their processes. "More value stream mapping wallpaper," we sardonically joke. People's neural pathways barely notice what is happening, as the brief wave of tool development passes through the brain painlessly, leaving barely a residue of interesting memories. Certainly there will be little evidence of behavior change in the core work process from wall-to-wall mapping.

Going narrow and deep is the only way to get deep learning. Yet we have been challenged by senior leaders who have called us to help them solve their problem and exclaim in frustration: "I have 35,000 people in 60 manufacturing plants globally, and you are suggesting that we change them one pilot line at a time. I will not be alive long enough to get through the first pass."

In other words, there are practical realities. The answer to this agonizing call for help is unfortunately not a solution but our old friend, the PDCA cycle. A good *sensei* answer to the frustrated chief operating officer might be

> *We did the model line. You saw the results. You were there with us and learned the power of PDCA. When we started the model line, we were not even sure what all the problems were, let alone what answers the team would develop. I would be a hypocrite if I tried to sell you on a 10-step plan for moving this from the one pilot area to 35,000 people in 60 plants. Instead, let's develop a plan for the next PDCA loop. We learned some things and have developed some people who can act as resources so that this next pass can be broader and more ambitious than the first.*

The Big Ship versus Small Ship comparison in Chapter 6 gave us a look at the difference in strategies. Small Ship started deep in the ball-valve area, creating a strong model. From that model sprung some spontaneous models in other parts of the shipyard, focused on some specific tools. Small Ship then intentionally spread the model deeply in a few other areas. Eventually that led it to focus on the overall submarine overhaul, and it approached this as a set of work cells, each of which needed

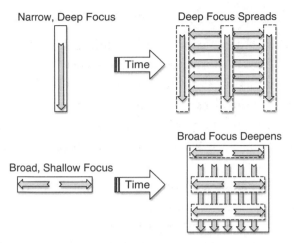

Figure 14.4. Changes in Breadth and Depth over Time

deep development. The top figure in Figure 14.4 illustrates how Small Ship started with a narrow, deep focus in the ball-valve area and then spread the process to other value streams by repeating the narrow, deep pilots. Each one took less time than the preceding one as the organization learned, but it still took several years before the company approached the overall submarine.

Big Ship, on the other hand, started broad and shallow, doing many projects superficially. Over time, when it got a chance to go back to some of the pilots, it would add additional tools, and then the managers were given targets for numbers of *kaizen* events, leading the whole organization to deepen across the shipyard. Layer by layer it burrowed down to deeper implementation, but the only areas where it got to the depth of the ball-valve area were in targeted pilot areas like the machine shop. In this case, the shop and its people were truly transformed, and the black belts who focused on the machine shop were also changed to the point where they viewed other black-belt projects as superficial and even misguided. Nonetheless, over a seven-year period, Big Ship and Small Ship, through different routes, eventually got to a similar place. They both achieved some level of balance between mechanistic and organic, though still far from the ideal. The ideal balanced approach is what Adler called "enabling bureaucracy."

Enabling Bureaucracy Is a Balanced Approach

If we return to Adler's concept of enabling bureaucracy, we get a picture of a balanced approach. Enabling bureaucracy takes advantage of the opportunities to structure routine aspects of the job so that they are repeatable, but involves employees in the application of the generic standards to their specific work. It will appear mechanistic, but if we take a second look, we will notice that team members are encouraged to improve on the standard so that it becomes new and better. What are enforced are higher-level principles. For example, visual management boards may be a requirement, and there may be some standards for the boards, but the specific metrics that are tracked, the targets that are set, and the details of how problems are highlighted can vary across work groups. Work groups have different situations, and they will not improve something if the organization insists that they do it exactly as the corporate staff specifies.

If we followed the Dreyfus model, we would start more mechanistically, teaching people to work through the PDCA problem-solving process in a regimented, prescriptive way, and then, over time, as they mature in their development, allowing more freedom to innovate with the process. Notice that what we are standardizing is the way to approach problems, not specific solutions.

The initial pilot areas are in a sense organic, but also mechanistic, as we saw in Alte Schule in Chapter 13. The teams do not start out with a precisely specified lean façade to copy, yet the *sensei* is quite strict about following the PDCA process. We find that to spread lean effectively, we need to teach the very fundamental tools of lean at an elementary level, which ends up looking mechanistic. It is a step-by-step process, and in the early stages of learning, there is little room for deviation in how the tools are used, although people are encouraged to try and allowed to fail. As the organization matures, and if things go as we would like, the process is increasingly turned over to the work groups, and innovation in the methods used is encouraged.

Focus on Core Business Goals

The challenge in having the patience to go narrow and deep is keeping senior management happy enough to allow the experiment to continue.

In some cases, senior management will be very patient, as we saw in the Japanese heavy equipment company in Chapter 7. In most cases, it will be critical to start the pilot by choosing a core business issue.

We saw this very clearly in the product development transformation of the automotive system supplier led by Charlie Baker. There was a major focus on cost reduction in this supplier, as it was in a crisis of downsizing and fighting for survival. Those involved agreed that a turning point occurred when they began to focus on cost engineering. When they developed should-be costs for subsystem components and related this to design features through cost tables, the design teams were off and running. The company had very challenging targets, but through creativity and hard work, it achieved the targets, reducing the total cost of each unit by about 30 percent. As you can imagine, this got the attention of senior management, but the design teams also learned deeply about lean in the process.

Under Charlie's direction, they learned true problem solving using PDCA. Figure 4.1 (p. 70) connected improvement activities to a purpose. We learned then that at the time the initial big target is set, it is not clear how the organization will achieve that target, but through smaller PDCA loops, we take steps toward the goal. Since the system supplier was struggling and this was a turnaround, the business purpose was clear to everyone. The cost engineering process provided clear and very challenging targets. The actual process involved breaking these overwhelming targets into smaller steps with their own mini-targets. We have found that a clearly defined purpose and targets, with the right coaching on a good process, will achieve the business results, keep senior management happy and engaged, and develop capable team members.

Moving into Support Functions

We often hear proclamations like, "We are not going to do lean manufacturing; we're going to do lean enterprise. We'll hit all the support functions and back offices in parallel with the shop floor." This is easy to say, but the result is usually broad and shallow deployment in a mechanistic way.

We caution you to proceed at a pace that your internal resources can handle effectively. If you have enough well-trained coaches who can be deployed to lead deep implementation across the enterprise, go for it. Few companies will be in this position. It is better to start in the core value-adding processes and add support functions as they become key enablers for your core functions. For example, we saw in Small Ship that as the ball-valve area made progress, it needed to bring in Engineering to get work instructions so that it could be self-reliant in some simple repairs. It also got Engineering to come to the floor and quickly prescribe repairs, teaching the engineers the importance of going to the *gemba*. This was much more meaningful than doing a generic workshop on "lean for engineering." It integrated the activities in the ball-valve area with the activities in Engineering and provided a model for collaborative relationships that could be applied in other areas.

Managing Change Is Political

When we talk about Toyota, we naturally emphasize fact-based problem solving, clear expectations, and people going about their business according to prescribed methods that they help improve. It sounds like a well-oiled machine. It is not, even at Toyota. Anyone who has tried to help an organization on its lean journey, whether the organization is mostly mechanistic or mostly organic, quickly finds that he is dealing with politics.

When was the last time you heard someone exclaim in frustration: "It's all political"? Immediately you know that that's a bad thing. If she's talking about a day at work, it means that some decisions were made that she did not like and that she believes were made for the wrong reasons. The right reasons for a decision are rational, devoid of emotion, and focused on what is best for the total organization. A person getting promoted because he "kisses up" to the boss is the wrong reason, unless he has achieved the level of performance required for the promotion. A person who is trying to build her department as an empire without thinking about how this will affect the customer or the enterprise is the wrong motive. Does politics therefore equate to misuse of power and influence?

In a general sense, *politics* means the use of power to move the organization in a certain direction. Sociologists have defined many sources of power, including *formal authority* (from one's position), *charisma* (from one's personality), *expertise* (from actual knowledge), *tradition* (based on accepted normative practices), *coercion* (the threat of a big stick), and *rewards* (dangling a carrot). Perhaps there are others, but without power, how could anyone get anything done, good or bad?

Leadership by definition involves power, and therefore politics—leaders need followers. Having followers means that we have influence, and thus we are using power and therefore "playing politics." A change agent must be a master politician. The change agent's job is to move the organization toward a vision. That becomes the political interest of the change agent. Some people believe in that vision, and others do not. The change agent must be able to read the political situation: Who is for lean? Who is against lean? Who is on the fence? What are the sources of power in the organization? How can these sources be used to move the organization toward the vision? When do you go up top to the executive, when do you work things out with the middle manager who is responsible for the project area, and when do you get the whole team involved?

Going back in history within Toyota, Taiichi Ohno and his students could be vicious. Their power came from the top leaders of the company, their position in the formal hierarchy, their charisma, and their deep expertise. They wielded that power like a mega battering ram, and nothing stood in their way. Certainly they had political enemies who did not agree with what they were doing. The modern incarnation of that group is the Operations Management Consulting Division (OMCD), and the new mantra is kinder and gentler. Battering rams have been replaced by gentle persuasion. On the other hand, everyone inside Toyota knows that TPS is sacred in the company and that these people from OMCD are experts. You shake a little when they are coming to see your operation, and it is not always a pleasant experience.

Respect for people, like it or not, is culturally specific. Being called stupid by Ohno might have been a badge of courage at one time in one culture and verbal abuse in another. Even the students of Ohno who seemed to be abused believed passionately that he loved them and cared deeply about their development. They all came out much stronger and more confident as a result of this tough love.

In some ways, a coercive bureaucracy is easier to deal with because the sources of power are predominantly formal authority, rewards, and punishment. The bad news is that people will comply, but lean needs far more than compliance. We need the hearts and souls of the people, or they won't bring problems to the surface and willingly undergo the pain of learning new skills. Organic organizations are messier because power is more dispersed and the power sources are harder to understand. But if the change agent does the hard work required to mobilize the work groups, the result can be far more satisfying.

Reflecting on the cases in Section Two, all of the *sensei* had to read the politics and become political actors in the system. In some cases that went really well, and in other cases it did not go so well. In part, the *sensei*'s success depended on their political skills and the political environment.

Companies with patience that are willing to go through the process to strive for long-term excellence are a delight to work with. Companies with short-term goals that are constantly seeking immediate return on their investment are frustrating, but we always hold out hope that we can teach them. There are many paths to success, and there is a lot of room for error in the early stages of lean deployment, when it is new and interesting. What is more telling is what happens 10 years later, when many people have changed seats and the environment has done its work of significantly changing the technology, market, regulations, competitive climate, stakeholders, and more. Has lean settled in as a cultural expectation, or has it morphed from an active program to a dormant set of slogans? We will take up in the last chapter the challenge of making continuous improvement a way of life.

Chapter 15

Continuous Improvement as a Way of Life

Deming Point 7: Adopt and institute leadership. Management must be empowered, beginning with senior leadership, to know the details of their business that will include operation of equipment because they must understand how to operate the work that they supervise.

—W. Edwards Deming, American consultant, statistician, and educator

We are very wary of the word *conclusion*, and are a mite hesitant to use it here in this book. It implies that in some way we have reached the end of something, which runs counter to the points we have been making in this book thus far. Instead of concluding, let's reflect.

We started this book with some rather harsh statements about how most companies' actions have them on a path to mediocrity instead of to excellence. Fighting words indeed. We discussed the differences between treating excellence as a hobby and treating it as an avocation, and all that was involved in the struggle to become excellent. Building on work done in the 1980s and 1990s, we discovered a common thread: the most successful American companies were driven by strongly held and widely shared values. However, there was also the caveat that companies that had achieved excellence in the past were just as vulnerable to decline as any other company. These companies had excellent leaders, but those leaders weren't teachers and didn't institutionalize learning, plan–do–check–adjust (PDCA) thinking, and so on. There were a few companies, however, that purposefully developed their next generation of leaders to succeed the current leaders and keep the passion for excellence alive. They understood that they were reaching for an ideal that can never be achieved, but the struggle to achieve excellence is what makes them excellent.

Being the frail creatures that we are, it is not possible for us to morph from just OK to excellence in one big flying leap. We need to take many steps here and there in the general direction of excellence, which we defined as a "True North vision." These many steps encompass continuous improvement . . . of ourselves, of our groups, and ultimately of the enterprise. The mechanism for continuous improvement is PDCA.

PDCA is a way of thinking, with the end of each PDCA cycle feeding into the beginning of the next, setting the problem-solving processes into perpetual motion. The focus is on thinking deeply and rigorously, based on the facts. We discussed the differences between solutions and countermeasures, with the latter being a specific trial response to a specific problem that probably would change over time as we learn more. We don't live in a static world, one in which deploying "standardized" solutions would be possible.

We emphasized that the groups that are doing the work must be thoroughly trained in PDCA so that they can immediately respond to problems as they occur, in real time. We discussed how, at Toyota, PDCA is more than a way to get results from improving processes; it is a way to develop the people who are doing the work. We always need to be aware of how people are developing as they go through the process, and we need to have a vision of what the ideal team member would be so that we can identify the gaps. Through repeated cycles of learning, eventually we can build a culture of true continuous improvement and respect for people.

We recalled a few case examples, discussing the differences between having a people development purpose during a lean transformation and simply chasing the bottom line and doing a "slash and burn" transformation. In the latter case, after two *kaizen* blitzes, the executive decided that the organization had spent enough money on consultants and that the plant managers now needed to "deliver the goods." In the former case, we watched how a young manager was developed through PDCA at Toyota. His boss understood both the business purpose and the people development purpose; our young manager was able to struggle and succeed, and the organization was stronger for the efforts.

Our efforts and focus then shifted to the importance of a company's having a purpose. We differentiated between measurable objectives, which most companies have, and a purpose, which too few do. Leadership needs to strive to create an institution, we observed, that will serve a greater purpose. The purpose begets the vision for the company and how that is transformed into planning horizons of varying lengths. We stressed the importance of the True North vision, the guidepost that helps us get a general sense of the right and wrong direction. An example of this is Toyota's contention that if a person is not being challenged and learning, she is not being respected. Respect for people is part of Toyota's True North vision. We then went on to contrast *hoshin kanri* with traditional management by objectives, with the latter typically being part of a "command-and-control" mechanism that leaves little room for learning and growth. If done right, *hoshin kanri* can align objectives and prioritize PDCA activities. Without this, individuals are randomly trying to fix things, and their collective efforts will not add up to any significant business purpose.

We discussed how targets give us a firm guidepost to which we can compare our current condition to give us a focal point for our PDCA activities. The managers' role is to coach the process; therefore, they must be experts in the process and will need, initially, coaching themselves. We also discussed the pitfalls of relying on "home run"–type breakthroughs. That isn't to say that Toyota doesn't have any breakthrough ideas or goals; it's just that its breakthrough goals are broken into smaller steps so that exploration and learning will move the company toward the breakthrough.

We finished our discussion of purpose by noting that the gap between the desired state and a company's current condition would determine what it worked on. There is no "one best" approach to lean transformation, so please let's put that thought to rest. Our infuriating response to that often-asked question will always be, out of necessity, "It depends." What are the business needs? What is your history? What is the maturity and culture? What is the skill level? The most important thought contained in gaining an understanding of the current condition is to always ask, "What is the purpose of this activity?" How will both the people and the processes be developed?

Through generations of managers, we have created cultures in which people start to think that everyone else in the organization is like a robot, and that their job is to keep the robots functioning within defined parameters. The robots do what they are programmed to do, and periodically we update the programs to increase the robots' productivity or deal with a major change in the environment (see Figure 15.1). Altering the programming in the robot takes an

Figure 15.1. Machine Land, Where Robots Manage Robots

investment in experts, so we had better carefully justify the investment in terms of cost savings.

Our next discussions dealt with the topic of "leaning out" a process versus building a lean system. We argued that if you simply focus on "leaning out" something, like a line, a department, or an area, you'll approach the task from a technical viewpoint. This type of thinking, machine thinking, treats all systems as though you can simply add or remove parts, update or upgrade the software, and the new system will perform as designed. You simply need to bring in the best experts to fix your machines and voilà, you now have a better-performing machine. Any improvement either will or will not return an investment in the short term—end of story (see Figure 15.2). This leads to the conclusion: "We need to do an ROI analysis for each *kaizen* event." (See the sidebar on "The Risks of ROI Ruling Lean Transformation.") Lean then becomes the next in a long line of technical programs to tinker with the mechanistic processes and make them more efficient.

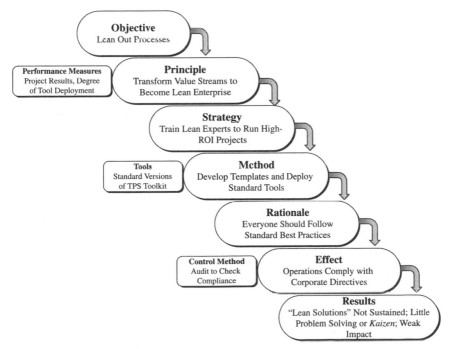

Figure 15.2. The Limitation of Getting Results by Implementing Lean Solutions

The Risks of ROI Ruling Lean Transformation

One of the companies that we attempted to teach seemed ideal for a top-to-bottom lean transformation. It was a retailer, and the founder's son was president. He was personally in charge of the lean transformation, or so we were told. Actually, his dad had brought in an outside CEO to "professionalize" the business. The outside CEO was a financial guy who had grown another similar business by several times. He claimed to use lean, but it quickly became apparent that it was mechanistic Lean Six Sigma to take out costs.

We started with our usual model line, in this case in a process that repaired product that had been damaged somewhere in the value stream, and hit a home run, improving productivity by 30 percent. The line had had a large backlog, and customers had sometimes waited weeks for their new product to get repaired. The president marveled at the level of employee engagement, which was beyond anything he had ever seen in the company, and wanted more. Life was good . . . for one month.

Six weeks into the engagement, the CEO, who had largely been quiet and absent from all lean activities, started demanding ROI calculations. What specifically had been saved through lean? A quick analysis showed that the 30 percent productivity gain was worth $400,000 annually. We were pleased. The CEO was not. He wanted a week-by-week breakdown of all costs for lean, including wages paid to employees who participated in the *kaizen* event, versus benefits attributable to that week's activities. Suddenly all lean activity—workshops, plans for training, follow-up coaching in the areas launched—came to a screeching halt. All hands were on deck to calculate ROI. Momentum was stalled, if not completely lost.

What we are really saying is not peculiar to "lean." Organizational systems are complex and dynamic, and a static machine view will lead to suboptimal results and a lack of learning and development on the part of the people who are directly involved with the processes. On the cost side of the ledger, it is easy to measure a reduction in inventory or the elimination of the costs of a person. On the positive side, it is difficult to forecast the benefits of an engaged workforce that is continually improving for decades. What is the net present value of highly developed, engaged people who are continually improving processes over the next 10 years? We have not seen anyone even attempt to calculate this.

Sustaining gains has been, and will be, of critical importance in lean transformations. We discussed the concept of entropy, or the organization's tendency to return to a "lower-energy state" by giving back the gains that were so recently won. Our position is that sustaining highly efficient, relatively waste-free, "lean" systems takes a tremendous amount of energy, and that the ideal power source is the commensurate development of the work groups at the *gemba*.

We then discussed the makeup of a true lean system. A lean system's purpose is to highlight problems immediately. These problems are then captured, reviewed, prioritized, and worked on, one by one, by the work groups. Through this PDCA activity, both the business needs and the people development needs are met. We went on to show the contrast between machine thinking and systems thinking when they are applied to moving toward a lean enterprise. Toyota's approach is to follow principles that work toward respect for people and continuous improvement (see Figure 15.3).

Getting from the current mechanistic thinking and waste-filled processes to a culture of continuous improvement based on PDCA is a long-term commitment, and there are many ways to do it. We distinguished between a mechanistic, broad approach and an organic, narrow approach to lean transformation. We maintain that there isn't "one best approach," and that you'll eventually end up with a balance between the two. If you've gone shallow and broad, you'll need to drive deeper into the organization, and if you've gone very narrow and deep, you'll need to expand the transformation across the rest of the organization.

What we have observed repeatedly is that in the first stage of lean, there are specific project-based efforts led by lean "experts," mostly based on applying tools that provide an initial bump in results. In fact, that is always our starting point. If there is a lot of low-hanging fruit,

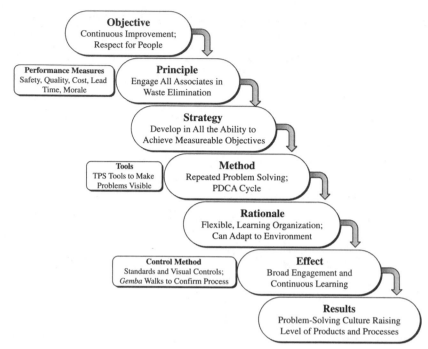

Figure 15.3. Toyota Method of Engaging People in Waste Elimination

the results can be significant, at least for the pilot area or the areas that are the focus of burst *kaizen*. Two key questions determine where the organization goes next:

What was the purpose of the first stage of using tools on distinctive projects?

Where does the organization go next in deployment?

Unfortunately, too many organizations view the purpose as leaning out processes, developing a lean façade, and never getting beyond this point. Then this initial burst tapers off and entropy sets in. On the other hand, if the purpose is learning, the first stage can

- Start to loosen up the organization to accept the concepts of TPS
- Create some awareness

- Generate the beginnings of a few believers.
- Start to win over senior management
- Start to develop a few managers
- Create a learning model

If management puts in the time to learn and then moves into the second phase of taking responsibility for improvement, there is another big bump in performance as a critical mass of projects provides some synergies, and at this point rudimentary *hoshin kanri* can be used to harness these gains and get to another level of results within business units. Again we will see a tapering off. The next frontier, and the biggest opportunity, is through a combination of culture change to get to continuous improvement at the work group level and true *hoshin kanri* to align activities with strategic business objectives, and then the breakthroughs in business performance can continue indefinitely (see Figure 15.4).

After laying the basic theoretical foundation for the journey to excellence, we then shared with you seven case studies from vastly different businesses and industries from around the world. Each story

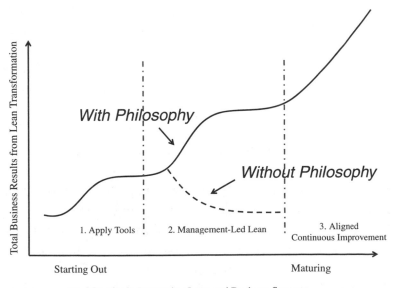

Figure 15.4. Results as Lean Evolves into Aligned Continuous Improvement

was told through the eyes of the external *sensei* or internal executive leader who was responsible for leading the transformation. Through these stories, you saw how each business was somewhere between crisis and stability, and how the different businesses faced very different challenges. While the specific solutions varied, the general PDCA approach was the same in all cases. Every situation is unique, and in every situation, an effective lean approach must solve the problems for that particular organization—not broadly apply tools in a scripted way.

The case studies were full of "*sensei* reflections" that provided many tips for transforming an enterprise. They all emphasized the need for a teaching approach to the transformation. The *sensei* is teaching the executive leaders, middle managers, and team members. The purpose of the teaching is to change their way of thinking, not simply to give them a new vocabulary. Then the leaders must learn enough to themselves become teachers at the *gemba*. Getting them to leave their pristine offices and conference rooms is often itself a major challenge. The effective *sensei* needs to become a confidante of the senior leaders and develop them so that they can develop others.

We continued our storytelling and presented a hypothetical company's first months of its lean transformation journey. The journey represented in this story was meant to show, as much as possible, the challenges facing any organization when it contemplates a lean transformation. We then reflected on this story to see what we had learned. We noted the transformation and development that the team members went through and the organizational resistance that they faced. Our old friend "machine thinking" made yet another appearance, this time exacerbated by the fact that the leadership was detached from the effort and wasn't invested in the process.

We then discussed the role of the *sensei* in a transformation and the need for experience, knowledge, and the ability to teach. We argued that the *sensei* can be either internal or external. We stressed that *sensei* are teachers, not process improvement engineers, and that they need to be skilled, passionate problem solvers. Identifying such a person is more like finding a life coach than like hiring a plumber. We discussed the importance of the *sensei*'s development of internal lean coaches and described the attributes of a successful lean coach. We again revisited some of the pitfalls of creating a mechanistic lean bureaucracy and the damage it can do to an organization. As a contrast, we spent a bit more time and effort describing how systems thinking can support the sustaining of the process.

Our next discussion involved differentiating between a lean façade and deep lean practices. We showed how the result of the first phase of lean is generally a superficial outer layer, or façade, of lean. If management is committed, lean progresses to the second phase, where it will move to a deeper implementation that includes management, but even this is only enough to stop entropy, and true gains come in fits and starts. In the third phase, a true "core" of deep lean practice within each work group, with strong group leadership, will stop entropy and support continuous improvement.

We then delved into the topic of "best practice replication" versus learning and argued that mindless replication of a best practice can actually lower organizational performance. This is due primarily to the loss of context during the replication phase. Many factors can be different, and therefore the countermeasure, while effective in the original location, might be of no benefit or, worse, detrimental to the new area to which it's being transplanted.

The topic of top-down or bottom-up was then reviewed. In this case, we did find that there is a sort of standard. Between us, we have never experienced a successful bottom-up transformation of an organization. Certainly, revolutions have had some success throughout history, like the one that led to the formation of the United States, but they are always led by strong, visionary leaders.

When lean is reframed as an endless quest for perfection, we recognize that any individual project is just one step on the journey. The success of the individual project is of consequence in terms of what the people who will be with us for the long term have learned from it. Their learning can have a multiplier effect that reverberates through the enterprise for years—if it is attended to.

If lean is a journey of striving for excellence, the starting point should be soul-searching. Are we really up for the challenge? Are we truly committed? Given the current governance of an enterprise, is it possible to be committed for the long term, and if not, is there a chance that we can change it? It may be hard to accept, but lean will never succeed as a one-off program of improving processes that stay improved.

Does Lean Ever Become Self-Perpetuating?

Recently, a CEO who was trying to drive his own organization to exceptional levels of performance suggested that at some point, lean becomes self-perpetuating, largely because the employees, being accustomed to problem solving, *kaizen*, and the like, would insist on continued improvement even in the absence of strong leadership. That may be true to a degree. As we noted at the Toyota plant, the work groups could maintain the Toyota Production System (TPS) for some time while new managers were learning on the job. On the other hand, the managers above the new hires and to each side were seasoned veterans.

Richard Zarbo, whom we met in Chapter 9 as the head of Pathology and Laboratory Medicine in the Henry Ford Health System, has a somewhat different view based on his experience.

> *"Lean never becomes self-sustaining. Never, ever, ever! No way, no how. It simply cannot.*
>
> *Why?*
>
> *There are infinite sources of friction and viscosity in an organization that can suppress the core behaviors that are critical to achieving exceptional performance. The friction and viscosity can be overcome only by the motive force of constant, vigilant, engaged leadership.*
>
> *Exceptional performance is possible. There is clear evidence that some organizations accomplish it, although most do not. Achieving exceptional performance requires generating and sustaining high-velocity, nonstop, broad-based improvement and innovation. In short, you can outperform the field only if you can consistently outlearn the field.*

Why?

Because the first version of everything that we design—product, process, or any complex system—will be grossly flawed. It has to be. Our brains are insufficient to anticipate all the structural needs and all the dynamic behaviors without practical tests. Therefore, we must have the skills to convert the ignorance that we originally incorporated into our designs into useful knowledge about how to design and operate the exceptionally complex products, services, and systems on which we depend and for which we are responsible.

Generating and sustaining high-velocity, nonstop, broad-based improvement and innovation is skill-based—not inspired genius, 'culture,' 'spirit,' 'servant leadership,' or any of that other fluffy kumbaya stuff that sounds good, but that isn't actionable."

At Toyota, the leaders can come across as challenging bosses, not mean or destructive, but tough in the same way that your best coach or teacher was tough: demanding, with high expectations, and giving constant feedback, encouragement, direction, and education. Achieving exceptional performance depends on skills, just like civil engineering, cooking, quality writing, or anything meritorious. There are deep skills required, and time and discipline must go into developing, nourishing, and applying them relentlessly or they will degrade.

What are those skills?

The skills necessary for an organization to outlearn its peers include

1. *Seeing and prioritizing problems.* Designing systems so that they both incorporate our current best-known approach *and* identify problems *immediately* when and where they occur. Those problems are broadcasting our current weaknesses.
2. *Solving problems.* Containing problems as soon as they are seen so that they don't propagate, and solving them rigorously (the scientific method, A3, PDCA, Shewhart—in essence rigorous diagnosis, treatment, and follow-up) so that what we learned by solving the problem is converted into useful knowledge.

3. *Sharing learning.* Both incorporating new knowledge locally and sharing it (and the discovery process behind it) systemically for broad effect.
4. *Developing people.* It is rare that we can out-technology our competitors. The key to competitive success is to outdevelop our people, relentlessly developing Skills 1 through 3 in others.

This may sound very basic, and like common sense, but in reality these are all very challenging skills for adults in general and leaders in particular to learn. Why is this so difficult for leaders who do not have these skills and experience using them?

1. Calling out problems makes them feel incompetent.
2. Solving problems rigorously takes a lot of discipline and doesn't provide the immediate gratification of a "solution."
3. Sharing learning requires that they expose their own work to critique.
4. Too much leadership education is about "decision making," implying that the key is having the right information and the right models to interpret the problems rather than being about discovery and development—finding new information and new ways to interpret the problems and solutions, and teaching others to do the same.
5. Developing people requires a different skill set from what got most managers promoted, which too often is firefighting that they lead through brute force, so they will themselves have to go back to school.

As we discussed in Chapter 1, the Shingo Prize team discovered that many of the candidates they evaluated that had seemed so promising had proved to lack leadership commitment and had gone backward. One of the more promising lean exemplars in America was a small manufacturing company called Wiremold, but after a decade of success, even that company went backward when it was sold to a company with leaders who lacked the vision (see the sidebar on "Changing Ownership of Wiremold: A Cautionary Tale.")

Changing Ownership of Wiremold: A Cautionary Tale[1]

One of a small number of successful transformations to a wall-to-wall lean enterprise was the Wiremold Company. This small family-owned manufacturing company made plastic wire protectors and cord covers used in homes and offices. The company had dabbled in quality programs inspired by Deming and in just-in-time methods, but it had never gotten beyond shallow programs. At the end of 1990, when the CEO was retiring, the company set out to look for a lean leader as the new CEO. It found Art Byrne, who had been a group executive for Danaher, a company made famous for its lean transformation in *Lean Thinking*.[2] Art had learned TPS from a Japanese consulting company, *Shingijutsu*, and was a true zealot. He turned the Wiremold plants upside down, personally leading *kaizen* event after *kaizen* event. More than half of his time was spent leading *kaizen* events. When Art started in 1990, Wiremold was losing money, the facilities looked chaotic, and there was inventory galore. Within two years, the company was still not very profitable, but inventory turns had doubled, which greatly improved cash flow. In four years, inventory turns had quadrupled. With bucketloads of cash, the company was able to make investments in sales, which grew revenue, while holding inventory constant, doubling inventory turns again. Over time, Art hired or developed an executive staff of lean leaders who took lean across all departments in the company.

Lean had started out as an operations improvement program, but it soon came to be at the core of the business strategy. As the company leaders reduced the lead time for giving quotes, delivering product, introducing new products, and responding to customer concerns at levels substantially better than the competition (90 or more percent better), they turned this into gains in market share and price premiums. They then started purchasing their

(Continued)

underperforming competitors and smaller companies (20 acquisitions) and turning them around using the same lean methods. From 1990 to 2000, ROI to shareholders was 34.7 percent per year vs. the S&P 500 ROI of 15.5 percent for the same period. Employees benefited because Wiremold shared 15 percent of the pretax profits with them, in cash, every quarter. It was also able to keep the promise that no one would lose his job because of productivity gains.

Ironically, Wiremold's incredible success with lean became its undoing. In 2000, four of the five children of the founder were alive, but they were in their nineties. Wiremold had a policy that if a shareholder died, the company would purchase back the shares, but the company had become so valuable that it could not afford to buy back the heirs' stock. So the executive team recommended that they put the company up for sale.

Legrand, a French company, purchased Wiremold. It was impressed by the 10-year results and said that it wanted to learn lean. In fact, the purchase agreement included golden handcuffs keeping the 10 top executives on board for two years. In the next two years, however, it became clear to these executives that Legrand had no serious interest in learning about lean. On the two-year anniversary of the sale, Art Byrne and two other senior executives retired. Soon the rest of the executives followed suit. Over time, the great lean enterprise degraded, and Wiremold became an average company. Most of the middle management bailed out. Many of the facilities were closed, and in some cases production was outsourced to Mexico. It was the end of an era of pursuing excellence.

We agree with Dr. Zarbo that the journey never ends and that entropy is always present. The discipline required, even for something as seemingly simple as PDCA, is far from natural. What is natural is doing what it takes to get through the day. It is only through passionate daily leadership at all levels that this unnaturally challenging journey will continue. On the other hand, the more capable and stable the organization becomes, the better it is able to weather short-term setbacks or the turmoil caused by management changes. There is a point where leaders can do more planning and checking and adjusting by coaching others and less doing just to keep the process running.

The Journey Needs Leadership

A lot has been written about "lean leadership."[3] Is it reasonable to say that there is a distinctive approach to leadership that is "lean" as opposed to not lean? We have argued that it is very different, and that in some cases it requires the opposite of the skills that made our current leaders successful. Many leadership books talk about vision and how we motivate and inspire others, which are certainly valuable in the case of lean leadership. But there is more to it than that. Decades ago, Deming wrote the principle at the beginning of this chapter: that managers, beginning with senior leadership, should "know the details of their business that will include operation of equipment." He was talking about quality, but the overlap with lean is clear. Managing at the *gemba* is a critical characteristic of lean leadership and is missing from the repertoire of many visionary, inspiring leaders. If the desire is operational excellence, we believe that the following characteristics are the minimum essential:

1. Is passionate about the business, customers, and quality.
2. Makes excellence a goal above and beyond short-term financial considerations.
3. Studies the business in order to know it inside out.
4. Obsessively checks on how things are going at the *gemba* in every part of the business.
5. Is dedicated to becoming an expert at true root-cause problem solving.
6. Values people who are committed to the business and want to improve themselves and their work.
7. Takes the time to coach and develop people who are committed to the business.
8. Has the skills to coach and develop people.
9. Is obsessed with improving herself as a person and a leader.
10. Is emotionally mature and can put developing others before her own egoistic needs.

In *Toyota Culture,* "servant leadership" was introduced as a concept in some parts of Toyota.[4] The idea is to think of the pyramid as being upside down, with the value-added workers on top and the management hierarchy supporting them through coaching, teaching, and removing obstacles. We have gotten questions from companies that want to know how to "implement servant leadership." These are the wrong questions. The right question to ask is: "What do we have to do to earn servant leadership?" Many of the statements about the ideal lean organization, such as servant leadership and turning the hierarchy upside down, are practical only after processes have achieved a level of stability and people have developed a level of maturity and trust in the organization (see Figure 15.5). This provides the foundation for servant leadership; if it is missing, servant leadership becomes delegation without support and the system will be unstable and topple.

Taiichi Ohno was the consummate teacher, and he personally had much to do with the creation of Toyota's culture of facing up to challenges with a positive spirit and remarkable persistence. It is still common today for his living alumni to speak of some learning moment as the most important in their lives. As one example, he asked a manager to pick up an empty box and follow him through the plant. The manager did as he was told, and after returning to the starting point Ohno

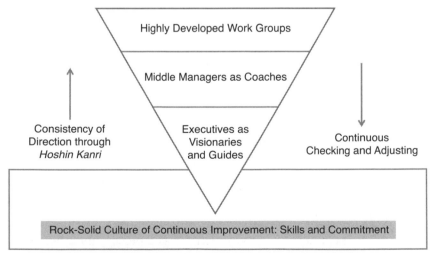

Figure 15.5. Servant Leadership Needs a Strong Foundational Culture

asked: "Didn't you realize there were many components lying on the floor? If you did, why did you not pick them up?" The manager said he noticed, but Ohno had not told him to pick up the parts. They made the same walk and this time the manager picked up the parts. Ohno asked: "Do you have any idea how much these components are costing us?" The manager admitted he did not, and Ohno one by one gave him the costs, to the penny, from memory, and the manager added them up, shocked at the total. Ohno said: "Everyone ignores these small items because they are insignificant, but what would you do if they were your money? I am sure you would pick them up." This changed the manager's thinking about waste, and after that there were never extra parts laying on the floor.[5]

One notable characteristic of a stable culture of continuous improvement is that people take responsibility and are accountable for their actions. In a traditional organization, people are accountable when they get caught, and then, if nothing bad happens to them as a result, they are still okay and have won. Getting away with what you can is not responsibility. Responsibility is that when my name is on the metric board by an action item, I will move heaven and earth to do what I said or feel awful because I have failed the team. Nobody needs to be watching over me to catch me. I will police myself relative to clear expectations and clear evidence that I was late or did not meet the targets. In this case, far less traditional supervision is necessary, and servant leadership becomes possible.

Is Continuous Improvement a Realistic Vision?

We have set the bar high. A True North vision is as high as it gets—a picture of perfection. Are mere mortals up to the challenge? The answer is no if the goal is to put the steps to perfection in a project plan and score ourselves on how quickly we achieve it. The answer is a resounding yes if the goal is to continue to progress toward excellence, and when we fail, pick ourselves up and rededicate ourselves. All of the cases in Section Two can be viewed as failures because the companies fell down at some point on their lean journey. On the other hand, each of these organizations made great strides through lean, achieving levels of performance, at least in parts of the business, that were beyond what they could have imagined. Even the companies that went backward after the initial surge of improvement had some residue of learning that could be ignited if the right leaders were to come in. For example, we do not believe that the capability for lean was dead and buried at the former Wiremold, and there have been reports of efforts by Legrand to reinvigorate lean.

We can get pessimistic about the prospect for growing lean enterprises when we look at individual companies that have gone backward, but as a bigger picture, let's consider the human quest to improve. Is the world a better place because so many organizations have tried some combination of Lean and Six Sigma? Has the needle moved as a result of the lean movement? In the big picture, the 10 to 20 years of lean experimentation is a blink of an eye, and we believe that we have come quite far.

When we started this in the 1980s, only a handful of companies understood more than the rudimentary tools. The quality movement was starting to gather steam, but it was often delegated to the quality department. There were a variety of experiments in motivating people through problem-solving groups, like quality circles and self-directed work teams. In other words, there were pieces, but they were scattered, and there were few models to turn to for a vision of lean progress outside of Japanese companies.

Now, a few decades later, lean is a household word. Understanding lean as a system of people, processes, and problem solving is not alien. It is almost an expectation that organizations have at least experimented with lean and had some degree of success. It is still hard to find a top-to-bottom, wall-to-wall example of a lean enterprise, but with a little searching, we can find at least a model value stream or model department for some process similar to our own without going to Toyota. Concepts of pull and flow are part of the general world vocabulary. And lean is being integrated with noble human pursuits like global sustainability.

We believe that over time, good lean thinking will simply become a good way of thinking about human progress. There is always a desire to eliminate waste. There is always a desire to better ourselves.

Eliminating waste in value streams gets us closer to one-piece flow, which is having what we need, in the amount we need, when we need it. Who does not want that for the health and welfare of the populace? The message here is that neither technology nor managers who are clever at manipulating global value streams will get us to that vision. It starts and ends with people who use their unique capability for reasoning and innovation to strive toward something that they care about. That more than anything is the lean message, and we describe it as the pursuit of excellence through continuous improvement.

So we've come to this point in our journey. If we've done our job properly, we've left you with more questions than answers. What is our purpose? What are our critical needs? What's my current environment like? Are we in crisis? What are the skills and abilities of my leadership team? What is our culture? What is our history? All of these questions and more should be swirling around your head as you contemplate your journey. Our best advice is to answer them all honestly, lace up your boots, pull on your jacket, and either get started on or continue your journey to excellence.

We'll see you out there!

Notes

Prologue

1. For a detailed analysis, see Jeffrey Liker and Timothy Ogden, *Toyota Under Fire* (New York: McGraw-Hill, 2011).

Section One

1. James P. Womack, Daniel T. Jones, and Daniel Roos, *The Machine That Changed the World* (New York: HarperPerennial, 1991).

Chapter I

1. Thomas J. Peters and Robert H. Waterman Jr., *In Search of Excellence: Lessons from America's Best-Run Companies* (New York: Harper & Row, 1982).
2. Ibid., p. 51.
3. Jim Collins and Jerry I. Porras, *Built to Last: Successful Habits of Visionary Companies* (New York: HarperBusiness Essentials, 2002).
4. Ibid., p. 28.
5. Steven Spear, *The High Velocity Edge: How Market Leaders Leverage Operational Excellence to Beat the Competition* (New York: McGraw-Hill, 2010).
6. Steven Spear, personal interview.
7. Hiroko Tabuchi, "Toyota Posts an Annual Loss," *New York Times*, May 8, 2009.

8. Industry Week/MPI Census of Manufacturers, released in November 2007; http://www.industryweek.com/articles/census_of_u-s-_manufacturers_—_lean_green_and_low_cost_15009.aspx?SectionID=10.

9. Walter Andrew Shewhart, *Statistical Method from the Viewpoint of Quality Control* (New York: Dover, 1939).

10. This was spelled out brilliantly by Robert Cole, who argued that American organizations tend to be strong only at individual learning and Japanese companies achieve both individual and organizational learning: Robert E. Cole, "Reflections on Organizational Learning in U.S. and Japanese Industry," in *Engineered in Japan*, ed. J. K. Liker, J. E. Ettlie, and J. Campbell (New York: Oxford University Press, 1995), pp. 365–379.

11. Jeffrey Liker and Michael Hoseus, *Toyota Culture* (New York: McGraw-Hill, 2008).

Chapter 2

1. Steven J. Spear and H. Kent Bowen, "Decoding the DNA of the Toyota Production System," *Harvard Business Review*, September/October 1999, pp. 96–106; reprint 99509.

2. See Jeffrey Liker, *The Toyota Way* (New York: McGraw-Hill, 2004), Chap. 9.

3. "The enormous saving of time and therefore increase in the output which it is possible to effect through eliminating unnecessary motions . . . can be fully realized only after one has personally seen the improvement which results from a thorough motion and time study, made by a competent man." Frederic W. Taylor, *The Principles of Scientific Management* (New York: Harper, 1911). The "competent man" is the trained industrial engineer.

4. Ibid.

5. James P. Womack, Daniel T. Jones, and Daniel Roos, *The Machine That Changed the World* (New York: HarperPerennial, 1991); James Womack and Daniel Jones, *Lean Thinking*, 2nd ed. (New York: Simon & Schuster, 2003).

6. See Jeffrey Liker and David Meier, *The Toyota Way Fieldbook* (New York: McGraw-Hill, 2006) or Jeffrey Liker and David Meier, *Toyota Talent* (New York: McGraw-Hill, 2007) for a discussion of the skills matrix.
7. Mike Rother, *Toyota Kata: Managing People for Improvement, Adaptiveness, and Superior Results* (New York: McGraw-Hill, 2009).
8. The process described here is the way we learn any complex skills; see H. Dreyfus and S. Dreyfus, *Mind over Machine* (New York: Free Press, 1982).
9. Rother, *Toyota Kata*.
10. The relationship between each step of Toyota Business Practices (TBP) and the Toyota Way values (called "drive and dedication") that should be taught at this step are described in Jeffrey Liker and Michael Hoseus, *Toyota Culture* (New York: McGraw-Hill, 2008), p. 151.

Chapter 3

1. In *Toyota Talent* (New York: McGraw-Hill, 2007), Jeffrey Liker and David Meier give a detailed discussion of Job Instruction Training and the right way to train people in the right way to do the job. What Yuri had learned was an additional key point to be added to the job instruction breakdown for each job, and he needed to retrain on that aspect of the standardized work.
2. Jeffrey Liker, *The Toyota Way* (New York: McGraw-Hill, 2004).
3. *The Toyota Way* includes chapters on the development of the first Prius and the development of the first Lexus, both of which are examples of planned innovation with a purpose.
4. For further insight into this process, see Mike Rother, *Toyota Kata: Managing People for Improvement, Adaptiveness, and Superior Results* (New York: McGraw-Hill, 2009).

Chapter 4

1. These two fictitious cases are composites of companies we have worked with or know of. They are not real cases, but they are realistic.
2. Jim Collins and Jerry Porras, *Built to Last: Successful Habits of Visionary Companies* (New York: HarperBusiness Essentials, 1994), p. xiii.

3. The examples in this paragraph are taken from Collins and Porras, *Built to Last.*

4. This example is based on a story that was personally communicated to Jeff Liker by Ron Lippitt in an organizational development workshop.

5. Larry Lippitt, *Preferred Futuring* (New York: Berrett-Koehler Publishers, 1998).

6. Yoji Akao, *Hoshin Kanri: Policy Deployment for Successful TQM* (New York: Productivity Press, 2004).

7. Jeffrey Liker, *The Toyota Way* (New York: McGraw-Hill, 2004).

8. Ibid., p. 18.

9. A detailed example of a year in the life of *hoshin kanri* can be found in Jeffrey Liker and Michael Hoseus, *Toyota Culture* (New York: McGraw-Hill, 2008), Chap. 15.

10. Mike Rother, *Toyota Kata: Managing People for Improvement, Adaptiveness, and Superior Results* (New York: McGraw-Hill, 2009).

11. James Womack and Daniel Jones, *Lean Thinking*, 2nd ed. (New York: Simon & Schuster, 2003).

12. Ibid.

Chapter 5

1. Daniel Katz and Robert L. Kahn, *The Social Psychology of Organizations* (New York: Wiley, 1978).

2. William Pasmore, *Designing Effective Organizations: The Socio-Technical Systems Perspective* (New York: Wiley, 1988); William Pasmore and John Sherwood (eds.), *Socio-Technical Systems: A Sourcebook* (San Diego: University Associates, 1978).

3. The most detailed discussion is in Jeffrey Liker and Michael Hoseus, *Toyota Culture* (New York: McGraw-Hill, 2008), Chap. 8.

4. P. Adler and R. Cole, "Designed for Learning: A Tale of Two Auto Plants," *Sloan Management Review*, Spring 1993; Christian Berggren, "NUMMI vs. Uddevalla," *Sloan Management Review*, Winter 1994 (with rejoinder by Adler and Cole).

5. The role of deep practice in developing talent is well described in Geoff Colvin, *Talent Is Overrated: What Really Separates World-Class*

Performers from Everybody Else (New York: Penguin Group, 2008) and Daniel Coyle, *The Talent Code: Greatness Isn't Born, It's Grown* (New York: Bantam, 2009).

6. Paul S. Adler, "Building Better Bureaucracies," *Academy of Management Executive* 13, no. 4 (November 1999): pp. 36–47.

Chapter 6

1. The original document was distributed as an electronic file, which then led to a summary article: Jeffrey Liker and Thomas Lamb, "What Is Lean Ship Construction and Repair?" *Journal of Ship Production* 18, no. 3 (August 2002): pp. 121–142.

2. At the time, the company was called Donnelly Mirror. For a description of this company, see Jeffrey Liker and Keith Allman, "The Donnelly Production System: Lean at Grand Haven," in *Becoming Lean: Inside Stories of U.S. Manufacturers*, ed. J. K. Liker (Portland, Ore.: Productivity Press, 1997), Chap. 8.

3. James Womack and Daniel Jones, *Lean Thinking*, 2nd ed. (New York: Simon & Schuster, 2003).

4. A short summary of the contrast between mechanistic Big Ship and organic Small Ship is provided in Jeffrey Liker and Michael Hoseus, *Toyota Culture* (New York: McGraw-Hill, 2008). This chapter provides a much more detailed account and analysis of their transformation and the implications for the pursuit of excellence in a complex bureaucracy.

5. Stephen Covey, *Seven Habits of Highly Effective People* (New York: Simon & Schuster, 1989); Mark Graham Brown, *Baldrige Award Winning Quality* (Portland, Ore.: Productivity Press, 2000).

Chapter 7

1. For an excellent overview of how to use A3 reporting as a people development tool, see John Shook, *Managing to Learn* (Cambridge: Lean Enterprise Institute, 2008).

2. See Jeffrey K. Liker and David Meier, *Toyota Talent* (New York: McGraw-Hill, 2007).

Chapter 9

1. Steven Spear and H. Kent Bowen, "Decoding the DNA of the Toyota Production System," *Harvard Business Review*, September/October 1999, pp. 96–106.
2. Ibid., p. 98.

Chapter 11

1. James Morgan and Jeffrey Liker, *The Toyota Product Development System* (New York: Productivity Press, 2006).

Chapter 13

1. This is an abbreviated version of the short story. The full version can be downloaded from the following Web site: www.mhprofessional .com/ContinuousImprovement

Chapter 14

1. Jim Collins, *Built to Last* (New York: HarperBusiness, 2004).
2. For further discussion of the lean coach's role and personal characteristics and skills, see Jeffrey Liker and David Meier, *The Toyota Way Fieldbook* (New York: McGraw-Hill, 2006), pp. 434–437.
3. H. Dreyfus and S. Dreyfus, *Mind over Machine* (New York: Free Press, 1982).
4. Liker and Meier, *Toyota Way Fieldbook*, p. 436.
5. Geoff Colvin, *Talent Is Overrated: What Really Separates World-Class Performers from Everybody Else* (New York: Penguin Group, 2008) and Daniel Coyle, *The Talent Code: Greatness Isn't Born, It's Grown* (New York: Bantam, 2009).
6. Mike Rother, *Toyota Kata: Managing People for Improvement, Adaptiveness, and Superior Results* (New York: McGraw-Hill, 2009).
7. The distinction between maintenance *kaizen* and improvement *kaizen* is discussed in Jeffrey Liker and Mike Hoseus, *Toyota Culture* (New York: McGraw-Hill, 2008), Chap. 6.

8. David Rock and Jeffrey Schwartz, "The Neuroscience of Leadership," *Strategy+Business* 43 (May 30, 2006): pp. 2–10.
9. Colvin, *Talent Is Overrated*, p. 71.

Chapter 15

1. An entire book was written detailing Wiremold's transformation into a lean enterprise and its subsequent decline under Legrand. See Bob Emiliani, David Stec, Lawrence Grasso, and James Stodder, *Better Thinking, Better Results*, 2nd ed. (Kensington, Conn.: Center for Lean Business Management, 2007).
2. James Womack and Daniel Jones, *Lean Thinking*, 2nd ed. (New York: Simon & Schuster, 2003), Chap. 7.
3. A quick search of the Web lists almost 200 titles concerning "lean leadership" from authors such as Bob Emiliani, Jamie Flinchbaugh, William Lareau, David Mann, Darrell Bender, and many others.
4. Jeffrey Liker and Michael Hoseus, *Toyota Culture* (New York: McGraw-Hill, 2007), Chap. 11.
5. Yoshihito Wakamatsu, *The Toyota Mindset: The Ten Commandments of Taiichi Ohno* (Bellingham, Wash.: Enna Products, 2009), pp. 6–8.

Index

About the Authors

Jeffrey K. Liker, Ph.D., is Professor of Industrial and Operations Engineering at the University of Michigan. He is co-owner of Optiprise and president of the Toyota Way Academy. Liker is author of the international bestseller *The Toyota Way: 14 Management Principles from the World's Greatest Manufacturer* (McGraw-Hill, 2004), and five other books about Toyota: (with David Meier) *The Toyota Way Fieldbook* (McGraw-Hill, 2005); (with Jim Morgan) *The Toyota Product Development System* (Productivity Press, 2006); (with David Meier) *Toyota Talent: Developing Exceptional People the Toyota Way* (McGraw-Hill, 2007); and (with Michael Hoseus) *Toyota Culture: The Heart and Soul of the Toyota Way* (McGraw-Hill, 2008). His articles and books have won eight Shingo Prizes for Research Excellence, and *The Toyota Way* also won the 2005 Institute of Industrial Engineers Book of the Year Award and 2007 Sloan Industry Studies Book of the Year. His latest book (with Tim Ogden) on how Toyota is transforming itself is *Toyota Under Fire: Lessons for Turning Crisis into Opportunity*. He is a frequent keynote speaker and consultant. Recent clients include Siemens, Kraft-Oscar Meyer, Caterpillar, Solar Turbine, Alcatel-Lucent, Hertz, Art Van, Wabco, Fortum, and Harley Davidson.

James K. Franz has over 24 years of manufacturing experience and learned lean as a Toyota production engineer in Japan. He began his journey at the Motomachi plant, then moved to NUMMI, and then finally worked in Georgetown, Kentucky. After leaving Toyota, he went to Ford to apply his lean knowledge beginning in production engineering. He was sent to Ford of Australia for three years and led its stamping, assembly, casting, and powertrain facilities to global leadership in lean. During this time he also worked with Tier 1 and Tier 2 supplier plants in their transformation efforts. Upon his repatriation, he became a lean advisor in powertrain for global alignment of lean practices. He left Ford to work with Dr. Jeffrey Liker as a senior lean consultant and is now a partner with Dr. Liker in the Toyota Way Academy. His continuing journey has taken him around the world to support companies such as Bosch, Caterpillar, the U.S. Air Force, Exxon Mobil, AMCOR, Android Industries, Benteler Automotive, Case New Holland, Dakkota, Fisher Coachworks, Grand Rapids Chair, Hertz, JLG, MENLO Logistics, Philips, Rio Tinto, SAF Holland, Continental VDO, Visteon, and WABCO. He also teaches at the University of Michigan's Center for Professional Development's Lean Certification course. He received his bachelor of science degree in Manufacturing Systems Engineering from General Motors Institute, and completed his master of science degree in Engineering at the University of Michigan.